INN

*By Nancy Webster and
Richard Woodworth*

SPOTS

&

*A guide to where to go, stay,
eat and enjoy in 30 of the
region's choicest areas.*

SPECIAL
PLACES

IN NEW ENGLAND

Wood Pond Press
365 Ridgewood Road
West Hartford, Conn. 06107

Prices, hours and menu offerings at inns and restaurants change seasonally and with business conditions. Readers should call or write ahead to avoid disappointment. The prices and hours reported in this book were correct at presstime and are subject, of course, to change. They are offered as a relative guide to what to expect.

The authors welcome readers' reactions and recommendations.

First Printing, April 1986.

Cover Design by Bob Smith the Artsmith

Cover Photo: Porch of the Inn at Thorn Hill, Jackson, N.H.

Contents

Introduction

This is yet another inn book. But it's far more than that, too.

We enjoy reading all the others. But they rarely tell us what we *really* want to know, such as where to get a good meal and what there is to do. And the inns often are not grouped by location, so you don't get a feeling for what the area is like. We've found that out by talking to innkeepers, reading all the guidebooks and brochures, visiting Chambers of Commerce and, best help of all, poring through the local newspapers.

That's what we now share with you. We start not with the inn but with the area (of course, the existence of inns or lack thereof helped determine the areas to be included). We sought out 30 extra-special areas, some of them New England's best-known and some not widely known at all.

Then we toured each area, visiting each inn, each restaurant and each attraction, as well as drawing on our experiences and memories of more than 30 years of vacationing in and 15 years of living in New England. We *worked* these areas as roving journalists, always seeking out the best and most interesting. We also *lived* them — staying in, eating in and experiencing as many places as time and budget would allow.

The result is this book, a comprehensive yet selective compendium of what we found to be the best and most interesting places to stay, eat and enjoy in these 30 special areas.

The book reflects our tastes. We want creature comforts like private bathrooms and comfortable reading areas in our rooms; we like to meet other inn guests, but we also value our privacy. We seek interesting and creative food and settings for our meals. We enjoy unusual, enlightening things to do and places to see. We expect to receive value for money and time spent.

While touring the past year to research this book, we were struck — as we have been while preparing our other books — by how times and places change. Many of the inns and restaurants that were "in" a decade or so ago have faded, their places taken by any number of newcomers not yet widely known. We're fortunate that our newspaper training and tight deadlines make this book as up-to-date as its 1986 publication date.

Yes, the schedule is hectic and we do keep busy on these, our working vacations which everyone thinks must be nothing but fun. One of us says she never wants to see another inn bedroom (especially up on the third floor); the other doesn't care if he never eats another piece of pate.

Nevertheless, it's rewarding to discover a little-known inn, to savor a great meal, to enjoy a choice museum, to poke through an unusual store.

That's what this book is all about. We hope that you will enjoy its findings as much as we did the finding.

Nancy Webster and Richard Woodworth
April 1986

About the Authors

Nancy Webster began her dining experiences in her native Montreal and as a waitress in sumer resorts across Canada during her McGill University years. She worked in London and hitchhiked through Europe on $3 a day before her marriage to an American newspaper editor, whom she met while skiing at Mont Tremblant. She started writing her "Roaming the Restaurants" column for the West Hartford (Conn.) News in 1972. That led to half of the book, *Daytripping & Dining in Southern New England,* written in collaboration with Betsy Wittemann in 1978. She since has co-authored *Weekending in New England,* and two more editions in the *Daytripping & Dining* series, as well as *Getaways for Gourmets in the Northeast.* She and her husband have two college-age sons and live in West Hartford.

Richard Woodworth has been an inveterate traveler since his youth in suburban Syracuse, N.Y., where his birthday outings often involved train trips with friends for the day to Utica or Rochester. After graduation from Middlebury College, he was a reporter for newspapers in Syracuse, Jamestown, Geneva and Rochester before moving to Connecticut to become editor of the West Hartford News and executive editor of Imprint Newspapers. With wife Nancy Webster and their sons, he has traveled to the four corners of this country, Canada and portions of Europe, writing their findings for Imprint Newspapers and others. He co-authored *Getaways for Gourmets in the Northeast* with his wife. Between travels and duties as publisher of Wood Pond Press, he tries to find time to weed the garden in summer and ski in the winter.

Historical marker tells about Dorset outside Dovetail Inn.

Dorset, Vt.
The Town that Marble Built

There is marble almost everywhere in Dorset, a town that marble helped build and upon which it has long prospered.

You see it on the sidewalks all around the picturesque green, on the porch at the historic Dorset Inn and on the terrace at the newer Barrows House, on the side of the turreted United Church of Christ and on the pillars of the Marble West Inn. An entire mansion built of marble fascinates passersby along Dorset West Road.

It seems as if all Dorset has been paved with marble — and good intentions. Here is what residents and writers alike have called the perfect village. Merchant Jay Hathaway phrased it well in a Dorset Historical Society lecture: What could be better than running "a small country store nestled in the mountains of Vermont in a town that is as close to perfect as Dorset?"

A village of perhaps 1,200 (about half its population during the height of its marble-producing days a century ago), it's a mix of charm and culture in perfect proportion.

Dorset is unspoiled, from its rustic Barn Playhouse (the oldest summer playhouse in the state) to its handsomely restored inn (the oldest in the state) to its Dorset Field Club (the oldest nine-hole golf course in the state) to its lovely white, green-shuttered homes (many among the oldest in the

1

state) to its two general stores, both of them in curiously different ways relics of 19th century life. Here is a peaceful place in which to cherish the past.

Yet barely 10 miles away is Manchester, one of the most sophisticated tourist meccas around. Many of its visitors don't know about nor are they particularly interested in Dorset, but people in Dorset can take advantage of all its urbane attractions as desired.

So the Dorset visitor has the best of both possible worlds — a tranquil respite amid a myriad of activities and attractions. What could be more copacetic?

Inn Spots

Dorset Inn, Church and Main Streets, Dorset 05251. (802) 867-5500.

Vermont's oldest continuously operated country inn, with a history dating back to 1796, was grandly renovated in 1984 and 1985 in what it bills as "the inspired revival of an historic site." That it is.

Under the aegis of new owners Alex and Hanneke Koks of the Village Auberge and Sissy Hicks, the former chef at the Barrows House and now co-inkeeper with Gretchen Schmidt, the restored inn is a fine blend of history and contemporary comfort.

Overnight guests are greeted by a stunning collection of blue glass displayed in lighted cases at the top of the stairway on the second floor. All 29 rooms on the two upper floors have been redone with wall-to-wall carpeting, modern baths with wood washstands, lovely print wallpapers and antique furnishings. Two of the nicest are the third-floor front corner rooms, one with twin sleigh beds, two rockers, Audubon prints and floral wallpaper and the other with canopy bed, marble table and wallpaper of exotic animals and birds.

Downstairs, the main sitting room is appealing with comfortable furniture around the fireplace, a collection of blue and white china on the mantel, scrubbed wide plank floors and a small television set. Beyond is a cheery breakfast room with Vermont-woven mats atop wood tables and green floral curtains against small-paned windows that extend to the floor. Out back is a pleasant tap room with big oak bar, a popular and inexpensive pub menu, and an attractive, country-style dining room (see Dining Spots).

Doubles, $90 to $100, MAP.

Dovetail Inn, Main Street, Dorset 05251. (802) 867-5747.

Nicely located in the heart of town just across from the Dorset Inn (in fact it was once an annex to the inn and housed chauffeurs and staff in the posh days) is the two-building Dovetail. Jim and Jean Kingston, he a marine engineer, moved up from Connecticut in 1984 and, as they say, picked a growing area.

They have redecorated the 12 rooms, all with private baths, in one structure; the other houses their quarters, an office and a cheery "keeping room" for guests' use. Rooms vary in size and have double, king or twin beds; most have a couple of easy chairs (ours had a sofa) and pretty new wallpaper and curtains. On the second floor landing is a nook with a window seat and many books for borrowing.

In the back yard is a 20-by-40-foot swimming pool, once the Dorset Inn's. The Kingstons have a beer and wine license and serve by the pool

Stone wall opens onto path to Little Lodge at Dorset.

or in the keeping room. They also serve tea and cookies in the afternoon at certain times of the year.

Breakfast consists of juice, muffins (the orange ones were delicious) and coffee or tea. You may have it brought to your room in a basket, if you wish.

Why the name Dovetail? "I like quality building and furniture," says Jim, "and a cutesy name didn't fit Dorset."

Doubles, $47 to $65.

The Little Lodge at Dorset, Main Street, Box 673, Dorset 05251. (802) 867-4040.

"We have more places to sit per guest than any inn we've seen," says Allan Norris of the appealing, five-room bed-and-breakfast home he and wife Nancy have run with T.L.C. since 1981.

Guests in those five rooms have access to a formal dining room with oriental rugs, shining silver and bone china for breakfast service, a living room with wood stove and large hooked rug, a large and luxurious den with barnwood walls, blue leather sofa, fireplace and shelves of books and games, an attached five-sided gazebo which has black garden furniture cushioned with yellow and green pads, a wet bar area with refrigerator and a hallway with separate entrance for shedding and stashing skis and boots. Outside are a rope hammock and a garden sitting area overlooking the trout pond, the verdant fairways of the Dorset Field Club and the mountainside beyond.

Given all these inviting public areas, one might expect the Norrises, transplanted Baltimoreans, to have skimped on their upstairs guest rooms. Not so. All five spacious rooms have private baths, are furnished with twin beds usually made up as kingsize, have paintings by Nancy's great-uncle

3

(Boston School of Impressionists) and bedspreads crocheted by Allan's sister, and exude an air of lived-in comfort.

Breakfast is continental-plus, Nancy supplementing juices and cereals with her homemade strawberry-pecan, orange-coriander and pear-walnut breads or muffins.

The grounds offer trails for cross-country skiing and hiking in the rear, a stocked trout pond (no fishing, but you can feed them) dug by a former owner of the home who runs the Orvis sporting goods company, and next door, an oriental garden with colorful red bridges. Enjoying all this with the guests is Columbine, an unusually friendly doberman pinscher who nuzzles up to one and all. "More people write in our guest book about Columbine than anything else," Allan reports.

Doubles, $60 to $65.

Barrows House, Main Street, Dorset 05251. (802) 867-4455.

We don't know what is more appealing about the Barrows House: the comfortable rooms and cottages amid six acres of park-like grounds with swimming pool, tennis courts and an intricate gazebo, or the meals in the smashing new greenhouse addition that extends the dining room to the outdoors. You don't really have to choose; the choice is made for you with an MAP rate schedule that requires you to take your meals and encourages long stays, which is just fine with the numerous repeat guests who sometimes stay for weeks at a time.

Black wicker rockers are at the ready behind the columns that front the main 200-year-old house, which has a fireplaced living room, a tavern beside a charming outdoor patio, the dining rooms and 10 upstairs guest rooms.

The most popular rooms, however, are scattered in a number of out-buildings converted into sophisticated lodging, the latest being the former living quarters of innkeepers Marilyn and Charlie Schubert, ex-New Yorkers who acquired the inn in the early 1970s. All but two of the 32 rooms in nine buildings have private baths. Most are carpeted, some have sofas and some in the cottages have fireplaces and sitting rooms. Many have co-ordinated wallpapers, draperies and quilts, and all are filled with nice touches like ruffled pillows and the adorable patchcraft hangings of Joan Stewart Neave, whose Patchcraft shop is down the street.

Doubles, $130 to $165, MAP.

Marble West Inn, West Road, Box 22, Dorset 05251. (802) 867-4155.

The historic Holley-West house two miles southwest of Dorset, a Greek Revival built in the 1840s by the owner of a marble quarry, is graced with seven marble columns in front. A marble sign designates the inn since its extensive restoration and opening in 1985.

The renovation was done with taste, incorporating family treasures, by two young educators-turned-innkeepers, Hugh Miller and Edward Ferenc, the latter a Dorset native. On our October visit, their artistic bent was evident in a spectacular fall arrangement of pumpkins, gourds, bullrushes and such on the front porch of the inn.

They salvaged the extraordinary stenciling (done by Honey West, one of the quarry owner's daughters) in the front entry and upstairs hall, and several other unusual decorative and architectural features, such as the low stairway banisters installed for a woman in the West family who was very short. Sofas and rocking chairs around the fireplace, a piano and, by the

Marble sign designates Marble West Inn.

window, a wood and copper Victorian bathtub (filled with gin at Honey West's wedding in the 1930s and now full of plants) beckon guests into the main parlor, open to the adjacent dining room used for breakfast and dinner. The library has a marble fireplace, small TV, stereo and a window seat. The ornate combination hat rack and walking stick stand in the hall still bears several old Victorian hats.

Upstairs off two different stairwells are seven guest rooms with private baths, plus a small single. Each is large and amply furnished, most with colorful afghans crocheted by Edward's mother (his uncle did most of the carpentry during the restoration). A rear corner guest room has windows on three sides, while a front suite has living room, bedroom and fireplace.

A full breakfast of blueberry pancakes, eggs or French toast is served from 8 to 9 a.m. (with continental breakfast available until 10). One-entree candlelight dinners at $10 per person are served to guests by reservation at 7:30. A typical meal might be fresh mushroom soup or gazpacho, salad and vegetables from the garden out back, baked breast of chicken souffle and, for dessert, gingerbread (everyone goes wild about it, says Edward), apple crisp or peach pie. Swedish lamb with dill sauce and veal marsala are other popular entrees.

A pond out back provides skating in the winter. The innkeepers also lead cross-country skiers on nearby trails.

Doubles, $70 to $90 with breakfast, $90 to $110 MAP.

Village Auberge, Main Street, Dorset 05251. (802) 867-5715.

The food is the chief draw at the Village Auberge, thanks to Dutch chef-owner Alex Koks and his wife Hanneke, who also are principal owners of the renovated Dorset Inn and who were restoring another Main Street house into a deluxe B&B for opening in 1986.

But not to be overlooked are the wide front porch, usually decorated for the season, the cozy dark-paneled bar and delightful accommodations, orchestrated by Hanneke, who was a professional interior decorator and fashion designer in Holland. The four upstairs rooms over the restaurant are pleasantly furnished with four-poster beds, antique dressers and patterned wallpapers, and all have private baths.

We liked best the accommodations (one a suite) in the converted cottage behind the inn, especially the plush large room in which we stayed with kingsize bed, loveseat, pine coffee table and upholstered chair matching the patterned bedspread (all portrayed in glorious color in the centerfold of the inn's brochure). It's the kind of room you hardly want to leave, especially since the common room in the main inn is rather small and busy with patrons passing through on their way to dinner.

Breakfast is served to inn guests in the cheery, plant-filled bay window end of the dining room at an extra cost of $3 for continental (with a big flaky croissant), $5.50 for full breakfast of eggs or omelet and a special pain perdu with various fillings.

When we last visited, Alex was excited about their new bed and breakfast down the street. They were restoring an old house and adding on the back, planning very spacious rooms in the $75 to $100 range.

Doubles at the Village Auberge, $55 and $65, $75 for a suite with private sitting room.

Birch Hill Inn, West Road, Box 346, Manchester 05254. (802) 362-2761.

Just across the Dorset town line and closely allied with it in spirit if not address, this imposing hilltop home was built in the late 1700s as a private home and has been in innkeeper Pat Lee's family since 1917. It was the home of her grandfather and her father; she and husband Jim live there and capitalize on the home-like atmosphere, serving breakfast and dinner and making their guests — many of them long-term and repeat — feel very much at home.

Guests dine family-style at two highly-polished tables in the gracious dining room. They gather for games, reading or conversation in a comfortably furnished, 40-by-20-foot pine-paneled living room. Outside is a marble terrace of similar dimensions where Jim may barbecue Cornish game hens or beefalo steak (the beefalo, providing meat that is low-fat and low-chloresterol, are raised on the Lees' farm next door). Large windows frame the grounds, where stone fences and cross-country trails abound. In back is a kidney-shaped swimming pool.

Three of the five large guest rooms on the second floor have private baths; the other two share. Each is decorated in country style with family furnishings. One has brass beds; another a four-poster and stenciling done by Pat, and one has a fireplace. Art by local painters (many by 85-year-old Luigi Lucioni, a friend of Pat''s father) is everywhere. Also available is a small cottage with bedroom, sitting room, bath and refrigerator.

For breakfast, Pat Lee serves fresh fruit, her popular homemade granola (and, in winter, hot cereal), and a choice of eggs (sometimes poached on English muffins) or pancakes.

At night, meals are the kind she'd serve at a dinner party with a single-choice entree (she was preparing a large salmon caught by a guest in British Columbia the night we visited). A soup (leek, tomato or zucchini tarragon are some favorites) usually precedes the entree. Green salad and vegetables from the large garden accompany, as do Pat's homemade chutneys, mustard sauce or herb jellies. Lemon souffle, rhubarb crunch, blueberry surprise or the Silver Palate's decadent chocolate cake might end the meal. Other

6

specialties are veal marsala, butterflied leg of lamb and chicken teriyaki. The Lees have a beer and wine license, and serve hors d'oeuvres as guests gather for cocktails prior to dinner at 7:30. Cook's nights off are Wednesday and Sunday, when guests are on their own.

Doubles, $70 to $86, including breakfast; $90 to $106, MAP.

Dining Spots

Village Auberge, Main Street, Dorset. (802) 867-5715.

Innkeeper Hanneke Koks, dressed in a Netherlands-style gown, greets diners in this white clapboard Vermont farmhouse-turned-inn. Striking built-in china closets filled with her collection from Holland are a focal point in the attractive, restful dining room with a large bay window at the far end. Tables are covered with moss green linens and topped with botanical service plates, and chairs are comfortable cane and bentwood.

Meals here are an inspired experience in country French and continental dining. A piping hot cheese fritter is served to each diner as the menu, which changes seasonally, is presented. It lists eleven hors d'oeuvres and soups, seven entrees plus changing specials, and six desserts.

Chef Alex Koks's appetizers ($2 to $6.50) are works of art. His cream of mustard soup (served hot or cold) is aromatic and spicy, his pate of lobster and halibut is served with a dollop of homemade mayonnaise, and his terrine of duck comes with raisin relish, his ragout of sweetbreads in puff pastry, and his smoked trout mousse with a cucumber sauce. Hot French bread and a mixed green salad with roquefort or strongly flavored vinaigrette dressings precede the main course.

Entrees ($10.50 to $17.50) range from sweetbreads braised in Madeira under a pastry crust to breast of pheasant stuffed with morels and poached in cabbage leaves, duck breast (undercooked, states the menu) in raspberry vinegar sauce, and the house specialty, rack of lamb ($37.50 for two). We savored the veal kidneys and sweetbreads with morels, both garnished with broccoli, tomatoes, spinach with nutmeg and potato balls duchess. Two or three seafood dishes vary nightly.

Bay window provides airy setting for dining at Village Auberge.

Desserts, if you can manage one after all this, are $3.50. They include a pastry from the tray, marquise au chocolat and a bavarois au chevre. We enjoyed a colorful dish of three homemade sorbets — lime, strawberry and pear — that was plenty for two.

Dinner nightly from 6; closed Monday in summer and fall, also Tuesday rest of year. Closed Nov. 15-Dec. 15 and April 15-May 15.

Chantecleer, Route 7, East Dorset. (802) 362-1616.

As far as area residents are concerned, there's a surprising unanimity as to the best restaurant around: the Chantecleer, along Route 7 in East Dorset, just north of the Manchester line. The food is consistent and the atmosphere elegant.

Swiss chef Michel Baumann and his Vermont-born wife Marie acquired the contemporary-style restaurant fashioned from an old dairy barn in 1981. The menu features Swiss and French provincial cuisine.

Ten appetizers run from $2.95 for fried cheese with dill sour cream sauce to $4.95 for poached shrimp and scallops with ginger vinaigrette or smoked salmon. Other interesting selections include escargots baked with hazelnuts and Pernod, vol-au-vent Zurichoise, tripes Napoli, and smoked marlin and mussels with two sauces.

Entrees are strong on veal dishes, the five running from wiener schnitzel to kidneys to escalopes oriental (the sauce including pink grapefruit and fresh ginger) to sweetbreads and priced from $10.95 to $13.95. Other entrees cost $9.95 for chicken with lemon sauce to $18.25 for sauteed baby pheasant with varying sauces. Among popular choices are braised rabbit with apple brandy sauce, roast duckling with apricot-walnut sauce, rack of lamb with herb garlic coating, frog's legs, beef fondue and any of the nightly seafood specials. All are served with salad and polenta, rice or roesti potatoes.

Favored desserts are coupe Matterhorn, frozen souffle grand marnier, chocolate fondue and Swiss Tobler chocolate cake. A number of Swiss wines are included on the wine list, and Swiss yodeling music may be played on tape as background music.

Dinner nightly from 5; closed Tuesday.

Dorset Inn, Church and Main Streets, Dorset. (802) 867-5500.

Some interesting, creative food has been emanating from the kitchen of this venerable inn since Sissy Hicks took over the chef's chores as co-innkeeper with Gretchen Schmidt in partnership with Alex and Hanneke Koks of the Village Auberge late in 1984.

The pleasant main dining room, which seats 85 at well-spaced tables, is predominantly blue, with frilly white curtains screening the windows from the street, oak chairs with upholstered seats, folk art paintings on the walls, beige over blue linen and pewter service plates. Fresh flowers, classical music and candlelight enhance the mood.

A practitioner of the new American cuisine, Sissy Hicks changes her menu seasonally. Pre-dinner drinks are served with a basketful of french-fry-size cheese sticks. The crabmeat mousse with a cucumber-mustard dill sauce and a few slices of melba toast makes a fine appetizer, big enough for two to share. Smoked Norwegian salmon, chilled scallops and shrimp with a green sauce, New England cheese chowder and french-fried mushrooms ($2 to

Dorset Inn faces the green.

$4.50) were other appetizers on the fall menu. Crusty French bread with sweet butter and green salads with excellent stilton or basil-vinaigrette dressings accompany.

Having been advised that the calves liver was the best anywhere, we had to try it. Served rare as requested with crisp bacon and slightly underdone slices of onion, it was superb. The fresh trout, deboned but served with its skin still on, was laden with sauteed leeks and mushrooms. These came with an assemblage of vegetables, including red-skin potatoes with a dollop of sour cream, and crisp cauliflower, broccoli and yellow squash. A Wente pinot chardonnay for $13.50, golden and oaky, was a good choice from about 30 selections on the reasonably priced wine list.

Entrees range from $10.50 for breast of chicken in pear and cider cream to $17.50 for rack of lamb with fresh mint sauce. Veal medallions with a lime ginger sauce and roast Cornish hen stuffed with wild rice and fruit were other possibilities.

Pies, wild rice pudding and lemon buttermilk cake were on the dessert menu. We settled for a kiwi sorbet, wonderfully deep flavored with the consistency of ice cream, accompanied by a big sugar cookie.

The inn serves a hearty breakfast (sourdough or fruit pancakes, all kinds of eggs, bacon, ham and sausage) for a prix-fixe $6, plus lunch in summer and fall. Many of the lunch items are available at night in the tap room, which is immensely popular with locals. Among the intriguing selections: warm chicken tenderloin salad, potato skins filled with creamed smoked salmon or poached eggs topped with hollandaise sauce, chilled scallops and spinach fettuccine provencale, and a vegetarian salad plate that includes navy beans, kidney beans and chick peas, most in the $5 to $6.50 range. Lunch daily in summer and fall, noon to 2; dinner nightly, 6 to 9; tap room menu, Sunday-Thursday 5:30 to 10.

Barrows House, Main Street, Dorset. (802) 867-4455.

The new greenhouse off to the left of the dining room is where we would choose to eat at the Barrows House, if we were lucky enough to get one of its seven tables. Not that the larger main room with ruffled curtains, flowered china, and dark green flowered and ferned wallpaper

9

isn't inviting; it's simply that the greenhouse is spectacular. "It's like sitting outside,"says innkeeper Marilyn Schubert, "and in the rain you think you're under a waterfall." The red tile floor and brick wall are graced with green plants and trees, and with the attractive grounds outside (flowers in summer, snow in winter), the setting is magical.

In the last few years the menu, which changes nightly, has been upgraded from the traditional New England fare by new chef Skip King, who trained in Paris and worked at Hemingway's near Killington. Four-course dinners including appetizer, salad and dessert are a prix-fixe $19.95.

After complimentary brie wafers with drinks, you might begin with Maryland crab cake meuniere, scallop quenelles with tarragon, or chilled sliced venison with mustard sauce, and proceed to blackened red snapper, New England oyster pie, ballotine of duck with pheasant and veal, or shrimp with dark rum and wild rice. Calves liver is always on the menu, sometimes served with port wine and sage, sometimes with onions and balsamic vinegar. The changing choice of vegetables — long a house specialty — is particularly enticing: cauliflower with walnut butter, snow peas with shallots, braised white cabbage with raspberry vinegar and caraway, spinach sauteed with garlic, and spaghetti squash with maple syrup and brown sugar.

Desserts are more standard, ranging from grasshopper pie to blackberry tarts.

Lunch, noon to 1:30; dinner 6 to 9, two seatings at 6 and 8:30 in season.

The Garden Cafe, Southern Vermont Art Center, Manchester. (802) 362-4220.

This nifty cafe, halfway up the mountain, is run in the warmer months by Marianne Koks, daughter of the Village Auberge owners. A dining room and outdoor terrace at the back of the Art Center is the setting, with sculptures all around in the sloping gardens, and a view of distant mountains through the birch trees. On a nice day it could not be a more idyllic setting for lunch or Sunday brunch.

Silk flowers in little baskets and Vermont woven mats decorate the tables; chairs are the ice-cream parlor type with flowered seats. Everyone gets a small dish of celery and carrots with a savory dip. Fresh fruit daiquiris are a specialty, and the blanc de blanc for $5 a half carafe goes well with most lunches.

Soups, sandwiches and salads, with a few daily specials, are the fare, but everything has special touches. The tomato orange soup, served in a glass bowl with a slice of orange and whipped cream on top, was wonderful, delicate yet tangy. Almost everyone we saw was ordering the chicken pot pie with croissant crust, a special, but we tried a sandwich of chicken salad and snow peas (all sandwiches are served open-faced on six-grain bread with homemade mayonnaise) and a pasta salad with parmesan cheese and mushrooms, both excellent. Crabmeat on a croissant and a burger with bearnaise sauce and avocado were other specials. A terrine of veal and sweetbreads on French bread, tabbouleh salad and a salad of thinly sliced raw filet of beef with mayonnaise, capers, shallots and gherkins are other interesting choices. Prices are $1.50 or $1.75 for soup, and $3.75 to $5.95 for main dishes (except for $7.75 for the filet).

Sunday brunch brings some of the lunch items plus fruit soup, eggs Benedict on a croissant, smoked salmon and scrambled eggs, ultimate chicken hash, and chicken livers Andalousian style, with tomatoes, ginger, mustard, sherry, bacon and onions. Prices are $5.25 to $7.75.

Open Tuesday-Sunday, 11:30 to 2:30, June to mid-October.

Diversions

Dorset Playhouse. Tucked away in the trees just off Church Street, the rustic, all-wood barn with the red and white awning on the side was the first summer theater in Vermont. For 10 years it has been home to the Dorset Theater Festival, a non-profit professional theater company committed to the revival of plays from the past and the development of new plays and playwrights. Its rediscovery of Cole Porter's 1938 musical "You Never Know" went on national tour; other new plays have gone on to New York and Washington, and in 1985 the company gave the world premiere of "Family Affairs," a comedy by Lynne Kadish of Boston. "The 1940's Radio Hour" was a musical highlight of the 10th anniversary season, which ran from mid-June through Labor Day in 1985.

Merck Forest & Farmland Center. These days it's rare to find so large and unspoiled an area so available for public use as this 2,700-acre preserve northwest of Dorset off Route 315 in Rupert. Twenty-six miles of roads and trails are available for hiking in the forests, meadows and mountains. Established by George Merck of chemical company fame, it is a non-profit outdoor education center open to the public year-round. Scholars study the organic garden, the maple sugaring and forest management. Hikers, campers and cross-country skiers enjoy the trails to Birch and Beebe ponds and the vista of the Adirondacks from the Viewpoint. The forest is a New England treasure.

General stores. Peltier's General Store has been the center of Dorset life since the early 1800s, the more so since it was acquired in 1976 by Jay Hathaway and his wife Terri, who have augmented its everyday goods with exotica like Scotch smoked trout, cheddar cheese from Shelburne Farm, aromatic coffee beans and fine wines. Just back from New York with an array of new items, Jay said his store "is ever-changing because we don't want to be routine." History he has, but "we have a ton to offer in real life."

Equally historic but thoroughly unchanging is the **H.M. Williams Department Store,** two attached barns marked by a small sign at the south edge of town and an incredible jumble of merchandise placed helter-skelter (foodstuffs amidst the hardware, boxes of ladies' shoes identified with a cardboard sign: "With this quality and these prices, let the big boys compete"). Prices are marked by crayon and the cash register is a pouch worn around his waist by proprietor Dennis Bromlee. While we waited for 50 pounds of sunflower bird seed for a bargain $13.10, the woman ahead of us bought 50 pounds of rabbit pellets and was told where she could find a bale of hay.

Two other Dorset stores are of special interest. At **Patchcraft** on Main Street across from the Dorset Inn, Joan Stewart Neave creates and sells her wonderful appliqued house portraits plus pillows, tea cosies, oven mits, pot holders and other items which you see all over Dorset. "They're so quiet," says Joan, "that they're made for this town." South of town is the **J.K. Adams Co.** factory store, which has an exceptional assortment of woodware and housewares made from native hardwoods. Butcher blocks, knife racks,

11

bowls, cutlery and homespun tablecloths are for sale at substantial savings.

More shopping. Since adjacent Manchester offers such fine shopping opportunities, here are a few favorites. Silk-screened greeting cards from the **Crockett Collection** are available at discount prices at the showroom on Route 7 north of Manchester; other cards and notes are available as well, and you can watch the cards being made. Fishermen gravitate to the **Orvis Retail Store** in Manchester Center where fishing rods are made (and can be tried out at the adjacent trout pond). **Southwicks Ltd.** is a large, rather preppy store with gifts and conservative clothing for men and women (although it sells Woody Jackson cow T-shirts). **The Jelly Mill** is a three-story barn crammed with gifts, cards, gourmet foods, kitchen ware and much more; the **Buttery Restaurant** on the second floor serves lunch and snacks. Across from the newly renovated Equinox Hotel is a building housing several new and glamorous shops. We liked the **Pat Estey Stencil Studio** and the **Equinox International,** where sweaters from Uraguay and fascinating wall hangings from Peru are among the wares for sale.

Southern Vermont Art Center. High up a hillside off West Road in Manchester on the road to Dorset is this special place not to be missed. Inside are changing exhibits from early June through foliage season, plus the Garden Cafe for lunch or brunch. A summer film festival and concerts (lawn tickets, $3) by such groups as the U.S. Military Academy Band, the New England Brass Consort and the Southern Vermont Chamber Orchestra are always well attended. The Manchester Garden Club restored and maintains the **Boswell Botany Trail,** a three-quarter-mile walk past hundreds of wildflowers and 67 varieties of Vermont ferns, all identified by club members. An hour's hike through the woods is another attraction, and the sculpture garden is bordered by amazing vistas.

Back roads. They're all around, but a few are special. Dorset West Road and adjacent West Road in Manchester take you past some interesting and impressive country homes. The Danby Mountain Road winds through secluded forests and, if you keep bearing right at every intersection, you eventually come to a dead-end with a spectacular wide open view across the hillsides toward mountain peaks 50 miles away. The sight at fall foliage's height actually produced a few "wows" out of us and lived up to Dovetail innkeeper Jim Kingston's promise of the best foliage trip in Vermont.

Extra-Special

We can't ever seem to get through Manchester Center without stopping at **Mother Myrick's,** the ultimate ice cream parlor and confectionary shop, but much, much more. One of the things that lures us is the fudge sauce, which is so good that a friend to whom we give it hides her jar in a cupboard and eats it with a spoon. Here you can buy the most extraordinary homemade chocolates, get a croissant and cappuccino in the morning, tea and a pastry in the afternoon, or a grand marnier truffle cake and espresso late at night. Sodas, milkshakes, floats, sundaes and pastries are served in a fantastic art deco setting with etched-glass panels, bentwood cases, light columns and the like done by gifted Vermont craftsmen. Mother Myrick's also carries, appropriately, a line of greeting cards about diets! Open weekends from 8 a.m. to 11 p.m., weekdays 10 to 9.

Village of Stowe nestles in valley beneath Mount Mansfield.

Stowe, Vt.
A Resort for All Seasons

When Olympic skier Phil Mahre first saw Stowe dressed in summer's green rather than winter's white, he was struck by its beauty. So were many in the Eastern Ski writers audience he addressed in August 1985 upon agreeing to run a series of racing clinics at Stowe.

Most downhill skiers haven't been to Stowe in what for them is the off-season, either. But the undisputed Ski Capital of the East is a year-round destination resort, more than its newer, less endowed competitors can hope to be.

For one thing, Stowe is Stowe, a village unto itself about eight miles from Mount Mansfield, a ski area unto itself. The twain meets all along the Mountain Road, which links village and mountain. Such a marriage between town and ski area is unrivaled in New England and rich in history — a history unequaled by any other ski town in the country, according to Mount Mansfield Company officials.

The ski resort was led for years by Sepp Ruschp, who left Austria in 1936 to be ski instructor for the fledgling Mount Mansfield Ski Club. The alpine mystique of the surrounding area was enhanced by Baroness Maria Von Trapp and her family, their story immortalized by "The Sound of Music," when they founded the Trapp Family Lodge.

The rolling valley between broad Mount Mansfield on the west and the Worcester Mountains on the east creates an open feeling that is unusual for northern New England mountain regions. In Stowe's exhilarating air, recreation and cultural endeavors thrive.

Cross-country skiing complements downhill in winter. Other seasons bring

13

golf, tennis, horseback riding, hiking, performing arts, art exhibits and enough sights to see and things to do to make credible the area's claim to being a world-class resort.

Foremost a ski center, Stowe is somewhat lacking in inns of the classic New England variety. Instead, it has resorts, motels, ski dorms, condominiums and more Alpine/Bavarian chalets than you'll find just about anywhere this side of the Atlantic.

Still, Stowe is Stowe, a storybook New England ski town dominated by Vermont's highest peak. It's a place to be treasured, by skier and non-skier alike.

Inn Spots

Edson Hill Manor, Edson Hill Road, Stowe 05672. (802) 253-7371.

A French Provincial-style manor with old English charm, built in 1940 as a gentleman's estate, became a country inn in 1954 and retains its original private-home flavor except in the two new carriage houses with motel-type accommodations added in 1984.

Set high amidst 500 secluded acres, the inn has a spectacular terrace beside a spring-fed, kidney-shaped swimming pool, a pond stocked for trout fishing, and a cross-country ski center. Nearby are stables for horseback riding.

The manor was a prime location in 1980 for the filming of winter scenes for Alan Alda's movie, "The Four Seasons." The famous Mercedes scene took place on the trout pond.

The manor's exterior was designed to resemble the log cabins with cottage-type roofs typical of French Quebec.

Inside are nine guest rooms, the pine-paneled parlor with Delft tiles around the fireplace, orientals, and more books and magazines than anyone could possibly read, plus a beamed dining room where dinner is served to the public by reservation (see Dining Spots). The beams in the large parlor are said to have come from Ethan Allen's barn. Some of the paintings were done by Effie Juraine Martin Heath, a grandmother of the Lawrence Heath family, innkeepers since 1954.

One family suite has a fireplace, sofa and armchair, and a large bathroom with tub. Next to it is a small room with shared bath and the best view of the mountains.

Each of the two new carriage houses, up a hill beyond the inn, has four spacious rooms done in the decor of the original manor with beamed ceilings, pine paneled walls, brick fireplaces and private baths. Billed as the inn's luxury units, they accommodate two to four people. An older annex has four rooms, some with kitchenettes.

All told, five rooms in the manor plus those in the carriage houses have working fireplaces — a great attraction for winter visitors. We'd happily settle any time for the manor's large Studio, which has queensize bed, fireplace, skylight (this was formerly an artist's studio) and an exceptionally nice sitting area with rust sofa, velvet chair and ottoman, and picture windows overlooking the pool, pond and gardens.

Doubles, $106 to $170, MAP only.

Stowehof Inn, Edson Hill Road, Stowe 05672. (802) 253-9722.

"Slow — Deer Crossing," the sign warns as you drive up the steep road

Tree trunks support porte cochere at entrance of Stowehof Inn.

to the Stowehof, whose soaring Alpine exterior is a hilltop landmark hereabouts. "No parking — sleigh only," reads the sign at the door.

Such touches reflect the character of this unusual, thoroughly charming place that grew from a private ski house into one of Stowe's larger inns.

At the front entrance, the trunks of two maple trees support the enormous porte cochere above the small purple door. More tree trunks are inside the spacious living room, nicely broken up into intimate nooks and crannies, the two-level dining room, the downstairs game room and the lounge. The bell tower, the sod roof laced with field flowers and the architecture are reminiscent of the Tyrolean Alps.

You'd never suspect that the owners are two couples from Hawaii, but their decorating flair is apparent in most of the 47 guest rooms, some of them unusually large and sumptuous. All rooms have balconies or patios with views in summer of lovely clumps of birches, a swimming pool, a trout pond, lawns and the mountains.

Breakfast and dinner are served in the well-appointed dining room with beamed ceiling, fireplaces and windows looking onto pool and mountains. One side of the dinner menu changes nightly; entree prices run from $13 for chicken with an apricot-walnut sauce to $19 for beef Wellington or rack of lamb. Wiener schnitzel, Dover sole macademia fileted at the table and roesti potatoes are among the specialties. The enormous wine list contains selections priced up to $420.

Locals advise going to Stowehof just to see it. We thought it an equally appealing place in which to stay.

Doubles, $120 to $170, MAP; off-season, $60 to $70, EP.

Ten Acres Lodge, Luce Hill Road, Stowe 05672. (802) 253-7638.

Built as a farmhouse in 1826 with several later additions, this rambling and picturesque red frame house with white trim on a quiet hillside off

15

the Mountain Road is better known for its restaurant (see below) than its accommodations.

The dining rooms and the small tavern are altogether appealing, and the parlor and front library could not be more comfortable. Cord, the fluffy orange and white inn cat who was found in a woodpile, is apt to be ensconced in front of the fireplace in the parlor, where the striking wing chairs and couches piled with pillows are popular with houseguests. The large bay windows look out onto ever-changing vistas of valley and mountains.

New innkeepers Dave and Libby Helprin have enhanced the guest rooms as well. On two floors, the lodge's 14 rooms (10 with private baths) vary. Some are tiny and spare; others are quite a bit larger and more luxurious. One with kingsize bed even has two bathrooms, one containing the tub and the other the toilet and wash basin. The rooms are carpeted, walls are pine-paneled or wallpapered with pine trim, and good-looking quilts cover some of the beds.

Two cottages offer two or three bedrooms, kitchens, working fireplaces and terraces with great views in every direction.

A continental buffet breakfast includes cereal and two kinds of breads and muffins.

The grounds contain a small pool, tennis court, and flower and herb gardens that are popular with white rabbits. Beyond, cows graze on neighboring farmlands. Who could ask for a more tranquil setting?

Doubles, $50 to $80.

Ye Olde England Inn, Mountain Road, Stowe 05672. (802) 253-7558.

Stowe seems an unlikely spot for an English coaching inn, but this newly restored and expanded inn fashioned from the tired old Sans Souci is British all the way from the bright red phone booth out front to the menu in Mr. Pickwick's Pub.

All 23 guest rooms have private baths. The new rooms added in 1985 are spacious, decorated in Laura Ashley style and, on the third floor, are notable for interesting shapes and views of the mountains. A few efficiency units are beside the swimming pool.

Transplanted Britons Chris and Linda Francis, skiers both, are more in evidence at their new inn than are many innkeepers in the area, casting personality to their still-in-progress inn.

An English breakfast and dinner are served in the beamed Dickens Room. A pub-type menu is available all day in the newly expanded pub with hearthstone fireplace or on the outdoor deck lined with umbrellas advertising British ale, presenting a scene straight from the English countryside.

The menu offers bubble and squeak, ploughman's lunch, bangers and mash, Scotch egg and Cornish pasties from $3.25 to $6.95, served from noon to closing. A few non-British items like chicken fingers and chili are listed. We enjoyed a lunch of spinach salad served in a tostada shell and a good steak and kidney pie served inexplicably with a side bowl of gravy (could it have been for dipping the french fries in?), all washed down with pints of Whitbread and Watneys ales, served in proper pub glasses. One can even get ale by the yard. In the evening, live jazz and folk music are enjoyed by the laid-back crowd.

Doubles, $90 including breakfast in winter, $45 in summer.

16

Green Mountain Inn, Route 100, Stowe 05672. (802) 253-7301.

Its deep red facade a landmark in the center of the village since 1833, the inn has been carefully restored and upgraded in the last few years.

The main-floor dining room is now considered one of the area's best (see below) and the legendary Whip downstairs is still where the action is, in the appealing bar as well as the cafeteria-style grill and outdoor deck by the pool. A couple of small parlors in front retain the New England inn charm.

Most of the 57 guest rooms are behind the inn in a motel-type configuration, albeit with an antique look. The twin or canopy-covered queensize beds, custom-designed reproduction furniture manufactured specially for the inn, period wallpapers and stenciling are accompanied by color television sets and phones, and all have private baths. A new health center offers a spa program.

The inn is connected by an enclosed upstairs walkway to the Old Depot shopping complex next door.

Doubles, $55 to $85, lower off-season.

1802 House, School Street, Box 276, Stowe 05672. (802) 253-7351.

You enter right into the kitchen, so it comes as no surprise that guests — who must be non-smokers — have the run of the house in this spiffy B&B with five bedrooms, three with private baths, and uncommonly nice public rooms.

Our guests share the house with us,'' says Rose Marie Matulionis, innkeeper with Richard Hubbard. "They can cook their dinners and we even provide the candlelight.''

Fresh flowers abound in the rooms, especially the large living room with a comfy rust velvet sectional in front of the wood stove, a wall of bookshelves and a piano with 1950s sheet music.

Rose Marie serves fresh fruits, breads and muffins for breakfast in the charming dining room with hanging copper pots, hooked rug and striking flower arrangements.

Cozy down comforters top the foam mattresses ("I think they're much more comfortable than inner springs,'' says Rose Marie) on the oversize beds in the spacious guest rooms.

In summer, guests enjoy the rear deck and a pretty back yard with yellow and white lawn furniture; in winter, they like the ski storage and waxing room, and at all times they like the laundry facilities and no-smoking policy.

Doubles, $34 to $50.

The Gables Inn, Mountain Road, Stowe 05672. (802) 253-7730.

What many consider to be the best breakfast in town is served from 8 to noon at the Gables, either under yellow umbrellas on the front lawn (facing a spectacular view of Mount Mansfield), on the front porch or inside on picnic tables.

Twelve guest rooms in the main building, and four in a small motel-type annex, have charming country furniture, homemade wreaths and, an unusual touch, all rooms (and even a couple of bathrooms) are decorated with a few fine china plates from the extensive collection of owners Sol and Lynn Baumrind. All have private baths, most gleaming white and modern, some in what Sol Baumrind laughingly calls a "toilet tower" he added just for the purpose.

Breakfast on the lawn is a tradition at the Gables Inn.

A landscaped swimming pool, hot tub, small plant-filled solarium and large, comfortably furnished den and living room with TV are other attractions in this homey place. In winter the downstairs den is used for apres-ski; the owners put out crockpots full of steaming hot soup, hot hors d'oeuvres, and cheese and crackers after 4 p.m. for hungry skiers, who BYOB.

As for that breakfast, it's open to the public, and some days the Baumrinds serve as many as 250. Says Sol with a smile, "service is leisurely — that's a code word for slow." Aside from all the old standbys, one can feast on kippers or chicken livers with onions and scrambled eggs, matzoh brei, and the Gables Florentine, two poached eggs on a bed of spinach, with a chipped beef sauce. Stuffed French toast made with raisin bread, and blueberry or banana pancakes are popular choices.

In ski season, family-style dinners are served in the dining rooms amid a wondrous collection of Royal Copenhagen plates. The picnic tables are covered with tablecloths, and candles glow.

Doubles, $90, MAP in winter; $40 to $45, EP in summer.

Foxfire Inn, Route 100, Box 2180, RD 2, Stowe 05672. (802) 253-4887.
An early 19th century Vermont farmhouse now is the home of an acclaimed Italian restaurant (see Dining Spots) and five comfortable guest rooms with private baths.

Innkeepers for 10 years, Art and Irene Segreto serve full breakfasts to inn guests on a sunny breakfast porch, which has white bentwood chairs, gold tablecloths and many plants in the windows on three sides.

The upstairs guest rooms are individually and handsomely decorated. One corner room has a bed with a crocheted curtain type of affair swathing the headboard, centered by a lace-covered hanging lamp. Another with an oriental rug, sofabed and blue corduroy chair has a quilt and ruffled pillows on the bed, while a third has an ingenious corner shower. Tiny vases filled with flowers are on the dressers.

18

Watch your step in the upstairs corridor — there's a well-disguised two-inch rise that we tripped over coming and going, several times no less. The comfortable downstairs sitting room has a fireplace; another parlor leads into the bar.

Out front is a lovely patio, lined with yellow lilies and redwood tubs ablaze with geraniums, under a huge maple tree.

Doubles, $48 to $56.

The Inn at the Mountain, Mountain Road, Stowe 05672. (802) 253-7311.

The once-renowned Lodge at Smuggler's Notch has been turned into condominiums, but next door the motor inn run by the Mount Mansfield Company continues with the next best thing.

A year-round resort with three heated pools, tennis courts, townhouses, kitchenettes and skiing almost at the door, the complex has 71 units, 33 of them in the comfortable three-story inn. Each has two double beds, refrigerator, TV, steam bath and sliding glass doors to deck or patio.

Downstairs are conference rooms and the Fireside Tavern. Down still more stairs is the **Toll House Restaurant,** serving lunch ($4.50 to $6.50) on the flower-bedecked outdoor terrace and dinner in the large, elegantly appointed dining room. Entrees ($9.75 to $14.95) have some creative touches: lamb and rhubarb ragout served over wheatberry rice pilaf or halibut basted with raspberry mayonnaise. The pastry chef is known for her desserts.

Doubles, $165 to $200, MAP in winter; $90, EP in summer.

Dining Spots

Ten Acres Lodge, Luce Hill Road, Stowe. (802) 253-7638.

The dining room is classically pretty — and the menus on the daring and innovative side — at Ten Acres, which usually is mentioned first when Stowe people are asked their favorite restaurants.

In summer, the airy porch with its small-paned bow windows and flowered wallpaper fills up first; the paneled interior dining room appeals more in winter. White-linened tables are set with Villeroy & Boch service plates in the Palermo pattern. The atmosphere is rather hushed, as Vivaldi music plays softly in the background, and young women in white blouses and long black skirts serve unobtrusively.

In an unusual arrangement, kitchen duties are shared by two head chefs, Jack Pickett and Bob Titterton, each of whom works five days, with three overlapping. Says Bob with a laugh, "one of us is right-handed and the other left-handed — that's how we get along so well!" Both have been at Ten Acres several years, so obviously it works.

They work hard at presenting an exciting and ever-changing menu, using whatever Vermont produce they can get, local lamb and veal and the like. Venison is flown in from New Zealand. Sherbets (one is starfruit) and ice creams are made in house; chocolate raspberry is a favorite.

The left side of the menu lists six appetizers and six entrees of the season; the right side has the night's two appetizers, soup (chilled blueberry bisque at our August visit) and three entrees. For a salad, how about one August version of spinach, endive, radicchio, apple and walnuts with port wine and stilton dressing?

We enjoyed generous drinks, crusty sourdough bread with sweet butter, an appetizer of lobster, shiitake mushrooms and creme fraiche in a cabbage leaf, and small house salads with excellent garlic-lemon and blue cheese vinaigrette dressings. Both the butterflied leg of lamb with preserved black currants and cracked peppercorns and the char-grilled Cornish game hen with tomato, basil and creme fraiche were superb, served with julienned zucchini and rice pilaf. A Sonoma merlot, for $14, was a perfect accompaniment.

Other entrees, which are in the $14 to $17 range, could be a saute of lobster, bay scallops, shiitake mushrooms, leeks, tomato, snow peas, red bliss potatoes, pancetta and cream; grilled veal chops with wild mushrooms and tarragon drambuie sauce; grilled duck steak with blood oranges, red flame grapes and orange muscat wine (how colorful can you get?), and sauteed breast and grilled marinated leg of pheasant with lobster-stuffed mushrooms. For $3.75 to $5.50, you could start with Wellfleet oysters on the half shell with American sturgeon caviar or a confit of duckling with balsamic vinegar, maple syrup and pecans, and go on to a soup of celeriac and fennel.

Our desserts were cherry ricotta pie and a goblet of bananas and fresh pineapple topped with Meyer's rum and coconut, both just right with the good strong coffee.

The huge wine list includes a page of old and rare vintages, most over $100 and going up to $260. Ten Acres is a place to cherish for special occasions.

Dinner nightly, 6 to 9:30.

Isle de France, Mountain Road, Stowe. (802) 253-7751.

Next door to the long-popular Shed but miles removed in terms of tone and atmosphere, this incredibly lavish (and almost out of place) restaurant was opened in 1979 by chef-owner Jean Lavina, a Frenchman from the Lyons area by way of the French Shack in New York City.

Formerly the Crystal Palace, the place shows its heritage: cut-glass chandeliers, mirrors, gilt ornamental work around the ceilings, rose-bordered service plates with gold edges, heavy silver and a single red rose on each white-linened table. Three tables have sofas for two on one side. The two dining rooms have plush round-backed chairs; the cozy bar has apricot-colored sofas.

Dining in the classical French style is serious business here. For appetizers ($3 to $5), you might start with pork and veal country pate or oysters bourguignon. The 20 entrees priced from $12 to $17 are supplemented by six to eight nightly specials like poached salmon in beurre blanc or fresh venison with a fois gras sauce. Eight beef presentations vary from entrecote bearnaise to chateaubriand; one is slices of tenderloin with a creamy bourbon sauce. There are sweetbreads, frog's legs, Dover sole meuniere and many other French standards.

Desserts range from frozen meringues Chantilly and creme caramel to bananas Foster, cherries jubilee and crepes Suzette for two. The large wine list is priced upward from the mid-teens.

Dinner, 6:30 to 10:30; closed Monday.

Green Mountain Inn, Route 100, Stowe. (802) 253-7301.

Chef Keith Martin has helped upgrade considerably this once-traditional

Ten Acres Lodge is known for fine dining in Stowe.

dining room, now country pretty with bare wood floors and nicely spaced tables flanked by bow chairs and set with white damask, candles, blue flowered plates and heavy polished silver. Lanterns and watercolors by the late Vermont artist Walton Blodgett adorn the walls.

Among appetizers ($3.95 to $5.50), you might try smoked Irish salmon or a sausage of salmon, shrimp, scallops and sole with red pepper puree. For main courses ($11.50 to $14.95), the chef innovates with fresh Idaho trout stuffed with a light shrimp mousse and finished with ginger hollandaise sauce, scallops sauteed with white wine and lime, stuffed quail with apple-prune sauce and breast of duck grilled with juniper berry butter.

For dessert, how about frozen amaretto souffle or "sac de bon-bon," a chocolate shell filled with mousse and fresh fruit ($6.50 for two)? The wine list is reasonably priced, five chardonnays ranging, for instance, from $11 to $29. Dinner nightly, 6 to 9:30 p.m.

Downstairs is **The Whip,** smartly redecorated and striking for the whips in the wall divider separating bar from dining room and over the fireplace. Just outside is a most attractive deck, where the garden furniture is navy and white and tables are shaded by white umbrellas.

The day's fare is chalked on blackboards above cases where the food is displayed. Many of the dishes are calorie-counted for those who are there for the spa facilities. Country pate with cornichons on toast points, smoked salmon with capers, tomato basil soup, salads with dressings devised by the Canyon Ranch in Arizona, crabmeat on a croissant with melted cheddar, open-faced antipasto sandwich — this is perfect "grazing" fare.

Main dishes like grilled yellowfin tuna, pork chops flamed with applejack, trout with lime and lamb chops with curry butter are chalked up at night. Prices are in the $8 to $11 range.

Lunch daily, 11:30 to 3; dinner, 6 to 9:30.

Edson Hill Manor, Edson Hill Road, Stowe. (802) 253-7371.

The inviting dining room of this manor estate high up Edson Hill is open to the public for dinner by reservation.

The beamed dining room is rustic, with rusty orange curtains on the windows overlooking forests and mountains. High ladderback chairs are at each table, set with woven mats for breakfast and white cloths for dinner. One particularly nice window table for two overlooks pool and pond.

The limited menu is a mix of New England and continental specialties. Appetizers ($2.50 to $3.95) range from chicken liver pate and marinated herring to baked stuffed mushrooms Italienne and escargots forestiere. A selection of raw vegetables is served with an unusual maple-curry dip.

Entrees are $9.50 for fettuccine Alfredo to $13.95 for sirloin steak. Sole amandine is sauteed with Dry Sack sherry, and veal, chicken and bay scallops presentations vary.

When the inn's ski touring center is open, a fireside luncheon is available in the downstairs cocktail lounge from noon to 2:30.

Dinner nightly by reservation, 6 to 9.

Hapleton's West Branch Cafe, rear of the Carlson Building, Main Street, Stowe. (802) 253-4653.

Some people think Hapleton's serves the most interesting food for the price in town. It's a cozy downstairs restaurant with wooden booths and bar and much stained glass, all crafted by local artists. Hanging green lamps and a huge fireplace create a comfortable spot in which people love to hang out. A small side patio with Perrier umbrellas and black wrought-iron furniture off the main floor operates in warm months.

Appetizers and light fare are served all day. The dinner menu ($9.50 to $13.50), augmented by blackboard specials, lists grilled lamb chops, sauteed liver, barbecued pork chops, and fish and veal of the night.

For lunch, try a "dog from Montreal," the Hebrew National brand, with pommes frites, or steamed shrimps en tabloid, served with complimentary newsprint.

At Sunday brunch, a popular choice is the Jamaican French toast with rum, coconut and cinnamon in the batter.

Open daily from 11:30, lunch to 3, dinner 6 to 9:30.

Foxfire Inn and Restaurant, Route 100, Stowe. (802) 253-4887.

North of the village is this small inn and large restaurant serving some of the best Northern and Southern Italian cuisine in Vermont.

A few oriental rugs dot the wide-plank floors of the large blue main dining room at the rear. Windsor chairs are at bare polished wood tables, topped by different woven or quilted mats, fresh flowers in carafes and occasionally yellow cloths. On the other side of the bar is a plant-filled enclosed porch.

The hot antipasto (rolled eggplant, mushrooms and shrimp, $8.50) and garlicked red peppers with cured beef ($4.50) are popular appetizers. Pasta dishes, including salad served after the meal, run from $6.50 for spaghetti with meatballs or sausages to $8.25 for fettuccine Alfredo.

Six veal dishes, five chicken, two steak and two seafood make up the entrees, $10.25 to $13.50. There's also a nightly special — lobster fra diavolo when we visited.

Italian cheesecake, frozen lemon or strawberry chiffon tortoni, a rum and coffee-flavored chocolate cake, cannoli and spumoni are among the luscious desserts. In cooler months, diners like to take their cappuccino with amaretto

Edson Hill Manor

or Foxfire coffee (with frangelico and Italian brandy, the whipped cream topped with an Italian flag) into the parlor to sit in front of the fireplace. The mainly Italian wine list contains some excellent values, a Torresella merlot for $9 and chardonnay for $10 among them.

Dinner nightly.

Stowe-Away Lodge, Mountain Road, Stowe. (802) 253-7574.

The blenders atop the tiled bar at Stowe-Away, which doesn't sound like a Mexican restaurant but is, hum most of the time in summer, when up to 13 gallons a night of chef-owner Michael Henzel's special homemade margarita mix get frothed up — $3.25 fetches a 12-ounce portion.

Two small dining rooms with hand-painted tile tables flank the bar; the back dining room looks onto a small terrace used for summer dining, where a redwood hot tub is on a platform at the side. Relax in this with one of the margaritas and you may never make it to dinner.

Mike Henzel, who has cooked in Wyoming and California, designed the menu himself and it is used in several other Mexican restaurants across the country.

Soups, served with garlic toast, include a chile verde and a vegetarian chili. Guacamole salad is $3.25; super nachos, $3.50. Seven kinds of burrito ($4.25 to $5.50), tostadas and tacos, combination plates and huevos rancheros regular and deluxe are listed, as are crab enchiladas, quesadilla grande, enchiladas mole, arroz con pollo and piccadillo. Fajitas, shrimp kabob, chicken Louie and large shrimp sauteed with garlic, butter, coriander, lime and white wine are in the $6 to $10 range. A party platter, serving three to five hungry gringos with ten dishes, is $35.95.

The homemade brownie is the only dessert in which the chef uses sugar; honey sweetens the sopaipillas, flan and homemade ice cream.

At Sunday brunch, egg dishes are $5.25, served with home fries, and the five versions of Eggs Louie are variations of eggs Benedict, $5.75 to $6.25.

Stowe-Away also has 11 bedrooms, in simple rustic style, six with private baths and five that share two, $42 to $50 a night.

Dinner, 5:30 to 10; Sunday brunch, 11 to 2:30.

Extra-Special

Austrian Tea Room, Trapp Family Lodge, Luce Hill Road, Stowe. (802) 253-8511.

In summer or foliage season, we know of no more appealing place for lunch or snack than the rear deck of the Austrian Tea Room, with planters of geraniums and petunias enhancing the view across the countryside and horses grazing nearby. It's a majestic setting where you feel on top of the world.

The fresh fruit salad looks great, as does the avocado stuffed with shrimp salad, and you can get broiled knockwurst or weisswurst served with sauerkraut and potato salad or an aufschnitt plate ($4.75 to $5.50). There are six open-faced sandwiches, fancy drinks, cafe Viennoise and Austrian wines by the glass or liter.

Those Austrian desserts we all know and love, sacher torte, linzer torte, apfelstrudel and the like, as well as Bavarian chocolate, peach torte and jailhouse pie, are $2.25 or $2.50 and — with a cup of cafe mocha — a delightful afternoon pick-me-up.

The trip up Luce Hill Road gives you a chance to see the rebuilt, exotic Trapp Family Lodge, which the locals consider the closest thing to Disneyland in Vermont. The tea room remains true to the lodge's heritage.

Open daily, 10:30 to 8:30.

Restaurant Swisspot, Main Street, Stowe. (802) 253-4622.

Skiers have always been partial to fondues, and they're the specialty at this small and enduring place, brought to Stowe in 1968 after its incarnation as the restaurant in the Swiss Pavilion at Expo 67 in Montreal.

The classic Swiss cheese fondue with a dash of kirsch is $16.95 for two, and made a fun meal for our skiing family. Also good is the beef fondue oriental ($13.95 for one), served with four sauces. There are six different quiches ($9.95) and a handful of entrees like bratwurst, manicotti, chicken Florentine and sirloin steak with a butter and herb sauce, $7.95 to $13.95.

Onion soup, eleven variations of burgers and many sandwiches ($3 to $7) are featured at lunch.

The dessert accent is on Swiss chocolate, including a chocolate fondue with marshmallows and fruits for dunking.

Open daily from noon to 10 p.m.

Diversions

Mount Mansfield. Skiing is what made Stowe famous, legions of skiers having been attracted to New England's most storied mountain since the East's first chairlift was installed in 1940 (the Mount Mansfield Company is its official name, but everyone calls the ski area Stowe). Today, Mount Mansfield has six lifts and about one-third of its slopes are for expert skiers, including the awesome "Front Four" — the precipitous National, Goat, Starr and Liftline trails, so steep that on the Starr you cannot see the bottom from the ledge on top; they almost make the Nosedive seem tame. There's easier terrain, of course, and the related Spruce Peak ski area across the way has four more lifts, a sunny southeast exposure and a special section for new skiers. Combined with accommodations and nightlife, the total skiing experience ranked Stowe among the top ten ski resorts in the world, according to a 1985 survey. Adult lift tickets are $28 daily.

Summer at Mount Mansfield. A four-passenger gondola takes visitors 7,000 feet up to the Cliff House, just below the summit (adults $6, open daily June 29-Oct. 14). Cars can drive up the 4.5-mile **Mountain Auto Road,** known to skiers who ease down it in winter as the Toll Road (cars $6, daily May 25-Oct. 14). The **Alpine Slide at Spruce Peak** appeals to the young at heart; you take a chairlift up and sled down (single rides, $3.75; open daily in summer, weekends in late spring and early fall).

Smugglers' Notch. Up the Mountain Road past the ski area you enter the Mount Mansfield State Park, passing picnic areas and the Long Trail. A couple of hairpin turns take you into Smugglers' Notch, a narrow pass with 1,000 foot cliffs on either side. It's the closest thing we've seen in the East to Yosemite, a quiet, awe-inspiring place to stop and gawk at such rock formations as Elephant Head, King Rock and the Hunter and His Dog. Stop at Smugglers' Cave and, farther on, hike into Bingham Falls. The road is not for the faint-hearted (it's closed in winter, for good reason). We drove back from Jeffersonville after a thunderstorm and found waterfalls which had been trickles on the way over suddenly gushing down the rocks beside the lonely road.

Special Events. Activities are scheduled all summer and fall, starting with the challenging Stowe Bicycle Race through Smugglers' Notch and including an Eight Mile Road Race, the Stowe Crafts Show, the Head Classic Tennis Tournament and an antique car rally, among others. The annual Stowe Winter Carnival (Jan. 17-26, in 1986) is the liveliest winter extravaganza between Quebec City and New Orleans.

The **Cold Hollow Cider Mill,** south of town on Route 100, is a large and intriguing red barn where you can watch cider being made (and drink the sweet and delicious free samples). For more than 20 years the Chittenden family also have sold tart cider jelly, cider donuts and other apple products as well as cookbooks, wooden toys, gourmet foods and about every kind of Vermont jam, jelly or preserve imaginable.

Shopping. Shops are concentrated in Stowe village and scattered along Route 100 and the Mountain Road. In the village, **Shaw's General Store** considers itself "90 years young" and carries "most everything," especially sporting goods, sportswear, gifts and oddities. Nearby is the new Old Depot Shops, an open meandering mall of a place with **All Things Special** crafts, **Purcell's Country Foods** (where sensational fruit butters like strawberry daiquiri and peach bourbon are made every day), **Annie Van's** handpainted clothing, **Stuffed in Stowe** gifts and **Bear Pond Books.** Up the Mountain Road at 108 West is the **Stowe Kitchen Co.,** with practical cookware and gadgets, and **Pinnacle Antiques,** an exceptional antiques and handicrafts shop on three levels featuring furniture, jewelry, antique quilts and such; we loved the limited edition cotton or wool sweaters, some with cow buttons, featuring pigs, horses, Vermont houses and other country things. Also on the Mountain Road is the **Christmas Place,** which speaks for itself; the excellent **Stowe Mountain Sports** is at Stowe Center. The West Branch Shops include **Betsy Snite Sports, Once Upon a Time** and **Samara,** an unusually good shop featuring works of Vermont craftsmen.

Waitsfield and Warren, Vt.
The Spirit of the Valley

Even more than most Vermont areas best known for skiing, the Mad
River Valley is a year-round paradise for sportsmen.

The focus, of course, is on skiing — at the venerable and spartan Mad
River Glen, a challenging area for hardy, serious skiers, and at the newer
Sugarbush and Sugarbush North, the toney resort spawned by and for jet-
setters. Both are very much "in" with skiers, for vastly differing reasons.

In the off-season, which extends from May into November, there are the
conventional athletic pursuits associated with other destination ski resorts,
such as golf and tennis. There also are the more unusual: mountaineering,
polo, rugby and soaring.

Off-mountain, activity centers along Route 100, which links the two
villages of Waitsfield and Warren. Ironically, Waitsfield (the home of Mad
River Glen) is busier and more hip in the Sugarbush style. Warren (the
address for Sugarbush) is in the Mad River Glen tradition, remote and
bypassed by the times.

The spirit of the valley — considered unique by its adherents — emerges
from its rugged, closed-in terrain as well as from the contrasting mix
attracted by its two skiing faces.

Unlike other ski resorts where one big mountain crowns a plateau, here
mountains crowd the valley on all sides, forging several narrow valleys
which leave some visitors feeling hemmed in. To understand, you have
only to stay in a remote chalet at Mad River, the mountains rising in silence
all around, or descend the back road from Roxbury Gap, one of Vermont's
more heart-stopping drives, which rewards the persevering with awesome
close-ups of some of the state's highest peaks.

The chic of Sugarbush joins with the rusticity of Mad River to present
choices from racquetball to backpacking, from boutiques to country stores,
from nightclubbing to roadhouses. For fine dining, the valley has no peer
among Eastern ski resorts.

Although the valley is at its best and busiest in the winter, its spirit spans
all seasons.

Inn Spots

Tucker Hill Lodge, Route 17, Box 147, Waitsfield 05673. (802) 496-
3983.

Emily and Zeke Church, who grew up five blocks from each other in
Wilson. N.C., have run this attractive inn since 1976; the South's loss is
Vermont's gain. In 1985 Zeke won the Vermont Hospitality Association's
"Restaurateur of the Year" award — so you can tell the dining room here
(see below) is well thought of.

This is one of the more lavishly landscaped inns we have seen. In summer,
the flower gardens are spectacular, with hanging clematis, flowering kale
and (we had to ask Zeke what this strange-looking thing was) decorative
mullen.

The 20 guest rooms vary in size and decor; 14 have private baths. Four
are in the "Cross Country" building across the way. All have handmade

Innkeepers Emily and Zeke Church in front of Tucker Hill Inn.

quilts on the beds and, of course, bouquets of flowers are in abundance in bedrooms and public rooms. A nicely furnished living room has TV and fieldstone fireplace; a big rec room offers a rustic bar and another fireplace. Tennis courts, a swimming pool and a large outdoor deck ringed with cedar trees are other attractions.

Breakfasts are hearty: seasonal fresh fruit, followed perhaps by cottage cheese pancakes with fresh peaches, a broccoli, tomato and mushroom omelet, or Vermont toast, which is French toast with shredded cheddar cheese between the layers.

The Churches recommend hiking the local trails (the Long Trail is not far away); you'll need to after one of their breakfasts or dinners! Guided mountain hikes are among the outdoor options they offer.

Doubles, $82 to $118, MAP.

The Waitsfield Inn, Route 100, Box 362B, Waitsfield 05673. (802) 496-3979.

If you detect a California flair injected into this New England setting, that's because the Campbell family emigrated from their corporate lifestyle in the Santa Cruz Mountains to take over the old Bagatelle Inn in 1983.

Ted and JoAnne Campbell and four children worked uncounted hours upgrading the original 1825 farmhouse from a ski lodge offering sleeping bag space in a barn loft into attractive dining rooms (see below) and ten colorful, comfortable guest rooms. Their crowning achievement is the plush sitting room in the attached barn and woodshed plus six new contemporary-style guest rooms on its upper levels. All sixteen rooms have private baths.

The spacious new sitting room is a beauty, sensitively done with rag rugs and orientals on the floors, the original wood on walls and ceilings, no fewer than five sofas plus velvet wing chairs, a huge fireplace, piano and game table.

27

The new barn guest rooms are particularly appealing, two with beamed lofts and skylights, and another very large with oriental rug, skirted tables and tufted comforter. JoAnne made all the attractive comforters, draperies, dust ruffles and curtains used throughout the guest rooms, while her husband did the stenciling. JoAnne also cans all the inn's jams, jellies and chutneys, offering them as well as interesting vinegars for sale.

Full breakfasts are served daily to guests and the public.

Doubles, $84 to $120, MAP.

The Sugartree, Sugarbush Access Road, Warren 05674. (802) 583-3211. *RR BOX 38*

Thanks to Chicago corporate expatriates Howard and Janice Chapman, the Sugartree also has undergone a facelift into an inviting inn from what essentially had been a ski chalet for 30 years.

Janice had never even seen skiing before they arrived in 1983. Summer's trees, gardens and window boxes envelop the inn in its own delightful island of greenery but, she says, when the leaves are gone "we get the most gorgeous views of the mountains and can watch all the skiers" across the way. And the fall foliage, she adds with her infectious, hearty laugh, "takes your breath away."

An artist at heart, she has outfitted her inn with an extravagant potpourri of folk art, Vermont handicrafts and inanimate animals of all sizes and kinds, from stuffed teddy bears to duck napkin rings, wood hens to mouse dolls. They're at their showiest in the entry hall and large paneled living room with fireplace, big windows and TV.

Colorful bedspreads, shams and dust ruffles perk up the 11 guest rooms, all with private baths. Furnished in country style, they vary in size from a large main-floor room with stove and sink to a small third-floor room with hearts and birds on the wallpaper. Some have quilts, and country curtains are being made for all the rooms.

Janice cooks a full country breakfast, which starts with as many fresh fruits as she can find, in a cheery breakfast room with four tables amidst a painted cow, a wooden pig and such. She leaves the kitchen open for guests to get ice and to make sandwiches, and says "it's like a party in ski season" when Howard serves hearty soups or sweet and sour meatballs to returning skiers.

Doubles, $40 to $60.

The Lareau Farm Country Inn, Route 100, Box 563, Waitsfield 05673. (802) 496-4949.

This really is a farm with gardens — the 1852 farmhouse lately converted into an inn, with barn, woodshed and appropriate country setting on flatlands that were farmed until a few years by the Lareau family. In the Mad River, just across the road, a 10-foot-deep swimming hole is flanked by rocks. You can dive into "water so clear you can see the brown trout," according to Susan Easley, innkeeper with her husband Dan.

The Easleys took over in 1984 and have added bathrooms and redone the 10 guest rooms, Sue piecing together the squares for 10 bed quilts in their first summer. The most dramatic changes are in the former woodshed, with four rooms on two stories. The dirt floors have given way to carpeting, but the rooms retain some of the original beams and posts amid modern touches like private baths. Brass bedsteads and rockers are mixed with a profusion of hanging plants.

The other six rooms, which share baths, are in the oldest part of the house, built in the 1700s. The main structure, which was added to it, now houses an enormous kitchen which is the center of activity, a dining room with two large tables, and a parlor full of Victorian furniture and stuffed animals. The wrap-around porch outside has comfy furniture in which guests like to laze.

Dan Easley is the breakfast chef, whipping up homemade muffins or breads and perhaps an egg souffle casserole on the wood cooking stove.

The Easleys provide hors d'oeuvres and setups for guests in the winter, and were thinking of serving dinners on Saturday nights (they had just catered a dinner for 25 polo players the night before we visited). Because the main entrance to the inn is via the kitchen, they planned to make that space into a common room and add a kitchen out back.

Doubles, $40 to $70.

The Inn at Beaver Pond Farm, Golf Course Road, RFD 2, Warren 05674. (802) 583-2861.

A farmhouse this may be, but an elegant one it is indeed. Located off a quiet country road overlooking several beaver ponds and the Sugarbush Golf Club fairways, the light green house with green roof has candles lighted in the windows even on a summer afternoon. Inside, the Hansens share their home with guests, who enjoy a stylish living room, a rear deck with a barbecue, a small bar where setups and hors d'oeuvres are provided in the late afternoon, and a lovely formal dining room with long table and oriental rug.

Full country breakfasts are served there in the morning, and gourmet dinners are presented on occasion at the owners' invitation.

Upstairs are five well furnished guest rooms, three with private baths and two sharing.

An advantage here is that guests are close to the clubhouse of the golf course, which in winter has a network of cross-country ski trails. A disadvantage for some is that standard booking periods are for two-day weekends and five-day weeks.

Doubles, $56 to $60.

Mountain View Inn, Route 17, RFD Box 69, Waitsfield 05673. (802) 496-2426.

One of the valley's first inns, occupying a bright red farmhouse built about 1830, this is a mellow, laid-back kind of place since it was taken over in 1979 by Fred and Suzy Spencer. The sign out front may or may not be up, the owners may or may not be home (the doors were open, but the family was off at church the Sunday morning we stopped by), the inn is heated by a wood furnace and the innkeepers serve hot mulled cider before the 6 p.m. dinner.

The seven guest rooms, all with private baths, are furnished with hand-made quilts, interesting hooked rugs and antiques, including high beds and one maple canopied bed.

A wood stove is the focal point of the pine-walled living room, where guests gather on old rockers or around the piano. They eat family style around the large antique trestle table in the dining room.

Both Spencers cook the meals, featuring their home-grown vegetables, homemade soups, breads and desserts. Eggs laid by their chickens and German apple pancakes are popular at breakfast, the hour for which is set by majority vote the night before.

Doubles, $90, MAP.

Dining Spots

Tucker Hill Lodge, Route 17, Waitsfield. (802) 496-3983.

The dining room is the big attraction at this inn, drawing people from all over the valley. The inner room is paneled and beamed; the outer addition is greenhouse-style, with skylights and brick floors. Quilts and watercolors decorate the walls; tables are white-linened and service is friendly.

Chef George Hamlin (who has worked at Cavey's and Apricots, two excellent restaurants in our home area) decides every morning what he will put on the dinner menu. He uses as many local products as he can, including veal and lamb, and the nearby Von Trapp Greenhouse (run by a grandson of Maria) supplies all kinds of lettuce and other vegetables ("leeks an inch in diameter, and perfectly clean," says George) for the inn. The assistant chef brings in eggs from his own chickens with which to make the pasta.

There are usually two soups and four appetizers to start. In summer, soups include mussel and clam, chilled broccoli, chilled fruit with fresh raspberries and creme fraiche, and cheese with scallions and red and yellow pepper.

We started with "a warm summer night's seafood salad," a colorful plate of smoked Maine brook trout and Maine lobster, garnished with smoked Maine mussels, julienne of celery and baby carrots, local spinach, marigold petals and warm fresh dill-raspberry beurre blanc with local red raspberries — whew! The roast sirloin of western Black Angus beef was, according to the night's menu, "rubbed with shallots, garlic and kosher salt, with a Madeira wine veal glace sauce with Italian porcini mushrooms, Vermont chanterelles and fresh savory." It was delicious, as were the medallions of pork loin with apples in a creme fraiche sauce with whole grain mustard and honey.

Soups are $2.25, appetizers in the $5 to $7 range, and entrees start around $12 for rock Cornish game hen (topped with coconut in a fresh pineapple dark rum sauce) and rise to around $19 (fresh Maine lobster with scallop sausage).

A special treat some nights is fresh New Zealand venison; one way the chef does it is with a kiwi fruit puree flavored with lime vinegar, chambord and creme fraiche, and an added touch of chestnut puree. The vegetables that garnish each dish are wonderful and ever changing.

Innkeepers Zeke and Emily Church are proud of their wine list, which is wide-ranging and fairly priced. Mirassou zinfandel Monterey for only $10 was a treat.

The eight or ten desserts (most $3) change every day as well; chocolate marquis, peach brandy tart, fresh strawberry-grand marnier mille feuille, white chocolate mousse with espresso sauce, and fresh raspberry Napoleon are possibilities. We were content with passion fruit sorbet and one of the lodge's special coffees with kahlua, brandy and cointreau. This is truly special-occasion dining!

Dinner nightly, 6:30 to 9:30; Sunday brunch, noon to 2.

Greenery and mirrors grace dining rooms at the Phoenix.

The Phoenix, Sugarbush Village, Warren. (802) 583-2777.

The Phoenix could only be in Sugarbush and its desserts — well, they're from nowhere else, either. Chef-owner Peter Sussman says his ratio of dinners to desserts is 106 percent desserts, because people often have more than one and some come only for dessert and coffee in the lounge.

Before dessert, however, comes the setting, the meal and a warning. "You can't have dessert until you eat your veggies," Peter admonished as we ogled the dessert cart he was wheeling by to another table.

The setting is multi-leveled with enormous windows filled with plants, twinkling lights even in summer, green-linened tables bathed in candlelight, bentwood chairs, mirrors and greenery everywhere. An old brick fireplace and hand-hewn beams support an intimate, narrow dining balcony. The two-level lounge has velvet sofas, skylights and beautiful stained glass. The bar was transformed from an old altar rail, there's an enormous espresso machine and even an old barber pole is in a corner. Too chic for words!

The meals, though fine, may be mere prelude to the desserts. Salads are extra, and appetizers like duck and scallion dumplings or wild mushroom tartlette ($4 to $6) might make you too sated for the finale. Anyway, the chewy rolls doled out with tongs helped tide us over and were good enough to ask for seconds. We had grilled chicken with pan-fried noodles (the noodles too crisp and the spicy sauce too salty and mostly soy) and a good breast of duck with raspberry and thyme. The vegetables, a wild rice pilaf and a tasty mix of snap peas and strips of red and green pepper, were superb.

At the appropriate moment and with due fanfare, Peter wheeled up two carts containing six desserts each. They ranged from white chocolate mousse and napoleons to fresh peach pie with pecan praline topping and banana kiwi fruit tart filled with custard creme, all of which we sampled because each can order two half-portions — though they turned out to be what most would consider full portions.

Peter makes up to 40 desserts daily from his repertoire of 280 or more. "I eat six or seven of them a day myself," he says. "I have a pretty bad sweet tooth," although you'd never know it from his build. His tastes are eclectic and he only makes what he likes, he said as he showed off his sparkling kitchen and climate-controlled wine cellar the next morning.

He was about to prepare napoleons with amaretto and grand marnier and a mocha macaroon pie with espresso cream topping among that evening's desserts. We groaned at the thought and toddled out into the noonday sun for a croissant at a nearby deli.

Dinner, nightly 6 to 10 (closed Wednesday in non-ski season); desserts also available in the bar.

The Common Man, German Flats Road, Warren. (802) 583-2800.

Here is the ultimate incongruity: a soaring, century-old timbered barn with floral carpets on the walls to cut down the noise and keep out wintry drafts, six crystal chandeliers hanging from the beamed ceilings and bare wood tables set simply with red napkins and pewter candlesticks, some exceptional French-Swiss-Vermont fare and a basket of herbed bread served without benefit of a side plate.

Needless to say, the whole mix works, and thrivingly so since its establishment in 1972 in the site we first knew as Orsini's. Co-owners Gusti Iten, the Swiss chef, and Mike Ware, the English-born maitre-d, operate one of the more popular places in the valley with an air of elegance but without pretension.

At our visit, Vivaldi's "Four Seasons" played rather prominently in the background, the better to mask lively conversations and produce what the partners call a soft baroque atmosphere. Winter's warming blaze in the massive fieldstone fireplace is replaced in summer by masses of fresh flowers.

Almost as you're seated, waitresses in long red printed skirts and white blouses serve smallish drinks with the aforementioned bread. The extensive wine list comes in two picture frames, hinged together to open like a book, and contains some fine bargains such as Parducci petite sirah for $10 or, our choice, a Chateau Ste. Michelle merlot for $12.75.

The escargots maison "served in our famous garlic butter with its secret selection of herbs" is the most popular and expensive of the otherwise rather standard appetizers ($3.75 to $4.50). More intriguing are the entrees, starting at $9.25 for chicken Frangelico or Vermont veal Zurichoise and topping off at $15.50 for rack of lamb provencale. With dishes like roast duckling in an apricot glaze, linguini with seafood or salmon poached in champagne all under $12, this is uncommon fare — not to mention value — for common folk.

Entrees arrive after house salads of romaine, carrot slices and croutons with a zippy dressing hinting of garlic and curry. The fresh Vermont rabbit sauteed in olive oil, garlic and rosemary was distinctive, and the Vermont sweetbreads Normande with apples and apple brandy were some of the best we've tasted.

Desserts include Bavarian apple torte and linzer torte, $1.75 to $2.75. The kirsch parfait sounded better than it turned out, the kirsch being hard to detect. Six different ports, offered by the glass or bottle after dessert, make a mellow finale for an uncommon meal.

Dinner, weekdays 6 to 10, weekends 6:30 to 10:30; closed Mondays in off-season. Reservations required weekends.

Sam Rupert's, Top of Sugarbush Access Road, Warren. (802) 583-2421.
Skiers heading for Sugarbush once stopped at the Sugarbush Sugarhouse
for pancakes and homemade syrup. Today, they stop at a vastly expanded
dining establishment with a smashing greenhouse room for chef Lyndon
Virkler's specialties, supplemented by a blackboard menu.

Beige linen with brown napkins sets the color scheme for the large dining
room with the greenhouse full of massed flowers at one end, flowered
lamps on tables spaced well apart, a wood stove and hanging plants all
around. The windows in the new greenhouse addition bring the outside
in.

An unusual touch: the wine list is presented in a heavy album with color
photos of the bottles against various backgrounds; one shows red roses in
the snow amid branches covered with ice. The prices are reasonable and
the choice extensive.

The dinner menu is a mixed repertoire of fresh seafood (snapper St.
Tropez the night we visited), chicken sate with an oriental peanut sauce,
rack of lamb with green peppercorns, a Basque duckling dish, Vermont
veal Normande, steak au poivre and the changing "vegetarian alternative,"
perhaps fettuccine with artichokes. Entrees are $9.50 to $18.50.

The snow pea salad with water chestnuts and mushrooms and the escargots with red pepper butter are popular starters. Finish with the house
specialty, a chocolate mousse pie topped with fresh whipped cream, frozen
peanut pie with hot chocolate sauce or peach melba deluxe with kiwi fruit
and strawberries ($2.75 to $3.50).

Dinner nightly, 6 to 9:30.

The Waitsfield Inn, Route 100, Waitsfield. (802) 496-3979.
A wide fieldstone path brightened by red geraniums leads to the main
entrance at the side of the Waitsfield Inn. The sprightly country look of
the inn's several small dining rooms is embellished by Laura Ashley wallpapers, frilly curtains and woven mats atop patterned tablecloths of burgundy and sprigged flowers. The main dining room opens onto a small
outdoor patio where breakfast and brunch are served at tables under bright
yellow umbrellas.

The chef, who had just catered Vincent Sardi's 70th birthday when we
visited, specializes in regional American cuisine (cioppino, ribs, etc.) on his
changing dinner menu.

Entrees start at $7.50 for country garden casserole (eggplant medallions
topped with imported cheeses) and go to $14.50 for two small filets served
with a port wine and ginger glaze. Others include roast duckling with
raspberry and Frangelico sauce, Louisiana shrimp Alfredo, pepper steak and
a daily veal special. Among desserts are a kahlua chocolate mousse pie,
strawberries Romanoff, raspberry tarts and a sensational angel food cake
served with rum custard, fresh blackberries, peaches, cointreau and whipped
cream.

Australian wines are popular choices among the 35 offered from six
countries. Dourthe and Robert Mondavi are the house wines, $2 a glass.

Breakfast or brunch in the sunny dining room or outdoors on the patio
is popular with the public as well as inn guests. A vegetarian quiche is
$4.25 and French toast with strawberries and cointreau-laced whipped
cream, $4.50.

Patio dining is an attraction at the Waitsfield Inn.

Dinner nightly except Tuesday, 6 to 9; breakfast 8 to 11, Sunday brunch to 2 (also Saturday in summer).

Chez Henri, Sugarbush Village, Warren. (802) 583-2600.

The longest-running of the valley's Big Six long runners, Chez Henri is starting its third decade as a French bistro with an after-dinner disco in the rear. It's tiny, intimate and very French, as you might expect from a former food executive for Air France.

Henri Borel offers lunch, brunch, apres-ski, early dinner, dinner and dancing, inside by a warming stone fireplace and marble bar in winter and outside in summer on a small terrace bordered by a babbling mountain brook.

The dinner menu, served from 6, starts with changing soups "as made in a French country kitchen," or a classic French onion soup or fish broth, and perhaps mussels mariniere, smoked trout with capers or fresh mushrooms in a garlic mayonnaise ($2.75 to $5.50).

Entrees range from $8.75 to $15.75; nearly half are under $10. Served with good French bread and seasonal vegetables, they include sauteed quails with gin and juniper, frog's legs provencale, tripes in casserole, rabbit with thyme and mushrooms, veal chop calvados and tournedos bearnaise.

Open from noon to 2 a.m. in winter; weekends in summer, hours vary.

Beggar's Banquet, Fiddler's Green, Route 100, Waitsfield. (802) 496-4485.

A canopied redwood deck with a view of the sheep at the Black Sheep Farm next door is a summer attraction at this casual place billed as "the valley's finest dining alternative." Inside, all is rustic with booths, hanging plants, hanging lamps and a wide expanse of windows along the south wall.

The menu contains something for everyone: light fare from eggrolls and escargots to potato skins, zucchini sticks and "hot shrooms" (broiled mushrooms stuffed with a spicy pastrami and vegetable mixture with white wine and cheese, $3), salads, burgers, sandwiches, pastas and entrees from $6.95 for lasagna to $10.95 for New York strip steak. Kushiyaki is cubes of sirloin and chicken with vegetables on a bed of rice. Sunday is Mexican night, entrees in the $5 to $6 range.

Open daily, 11:30 a.m. to 11 p.m., Sunday 6 to 10.

Bridge Street Cafe, Bridge Street, Waitsfield. (802) 496-3474.

Located near the covered bridge, this intimate storefront restaurant lives up to its claim: "the smells and tastes of Mom's kitchen." Homemade muffins, soups and salads change daily; the tacos are piled high with choice of beef or guacamole and fresh vegetables or both (two for $3), croissant sandwiches are filled with cheese and ham or turkey, and a bagel with melted cheese, tomato, onion and sprouts is $1.50.

Breakfast includes French toast, pancakes, and waffles as well as eggs; the special of two eggs, homefries, toast and coffee at $2.20 is a hearty bargain for skiers. Sunday brunch brings eggs Benedict plus changing specials.

Open Monday-Saturday from 8 to 2:30, Sunday brunch from 10 to 2.

The Odyssey, Sugarbush Village, Warren. (802) 583-2001.

Located underneath and run by the Phoenix, the Odyssey claims to be the least expensive place to eat in the valley. Italian dinners with freshly made pasta run from $3.50 to $5.25 (for lasagna), but pizzas are the popular item here. Mexican pizzas are $4.50 and $7.50, vegetarian $4.80 and $8. Ice cream sundaes are the dessert forte; beer, wine and liquor are served.

The decor is funky: blue or red checked tablecloths, blue bentwood chairs, bare floors, mirrors with infinity lights over the bar and a 20-foot metal sculpture welded to the wall.

Open daily, 5 to 11.

The Deli-Bakery at the Warren Store, Warren. (802) 496-3864.

At the rear of the old Warren Store is a delightful place for breakfast or lunch. You can get egg McWarren for $1.25 and, on Sunday, eggs Benedict for $3.25. A veggie pita pocket, salad Nicoise, chef's salad and fruit salad plate are $2.50 to $4.50, and "le pain et pate" is $3. Finish with a fresh pie or pastry or a Haagen-Dazs milkshake. You can take it all outside to tables on a deck under a green striped canopy beside the falls of the Mad River. The store also has a fine selection of rare wines. Open seven days a week.

Diversions

Downhill skiing reigns supreme and gives the valley its character.

Mad River Glen. Billed as a serious place for serious skiers, Mad River has been challenging hardy types since 1947. There are no frills here: little snowmaking, the original single chairlift (with blanket wraps provided to ward off the chill) to the summit, hair-raising trails like Paradise and the Fall Line, plenty of moguls and not much grooming, and a "Practice Slope" so steep it scares the daylights out of beginners. The Birdland area is fine for intermediates. There's a Mad River mystique (bluejeans and milk runs) that you sense immediately and attracts you back. Adult lift tickets: $22 on weekends, $20 weekdays.

Sugarbush. Founded in 1959 and among the first of Vermont's destination ski resorts, Sugarbush with its own "village" at its base appealed immediately to the jet set. From its original gondola lift to its expert Castle Rock area, from its clusters of condos and boutiques to its indoor Sports Center, Sugarbush appeals to those who appreciate their creature comforts — and good skiing as well (we think the Glades offer the best glade skiing in the East). Since Sugarbush acquired neighboring Glen Ellen (which has the valley's greatest vertical drop, 2,600 feet) and rechristened it Sugarbush North, Sugarbush boasts a new diversity of skiing and mood; the two areas are not yet linked by trails, but a bus shuttles skiers back and forth. Adult lift tickets are $28.

Other sports. This is a four-season sports area with a difference. Yes, there is golf, at the Robert Trent Jones-designed **Sugarbush Golf Club** par 72 course with water hazards (pond or brook) affecting eight consecutive holes. Yes, the **Sugarbush Sports Center** has three indoor and ten outdoor tennis courts, racquetball and squash courts, indoor and outdoor pools, whirlpools and exercise facility.

But there's much more: this is something of an equestrian center with a number of stables offering trail rides. The **Sugarbush Polo Club,** started in 1962 by skiers using ski poles and a volleyball, now has three polo fields for games and tournaments, staged Saturday and Sunday afternoons June through September. Also for horse fanciers is the annual Sugarbush Horse Show in late July.

Soaring via gliders and sailplanes is at its best from the Warren-Sugarbush Airport, where instruction and rentals are available. Biplane rides for one or two persons also go from the airport, which hosts an annual airshow early in July.

For hiking and backpacking, the Long Trail is just overhead; innumerable mountain peaks and guided tours beckon. The Mad River and Blueberry Lake are ready for swimming, canoeing and fishing. The Mad River rugby team plays throughout the summer and fall at the Waitsfield Recreation Field. Finally, a round-robin Victorian croquet tournament is open to teams of two players in mid-summer.

Scenic drives. The Lincoln Gap Road, the McCullogh Turnpike (Route 17) beyond Mad River Glen and the steep Roxbury Gap Road each have their rewards. For the most open vistas and overall feel, traverse Brook Road and Waitsfield Common Road out of Warren, past the landmark Joslin Round Barn, Blueberry Lake and Sugarloaf Airport, and come the back way into Waitsfield.

Extra-Special

All Things Bright and Beautiful, Bridge Street, Waitsfield. In a shop next to the covered bridge is the ultimate collection of stuffed animals, mainly bears, outfitted in everything from a London bobby's uniform or a wedding dress to ski vests that proclaim "Save the Bear." The Victorian house has 10 rooms and porches presided over by two sisters and Malcolm the cat perched atop the cash register. It's a bit overwhelming, but not to be missed.

Skiers enjoy fresh powder at Sugarbush.

Shopping. Waitsfield has three shopping complexes, each worthy of exploration: The Mad River Green and the Village Square along Route 100 and the new Bridge Street Marketplace beside Vermont's second oldest covered bridge. Among our favorites: The well-known **Green Mountain Coffee Roasters,** founded in Waitsfield with a retail store in Mad River Green, roasts 30 varieties of coffees and decafs, including founder Jamie Balne's special blend, and offers teas, coffee grinders and accessories, plus a cafe and espresso bar that's good for breakfast and lunch. **The Store** in the 1834 Red Meeting House along Route 100 includes antiques and gourmet gifts as well as **Cabin Fever Quilts,** a lovely collection of handmade quilts and pillows. In Village Square, the **Blue Toad** gift shop specializes in particularly nice, inexpensive baskets from 20 countries, and **Tulip Tree Crafts** shows Vermont crafts and art, including lots of cows and many of the prints by Sabra Field, our favorite Vermont artist. South of town next to Fiddler's Green at the Black Sheep Farm is **Three Bags Full,** featuring wool, handmade sweaters, blankets, fleece and, of course, lots of grazing black sheep for the watching.

In tiny Warren, the premiere attraction is the **Warren Store,** an old-fashioned general store with provisions, fine wines and deli (see Dining Spots), plus upstairs, the **More Store,** with kitchenware, jewelry, apparel and cards. Across the street, blue and white stoneware made on the premises is displayed on the lawn in front of the Warren Village Pottery.

The Von Trapp Greenhouse, run by a grandson of Maria off a dirt road east of Waitsfield Common, is worth a visit (limited hours). Beautiful flower and vegetable gardens surround the family's Alpine house; there's a retail shop in front of one of the two greenhouses, which furnish many of the lavish floral displays and some of the produce for the valley's inns and restaurants.

Woodstock-Quechee, Vt.
A Chic Blend of Old and New

Picture the perfect Vermont place and you're likely to picture Woodstock, the historic shire town portrayed by the media as the picture-perfect New England village.

Picture an old river town with handsome 19th century houses, red brick mill, waterfall and covered bridge and you have Quechee, the emerging hamlet being restored to reflect Vermont as it used to be.

Join them with Rockefellers, Billingses, Pearces and other old names and new entrepreneurs, and you have an unusual combination for a chic, changing dynamic.

Carefully preserved and protected, Woodstock has such an impressive concentration of late 17th and 18th century architecture that National Geographic magazine termed it one of the most beautiful villages in America. That it is, thanks to its tradition as a prosperous county seat following its settlement in 1765 and to its early popularity as both a summer and winter resort (Vermont's first golf course was established south of town around the turn of the century and the nation's first ski tow was installed on a cow pasture north of town in 1934).

That also was the year when Laurance S. Rockefeller married a local woman named Mary Billings French, granddaughter of railroad magnate Frederick Billings. The Rockefeller interests are Woodstock's largest landowner and employer; they buried the utility poles underground, provided a home and much of the impetus for the Woodstock Historical Society, bought and rebuilt the Woodstock Inn, acquired and redesigned the golf course, bought and upgraded the Suicide Six ski area, opened the Billings Farm Museum, and built a new indoor sports center in 1986.

New entrepreneur Simon Pearce, the Irish glass blower, is providing some of the same impetus for neighboring Quechee. He bought an abandoned mill as a site for his glass-blowing enterprise, powered it with a 50-year-old turbine using water from the river outside, added more craftsmen and a restaurant, and sparked a crafts and business revival that is enlivening a sleepy hamlet heretofore known mainly for its scenic gorge.

In this inspirational setting of old and new, entrepreneurs are supported and crafts are appreciated.

Inn Spots

The Quechee Inn at Marshland Farm, Clubhouse Road, Box B84, Quechee 05059. (802) 295-3133.

This venerable establishment — a beautifully restored 1793 farmstead built by Vermont's first lieutenant governor — is every Hollywood set designer's idea of what a New England country inn should look like: a pure white rambling Vermont farmhouse, red barns out back against a backdrop of green mountains, and across the quiet road the Ottauquechee River heading into Quechee Gorge.

The interior lives up to expectations as well: the most welcoming beamed and barnwood living room, lately expanded and so carefully integrated that innkeeper Barbara Yaroschuk asked if we had noticed it. The rustic, stenciled

The Woodstock Inn and Resort is a local institution.

dining room (see below) in which some locally acclaimed fare is served. The new library, dressed in elegant draperies and valances, for reading or meetings. The new gift shop specializing in Vermont crafts. And 22 comfortable guest rooms, all with private baths, Queen Anne style furnishings, brass and four-poster beds, wing chairs, braided and Chinese rugs on wide-plank floors and — the only jarring note, the purists would say — cable TV.

All this was produced with T.L.C. by Barbara Yaroschuk, her late husband Michael, and their three children. Since her husband's death in 1985, Barbara has been running the inn under the auspices of the Romantik Hotels association.

With fifteen rooms in the original farmhouse and seven more on the second floor of a new wing housing the expanded common rooms and dining room, the inn is large enough to be a focal point of activity: a Christmas Eve open house for inn guests and townspeople, cocktails before a crackling fire in the lounge, summer get-togethers on the canopied patio, a new cross-country learning center in the smallest barn (preparing skiers for touring through Quechee Gorge, in the upper meadow behind the inn or in what Barbara describes as "a lovely tunnel through the pines").

A continental breakfast includes help-yourself coffee, English muffins, fresh rolls and the inn's famed coffee cake.

Doubles, $66 to $102, lower rates midweek November-May; closed April and early December.

Woodstock Inn and Resort, 14 The Green, Woodstock 05091. (802) 457-1100.

The biggest institution in town, the Woodstock Inn sits majestically back from the green, its front facing a covered bridge and mountains, its back looking across the pool and putting green and down the valley toward its golf course and ski touring center. The resort's other leisure facilities include the Suicide Six ski area, ten tennis courts and two lighted paddle tennis courts, a new indoor racquet and sports center, and such attractions as sleigh rides, dogsledding, horseback riding or touring in the inn's Stanley Steamer car.

The interior of the inn is just as impressive. Built by Rockresorts in 1969 after Laurance Rockefeller found the original Woodstock Inn beyond salvation, it contains a lobby warmed by a 10-foot-high stone fireplace around which people always seem to be gathered, a large dining room, coffee shop, Pine Room lounge and gift shop.

The 120 guest rooms are among the more luxurious in which we've stayed, with handmade quilts on the beds, upholstered chairs, three-way reading lights, television, telephones and large bathrooms and closets. Walls are decorated with paintings and photographs of local scenes.

The long main dining room has large windows onto a spacious outdoor terrace overlooking the pool and gardens. It offers a luncheon buffet Monday through Saturday and dinner nightly.

The Sunday brunch is popular, as is the Saturday night buffet, for which people start lining up before 6 o'clock for first crack at the 50-foot table laden with 200 items from stir-fried beef to halibut with a seafood sauce.

Otherwise, dinner entrees run from $14.75 for Cornish game hen Madeira accompanied by apple compote to $18 for lamb noisettes with a light peppercorn sauce. To the limited menu add daily specials, sometimes sauteed veal with Vermont cheddar cheese and fresh morels gathered from the nearby woods or roast loin of pork glazed in maple syrup with apple prune stuffing. Billings Farm ice creams and sherbets are among the desserts. Regional Alpine dishes, such as raclette and apple fritters Matterhorn, are served in the Coffee Shop, which is more attractive than most.

Doubles, $78 to $125; many package plans available.

The Charleston House, 21 Pleasant St., Woodstock 05091. (802) 457-3843.

When we first saw the Charleston House, it was festooned for Christmas, inside and out, and looked like a spread for House Beautiful.

But the red brick 1835 Greek Revival house is gorgeous at any time of year. Named for the hometown of Betsy Bradley, who with husband Laird owns the inn they opened in 1985, it is the epitome of Southern charm and hospitality.

All seven comfortable bedrooms have private baths, most have four-poster queensize hand-carved Charleston rice beds decked out with lace trimmed sheets and stenciled pillows of cats or ducks, three-way reading lamps, fresh flowers and a small basket of fruit and a chocolate bar.

A fire is usually going in the living room where there are TV and books and soft sofas. Everything is decorated to "my taste," says Betsy, which is to say in the proper Charleston style.

Guests congregate in the elegant dining room, filled with silver, crystal and Chippendale furniture and the traditional Southern portrait of the hostess, for a full breakfast that might feature apple-cinnamon pancakes, eggs or French toast. Once in a while, Betsy makes Vermont cheddar cheese grits. Those who like to sleep late may have continental breakfast in bed.

Doubles, $74 to $84.

The Jackson House at Woodstock, Route 4 West, Woodstock 05091. (802) 457-2065.

If ever every room in a small country inn were worthy of coverage in an antiques or decorator magazine it would be these. All nine guest rooms are different and eclectically furnished with such things as antique brass lamps on either side of the bathroom mirror, a marble-topped bedside table, an 1860 sleigh bed, a $2,000 ceiling fan from Casablanca, Chinese carved rugs, old steam radiators painted gold, handmade afghans coordinated to each room's colors, bamboo and cane furniture, a blanket box made of tiger maple and so much more.

Suffice to say that the rooms vary from French Empire to British Oriental to old New England and bear such names as Gloria Swanson, who once stayed here when it was a guest house, and Mary Todd Lincoln, with furniture of the period. The floors in each room are of different woods because the house was built in 1890 by a sawmill owner. A lovely celadon collection is housed in a lighted stand at the top of the staircase with its highly polished banister of cherry wood.

Each bathroom has a new glassed-in shower, but that's about the only modern touch beyond the idea of luxury espoused by innkeepers Jack Foster and Bruce McIlveen: elegant guest rooms, a parlor in which eggnog or wassail are served in winter (champagne and pate or caviar are frequent substitutes), an adjacent library where you can shut the door, turn on the 1937 Zenith radio and curl up with a classic, and a formal dining room in which elaborate breakfasts are served.

There's more, for Jackson House opened only in August 1984 and the innkeepers say they are not yet finished. When we visited at Christmas 1985, they were about to put in a pond for swimming and ice-skating behind the brook that cuts through their three-acre property out in the country west of town. They were planning to add one more bathroom so that every room would have a private bath, as well as two deluxe suites on the third floor. And sometime in the future they were hoping to hire a chef to serve dinners with a limited menu at two sittings.

Meanwhile, they give you fuzzy brown slippers from K-Mart so your shoes won't mar the floors and a bedroom that would do justice to a museum. At breakfast, you gather around a Jacobean gate-leg table (acquired from an English pub) and feast on a plate of honeydew, canteloupe and kiwi followed by a mushroom and sausage omelet or walnut pancakes or cheese blintzes or Sante Fe French toast with whipped cream.

Doubles, $85. No smoking allowed.

Quechee Bed & Breakfast, 753 Woodstock Road (Route 4), Box 0080, Quechee 05059. (802) 295-1776.

The waters of the Ottauquechee River can be seen from the back yard and rear upstairs guest room of this large gray 1795 house perched on a cliff not far from Quechee Gorge. It was converted into a luxury bed and breakfast establishment in September 1985 by Susan and Ken Kaduboski, transplanted Boston accountants, who restored five spacious bedrooms with private baths and had plans for four more.

Guests enter a large living-dining area with comfortable sofas around a huge fireplace, television set and four breakfast tables topped with dusty rose cloths and paper narcissuses in pots. A large cactus stands in one corner, and an interesting art collection is on display.

A smaller parlor leads through heavy doors into the original house and the guest quarters, nicely secluded and private with a separate entry hall and staircase. Three rooms are on the first floor and two slightly larger with beamed, half-cathedral ceilings are on the second. Each is suavely furnished with queensize beds (one a rice-carved four-poster) or, in one case, twin sleigh beds, antique dressers, wing chairs, sprightly wallpapers and decorative touches like swags and stenciled lamp shades, and large bathrooms with colorful towels. Sheets and pillowcases are white and lavishly trimmed with lace.

The Kaduboskis serve a full breakfast of juices, baked apple or broiled grapefruit, homemade breads and main dishes like eggs, apple pancakes or French toast stuffed with cream cheese and nuts.

Doubles, $65.

Parker House, 16 Main St., Quechee 05059. (802) 295-6077.

This elegant red brick and white frame Victorian mansion with steep black mansard roof crowned by an ornamental wrought-iron railing is a registered National Historic Site. It has been better known for its dining than its lodging, but the attractive overnight accommodations opened in 1984 are becoming a draw as well.

A Vermont state senator and mill owner, Joseph C. Parker, built the mansion in 1857 next to his mill on the Ottauquechee River. By happy coincidence, it was acquired several years ago by Virginia and Frank Parker (no relation). After putting their restaurant on the culinary map, they restored four large upstairs guest rooms with sitting areas and private baths.

Emily's room in front, named for the original Mrs. Parker, has twin white enamel and brass poster bedsteads joined with a kingsize mattress, oriental rug, a small sofa, dressing room with desk and an enormous modern bathroom with rust carpeting and deep blue and rust wallpaper. Even larger is the Empire Room which runs the width of the back of the house and has a fine view of the river. Joseph's Room, actually a sitting room plus a bedroom, has a double bed in an alcove with towering windows on three sides (no doubt so the owner could keep his eye on the mill outside; today, the view toward the falls and covered bridge is reason enough). Each room is furnished with a small table set with mats for breakfast, and two chairs.

A full breakfast is served in the bedrooms, one of the dining rooms, the lounge or outside on the rear balcony. The Parkers also have been known to serve dinner to guests in their rooms.

Doubles, $60 to $80.

Lincoln Covered Bridge Inn, Route 4, RR 2, Box 40, Woodstock 05091. (802) 457-3312.

Located next to the westernmost of Woodstock's covered bridges, this former farmhouse also is known for its dining (see below).

Upstairs, Pat DiPietro, co-owner with her chef-husband Phil, has furnished six small, homey bedrooms, each with modern private bath and three with queensize beds. In 1985, the DiPietros added two far larger guest rooms in the carriage house out back; each has a queen or king bed and a sitting area with sofabed. Fresh flowers are in all the rooms, and mints are placed on the pillows when the beds are turned down at night.

Guests gather in a living room with woodstove and TV. Continental breakfast is taken in the Fireside Room or outside on a porch overlooking the Ottauquechee River. Homemade croissants, muffins and breads are served with preserves made by Pat DiPietro's mother.

Doubles, $60 to $75.

Three Church Street, 3 Church St., Woodstock 05091. (802) 457-1925.

Classical music is heard throughout the several common rooms of this 1830s brick and white-pillared Georgian mansion listed in the National Register of Historic Places. Fires are ablaze in a small front sitting room with sofa and parquet floors, way out back in a more casual room with modern black wood stove and tea and coffee at the ready, and sometimes in others of the nine fireplaces, some made of marble with hand-carved mantels.

Except for the kitchen-apartment of innkeeper Eleanor Paine, the entire downstairs — including large formal parlor and music room with plush sofas and oriental rugs, spacious dining room and rear gallery overlooking the lawn leading to the Ottauquechee River — are available for guests. So are the tennis court and swimming pool with changing room and cabana out back.

The Spanish-style foyer has a spindled staircase leading upstairs, where six of the eleven guest rooms have private baths and beds are about equally

Three Church Street.

split between doubles and twins. Rooms are spacious, nicely decorated and enhanced with striking art works.

Eleanor Paine, who raised eight children in her home, offers what she calls "more than bed and breakfast at reasonable prices." Guests have the run of her house, and are served bountiful breafasts at half a dozen tables in the large dining room. Among her repertoire are apple pancakes, oatmeal, homefries and grits.

Doubles, $46 to $58; one three-room suite, $160.

Dining Spots

Simon Pearce Restaurant, The Mill, Quechee. (802) 295-1470.

The restaurant which opened in 1985 has just as much integrity as the rest of the mill complex. Irish chef Hester Cowhig even imports flour from Ireland so she can make Irish soda and Ballymaloe brown bread.

You sit on sturdy ash chairs at bare wood tables topped with small woven mats. The brown and white tableware and heavy glassware are all made by Simon Pearce and his family. Irish or classical music plays in the background. Through large windows you have a view of the river, hills rising beyond (in summer, a canopied outdoor deck is almost over the falls). The setting is spare, but plants and antique quilts soften the brick walls and bare floors.

Several wines are available by the glass; at lunch we tried a Fetzer white and Monterey red, $2 a glass, while nibbling the absolutely sensational bread (seconds were offered and accepted).

Table for two at Simon Pearce restaurant.

The menu changes every week but there are always speciallties like Irish stew (which we tried — for $6 a generous serving of fork-tender lamb and vegetables, plus a small side salad of julienned vegetables). Soups at our visit were corn chowder and split pea with ham ($2.50 or $3) and entrees, which included curried lamb and rice, brie with fresh fruit, a roast leg of lamb sandwich with mustard and cucumber, and smoked ham sandwich with boursin, were $4.50 to $6. The pasta salad, a huge heap of spirals, included many vegetables and a superior dressing of oil, vinegar, basil and parmesan cheese.

Although the restaurant had been open only six months when we visited, Hester's hazelnut meringue cake with strawberry sauce was already well known, and justly so. Topped with a mountain of whipped cream, it was crisp and crunchy and melted in the mouth. Chocolate rum cake, Irish apple cake and pecan pie are other possibilities, but if we go back, which we certainly plan to, nothing but the hazelnut meringue will do.

At night, a candlelight dinner might start with Irish smoked salmon with

44

capers or smoked rainbow trout with horseradish sauce, or perhaps clam and mushroom soup. Entrees ($10 to $15.50) could be tenderloin of beef with mushroom and red wine sauce, baked swordfish with garlic butter, or stuffed breast of chicken with a creamy mustard sauce.

Lunch, 11.30 to 2:30 Monday-Saturday; dinner from 5:30, Wednesday-Sunday (Friday-Sunday in winter); Sunday brunch, 11:30 to 2:30.

Parker House, 16 Main St., Quechee. (802) 295-6077.

The food is creative and the atmosphere elegant in the two small dining rooms of this delightful Victorian inn. Heavy gold brocade draperies frame the tall windows, and lighting comes from crystal chandeliers, wax candles in the wall sconces and candles on the tables covered with crisp white and gold linens. At holiday time, a wondrous Victorian Christmas tree sparkles with old-fashioned ornaments and hundreds of tiny white lights.

Delicate, light cheese puffs are served with drinks, the bread is so good you'll probably ask for seconds, and an interesting salad of assorted greens brightened by bits of colorful vegetables is served with a fine Dijon honey dressing.

The innovative menu changes seasonally and the prices are written out, perhaps so as not to be so noticeable — when was the last time you saw an entree for "fifty-four dollars" (boned sirloin of lamb for two)?

Smoked goose breast with fresh fruit, duck liver pate and an array of smoked sea and lake fish appeal among appetizers ($4.50 to $6). Entrees start at $14 for the chicken special, rise sharply and include duckling with gooseberry plum sauce, veal bigarade and a shelled lobster witih mushroom duxelles and truffle shavings. We enjoyed the braised young pheasant with pear pecan stuffing and green peppercorn cream and chef Kenneth Thompson's prize-winning pork McIntosh, rubbed with Vermont maple syrup, filled with McIntosh apples, wrapped in bacon, roasted, glazed and finally served tableside with a flaming sauce. Vegetables on the December night we dined were pea pods, broccoli with hollandaise and a mixture of white and dark rice.

Innkeeper Virginia Parker makes the chocolate cake, each layer drizzled with kahlua and frosted with chocolate ganache. Chef Thompson's cheesecake is another prize-winner, and we found the parfait Lisa with raspberries and creme de cassis ($4.50) and Quechee coffee laced with creme de cacao, brandy and cinnamon ($3.80) festive endings to a memorable meal.

The wine list is extensive and expensive, starting at $11 and rising rapidly to a $175 Chateau Lafitte.

Dinner 5 to 10, closed Wednesday.

The Prince and the Pauper, 34 Elm St., Woodstock. (802) 457-1818.

A new cocktail lounge with a wine bar and the shiniest wood bar you ever saw has freed up space for more tables in what many consider to be Woodstock's best restaurant.

Tables in the expanded yet intimate L-shaped dining room (some surrounded by dark wood booths) are covered with brown linen, oil lamps and flowers in small carafes. The lamps cast flickering shadows on dark beamed ceilings, and old prints adorn the white walls, one of which has a shelf of old books.

Chef-owner Chris J. Balcer refers to his cuisine as "creative continental"

— his soup of the day could be duck and barley, the pasta perhaps fettuccine primavera with pignoli nuts, and his pate a mixture of veal, pork and duck livers topped with lingonberry sauce.

For other appetizers ($4.75 to $6.25), how about cracked Florida stone crab claws with sauce ravigote or smoked breast of goose with an orange ginger sauce? Entrees go from $12.95 for Indonesian curried lamb to $18.95 for rack of lamb Royale. Veal saltimbocca, sweetbreads Madeira, shrimp Nantua in puff pastry and ragout of lotte diable are other intriguing choices. Homemade bread, house salad and seasonal vegetables accompany, and the interesting wine list is heavy on Californias.

Desserts include strawberry sabayon with triple sec and pears Helene.

Dinner, nightly 6 to 9 or 9:30; reservatons essential.

Quechee Inn at Marshland Farm, Clubhouse Road, Quechee. (802) 295-3133.

Most people enjoy a drink by the fire in the expanded living room-lounge before dinner in the antiques-filled dining room. Beamed ceilings, wide-planked floors and lovely stenciled borders on the walls provide the setting for some inspired cuisine.

The stenciling is repeated on the good-looking covers of the menu, wine list and the new Quechee Inn Dessert Cookbook, a wonderful collection of the recipes of the inn's baker and dessert chef, Erma J. Hastings, including her renowned French silk pie (the recipe for which also appeared in Gourmet magazine).

Chef Gene Esquively's dinner menu changes seasonally and the entree price includes Erma's bread, appetizer, salad, potato and vegetable. The winter offerings start with baked apple soup (baked apples and cinnamon with a touch of onion and cream), sliced mushrooms provencale, escargots in artichoke bottoms and baked avocado stuffed with mushroom, artichoke and cheese. The garden salad of mixed greens and vegetables comes with a choice of homemade mustard vinaigrette, blue cheese or creamy dill dressings.

The seven entrees run from $15.50 for chicken cassis to $21.95 for rack of New Zealand lamb. Others include roast duckling with honey Madeira sauce, veal sauteed with white wine and lime juice, and pork with mustard and wine-cream sauce.

The interesting wine list starts in the low teens, has some fine choices in the $20s and $30s and a page of "rarities" up to $100.

Desserts by Erma Hastings run the gamut from almond cream chocolate layer cake and cranberry apple pie to maple walnut cheesecake, pumpkin mousse and rum mocha cream puffs with fudge walnut sauce. Many of her desserts are works of art, as is the gingerbread village she creates for the inn at Christmas.

Dinner, Wednesday-Sunday 6 to 9, also Monday mid-July to mid-October. Reservations required; jackets requested.

Bentleys, 3 Elm St., Woodstock. (802) 457-3232.

Entrepreneurs David Creech and Bill Deckelbaum Jr. started with a greenhouse and plant store in 1974, installed a soda fountain, expanded into a restaurant catering to every taste at every hour, added a specialty foods shop, opened another Bentleys in 1983 in Hanover, N.H., and last we heard were developing Waterman Place with 10 retail stores and a 75-seat restaurant in a 100-year-old house along Route 4 in Quechee.

The flagship of it all is the original Bentleys, a casual and eclectic spot at the prime corner in Woodstock. On several levels, close-together tables are set with small cane mats, Perrier bottles filled with flowers and small lamps or tall candles in holders. Old floor lamps sport fringed shades, windows are covered with lace curtains, the plants are large potted palms, and walls are covered with English prints and an enormous bas-relief.

The menu is eclectic as well. For lunch, we enjoyed a house specialty, torta rustica ($6.95), a hot Italian puff pastry filled with prosciutto, salami, provolone and marinated vegetables, and a fluffy quiche ($5.95) with turkey, mushrooms and snow peas, both accompanied with side salads. From the dessert tray we shared a delicate chocolate mousse cake with layers of meringue, like a torte, served with the good Green Mountain coffee in clear glass cups.

Appetizers, salads, sandwiches and light entrees (all but one $6.95 or less) such as the torta rustica, chicken chimichanga and cold sliced marinated flank steak make up half the dinner menu. The other side offers such entrees as three-mustard chicken, duckling with cranberry bourbon glaze, veal Romanoff, Jack Daniels steak, Shanghai stir-fry and four Cajun-Creole specialties ($13.95 to $17.50).

With choices like these, it's little wonder that Bentleys is always crowded and bustling.

Lunch, daily 11:30 to 2:30, dinner 5:30 to 9:30, Sunday brunch noon to 3.

Lincoln Covered Bridge Inn, Route 4, West Woodstock. (802) 457-3312.

Highly touted northern Italian cuisine is served up by chef-owner Phil DiPietro in the pretty Victorian dining room with heavy linen, crystal globes and huge vases filled with plants.

Maryland crabmeat cocktail, escargots bourguignon, and mushroom caps stuffed with sweet sausage, herbs and chopped mushrooms are among appetizers ($4.50 to $6). Five homemade pastas also are offered.

Four veal dishes head the list of entrees ($11.50 to $17.95). Others are chicken macadamia, poached rainbow salmon with an ever-changing sauce, pork Wellington, shrimp and scallops Florentine, roast rack of lamb and steak pizzaiola.

In winter, a blackboard menu changes weekly. Pat DiPietro says the chef's selected dinner (a prix-fixe $15 from appetizer to dessert) is "the best value in town."

Dinner, nightly 6 to 9:30.

The Village Inn of Woodstock, 41 Pleasant St., Woodstock. (802) 457-1255.

Kevin and Anita Clark have upgraded this old inn, especially the three small dining rooms done up in white linen, lace curtains and Victorian decor, with working fireplace, oak woodwork and tin ceilings. Adjacent is a small cocktail lounge and antique oaken bar.

The dinner menu — fancily presented on oversized, heavy parchment — mixes appetizers like chicken tempura, vegetable eggroll and chicken liver pate with fresh fruit cup and stuffed potato skins. Maple baked beans, creamed baby onions and fried eggplant are offered for a price as "accompaniments" with the nightly vegetable and rice pilaf or potato, but most people don't need an extra vegetable after the relish tray, garden salad, hot breads and popovers that come with dinner. Entrees start at $8.50 for roast Vermont turkey and $8.75 for grilled calves liver, topping off at $17.95 for roast rack of lamb. Roast duckling with a cognac-orange sauce is a house specialty, $12.95.

Upstairs are nine old-fashioned guest rooms, two with private baths, priced from $42 to $50.

Dinner, Monday-Saturday 5 to 9 or 9:30; breakfast daily; Sunday brunch 10 to 1.

Spooner's Restaurant, Sunset Farm, Route 4, Woodstock. (802) 457-4022.

The lower floor of the old Spooner Barn built in 1850 at the east end of town was converted into a handsome restaurant in 1983. It's all bare woods, dark greens and beiges, with bentwood chairs and inlaid tables in a modern greenhouse section, and velvet covered benches from the old Woodstock Inn as well as booths made of old church pews in other sections. Colorful Sabra Field prints hang on the walls, and a classy bar centers the whole affair.

Fresh seafood is featured on the dinner menu, the offerings ranging from Philly Jim's homemade crab cakes with shrimp sauce ($9.95) to grilled marinated shrimp on linguini ($12.50). Crabmeat imperial is served in a puff pastry shell and spicy shrimp is stir-fried with vegetables, water chestnuts and snow peas. The menu also lists stir-fried spicy beef, Chinese crispy duckling, crabby nachos, salads, burgers, pastas and vegetarian dishes. The wine list is one of the area's more reasonable and appealing.

Lunch was reinstated in December 1985, the changing daily menu featuring Chinese specials as well as sandwiches (turkey and boursin on a croissant is one) and burgers. Beef stew with buttermilk biscuits, fried oyster platter and smoked salmon omelet are in the $3.95 to $5.50 range.

Lunch, Monday-Friday 11:30 to 2:30; dinner, 5:30 to 9:30; Sunday brunch, 11:30 to 2.

Rumble Seat Rathskeller, Woodstock East, Route 4, Woodstock, (802) 457-3609.

The cellar of the 1834 Stone House houses this casual-elegant little establishment with intimate niches and crannies in three small dining rooms, one with four tables — "a cozy little room for cozy little couples," according to the hostess. It's well away from the large lounge beyond.

The original stone and brick walls have been lacquered, gray linens are accented by cranberry napkins, and it's all more attractive than one might expect from the name.

When we last visited, new owners were revising the dinner menu. Entrees ($8.95 to $12.95) included veal francais, sirloin au poivre, Cornish game hen with honey and almonds, vegetable stir-fry and pasta with broccoli. Appetizers went from potato skins to sole and scallop mousse, and salads and sandwiches were available as well.

Open daily, noon to 11.

The Mill at Quechee houses Simon Pearce enterprises.

Extra-Special

Simon Pearce, The Mill at Quechee.

Every time we're in the area, we stop at Simon Pearce's magnificent mill, partly because it's all so fascinating and partly because there's always something new. Simon Pearce is the 40-year-old Irish glass blower who left Ireland in 1981 to set up business in the abandoned flannel mill beside the Ottauquechee. The site is inspiring: thundering waterfalls, covered bridge, beautifully restored mill and classic white Vermont houses all around. The interior has a new restaurant (see above) and a wondrous shop offering glass, pottery and Irish woolens, all beautifully displayed. Downstairs is a glass-blowing area where you can watch Simon Pearce and eight associates turn out 120 pieces a day, the pottery where Miranda Thomas is at work, the hydro station with enormous pipes from the river and a steam turbine which provides enough power to light the town of Quechee as well as serve the mill's energy needs (melting sand into glass, firing clay into porcelain and stoneware). "The whole idea was to become self-sufficient and provide an economic model for small business in Vermont," says Steve McDonnell, Simon's brother-in-law. The mill is zoned utility in the subbasement, manufacturing in the basement, retail in the restaurant and shop, office on the second floor and residential on the third, where Simon lived with his family until he moved out in 1985 and bachelor Steve moved in. The enterprise is growing all the time, expanding to other outlets (Cambridge, Greenwich Village and Keene, N.H.) and adding ventures (furniture, wooden bowls, brother Stephen Pearce's Irish pottery and Shanagarry by their father, Phillip). We defy anyone not to enjoy, learn — and probably buy! Beautiful clear glass balls, $8 each, are marvelous ornaments for a Christmas tree.

Open daily, 10 to 5; glass-blowers work Monday-Friday except for lunch from 1 to 2.

Diversions

The sportsman and the sightseer have plenty to do in the Woodstock-Quechee area. You can ski at Suicide Six, not far from Gilbert's farm where Woodstockers installed the nation's first rope tow in 1934 (or you can ski at nearby Killington, the East's largest ski area). You can golf at the historic Woodstock Country Club, site of Vermont's first golf course and home also of the fine Woodstock Ski Touring Center, or at the newer golf course in Quechee. You can hike through the Quechee Gorge area or the hundreds of acres of forests maintained by the Woodstock Inn. You can walk around the village green and center, marveling in the architectural variety and browsing through the Woodstock Historical Society. But it is arts, crafts and shopping that make Woodstock so appealing for many.

Shopping. The Vermont Workshop of Nancy Wickham Boyd, 73 Central St., is said to be the oldest gallery in Woodstock, having evolved from a summer workshop established in 1949. Her pottery is in the basement of her home next door; her wares are on display and for sale in this historic building with those of other craftsmen — everything from woven mats and interesting shades on her own Wickham lamps to wall hangings and cookware — in room after room of great appeal.

Nearby on this artsy section of Central Street are the two locations of **Gallery 2.** The print room at 63 Central has lots of Woody Jackson cows and woodcuts of Sabra Johnson Field, whose studio in nearby East Pomfret, Tontine Press, is worth a visit (by appointment). The new location at 43 Central has paintings, sculpture and art glass pieces.

The **Pomfret Shop** offers unusual garden ornaments, plant containers, fine arts and handicrafts, and a **Christmas Treasures** shop upstairs. **Log Cabin Quilts** has everything for the quilter plus the finished products, including a marvelous selection of pillows. Next door is the **Unicorn,** a gift shop with jewelry and woodcrafts by New England artisans.

F.H. Gillingham & Co. at 16 Elm St. is the most fun store of all. Run by the Billings family for 100 years, it's a general store, but a highly sophisticated one — everything from specialty foods and wines to hardware — and so popular that it does a land-office mail-order business.

In Quechee, the new **Shop on Main Street** features country gifts and artifacts, almost all American and handmade. Proprietor Jill Rustici likens it to "a small museum for people who like to browse." Her dried peonies amaze people who didn't think it could be done. New shops were expected to open in 1986 on three levels at **Waterman Place,** a 100-year-old restored house with new glass atrium above Quechee village off Route 4.

Billings Farm & Museum, Route 12 north of Woodstock. This is an artfully presented display of life-like exhibits portraying the Vermont farm year of 1890. Housed in four interconnected 19th century buildings on the working Billings Farm, it shows how crops were planted and harvested. Farm life also meant making butter and cider, cutting ice and firewood, sugaring and darning socks, as well as going to school and the general store and participating in community life; such activities are imaginatively shown. Down a path the modern farm is evident: visitors can see the Jersey herd, calves, sheep, oxen and two teams of Belgian horses, and the milking barn is open. Special events include a 19th century crafts day and a cow-milking contest. Open daily June-Oct. 20 from 10 to 4; adults, $3.

Newfane-West River Valley
The Essence of Vermont

There's not much to do in Newfane and Vermont's surrounding West River Valley. And that's the way the inhabitants like it.

The interstates, the ski areas, the toney four-season destination resorts are some distance away. This is the essence of old Vermont, unspoiled by tourism and contemporary commercial trappings.

The meandering West River creates a narrow valley between the mountains as it descends toward Brattleboro. Along the way are covered bridges (one is the longest in Vermont), country stores, flea markets and a couple of picture-book villages.

The heart of the valley is Newfane, the shire town of Windham County without so much as a brochure to publicize it. In 1824, Newfane "moved" to the valley from its original site two miles up Newfane hill and now has fewer residents than it had then. The Newfane green is said to be Vermont's most-photographed. Clustered around the green are the white-columned courthouse, the matching Congregational church, the town hall, two famed inns, two country stores and, beyond, some houses — and that's about it.

Upriver is Townshend ("Historic Townshend," one of the area's few tourist brochures calls it), with a larger green and more business activity, though that's relative.

There are back roads and country stores to explore, but for many visitors this quiet area's major blessing is its fine inns and restaurants amidst a setting of Vermont as it used to be.

Inn Spots

The Four Columns Inn, Off Route 30, Newfane 05345. (802) 365-7713.

Ever since French chef Rene Chardain left the Old Newfane Inn to open the Four Columns, this inn has been widely known for outstanding cuisine (see Dining Spots). Under the auspices of subsequent innkeepers Jacques and Sandy Allembert, it has become known for tasteful overnight accommodations as well.

Nine guest rooms and three suites, all with private baths and most with king or queensize beds, are located in the main columned inn. built in 1830 by General Pardon Kimball for his Southern-born wife as a replica of her girlhood home. Another four rooms, two with working fireplaces, were in the works in an outbuilding for the summer of 1986.

All rooms are colorfully decorated with antiques, hooked rugs, handmade afghans and quilts. An 84-year-old local craftsman made the canopied four-poster bed in one room.

A former New York actress, Sandy Allembert is especially fond of the new third-floor hideaway she decorated from scratch. Centered by an exposed chimney that divides the room into unusual spaces, it has a canopied bed set into an alcove, a sitting room with a private front porch overlooking the Newfane green, thick beige carpeting and Laura Ashley fabrics.

Several common rooms are good for relaxing or watching television, and the tavern to the rear of the dining room is a popular gathering spot.

Guest rooms are in front and restaurant at rear of Four Columns Inn.

Continental breakfast is served to house guests, who can order a full breakfast for an extra charge.

The Allemberts have been working hard to improve their spacious and attractive grounds, which include a landscaped swimming pool, a trout pond beloved by ducks, rock gardens and Jacques Allembert's large herb garden behind a vine arbor. Beyond are a trout stream and hiking trails up the inn's own little mountain.

Doubles, $55 to $70.

The Inn at South Newfane, Dover Road, South Newfane 05351. (802) 348-7191.

What better way to approach a country inn than through a covered bridge? The one we have in mind is in Williamsville, the town next to South Newfane, where the handsome Inn at South Newfane, with its olive green trim and masses of pink impatiens surrounding the porte cochere, opened in late 1984.

A private turn-of-the century estate on 100 acres, it was purchased by Connie and Herb Borst of Westchester County. They had traveled extensively in Europe, always enjoying small inns more than hotels, so decided to open one of their own. Their daughter, Lisa, is the exceptional chef (see Dining Spots).

Herb Borst does the baking for breakfast, when dishes like French toast or blueberry pancakes and country bacon are served in a sunny morning room.

A cozy and well-furnished living room with fireplace and the "Great Room" that is just beyond the front door, in shades of gold and with shelves full of books, are available for guests' use.

The porch in back is set with garden furniture and beyond are extensive grounds, embracing grand gardens and a fair-sized pond for swimming in summer and skating in winter. Hiking and cross-country trails abound, some on the mountain that rises behind the inn.

The six bedrooms, of different sizes, have queen or twin beds and all

52

have been totally redone by the Borsts, who added private baths. Quilts made by "the ladies in the church across the street," floral wallpapers, frilly curtains, and stuffed animals or quilted cat pillows on the beds add to the charm. One room has a reproduction of an old Colonial bed, so high you must use a stool to climb up, and another has twin cannonball beds. The Borsts supply terrycloth robes in the two rooms which have their private baths across the hall. The windowed back room has a bathtub in which, says Connie, you can soak and look out at the birds and trees. Flowers and small bowls of fruit are in the rooms.

In the big hall upstairs is a reading and writing alcove, where a chest holds all kinds of good books and magazines, and old glass bottles of many colors are displayed by the window.

Doubles, $100 to $160, MAP; $70 to $130, B&B. No credit cards.

Windham Hill Inn, West Townshend 05359. (802) 874-4080.

Up a steep hill so far off the main road that we had to stop to ask if we were on the right track is this gem of an inn, a speckled brick and white wood structure built in 1825 and distinguished by a suave oval sign and a commanding view of the West River Valley. Ken and Linda Busteed took over the inn in 1982 and, with skilled decorating touches and hospitable nuances like small decanters of Harvey's Bristol Cream in each room, have turned it into a destination unto itself. "There's not much to do but relax, admire our 150 acres of trees and hills, and enjoy two good meals a day," says Ken.

Linda's touch as an interior designer is evident throughout the inn's common rooms and guest rooms, which rated a six-page photo spread in Country Decorating magazine. The 15 spacious guest rooms, all with private baths, are furnished with oriental rugs, old photographs and paintings, old quilts and such delights as handmade wreaths, high-button shoes, a christening dress on a wall and a hat over a bed.

One rear room Linda calls the tree house because "when you wake up in the morning you feel you're in the trees;" it has a sofa, a corner window seat and a private balcony. An upstairs corner room has dainty wallpaper, a quilt on a stand in front of the fireplace, candlesticks atop the mantel, and old farm furniture painted, Ken tells guests, with milk and manure. Among the most coveted rooms are the five new ones fashioned from nooks and alcoves in the White Barn annex, particularly the two sharing a large deck overlooking the mountains.

Guests are served full breakasts, Ken offering eggs, pancakes or homemade granola (hot cereal in winter) amidst a background of taped chamber music, antique silver and crystal.

Linda cooks five-course dinners, which are served at large mahogany and maple tables in the main dining room or at four tables in the Frog Pond Room overlooking the pond and lawns. Seatings for dinner are at 6 and 7:30, and the public may be served by reservation ($20) if the inn is not full. Linda's aim is to "make basic things interesting." Dinner the night we visited was tomato bisque, mushrooms under glass, breast of chicken with tarragon or mustard sauce, and fresh peach clafouti.

Other rooms at guests' disposal are a cozy parlor with blue velvet sofa, a small service bar area with all kinds of old rugs and a victrola, a back room filled with wicker furniture, wood stove, television set and game table, and in the barn annex, an acoustically fine space in which Musica Vermont of the Brattleboro Music Center presents the occasional concert.

Doubles, $110 to $130, MAP.

The Old Newfane Inn, Route 30, Newfane 05345. (802) 365-4427.

Built in 1787, this classic New England inn along the green proclaims itself "virtually unchanged for nearly 200 years" and proud of it. Even the spectacular banks of vivid phlox outside the entrance have stood the test of time.

German chef Eric Weindl and his wife Gundy run the place in the continental style, with an emphasis on their dining facility. Theirs is one of the few area inns we've heard of with a two-night minimum stay.

The 10 old-fashioned guest rooms upstairs are meticulously clean, most furnished with twin beds, pretty floral wallpapers, samplers and wall hangings, wing chairs and rockers. Eight have private baths and one is a suite. Several rooms, which once were part of the ballroom, have gently curved ceilings and access to a side balcony looking onto the green.

Off the entry on one side is a dark, beamed parlor with fireplace, upholstered chairs and sofa. On the other side is a narrow and dark beamed dining room, with white lace curtains, pink linens, lamps on the window tables, shiny wood floors, floral wallpaper and a massive fireplace.

Eric Weindl, who trained in a Swiss hotel, cooks in what he calls the Swiss-Continental style. The food is as predictable as when we first went out of our way to dine there nearly two decades ago during a ski trip to Mount Snow — that is to say, good but not exciting.

A few daily specials spark up the enormous printed menu, which lists most of the standards starting with a slice of melon for $2.50 through marinated herring and escargot bourguignon to Nova Scotia salmon for $6.75. Capon cordon bleu, duckling a l'orange, veal marsala, brochette of beef bordelaise, frog's legs provencale, shrimp scampi and pepper steak flamed in brandy are a few of the tried and true dishes, priced from $12.25 to $17.95 and accompanied by seasonal vegetables and salad. Peach melba, Bavarian chocolate cream pie, cherries jubilee and pear Helene are featured desserts.

Dinner nightly 6 to 9; lunch noon to 1:30, late May through October. Closed late fall and spring. No credit cards.

Doubles, $68 to $75, including continental breakfast.

Dining Spots

The Four Columns Inn, Off Route 30, Newfane. (802) 365-7713.

Beamed timbers from the original barn, a huge fireplace, antiques on shelves and walls, and tiny white lights aflickering make the dining area at the rear of the inn a charming setting. Add the magnifcent old French pewter bar decorated with country things like calico hens and an inventive menu that changes seasonally and you have one of the premiere dining experiences in southern Vermont.

The tradition launched by Rene Chardain, who left to open a restaurant bearing his name in South Salem, N.Y., is continued by Sandy and Jacques Allembert and their head chef, Gregory Parks, who was sous-chef under Rene.

The hand-written dinner menu is limited but supplemented with blackboard specials so that chef Parks can take advantage of local seasonal products. Appetizers ($4.75 to $7) might be creamy duck liver and hazelnut pate, snails with walnuts, cream and Vermont smoked ham, or smoked salmon and buffalo mozzarella with basil and peppers.

For entrees ($15.95 to $19), it would be hard to choose among such dishes as free-range chicken grilled over applewood with wild mushroom and garlic sauce, veal scallops in port wine and cream, rabbit braised with tomato, mustard and cream, or saute of shrimp, sea scallops and vegetables with ginger and dark sesame oil.

Desserts change nightly, and you can stop in the lounge to pick one from the cart, even if you haven't dined at the inn.

Lunch is served in season. After starting with cold sorrel soup or a saute of mixed wild mushrooms with garlic and tarragon, perhaps, you might try the white bean, anchovy and red pepper salad served with cornbread, the charred raw tenderloin with spicy mayonnaise or barbecued shrimp Creole style. The prices can be high ($6.50 to $12.95), but the fare is worth it.

Lunch, daily except Tuesday noon to 2, July-October; dinner, nightly except Tuesday, 6 to 9. Reservations required; jackets required at dinner.

The Inn at South Newfane, South Newfane. (802) 348-7191.

Lisa Borst, who loves to cook, reigns over the big kitchen at her parents' new inn. "I enjoy what I do so much," says she, "that it rubs off in the presentation of the food." Always looking for that extra oomph, she gets drenched picking blackberries early in the morning from her extensive vegetable, herb and fruit garden out back, and she makes preserves, purees and sauces (even watermelon pickles) from her produce to carry over the winter.

The summer menu featured shanks of spring lamb with tomatoes, onion and lots of garlic, California duckling served with a ginger oriental sauce, Pacific coho salmon with bearnaise sauce and a loin veal chop with sorrel sauce, among entrees from $14.25 to $17.50. One could begin with smoked

The Inn at South Newfane.

Idaho trout with a curry mustard sauce or baked Montrachet cheese, served warm with olive oil, herbs and saffron, and end with a fresh raspberry tart.

Soup, at our July visit, was curried cream of summer squash.

In winter, you might find a prime rib of buffalo ($19.50) or Lisa's "killer" rack of lamb for one with a sauce of red wine vinegar and rosemary.

Grand marnier cheesecake (so light that it vanishes on the tongue), chocolate walnut torte — the inn's signature dessert" — and homemade ice creams like fig cinnamon are some of the yummy desserts.

The large wine list is interesting as well, with many bottles from Idaho. House wines are DuBoeuf Beaujolais Villages and Glen Ellen chardonnay, $2.50 a glass.

From the French bread at the meal's beginning to the chocolate truffle at the end, everything is homemade and served in a serene dining room with comfortable bow chairs, beige linens, candles in brass holders, crystal water glasses and proper large wine glasses. The Mikasa china is rose colored, and the wallpaper features big tulips in beiges and mauves, with matching valances and draperies.

Dinner nightly except Monday, 5:30 to 9 or 9:30. No credit cards. Reservations required by 4 p.m.

West Townshend Village Cafe, Route 30, West Townshend 05359. (802) 874-4152.

The outdoor deck high up in the trees over a creek and a casual, semi-contemporary interior are draws in this attractive blue wood building down a steep hill. Richard and Debbie Carusona opened in 1982 and renovated in 1984 to produce a dining room with knotty pine paneling and a large bar and lounge with a pool table. It's a mix of gold cloths and white paper mats and napkins, old wood beams and fireplace, herbal wreaths and hanging plants.

The all-day menu lists sandwiches, salads, light dinners and full dinners (the last from $7.95 for rib eye steak to $14.25 for prime rib, Saturdays only). For dessert, besides ice cream, two or three kinds of pies are baked every day — maple pecan and apple, on our visit. The soup and salad bar (all you can eat for $4.50) would be fine for lunch under the colorful Bolla umbrellas on the deck above Tannery Brook.

Open daily from 11 a.m.

Extra-Special

Maison Chardain, Main Street Gallery, Brattleboro. (802) 257-7887.

If you tire of rural pleasures and seek urban chic, southeastern Vermont style, tool down to Brattleboro for some shopping and lunch or dinner in a fine restaurant right above the Connecticut River at the rear of a downtown shopping mall.

Wes and Monika Chardain revived the Chardain family's Vermont tradition in 1985 on the site of the former Autumn Winds restaurant, renovating a solarium and dining room in smashing style. The menu is classic French/continental — "we felt people here missed what Rene Chardain had offered," Monika Chardain said of her father-in-law.

At dinner, the pate du chef ($4.50), two slabs of a hearty rabbit and pistachio terrine, was more than enough for two. Among entrees ($13 to $16.50), we liked the pungent chicken curry Indonesian style and a blackboard special, venison steak, amazingly tender and un-gamy. A smooth Willow Creek cabernet sauvignon for $12, from an interesting wine list, was served in delicate wine globes. The rum-raisin cheesecake was light and garnished with mint and strawberries.

Some of the dinner specialties are included on the lunch menu, with prices generally are in the $4 to $5 range.

Lunch, Monday-Friday 11:30 to 2; dinner, Monday-Saturday 6 to 9.

Vermont's longest covered bridge crosses West River near Townshend.

Diversions

There aren't many diversions — at least of the traditional tourist variety. For those, head for Brattleboro, Wilmington, Weston or Manchester, all within less than an hour's drive. In the West River Valley, you simply relax, hike or drive scenic back roads, and browse through flea markets and country stores.

Shopping usually begins and ends at the **Newfane Country Store.** Mary and Peter Loring claim the best selection of custom-made quilts in all New England in their store chock full of "country things for country folks." Some of the quilts, which the Lorings say represent a local cottage industry, hang outside and beckon passersby in for herbs, jams and jellies, penny candy, maple syrup, sweaters, Christmas ornaments and such. The formula obviously works; in 1985 the Lorings opened another Newfane Country Store in Amherst, N.H.

Other general stores are the **Newfane Store,** a family-operated business for 38 years across from the Newfane green, the **South Newfane General Store** ("experience nostalgia in a working general store and post office"), and the **West Townshend Country Store,** a fixture since 1848 with foods, gifts, cookware, old pickle and cracker barrels (would you believe pickled limes?), spruce gum and two-cent penny candy. Along Route 30 in Townshend, **Lawrence's Smoke Shop** has maple products and corn-cob smoked bacon, ham and other meat products. The factory outlet for **Mary Meyer** stuffed toys is also on Route 30 in Townshend. The **Townshend Furniture Co.** factory has an outlet store with Colonial, country and contemporary pine furniture, plus English country antiques and used furniture in the **Back Store.**

Flea markets seem to pop up all along Route 30. The original Newfane flea market, Vermont's largest now in its 20th year, operates every Saturday and Sunday from May through October one mile north of the Newfane common. New in 1985 was the Townshend flea market, beginning at the ungodly hour of 6 a.m. every Sunday from May through October.

Swimming is extra-special in the Rock River, just off Route 30 up the road to South Newfane. Cars and pickups in a parking area identify the path, a long descent to a series of swimming holes called locally "Indian Love Call," with sections for skinny-dippers, the half-clothed and the clothed. More conventional swimming is available in the West River reservoir behind the Townshend Dam off Route 30 in West Townshend.

West Dover, Vt.
Fun in the Sun and Snow

If it weren't for ski pioneer Walter Schoenknecht and his vision for a showy ski resort called Mount Snow, West Dover might still be little more than a stagecoach stop on the back road from Wilmington to who-knows-where.. It could have followed the path of Somerset, the sprawling township beyond Mount Snow's North Face, which has one of Vermont's largest lakes and nary a single resident — just the remnants of a ghost town lost in the wilderness.

Flushed with success from his Mohawk Mountain ski area in northwest Connecticut, where he was the first to make artificial snow more than 30 years ago, Walt Schoenknecht developed something of a skiing Disneyland on a 3,556-foot peak above West Dover. It had a glitzy gondola, enclosed bubble chairlifts, easy wide slopes and, after a day's skiing, you could frolic in its heated outdoor swimming pool. Here was the the closest major ski and fun resort to Eastern metropolitan areas, and the snow bunnies turned out from the city in droves.

Other ski areas, inns and lodges, restaurants and condos followed, and the boom was on along the river that gives the Deerfield Valley its name. Mount Snow pioneered as a four-season resort with its own Snow Lake Lodge and an 18-hole golf course. Two pioneering inns, catering to an affluent clientele, set a new standard for elegance and dining among New England inns.

Still, winter fun reigns around West Dover, and cross-country skiing is growing faster than the downhill variety. High season is winter. Lodging rates generally are lower in summer, and vary widely depending on weekday or weekend, length of stay and holiday periods.

While Mount Snow has evolved since its acquisition by the owners of Killington, so has the Deerfield Valley. Inns and restaurants are proliferating as West Dover takes ever more advantage of its place in the sun and snow.

Inn Spots

The Inn at Sawmill Farm, Route 100, Box 367, West Dover 05356. (802) 464-8131.

To hear Ione and Rod Williams tell it, they never planned to live in Vermont, much less run an inn. He was an architect and she an interior designer in New Jersey. On a ski trip to Mount Snow, a blizzardy day forced them off the slopes and into a real estate office. The agent took them directly to the old Winston Farm they had been admiring for years. "We've never been sure who was more surprised that day when we bought the farm — we or the realtor," the Williamses recall.

That was in February 1968. Their creative minds went to work and the idea for an inn evolved. They spent the next few years turning the 1799 columned farmhouse, a dilapidated barn, a wagon shed and other outbuildings on the site of an 18th Century sawmill into an inn that is a model of sophistication and distinction.

Not the usual country inn, this — even though it's in the country and indeed one of the world's most perfect hideaways, as Travel & Leisure

Clock tower and gondolas are trademark of Mount Snow.

magazine once described it. Rod Williams kept elements of the barn (hand-hewn beams. weathered posts, boards and doors) so guests would know they're not in the city. A New Jersey birch tree grows up through an enclosed courtyard outside a dining room window; dining rooms, the small bar, living room, loft room, entry, lobby and corridors to guest rooms all meld together fashionably and with unfolding fascination.

Public and private rooms are a decorator's dream. The 21 guest rooms in the inn, sawmill studios and fireplace cottages are large and unusually comfortable. Our mid-price master bedroom typified the place. Extra-spacious, it had a kingsize bed, a desk-like table and chair, three upholstered chairs in a sitting area around a wood table with a good porcelain reading lamp, two sinks in a dressing area outside the bathroom, a dresser and a large plant in a dark wood stand. Wallpaper, upholstery, bedspread and even the shower curtain were in the same country floral print, and the lush green towels matched the thick carpeting. Beyond was a small balcony overlooking the pool.

And then there are the extras: little packages of Godiva chocolates in your room, afternoon tea with nut bread and ginger cookies in front of the large brick fireplace in the living room, superb dinners (see Dining Spots), hearty breakfasts, a sparkling swimming pool, a spring-fed trout pond, a tennis court and the historic part of West Dover just below.

The hearth of the cathedral-ceilinged living room, festooned with copper pots and utensils, is the focal point for guests who luxuriate on comfortable sofas or wing chairs and read the magazines displayed on a beautiful copper table. Other groupings are near the huge windows which give a perfect view of Mount Snow. The loft room upstairs has more sofas, an entire wall of books and the inn's only television set, which is rarely in use.

Breakfasts are a delight in the sunny greenhouse dining room facing the pool in summer and a flock of chickadees at the bird feeders in winter. You get a choice of all kinds of fruits, oatmeal and fancy egg dishes. We especially liked the baked eggs Portuguese and the eggs Buckingham, the latter an intriguing mix of eggs, sauteed red and green peppers, onion and bacon seasoned with Dijon mustard and Worcestershire sauce, served atop an English muffin, covered with Vermont cheddar cheese and then baked. What a way to start the day!

Doubles, $160 to $190, MAP; cottages, $200 to $220; September, October and holidays, add $10.

Deerhill Inn, Valley View Road, Box 397, West Dover 05356. (802) 464-3100.

We were sad to hear that Ole and Patti Retlev had sold the Deerhill Inn and moved to the Brandywine Valley, but on our last visit were pleased to find enthusiastic new owners Eileen and Ronald Armonath from Fairfield County. Both are clearly enjoying being innkkeepers.

High on a hill overlooking the valley and the Green Mountains, the inn is quiet and comfortable. All but two of the seventeen rooms, some in the main inn and some in a wing by the swimming pool, have private baths. They and the public rooms were decorated by Ione Williams of the Inn at Sawmill Farm, Patti Retlev's aunt, which explains their flair.

The large first-floor living room, with sofas, wing chairs and massive fireplace, pewter candlesticks and tankards on the mantel, is most welcoming, as is the second-floor living room with its copper table and another large brick fireplace. A reading alcove with shelves of books is also on this floor.

Bedrooms are furnished with queen and kingsize beds, some with canopies, and modern bathrooms with thick colorful towels. We like the room that looks over the swimming pool, with print canopy over the bed.

Besides the 20-by-40-foot pool (a great setting for cocktails on the deck while watching the sunset over the mountains), there is a tennis court.

Eileen gets up at 6 a.m. to prepare breakfast, served in the handsome dining room (see Dining Spots). Fresh orange juice, pancakes, French toast, bacon from Lawrence's Smokehouse in Townshend and omelet of the day (maybe cheddar cheese and tomato) are the fare.

Doubles, $110 to $140 MAP, midweek; $130 to $155 weekends.

The Hermitage, Coldbrook Road, Wilmington 05365. (802) 464-3511.

Nestled into a hill overlooking the Haystack Mountain ski area stands an 18th century farmhouse that once was the home of the editor of the Social Register, the blue book for blue-blood society. Today it's the nucleus of an acclaimed inn, restaurant and enough other enterprises to stagger the imagination.

"Please do not ask if you may bring you pets," the room confirmation card warns. Any doubts as to why are dispelled as you near the inn at the end of a dirt road. You hear the quacking of ducks and the squawking of geese. Off to the side is the liveliest group of game birds you ever saw. You can ogle the inn's peacocks and English setters, try your hand at fishing in the trout pond, cross-country ski at a large touring center, see the results of a vast maple syrup operation, and examine some of the bottles that

Entrance to the Deerhill Inn.

comprise the largest wine list of any New England restaurant in the inn's wine and gift shop.

Now with a large new dining addition that also triples the size of the wine cellar, the Hermitage is the expanding restaurant-turned inn-turned hobby of owner Jim McGovern, a man of many talents and interests. He pursues most of them 18 hours a day through the changing seasons on his 24-acre property. Part of the Hermitage experience is to wander the grounds, viewing the maple-sugar shed in which the innkeeper also produces more than 10,000 jars of preserves and the outdoor pens with as many as 60 different species of game birds, which are for sale and which also turn up on the lunch and dinner menus.

If the lodging almost seems an adjunct to all the other goings-on, no matter. The 16 guest rooms in the main inn, the converted carriage house and the new Wine House have private baths, and 10 have working fireplaces. Rooms are generally large and modern, but individually decorated and furnished with antiques. In the Wine House, where pictures of ducks grace the small parlor, one room has a heavy carved bed with chenille spread, fringed curtains and a tiny sofa; another has old wood and leather rockers in front of the fireplace. The carriage house with four guest rooms has its own living room and sauna.

For breakfast, guests have a choice of eggs, omelets, pancakes and the like. All the maple syrup and preserves, of course, come from the Hermitage enterprises.

Doubles, $140 to $160, MAP.

West Dover Inn, Route 100, Box 506, West Dover 05356. (802) 464-5207.

Built in 1846 as a stagecoach shop and once the site of the town offices, this historic, pillared and porticoed inn was acquired in July 1984 by Long

61

Islanders Don and Madeline Mitchell. And just in time, we might add, since the inn was suffering from benign neglect.

"People thought we had to be insane," Don recalls. He did most of the wallpapering (it took 80 rolls and enough acquired skills that "he's going to hire himself out," quips Madeline). She masterminded the decorating, and together they refurbished every room. Instead of the two rooms with private baths and ten shared which they inherited, now ten rooms have private baths and two share.

Rooms are nicely decorated with antique furnishings, bright quilts hand-sewn by a woman from Arkansas, brass and wicker bedsteads and those colorful wallpapers hung by Don. Most have comfortable chairs and color TV. Over the dining room is a deluxe room big enough for a family, with a huge bathroom as well.

The organ in the downstairs common room, with walls of barnwood and comfy sofas, is often in use. Beyond is a small cocktail lounge and restaurant called Capstone (see Dining Spots).

The Mitchells share cooking duties in the morning, offering full breakfasts — pancakes, French toast, eggs, sausages — as part of the room rates.

Doubles, $60 to $90, B&B; $90 to $120 MAP; lower rates weekdays and summer.

Doveberry Inn, Route 100, West Dover 05356. (802) 464-5652.

The former Tollhouse bed and breakfast establishment was upgraded in 1984 into the Doveberry Inn, with a pleasant restaurant, a great outdoor dining deck with colorful Schweppes umbrellas and eight fine guest rooms, all with private baths.

The renovated inn has a contemporary air, some rooms having skylights and one luxury suite having private deck and sitting area with color TV. The deluxe Blue Room has two double beds, a duck cushion resting on one and a butterfly cushion on the other, and a basket of apples at our fall visit. A typical smaller double has two cat pillows on the chairs, flowered curtains matching the wallpaper (which also covers the ceiling) and a bathroom with copper in the sink and shower. The North Room is mostly rose with kittens on the curtains; Heidi's Room, all in green, has a peach-colored pillow with flowers and paintings of ducks. "Ellen's into ducks and flowers," innkeeper David Richardson says of his decorator-wife, Ellen Kempton. She collects the pillows from a woman who sells them at the local flea market on summer Saturdays.

Wood stoves and an open brick fireplace warm the common rooms. Overstuffed dark blue sofas are grouped around the hearth; classical music plays on tapes, and books and games are available. Afternoon tea is served with breads and cookies.

David cooks up a full breakfast of the guest's choice: perhaps eggs and bacon in summer, French toast or blueberry pancakes in winter.

Doubles, $48 to $78; suite $68 to $88.

Brook Bound, Coldbrook Road, Wilmington 05363. (802) 464-5267.

Mounds of snow surround this white, dark-shuttered inn in the winter, which is appropriate, for Brook Bound conveys a ski lodge atmosphere through and through. A side entry — where you store your skis and your beverages — leads along a hall past the original small bedrooms into a pine-paneled common room with two sofas for watching television, a fireplace and a piano. Guests eat around an oval table in the small breakfast room. Beyond are the larger guest rooms.

Of the 13 rooms, 11 have private baths. Most are paneled, some have shelves of books, and all are pleasantly if spartanly furnished in a cross between country-inn and ski-lodge style.

The attractive grounds astride a hill off Coldbrook Road contain a swimming pool and tennis courts.

The inn was acquired in 1985 by Jim McGovern of the nearby Hermitage. Asked his plans for the inn, he demurred, but noted that he has never been known to remain idle.

Brook Bound guests are served a full breakfast of their choice. Dinner at the Hermitage is included in the rates.

Doubles, $110 to $140, MAP.

Snow Den Inn, Route 100, P.O. Box 615, West Dover 05356. (802) 464-9355.

This 100-year-old farmhouse became the first ski lodge in the Mount Snow area in 1952, and although it has been upgraded into an inn since Milt and Jean Cummings took over in 1977, it remains a bit of a ski lodge at heart.

All eight guest rooms have private baths, and five have fireplaces and color TV. Among the furnishings are canopy, brass and oak beds, a number of antiques, oriental scatter rugs and quilts.

The main sitting room has recreation-room type furniture around a hooked rug, a wood stove and color TV.

Hitchcock chairs are at tables covered with green mats in the dining room, where a teacup collection is on display.

Doubles including breakfast, $60 to $90 in winter, $45 to $55 in summer; MAP offered in winter.

Dining Spots

The Inn at Sawmill Farm, Route 100, West Dover. (802) 464-8131.

The food served up by engineer-turned-chef Brill Williams, son of innkeepers Rodney and Ione Williams, is worthy of the magnificent setting they created.

The three candlelit dining rooms are as attractive as the rest of the inn and display the owners' collection of folk art. The most formal has wrought-iron chandeliers, chintz draperies and Queen Anne-style chairs contrasting with a cathedral ceiling and barnwood walls. The main dining room has white beams, theorem and oil paintings, rose and ivory wallpaper (even on the ceiling), a lovely china cabinet and tables set with white linens, heavy silver and pretty flowered china. We like best the Greenhouse Room beyond, a colorful plant-filled oasis. And, for the ultimate in coordination, the waitresses wear long peasant-style dresses made of the same print as the wallpaper.

The menu is rather larger and more ambitious than one might expect, comprising more than a dozen appetizers and nearly two dozen entrees. For starters ($5.50 to $8.50), how about salmon mousse with black American caviar, backfin crabmeat cocktail, poached lemon sole with white and red butter sauces or shrimp in beer batter? We liked the thinly sliced raw prime sirloin with a shallot and mustard sauce better than the dry cured smoked salmon, and dug into the delicate green salads and a basket of good hot rolls and crisp homemade melba toast.

Entrees run from $16.50 for Indonesian curried chicken breasts to $24 for steak au poivre flambe. Duck is prepared three ways (one version the creation of Brill's wife Luz). A roasted baby chicken stuffed with shallots and mushrooms is available for two; pork is sauced with cognac, cream and walnuts, and veal loin steak with morels and calvados. We found outstanding both the rabbit stew and the sweetbreads chasseur garnished with french-fried parsley.

Desserts are grand. A chocolate whiskey cake with grand marnier sauce, bananas Romanoff and apple brandy cake were among the choices when we visited. The espresso is strong and coffee is served in a silver pot.

Brill Williams's wine cellar, which he says he has developed "more as a hobby than a business," has been ranked one of the top 100 in America by the Wine Spectator. Prices start in the high teens and rise sharply, but you can find some rare treats for a splurge.

Dinner nightly by reservation, 6 to 9. Jackets required; no credit cards.

The Hermitage, Coldbrook Road, Wilmington. (802) 464-3511.

The dinner menu at the Hermitage rarely changes. It doesn't have to. Innkeeper Jim McGovern, one of whose talents is cooking, specializes in game birds which he raises on the inn's property. He also is a connoisseur of wines. Combine the three interests and he has a going concern indeed.

Lunch and brunch are served outside on a marble patio, inside on an intimate sunporch or in one of the two small, elegant dining rooms. The large new rear dining room is simply gorgeous, with upholstered and wing chairs around well spaced tables set with white linens and blue overcloths, fresh flowers, white china and heavy silver. Walls are covered with the "naif" prints of Michel Delacroix; pretty patterned carpeting, huge windows looking onto the grounds, a grand piano, and hand-carved decoys everywhere complete the picture. A wreath made of corks graces one wall in the lounge.

The relatively small dinner menu lists eleven entrees from $12 to $20. You can get filet of sole, boneless trout, frog's legs provencale, veal marsala, wiener schnitzel or filet mignon. But who wouldn't opt for the nightly game specials — perhaps pheasant, quail, duck, goose or, the last time we visited, partridge?

Dining table at the Hermitage.

As you dine, Jim McGovern may table-hop, chatting about his game birds or the wine cellar, now containing 25,000 bottles, remarkable for their quality and variety. The black-bound, typeset wine list has more than 500 choices (86 California chardonnays, for instance), priced from the low teens to $1,000.

For a weekend brunch (the same menu is offered weekdays for lunch), we sampled the mushroom soup with a rich game pate on toast triangles plus a house specialty, four mushroom caps stuffed with caviar and garnished with a pimento slice and chopped raw onion on a bed of ruby lettuce. Chicken salad for $5.95 was a winner: an ample plateful colorfully surrounded by sliced oranges, apples, green melon, strawberries, grapes and tomatoes on a bed of bibb lettuce. The portions were large enough that we could not be tempted by such desserts as a hot Indian pudding, a maple parfait made with Hermitage syrup or fresh strawberries on a homemade shortcake.

Lunch weekdays in season, noon to 2; brunch weekends and holidays, 11 to 3; dinner nightly 5 to 11, Sunday noon to 11.

Two Tannery Road, 2 Tannery Road, West Dover. (802) 464-2707.
Since Linda and Michael Anelli opened Two Tannery in 1982, it has been a favorite of summer and winter visitors as well as locals. Now they've renovated the historic house to perfection. A large and inviting bar-lounge is where the kitchen used to be, and a new kitchen has been added behind it. A large new entrance hall is decorated with quilts and a deacon's bench.

The focus of the lounge is the dark oak and mahogany bar, purchased at auction in upstate New York in 1983 and from the original Waldorf-Astoria Hotel. A jukebox in the corner plays oldies like Glenn Miller.

The Garden Room in back, with a new wall of windows looking onto it from the Fireplace Room, is as smashing as ever; large windows on three sides look onto the spotlit lawns and trees. Copper pans and pots glow on the brick fireplace; the lushest poinsettias we've seen hang in profusion from the beamed ceiling, and folk art is everywhere. Charming stenciling, done by energetic Linda, runs around the walls and some windows, different patterns in each room. Tartan mats on the dark wood tables are topped with her new Aynsley bone china in Leighton Cobalt pattern. The Fireplace Room and two more small dining rooms are beamed; oriental patterned rugs dot the wide plank floors.

Michael, who was chef at the Hermitage for eight years, is head chef, while Linda does baking and desserts, and puts together the wine list. The menu, marked with asterisks to show "last season's most popular items," is augmented by specials like candy stripe fish, layers of sole and salmon with a dill hollandaise sauce.

Appetizers ($5.50 to $7) include scungilli vinaigrette, Acadian pepper shrimp, and fettuccine with sausage and mushrooms. Soup of the day could be tomato basil or salmon bisque; we remember a good summer soup of cold cucumber with dill.

Entrees, from $12 for grilled chicken breast Dijonnaise to $18 for steak au poivre or filet mignon, include holstein schnitzl, sauteed chicken medallions with frangelico and Two Tannery mixed skillet, a combination of chicken breast, shrimp in a sauce of veal stock, wine and heavy cream, and a small tournedo.

For dessert, apple cake with hot caramel sauce, zuppa inglese, mud or chocolate silk pie and parfaits are winners. The flavor of the cheesecake changes every few days; it was a luscious lemon with whipped cream and strawberries at our visit. Linda reported the eggnog cheesecake served at Christmas was really something. Homemade ice creams include peanut butter chocolate chip.

The wine list is huge and richly varied, at reasonable prices. Thirty-one cabernet sauvignons, for instance, are priced from $12 to $75.

The house, moved to its present location in the 1940s, is the oldest frame building in Dover. In the early part of the century it belonged to President Theodore Roosevelt's son and daughter-in-law; the President is reported to have used it as a retreat. We think he'd approve of the hearty food and delightful atmosphere it offers today.

Dinner, Tuesday-Sunday 6 to 10, open Monday of holiday weeks. Closed mid-April to Memorial Day and first two weeks in November.

Deerhill Inn, Valley View Road, West Dover. (802) 464-3100.

Innkeeper Eileen Armonath told us, "A couple who came here last summer after traveling up the whole coast said this was the best food they had the entire trip." That's a credit to new chef Wade Hoover, graduate of the up and coming Culinary Institute of New England in Montpelier. But even Eileen's husband Ronald can be found in the kitchen (he was making little roses out of tomatoes to garnish every plate the night we were there).

The two dining rooms at Deerhill are light and airy, their expansive windows looking over the valley to the mountains beyond. One has a tartan rug and fireplace, and the other a lovely moss green carpet with round oriental-style inserts. Pink and white linens, huge wine glasses and candles with flowered bobeches create an elegant backdrop.

Soup of the day ($2.25) could be cream of watercress or mushroom, or tomato dill. The terrine ($5) changes nightly. Sweetbreads in puff pastry, escargots under puff pastry, scallops with hiziki and shrimp remoulade are other appetizers. Nine entrees ($12.50 to $17.50) are augmented by a couple of daily specials, coulibiac when we visited. Grilled swordfish in tomato noisette sauce, chicken paillard with chutney, sirloin steak with stilton butter, roasted duck with date and port sauce, and scallops and shrimp sauteed with pine nuts are some.

Finish with the ever-changing desserts ($3.50 to $4.50), maybe a flourless chocolate cake with raspberry sauce called chocolate sin, or chocolate amaretto mousse.

Dinner nightly.

Le Petit Chef, Route 100, Wilmington. (802) 464-8437.

The outside of this low white 1850 farmhouse smack up against the road to Mount Snow looks deceptively small. The inside houses three intimate dining rooms, a spacious lobby abloom with spring flowers in midwinter, and an inviting lounge. Tables are set with white cloths, blue napkins, handsome white china and cutlery, and oil lamps. Cabinets full of antique china and glass, oriental rugs and grapevine wreaths are accents.

Chef-owner Betty Hillman, whose mother Libby is the cookbook author, studied in France and her menu is fairly classic. Appetizers ($4 to $6.25) include eggplant roulade, escargots with roquefort, mussels in a casserole, carpaccio and gravlax.

Entrees run from $11 for stir-fried vegetables to $18.75 for noisettes of venison with red currant sauce. Among others are fish of the day poached Mediterranean style, duckling with maple vinegar sauce and cranberry chutney, two versions of veal (cream or herbs), and filet of beef with green peppercorns and a mustard cognac sauce.

Fresh fruit tarts, chocolate torte, and special ice creams and sorbets are among the homemade desserts.

Dinner nightly; lunch in season.

Elsa's European Deli & Cafe, Route 100, West Dover. (802) 464-8425.
Since Elsa's is one of the few places where you can have lunch in the area, we're happy to report that it is worth the stop. It's small, but in summer you can eat at decks in front by the road or in back by a stream. Inside, six or seven chairs face a right-angle counter; green paper mats and dried flowers in mustard jars top the small tables. The open kitchen where copper pots hang is bordered by a canvas awning in many colors, and skylights make the place bright and cheery, especially in the brick-floored small front room. Posters, lots of tile, a wood stove, and shelves with pastas, pickles and such for sale add to the cafe feeling.

A blackboard lists many specials to supplement the menu, which is comprised mostly of sandwiches, burgers, omelets and salads. Bratwurst with potato salad, barbecued ribs, chili and cream of mushroom soup were some specials at our winter stop. We enjoyed a plate of duck liver pate (all the pates come from Trois Cochons in New York) with a delicious Cumberland sauce, served with crusty warm French bread, and an unusually bountiful salad Nicoise ($5.25). Sandwich prices are in the $1.50 to $4.50 range; the latter includes the Hans C. Andersen, a warm croissant with pate, bacon and horseradish sauce.

Wines and beers are served; the house Meribeau is $2 a generous glass. For dessert, carrot cake, brownie a la mode, tollhouse cookie pie and chocolate almond pie are in the $2.50 to $2.95 range.

Elsa's also puts up box lunches for two, and is a good place for a late breakfast of bagel and cream cheese ($1.50) or Vermont cheddar and ham omelet ($4.25).

Open daily except Tuesday, 11 to 8, to 10 on weekends. No credit cards.

The Capstone, Route 100, West Dover. (802) 464-7264.
This adjunct to the West Dover Inn is leased by Doug Mitchell, son of the innkeepers, and gets its name as the crowning achievement of the inn's restoration. Culinary Institute-trained chef Scott Fredericksen, a boyish-looking 26-year-old, has quite a local following.

If the small dining room seems simple and unprepossessing, the limited dinner menu does not. Entrees ($9.95 to $13.95) include veal Hongroise, shrimp and scallops with oriental sauce, swordfish chasseur blanc and lamb Houstonian, a complex dish of lamb tenderloin wrapped in spinach and puff pastry. Fall appetizers ($2.95 to $5.95) included apples sakoda, clams nordique, wild and shiitake mushrooms in puff pastry, and a country-style pate of veal, chicken and pork. The dessert cart might contain three pastries — chocolate mousse cake, carrot cake and New York-style cheesecake when

Outdoor dining on the deck is popular at Doveberry Inn.

we were there. The bound wine list has interesting choices at fair prices.

Five kinds of omelets are $3.95 at lunch, when the special might be tuna steak in shallots and ginger butter, with salad, for $6.95.

Lunch, daily; dinner, nightly.

Doveberry Inn, Route 100, West Dover. (802) 464-5652.

Chef-innkeeper David Richardson, a former Boston lawyer, is aiming for the middle market in the small restaurant at the far end of his renovated inn. "The whole idea is to appeal to those who want to pay maybe $15 a person for a nice dinner with wine," he says. "We're trying to be something between the best and the pizza places."

From the looks of things, the formula is succeeding. Two country-style dining rooms, one with a wood stove, have ladderback chairs and bare wood tables topped with woven mats and cutlery tucked inside brown napkins. A tartan rug covers the floors.

Dinners are simple but hearty: homemade soups and a couple of appetizers, crusty Canadian oatmeal bread and garden salad, and entrees ($7.95 to $10.95) from chicken bearnaise or parmigiana to veal bearnaise and petit filet mignon bordelaise. Lasagna, bay scallops, gulf shrimp and three old-fashioned roasts — turkey, leg of lamb and pork loin — round out the menu. A small wine list is priced from $8 to $15.

In summer, the new front deck is popular for lunch. Sandwiches, salads and platters of such things as double knockwurst and potato salad or tomato stuffed with crabmeat salad are available from $2.25 to $5.95.

Lunch in season; dinner nightly.

Diversions

Skiing. Mount Snow virtually put West Dover on the map, and skiing remains the stellar attraction today. Long known as a great beginners' area and a lively place for apres-ski (with the stress on apres more than ski), it nonetheless always has appealed to us for its wide-open, almost effortless intermediate skiing. Since founder-showman Walter Schoenknecht sold to the business types from Killington, Mount Snow has been upgraded in terms of snowmaking and lift capacity. Gone is the heated swimming pool; more emphasis is on the North Face, a challenging area for advanced skiers, blessedly away from the crowds. Now any skier can find his place — and space — at Mount Snow. Adult lift rates: $28 weekends, $26 weekdays.

More skiing. Haystack, a smaller mountain (1,400-foot vertical, compared with Mount Snow's 1,900), has had its ups and downs, but the 'Stack is back, as its advertising proclaims, with two new triple chairlifts, base-to-summit snowmaking and uncrowded, family-type skiing (adult lift tickets, $22 on weekends, $18 weekdays). Also operating on and off is still smaller **Carinthia** (1,100 vertical), lately on with a new double chairlift to the summit and in transition since being acquired by Mount Snow.

Cross-Country Skiing. Where skiers gather, cross-country is usually available, too. So it is with the Deerfield Valley, which has three major touring centers. The best is the **Hermitage Touring Center,** run by the Hermitage inn, which has 55 kilometers of groomed trails next to Haystack. It is part of the rugged new Ridge Trail, a five-mile-long mountaintop touring trail that winds up and down four peaks between Haystack and Mount Snow. The **Sitzmark Ski Touring Center** offers 25 kilometers of trails on its golf course and adjacent wooded hills off East Dover Road in Wilmington. The **White House Ski Touring Center,** run by the White House Inn in Wilmington, has 14 miles of trails through woods and hills east of Wilmington.

Other Seasons. Two of southern Vermont's largest lakes are close at hand for boating, fishing and swimming, Somerset Reservoir in the wilderness north of Mount Snow and Lake Whitingham southeast of Wilmington. Golf is available at the 18-hole Mount Snow Country Club, the par-three Sitzmark golf course and the new 18-hole Haystack championship course. Special events are scheduled throughout the summer and fall. Gondola rides to the top of Mount Snow are available during the fall foliage season.

Shopping. West Dover is little more than a hamlet with some landmark structures that make up what innkeeper Madeline Mitchell says is an emerging "Historic Mile." Even the ski areas have failed to attract the usual shops; most of the shopping opportunities are down the valley in Wilmington. An exception is **von Schreiner's Delectables,** an ice cream emporium at Route 100 and Coldbrook Road. Here are room after room of gifts, toys and Christmas decorations as well as an old-fashioned soda parlor offering all kinds of ice cream confections. Who could resist the sap bucket, a Vermont sundae of butter pecan ice cream, butterscotch-maple sauce and chunks of maple-peanut brittle?

Extra-Special ⎯⎯⎯⎯⎯⎯⎯⎯⎯⎯⎯⎯⎯⎯⎯⎯

The Marlboro Music Festival. Popular with West Dover visitors is the summer tradition at Marlboro College in Marlboro, where three chamber music concerts are presented each weekend from early July to mid-August. Since 1952, Rudolf Serkin has directed the 70 festival players whose concerts are incidental to their studies. Tickets usually are sold out by spring, but seats may be available on the canopied porch outside the 650-seat concert hall.

Lake Sunapee Region, N.H.
Sports Galore and a Clubby Air

The fortuitous combination of lakes, mountains and meadows makes the Sunapee Region a choice year-round attraction, especially for the sportsman.

Lake Sunapee, New Hampshire's third largest, and its neighbors, Little Sunapee and Pleasant Lake, provide all kinds of water pleasures within view of Mount Kearsarge, central New Hampshire's highest peak with two state parks on its slopes, and Mount Sunapee, a state park and ski area. In between on the rolling flatlands are four golf courses and two tennis clubs.

So it comes as no surprise that historic New London, the largest village in the region (year-round population, 1,335, but swelled by second-home residents, tourists and students at Colby-Sawyer College), is a mecca for the affluent. Its hilltop setting with posh contemporary homes, trendy shops and country clubs casts an unmistakable aura of prosperity. Legend has it that the song made famous by Kate Smith, "When the Moon Comes Over the Mountain," was written by a Colby student as she watched it rise above Mount Kearsarge.

Little Sunapee and Pleasant lakes, hidden from the tourists' path, are happily unspoiled. Some of the Lake Sunapee shoreline is surprisingly undeveloped as well, and old Sunapee Harbor — the heart of the lake resort region — looks not unlike a cove transplanted from the coast of upper Maine.

The area's inns, most of which have been around a while and bill themselves as self-contained resorts, reflect the solitude and variety of the region. Somewhat detached and above it all, many succeed on tradition and clubbiness, knowing that their legions of regulars will return with the seasons.

Inn Spots

Seven Hearths, Old Route 11, Sunapee 03782. (603) 763-5657.

While this inn might look like an old farmhouse from the outside, take one step inside and you know that sophistication reigns. A small table in the middle of the reception area holds a large round clear bowl with a beautiful arrangment of flowers, brilliantly spotlit from above; beyond it is another table with a display of wine bottles. To the right, through glass doors, is a stunning living room dominated by a huge fieldstone fireplace and two plush mushroom-colored velvet sofas.

The farmhouse dates from 1801 and its last incarnation was as an antiques store. Vacant for a period, it was acquired in 1983 by a Harvard School of Design graduate and his wife, who restored it with taste and tender loving care, opened it as an inn in the summer of 1984, and then decided they didn't like the inn business. They sold a few months later to Mary Ann Callahan and Miguel Ramirez, corporate types from Boston, who brought their extensive art collection to the inn, but otherwise didn't have to do much else.

There really are seven hearths, one in the dining room and five in the

70

Lake Sunapee is quiet in early morning in this view from Three Mile Loop.

bedrooms (there are 10 guest rooms, all with private baths). We certainly enjoyed ours in a large front corner room on a chilly September night.

Rooms vary in size from very large to quite small; some have twin beds, but most have queensize. All are elegant, with touches like needlepoint luggage racks, velvet wing chairs, interesting area rugs and antique furnishings. The back corner room has a round window through which you can see white birch trees; a picture of birches hangs on the opposite wall. Bowls of fruit are placed in each room.

Spacious grounds contain flower gardens, a large vegetable garden well-used by the chef and, in back, a swimming pool up a slope landscaped with rocks and flowers.

Before dinner (see Dining Spots), guests gather in the Hearth Room for cocktails and hors d'oeuvres. Breakfast at Seven Hearths is an event, from the freshly squeezed orange juice ("I get up every morning at 6:30 to squeeze it," says Mary Ann) served as a first course with homemade croissants, to the dish of fresh fruit with creme fraiche (nectarines and blueberries at our visit), accompanied when we were there by a slice of spicy gingerbread and a piece of brie. Hearty eaters may then order eggs any style, pancakes or waffles. One of us thought the preceding was more than enough. Accompanied by good coffee and music from "The Magic Flute," it was a breakfast fit for a monarch, which may be what you feel you ought to be when it comes time to settle the bill.

Doubles, $130 to $170, MAP.

Hide-Away Lodge, New London 03257. (603) 526-4861.

The name says it all: Hide-Away Lodge, hidden away on a hill in the woods off a private driveway beyond Little Lake Sunapee, and a "lodge" in the true sense, from the head of the deer over its huge granite fireplace to the Oregon fir paneling used throughout.

But the name does not convey the stature of its dining room nor the hospitality of longtime innkeepers Wolf and Lilli Heinberg, who sold in September 1985 to Californians Bill and Bonnie Sroth. The Sroths planned to carry on in the Heinberg tradition and, happily, to open the operation year-round.

In searching for "the perfect inn," the Sroths inherited an elegant, club-like masterpiece maintained with old-world traditions over two decades by the Heinbergs. Built in 1930 as a summer residence by Maryland poet Grace Litchfield, the place is what you'd expect a lodge to be (except for all the space naturally given over to the restaurant operation).

You arrive by a private driveway, part of the historic Daniel Webster Highway leading into forests laced with logging roads and cross-country trails. You enter through a long, geranium-lined front porch filled with wicker furniture into the living room-foyer with its enormous fireplace. Beyond are several dining rooms, a cocktail lounge on a screened terrace and, downstairs, the Pipedream Pub and the showplace wine cellar developed by Wolf Heinberg.

Upstairs are two guest rooms and a suite, paneled in the Oregon fir and furnished simply in lodge style. One corner room has a delightful little claw-foot tub that makes you want to hop right in for a soaking bath. Four other rooms with private bath are located across the driveway in a guest house that Bonnie calls "the cottage."

Guests have beach privileges at Little Lake Sunapee, a short walk away, as well as golf privileges at the Twin Lakes Villa nine-hole course nearby. But what they have most of all is utter peace and quiet with unparalleled dining (see below) in a small, hidden lodge.

Doubles, $34 EP, $82 MAP.

Dexter's Inn and Tennis Club, 150 Stagecoach Road, Sunapee 03782. (603) 763-5571.

Its amenities and location up a country lane, high above Lake Sunapee, make this self-contained small resort a retreat for sports enthusiasts.

The main house, painted a pale yellow, was built in 1801, extensively remodeled in 1930 and converted into an inn in 1948. Dartmouth men have owned and operated it ever since, Frank Simpson and his wife Shirley having acquired it in 1970. They added "Tennis Club" to the name in 1973; tennis buffs have use of three all-weather courts, with a tennis pro and tennis shop at hand, "and we've never heard of anyone who didn't get enough court time," Frank says proudly.

Tennis players — and others, for this is by no means exclusively a tennis resort — can cool off in the attractive swimming pool. The 200-acre property offers shuffleboard, croquet and a horseshoe pit as well as secluded paths and hiking trails plus a wildlife and bird sanctuary at Beaver Pond.

The sports theme continues inside the large barn recreation room, with bumper pool and ping-pong tables. One of the regular guests, an 80-year-old widower, is always ready for a rousing game of ping-pong.

The main inn has a long narrow entry with red velvet Victorian chairs, a living room with a grand piano and walls of books, a lounge with TV and fireplace, and a small gift shop.

All ten guest rooms in the main inn and seven in the annex have private baths. Each is decorated in vivid colors coordinated with the striking wallpapers. The front rooms have views of the lake. Rooms in the annex and barn are larger; one has twin canopy beds, several have sliding doors leading to a patio, and all are bright and cheery.

Hide-Away Lodge really is hidden away on wooded property.

Coffee and juice are served in the bedrooms (and you could have your whole meal there), but most guests gather for breakfast by the bay window in the dining room for a view of the lake. In summer, salads and sandwiches are served for lunch on an outdoor terrace.

Dinners are table d'hote, the limited menus rotating every two weeks in summer and weekly in fall. A soup like gazpacho, cold cucumber or French market soup leads off the meal. Entrees might be beef kabobs, veal scaloppine or pork tenderloin with an apple-walnut stuffing. Homemade pies and cakes and Dutch apple crisp are among desserts. The dining room is open to the public daily except Tuesday by reservation although, Frank advises, "this is a dining room, not a restaurant."

Doubles, $100 to $120, MAP. Bed and breakfast available May, June and September, $75 to $95 double. Open May-October. No credit cards.

The Inn at Sunapee, Burkehaven Hill Road, Box 336, Sunapee 03782. (603) 763-4444.

Kate Crawford, who formerly managed the Highland House in Vermont and before that was a Washington lobbyist, has found a home for herself and her possessions at the Inn at Sunapee, which she acquired in late 1985. Although the previous owners had done basic renovations, the inn was in need of some cosmetics and deplasticizing, which Kate has enthusiastically pitched in to do.

Perched high on a hill, with a distant view of Lake Sunapee and the surrounding mountains, the inn has spacious grounds with swimming pool and tennis courts, and there's a decidedly "out in the country" feel to it. Beyond the pool are four motel-like units and an old milk house that was being turned into a honeymoon cottage.

The rest of the 22 rooms are on two floors of the main inn. All have

Lake Sunapee is on view from the Inn at Sunapee.

private baths and there are two suites, one with two bedrooms and one with three. All have been, or were about to be, newly painted, with new wallpaper, painted floors and scatter rugs. A local seamstress was making pillow covers from Kate's grandmother's linens. Dried flower arrangements are in all the rooms. Armoires and dressers from her family are in some.

Guests gather on overstuffed chairs or at the bar in a cheery fireplaced lounge, where the walls are decorated with grandmother's gilt paintings on glass and an old ship's masthead.

Breakfast, which on summer days can be taken on the back deck, includes pitchers of orange juice on the tables, and a choice of eggs, pancakes, French toast, sausage or bacon. On terribly creative mornings, says Kate, "we might do omelets or eggs rancheros." Skiers could find hot cider and cookies in the lounge when they come back, tired and hungry. As for dinner (see below), since the inn reopened customers have been returning again and again.

Doubles, $60.

Pleasant Lake Inn, Pleasant Street, Box 1030, New London 03257. (603) 526-6271.

Down a long hill north out of New London at the end of Pleasant Lake is the area's oldest operating inn.

"The view from our front window is the most spectacular in the area," say new innkeepers Grant and Margaret Rich, and they could be right. The exceptional setting with a beach across the road and Mount Kearsarge at the far end of the lake have attracted visitors for more than 100 years.

Five of the 13 guest rooms on the second and third floors have private baths. Each is furnished differently with beds of varying sizes, some canopied, and antiques.

The guests' living room has cable television and a bumper pool table, and is home to two lively cockatiels named Poco and Polly.

For many, the handsome dining room is the main attraction (see below). Meals are served in the 1790 bar room with fireplace, part of the original homestead, or beyond in the wrap-around flagstone patio room, which offers a smashing view of Pleasant Lake.

Inn guests have beach and boating privileges at the Slope and Shore Club across the road.

Doubles, $40 to $60, EP.

Maple Hill Farm, Newport Road, RR 1, Box 1620, New London 03257. (603) 526-2248.

A 160-year-old farmhouse just off Interstate 89 was converted in 1985 into a bed and breakfast establishment by corporate dropout Dennis Aufranc and his wife Roberta, who commutes weekends from her job in New York.

Perhaps because Dennis is resident innkeeper and chief cook and bottle washer, a masculine air prevails about this place with three dogs, six cats and ten guest rooms. Once a boarding house with one bathroom and eight bedrooms — "not one of which you would want to sleep in," Dennis relates — he has renovated and refurnished them with new plumbing and beds. Decor is spare, but the rooms on the second and third floors are serviceable and about half have private baths.

The public rooms downstairs are more comfortable. A front common room has one wall of red tin, an old wood stove, a pretty corner hutch and a real oldie of a radio that belonged to Dennis's grandmother from Saskatoon. Another parlor has mushroom-colored velvet sofas and a round oriental rug.

The large dining room is exceeded in size only by the kitchen, where guests often gather to watch Dennis prepare breakfast or group dinners by reservation. Breakfast involves a choice of the tummy warmer, hot oatameal with dried fruit; the continental, custard with fresh fruit and toast; the farm special, a huge meal, and the traditional, with blueberry pancakes. Orders are placed the night before. Meals are taken in the dining room at tables covered with blue and white checked cloths and fresh flowers, or on a small outside porch.

A path behind the house leads through the woods to Little Lake Sunapee, where guests have use of a small beach for swimming, boating and fishing.

Doubles, $35 to $45, including breakfast.

New London Inn, Main Street, New London 03257. (603) 526-2791.

This village hotel next to the Colby-Sawyer College campus has been around since 1792, and looks and feels it.

Each of the 26 guest rooms on three floors has a private bath. They vary in size and decor, with subdued wallpapers and white the prevailing color from bedspreads to wicker chairs. Even the exposed pipes from the new sprinkler system have been wallpapered to make them unobtrusive. The corner rooms are larger; those like the one in which Ronald Reagan stayed when he campaigned in the New Hampshire primary have oriental-style rugs and a separate sitting area created by a large closet in the center of the room.

Light meals and cocktails are served in Nelson's Tavern. Besides soups, salads and sandwiches, there are hot entrees like beef burgundy, chicken pot pie, fish and chips and stuffed Cornish pasties.

Continental fare is offered in the two main dining rooms, brightly wall-papered and more formal with yellow cloths and red napkins. Dinner entrees run from $8.95 for pork Normandy or chicken a l'orange to $13.95 for steak au poivre. Rock Cornish game hen, shrimp remoulade and sole Foster with bananas and rum are among the offerings.

Doubles, $34 to $49. Three meals daily.

Dining Spots

Hide-Away Lodge, New London. (603) 526-4861.

New owners Bill and Bonnie Sroth knew a good thing when they found it in 1985. They took over the prestigious Hide-Away Lodge in September and planned to run it year-round in the manner of their predecessors, Wolf and Lilli Heinberg, who were helping them every bit of the way, Wolf remaining as a menu and wine consultant.

Dinner here is a special occasion, the more so because of its broad range and exceptional value. It begins when the young valet whisks away your car and the hostess greets you at the door, ushering you for cocktails to the screened terrace in summer or the Pipedream Pub downstairs the rest of the year.

Drinks are accompanied by crackers and a zesty cheese spread as you study the menu, hard-covered and hand-lettered, offering intriguing choices for four-course meals. Depending on choice of entree, the unusually gentle prices range from $13 to $21 (except for a few surcharges). You also choose your wine from an enormous and reasonably priced selection, either from the written list interspersed with humorous graphics and quotes or verbally from the special wine cellar. One recent party was able to order a 1978 Heitz cabernet sauvignon for a bargain $27, Bonnie Sroth reported.

Your choices made, you move to one of five small dining rooms seating a total of 65. Tables are set simply with white linen, green napkins and fresh flowers.

The menu changes yearly, the innkeepers believing that since their guests don't change, their food must. Meals begin with such choices as smoked trout in celery aspic, mussels marinated in olive oil and garlic, the house pate flavored with brandy or one of five soups — cold Danish fruit, watercress and celery vichyssoise, duck broth, Spanish garbanzo or French onion. We liked the shell of garlic bread filled with mushrooms in snail butter and a herring salad with cranberries and sour cream. A choice of salads includes asparagus flan with dill mayonnaise, mushrooms malabar, spinach greens with creamy egg dressing, and apricot and cottage cheese with chantilly dressing. Caesar salad prepared at the table costs an additional $2.50.

The dozen entrees include chicken curry, rainbow trout poached in chablis and coriander butter, breast of capon with truffles and Madeira, veal scallops jardiniere, grilled lamb steak with minted bercy sauce and game dishes like vol au vent of venison, pheasant baked with juniper, or rabbit with burgundy. We still remember delectable mignonettes of veal Nicoise and pork loin braised in maple syrup with pineapple mustard relish.

The lavish desserts include a Hungarian poppyseed and honey parfait, pumpernickel-raspberry pudding with creme de cassis, raspberry mousse cake, cheese strudel with fruit sauce, amaretto chocolate mousse and, for

$3 extra, a house specialty of praline crepes flamed in apricot brandy.

After dinner, guests who ask may get a tour of the wine cellar, a showplace with museum-type displays and a large dining table for private parties. It's part of the tradition of Hide-Away — in Bonnie Sroth's words, "there's a real spirit to this place that we sensed immediately and want to keep up."

Dinner, 6 to 9 nightly except Tuesday; closed April and first two weeks of November.

Seven Hearths, Old Route 11, Sunapee. (603) 763-5657.

The suave handwritten menu changes nightly in the restaurant at this elegant new inn. Candles, lanterns and recessed lighting illuminate the dark main dining room, pretty as a picture with pink and plum linens accented with vases of fresh flowers, wide pine floors, bay window and a hearth with beehive oven. A smaller room behind the dining room is good for private parties, of which Seven Hearths seems to have many.

Meals are preceded by cocktails in the inn's large living room. Inn guests are urged to be there 45 minutes before their dinner reservations for drinks and complimentary hors d'oeuvres (brie with crackers and hot cheese quiche strips, very good and very filling, the night we stayed). Co-innkeeper Miguel Ramirez, clad in white trousers, is a genial host and mixes hefty drinks. Whether the cocktail get-together works, however, depends entirely on the crowd. The two of us shared the room with an outside party of five retired couples chatting about their golf games and, later, 11 women educators; we felt somewhat conspicuous first by ourselves at one end of the room and then trying to mix around the hors d'oeuvres table.

Chef John Rego's menu is $20, prix-fixe, including the hors d'oeuvres in the living room. Dinner begins with the night's soup, perhaps creamy celery sherry, tomato garlic bisque or creamy scallop, or a Scarborough crepe with scallops in tomato sauce.

Three or four entrees are offered, among them shrimp and mussels fra diavolo, halibut steak sauteed with mushrooms and sherry sauce, either filet mignon with tarragon butter or prime rib with shallot duxelle sauce, and a house specialty, chicken breasts with mushrooms, scallions and artichoke hearts Dijonnaise. We thought the last was excellent, as was a spicy shrimp dish with such bite as to leave the mouth burning. A good rice pilaf and crisp julienned slices of summer squash and zucchini were accompaniments, and the plate was decorated with nasturtiums.

A green salad with poupon red basil vinaigrette followed the main course. It's the first dining room we can recall where no bread was served with dinner.

One or two desserts are offered daily: perhaps a tart green apple cake with cream cheese frosting, homemade mandarin chocolate ice cream on a cloud, frangelico mousse with strawberry cognac puree or toasted almond chocolate torte.

The wine list is interesting but limited, with most priced in the high teens. The house Chantefleur is $2 a glass, $9 a carafe.

Lunch entrees ($4.95 to $6.95) include frittata, croque monsieur, chicken breast with barbecue sauce and tenderloin tips with mushrooms.

Lunch, Tuesday-Saturday 11:30 to 2, July-October; dinner, Tuesday-Saturday 6 to 9, year-round; Sunday brunch, 11:30 to 2. Reservations required.

Pleasant Lake Inn, Pleasant Street, New London. (603) 526-6271.
The wrap-around patio room with the great view down Pleasant Lake toward Mount Kearsarge is popular with inn guests and public alike.

Dining at Pleasant Lake Inn.

Sleek cane and chrome chairs flank well-spaced tables dressed with white cloths, pink napkins, candles in hurricane lamps and dried flowers. A fireplace takes the chill away in an interior dining room.

Dinners begin with a choice of appetizers ($1.50 to $3.95), among them crabmeat bisque or snails in puff pastry. Entrees run from $9.25 for baked filet of sole to $14.75 for veal Victoria, laced with cognac and topped with mushrooms, crabmeat and mozzarella cheese. Chicken apricot or Madeira, roast duck a l'orange, beef stroganoff, broiled scallops and shrimp South Pacific are other possibilities. Irish coffee cream pie, a frozen Bavarian cream pie and the Rich family's favorite chocolate icebox cake are popular desserts.

Dinner nightly except Monday, 6 to 9, weekends to 10, Sunday brunch, 11:30 to 2.

The Inn at Sunapee, Burkehaven Hill Road, Sunapee. (603) 763-4444.
The dining room at the Inn at Sunapee is cheery, granting wondrous views of the lake and mountains through bay windows. Paper narcissuses in the windows and primroses on the white-linened tables add to the color, and a gorgeous accent is the breakfront that belonged to innkeeper Kate Crawford's grandfather, who was involved in the China Trade era, filled with her grandmother's Royal Worcester plates.

Chef Blair Maiers, former owner of Autumn Winds in Brattleboro, Vt., has devised a menu that keeps diners coming back for more. Appetizers ($2.50 to $3) include Danish country pate with lingonberry sauce, savory phyllo puffs and escargots in puff pastry. For entrees ($8.95 to $13.95), choose among Indonesian chicken with a hot peanut sauce, ducking with raspberry sauce, tortellini with mushrooms and gruyere, lemon veal, and tenderloin of beef with mushrooms, sherry, cognac and chive butter. Kate's aim is for "sophisticated country dining" and she feels strongly about using local produce, going so far as to find someone to raise corn-fed chickens for her.

Desserts might be lemon tarts, a "killer" chocolate cake, creme caramel, cheesecake with blueberry sauce, and homemade lime or raspberry sherbet. The wine list, with four whites and four reds, is most reasonable and the Folonari house wine is $1.75 a glass, $5.25 a liter.

A Mexican menu is offered Monday nights. Start with melted cheese tortillas and two salsas, then have Mexican Christmas salad, then red snapper with avocado sauce, chicken enchiladas or tacos, and end with flan or sherbet with Mexican cookies. Quite a bargain for $11!

Dinner nightly, Thursday-Sunday; Mexican menu Monday.

Woodbine Cottage, River Road, Sunapee Harbor. (603) 763-2222.

Eleanor Hill, a very peppy 80, is still much involved in the restaurant she and her late husband Bob began 59 years ago in their home. They had a small screened porch which they built around, and, says she, it just grew from there. Now a thriving enterprise, the vine-covered cottage incorporates an inner dining room and a garden room, as well as a large gift shop, for which Mrs. Hill is the buyer. Next door is the Holly Shop, chock full of everything for Christmas.

Breakfast, lunch, tea and dinner are served daily. In fact, the atmosphere is rather tea roomish, with lacy paper mats on the tables. An arrangement of mums and berries is over the mantel of the fireplace (which is lit on cool days), and gorgeous flower gardens, spotlit at night, are outside. Each table sports a different colored candle and flowers to coordinate.

Breakfasts are from $1.85 for continental to $4.75 for full; a la carte blueberry griddle cakes are $2.35. Full-course luncheons are from $8.50 for turkey pie to $11.95 for lobster salad or newburg; sandwiches and salads are in the $2 to $5 range. At teatime you may have, for $3.50, tea sandwiches and cake, with tea in a proper pot.

Full dinners, from $12.50 for chicken and mushroom casserole to $16.50 for planked steak, include the famous salad wagon and butterscotch buns. This is good solid New England fare — broiled halibut, salmon or Cape scallops, lobsters boiled or broiled, roasts and chops.

Desserts get the most raves at Woodbine, however. Among the goodies are strawberry shortcake, pecan, date macaroon and chiffon pies, tortes, cheesecake, homemade sherbets and ice creams, served with a choice of

Woodbine Cottage started as a porch and grew from there.

six sauces including French apricot and ginger, and frozen cake balls (choose your own flavor of ice cream and sauce). Fresh fruit in season, meringue glace and Dixie crunch ice cream ball are more.

A little cookbook of "Our Favorite Recipes" is for sale in the gift shops, as are jars of the famed house Caesar salad dressing.

Breakfast, lunch, tea and dinner daily; Sunday dinner, noon to 4; May to mid-October.

Millstone Restaurant, Newport Road, New London. (603) 526-4201.

A lofty cathedral ceiling with skylights lends an airy feel to this casually elegant place which is popular with the Colby-Sawyer College crowd. Owned by Tom Mills, who owns another Millstone in Concord, it has a pleasant, canopied brick terrace for dining in the summer. Inside are well-spaced tables, covered with beige linen and blue napkins.

Entrees ($8.95 to $14.95) on the large and varied dinner menu run the gamut from pasta dishes (angel hair scampi is one), veal picatta and Bavarian schnitzel to pork tenderloin oriental (served with the house sweet and sour apricot-plum sauce), sweetbreads mimosa (glazed in an orange champagne sauce) and baked stuffed quail. A sole dish is surrounded by Gulf shrimp and topped with lobster sauce. Grilled chicken has been marinated in lime juice; chicken Elizabeth is stuffed with crabmeat and white asparagus and baked in puff pastry.

Among appetizers are broiled tomatoes stuffed with pesto sauce, grilled seafood sausage with lobster sauce, and hummus served with Syrian bread points. Desserts include profiteroles aux chocolat, praline flan, chocolate chip coconut pie and a maple-lemon custard.

The same desserts are on the lunch menu, as are some of the interesting entrees ($3.75 to $7.95), plus an array of salads, sandwiches and omelets.

Lunch daily, 11:30 to 2:30; dinner from 5:30.

The Velvet Green, Lake Sunapee Country Club and Inn, Route 11, New London. (603) 526-6040.

It's advertised as "gracious country inn dining," but we'd mislead if we called it anything other than your typical country club experience — from the large (and low-priced) drinks to the clientele to the lovely views of fairways and greens with Mount Kearsarge as a backdrop.

For lunch in what we would call the grill (with paper mats over bare tables, upholstered cane chairs and a couple of lighted ficus trees framing the expansive windows), we enjoyed a veggie pouch sandwich, chock full of things like artichoke hearts and alfalfa sprouts, and a spinach salad. We did not enjoy the basket of rolls which turned rock-hard when they cooled.

Dinner in the adjacent dining room is more formal, with brown and white linen and again the wonderful views (they're even better outside at tables with yellow and white chairs and umbrellas on the back lawn). Entrees are standard club fare, from $7.95 for fettuccine Alfredo to $13.50 for filet mignon. The chef gets to show his stuff with steak Diane and chateaubriand or rack of lamb, finished tableside for two.

Dessert are parfaits, walnut pie, carrot cake and strawberry shortcake, plus a daily special of the same ilk.

The club also has 30 guest rooms and cottages, available at $45 double.

Breakfast, lunch and dinner daily.

Picnic tables at the Dock and Boathouse Tavern.

Extra-Special

The Dock and Boathouse Tavern, Sunapee Harbor. (603) 763-2227.

The setting is the thing at this otherwise nondescript restaurant, which amounts to a long, narrow room with pine tables and booths beside the screened windows and a rear deck with open air bar, picnic tables and colorful umbrellas. The vantage point for viewing the harbor goings-on is great — you can't get much closer to the water without being on or in it.

Soups, salads and sandwiches are the all-day fare, plus a few more substantial items like shish kabob, fresh filet of fish or barbecue ribs ($5.95 to $8.75) and, after 5 o'clock, pizza. A blackboard menu keeps up with the times: nachos, potato skins, ham and cheese quiche, wings 'n things.

Open daily from 6 a.m. to 1 a.m. in summer, from 11:30 Friday-Sunday in the fall.

Peter Christian's, Main Street, New London. (603) 526-4042.

A spinoff of its Hanover namesake, Peter Christian's occupies intimate, dark quarters with low beamed ceilings and booths in the mid-section of what used to be the Edgewater Inn.

The fare and prices are geared to the college crowd. Dinner entrees run from $6.25 for beef stew, served with salad and bread, to $8.95 for hot crab and cheese bake, chicken parmesan or shrimp and rotini noodles mornay, served with salad and lemon muffin. There are Chinese chicken stir fry, quiche du jour (summer squash when we visited) and, for starters, spinach and ham balls to be dipped in mustard, boursin cheese and crackers, parmesan artichoke dip and vegetable board ($4.50 and plenty for two) and, natch, nachos. Desserts include rum fudge mousse, fudge swirl cheesecake, hot fudge sundae and, if you're not into fudge, strawberry cream puff. The few wines are appealingly priced, by the glass or bottle.

The lunch menu is as casual as the dinner menu, with a couple of salads and soups, eleven sandwiches, the daily quiche and cheese or meat boards. Open daily, 11:30 to midnight.

Diversions

Cultural offerings. For 52 years, the **New London Barn Players,** New Hampshire's longest operating summer theater, have presented matinee and nightly performances of musicals and comedies from mid-June to Labor Day. Guest events in the **King Ridge Summer Music Series** are staged every two weeks or so from late June through August. Despite its generally low-key flavor, the area bustles during the League of New Hampshire Craftsmen's annual crafts fair, the nation's oldest, which attracts 1,500 craftsmen and 50,000 visitors the first week of August to Mount Sunapee State Park.

Mount Sunapee State Park. A 700-foot-long beach is great for swimming in the crystal-clear waters of Lake Sunapee. Across the road is the 2,700-foot high Mount Sunapee, criss-crossed with hiking and ski trails and its summit lodge accessible in summer and winter by a 6,800-foot-long gondola lift. The park is also the site of such special events as a gem and mineral festival, the Great American Milk Bicycle Race and the New England championship Lake Sunapee Bike Race.

Sports. All the usual are available, plus some in abundance. Golfers have their choice of four semi-public country clubs and smaller courses: the venerable Lake Sunapee Country Club and Inn, the hilly and challenging Eastman Golf Links in Grantham, picturesque Twin Lakes Villa beside Little Sunapee, and the Country Club of New Hampshire, rated one of the nation's top 75 public courses by Golf Digest. Downhill skiers get their fill at Mount Sunapee or King Ridge ski areas, and cross-country skiers take over the fairways at the area's golf clubs in winter.

Lake excursions. From Sunapee Harbor, the 150-passenger M.V. Mt. Sunapee II gives 90-minute narrated tours the length of Lake Sunapee at 10 a.m. and 2:30 p.m. daily from mid-June to Labor Day, and 2:30 weekends in spring and fall. Its companion steamer, the M.V. Kearsarge, offers buffet supper cruises at 5:30 and 7:45 nightly in summer. Another way to view the lake is to drive the Scenic Three-Mile Loop around Sunapee Harbor; you'll find striking new houses interspersed with old traditional cottages.

Shopping. For a town its size, New London has more than its share of good shopping — spread out along much of the length of Main Street and clustered in shopping centers and a new mall along Route 11 on the southwest edge of town. **Campion's** for clothing and **Kearsarge Bookshelf** are highlights of the attractive new Gallery Mall. Featured at the Village Green are **Deming Art Gallery** and the **Menagerie,** "a unique boutique for a menagerie of people." Along Main Street are shops like **Basics** (clothing for the family, with a branch in Sunapee Harbor), **Artisans Workshop,** the **Crafty Goose,** the **College Sport Shop** and **C.B. Coburn Co.,** a general store turned gift shop. In Guild, to the southwest of Sunapee, is the **Dorr Mill Store,** a large and attractive shop specializing in woolens. Despite its location at the mill, this is no mill outlet and the prices are what you'd expect to pay back home.

Robert Frost worked at this desk in Franconia with view of Cannon Mountain.

Franconia-Sugar Hill, N.H.
The Road Less Traveled

The lines are from Robert Frost: "Two roads diverged in a wood, and I — I took the one less traveled by, and that has made all the difference."

They were written when the poet lived in Franconia beneath Cannon Mountain, and the road less traveled has made a difference historically in maintaining the Franconia area as an island of serenity just north of the crowds.

"Many people don't know about our history and beauty," says Richard Bromberg of the Sugar Hill Inn. "They think that to the north beyond the Old Man of the Mountains, there's just woods and Canada."

Indeed, Franconia and its upcountry neighbor, Sugar Hill, are remote and almost untouched by the usual trappings of tourism. They retain much of the look and the flavor of the late 19th century when they were noted mountain resort areas. In the 1930s, Austrian Sig Buchmayer established the country's first ski school at Peckett's-on-Sugar Hill (now designated by a primitive historic marker) and Cannon Mountain dedicated skiing's first aerial tramway.

But for the mystique of the name, one might not be aware of the area's storied past. Gone are the large hotels and, as ski areas go, Cannon keeps a low profile. Today, the crowds and the condos stop at Franconia Notch to the south, leaving Cannon Mountain, Franconia, Sugar Hill and even the town of Littleton for people who appreciate them as vestiges of the past.

For those who want action, the magnificent Franconia Notch State Park stretching eight miles through the notch offers some of the Northeast's most spectacular sights and activities.

But the road less traveled takes one beyond. We can think of no better place for fall foliage viewing than from Sunset Hill or the ridge leading up to Sugar Hill above Franconia. The heights afford sweeping vistas of the towering White Mountains on three sides and toward Vermont's Green Mountains on the fourth.

In winter, downhill skiers can revel in the challenges of Cannon Mountain, the venerable World Cup area so much a part of skiing history that the New England Ski Museum is located at its base.

In spring and summer, the quiet pleasures of an area rich in history and character suffice. The Frost Place, the Sugar Hill Historical Museum and the Sugar Hill Sampler are classics of their genre.

Don't expect luxury inns, fancy restaurants or trendy shops. Immerse yourself instead in the beauty and the serenity of New England as it used to be.

Little wonder that long after he left, poet Frost wrote, "I am sitting here thinking of the view from our house in Franconia." It's unforgettable.

Inn Spots

Sugar Hill Inn, Route 117, Franconia 03580. (603) 823-5621.

Nestled into the side of Sugar Hill, this old white inn, built as a farmhouse in 1789, its wrap-around porch sporting colorfully padded white wicker furniture and a telescope for viewing Cannon Mountain, welcomes guests all year except for spring mud season.

Carolyn and Richard Bromberg, both from Connecticut (they met while skiing in Vermont), moved here in 1983 after corporate careers in Pennsylvania and Illinois. "Our moving truck left on a Wednesday," said Richard. "We were fully booked starting on Friday and we had nothing to put on the walls." They've managed since to fill them up with pretty stenciling, old pictures, samplers and wreaths made by Carolyn.

The 10 rooms, all with private baths, exude country charm, with rocking chairs, quilts, towels in bright colors, and even a teeny pillow shaped like a duck on most beds. All the rooms are different, with choice of twin, double, queen and king beds.

The six cottages in back (not open in winter, because the water lines freeze) are equally nicely done, some with stenciling on the country chests, and with plush carpeting and television sets.

Two living rooms in the main inn are available for guests. One is quite formal, containing the couple's fine collection of antiques, and the other has a large TV and sofa.

Breakfast, served from 8 to 9:30, is a real occasion, with enough food for a lumberjack, as our waitress said. First course is choice of juice and a homemade muffin (ours was zucchini-walnut and outstanding), then a dish of fresh fruit in season (blueberries and peaches at our September visit) followed by a choice of several hot dishes. We can only say that the eggs Benedict were splendid and after trying the country souffle, we requested the recipe to add to our repertoire.

Carriage is trademark of Sugar Hill Inn.

As we were warned upon making our reservations, there is no smoking anywhere in this inn (we did spot an ashtray on the porch), a rule we heartily endorse.

Doubles, spring and summer, $64 to $70, including breakfast. Rest of year, MAP, fall $128 to $140, winter $100 to $120.

Franconia Inn, Easton Road, Franconia 03850. (603) 823-5542.

Classically situated by a meadow with Cannon Mountain as a backdrop, this rambling white structure, which looks the way you think a country inn ought to look, is the area's largest and busiest. "We have a reputation for lots of activities," says Alec Morris, innkeeper with his brother Richard for their parents who run a resort in the Ozarks.

Thirty-two rooms on two floors have been gradually upgraded since the Morrises took over the vacant inn in 1980 after it had lapsed into bankruptcy. Most of the changes were cosmetic, but every guest room now claims a private bath and carpeting.

Rooms vary in size and beds; some connect to become family suites. Generally, room decor is rather plain, although there are exceptions such as twin-bedded Room 14 in which the ducks on the lamps match the ducks on the bedspreads. The corner rooms are best in terms of size and view.

The main floor has an attractive dining room (see Dining Spots), living room and oak-paneled library with fireplaces, a pool room, a game room with pinball machines, and a screened porch with wicker furniture overlooking a large swimming pool. Downstairs is a spacious Rathskeller lounge, with entertainment at night, and beyond, a hot tub in a large redwood room.

Outside there is swimming in the pool or in a secluded swimming hole in the Ham Branch River. Four clay tennis courts and a glider/bi-plane facility are across the street ("soaring lets you see the mountains at the ultimate vantage point — from the sky," says Alec Morris). The stables next door shelter five horses for trail rides in what the inn touts as a western adventure. In the winter, the barn turns into a cross-country ski center; sleigh rides and snowshoeing are other activities. Movies are shown every night.

Double rooms, $57 to $65; family suites with connecting bath, $90 to $110. MAP, add $23 per adult. Numerous package plans available. The inn closes for most of April and May, and from mid-October to mid-December.

Lovett's Inn By Lafayette Brook, Profile Road, Franconia 03580. (603) 823-7761.

Although this inn, a fixture for two generations, recently added a swimming pool for its summer clientele, it's at its best in the winter — and we'll always remember it that way. We were lucky enough to stumble into one of its fireplaced cottages during a snowstorm 15 years ago and liked it so well we stayed for two days.

Many of the patrons have been coming here for years, such is the spell that innkeeper Charles H. Lovett Jr. and family have cast on his inn and dining room.

Not quite a traditional New England inn, Lovett's is a cross between a bed-and-breakfast facility which also serves dinner and a motel-chalet colony.

The main house, dating from 1784, has eight guest rooms with shared baths upstairs, an acclaimed dining room, a basement rec room, a living room with TV and an adjoining sunporch full of video games — great for the kids while parents linger over dinner. The rooms here are simple but adequate and bear a few interesting decorative touches. The nicest is the Antique Room, with private bathroom, air-conditioning and television.

Summer or winter, we'd choose one of the chalets, duplex units scattered beside the pool and around the lawns. Each has a small patio with chairs for gazing upon Cannon Mountain in summer; the nine with fireplaces are positively idyllic on winter nights. All have sitting areas and small television sets; the elongated narrow bathrooms at the rear are ingenious as well as serviceable.

A full breakfast, including shirred eggs with mushrooms or herbed tomatoes, and several renditions of pancakes (chocolate or parsnip!), is served, as is dinner (see Dining Spots).

Doubles, $72 to $128, MAP.

Beal House Inn, 247 W. Main St., Littleton 03561. (603) 444-2661.

A large, cheery breakfast room chock full of antiques, where guests eat on blue and white willow china at a long table covered by a red cloth, is the central feature of the bed-and-breakfast establishment and antiques shop run by Doug and Brenda Clickenger in the heart of Littleton. A calico hen sits on a basket on the table and even the salt and pepper shakers are antiques.

All the antiques here — as well as in the cluttered, cozy parlor, the glassed-in wicker-furnished front porch, up the various staircases and in the 14 guest rooms — are a logical extension of the Clickengers' antiques shop in the barn, connected to the inn by a carriage house. And except for family pieces, all are for sale. The striking highboy in the corner Washington Room when we visited, for instance, was available for $1,600. So was the four-poster bed, although it could not be delivered until a replacement was found.

Besides the public rooms, guests also have use of an outdoor deck up a hill in back of the house, illuminated at night.

Rooms are furnished with four-poster, canopied, brass and spool beds, colorful quilts, hooked and braided rugs, wing-back chairs and rockers. Two pillows depicting a bride and a bridegroom decorate the white iron bedstead in the Honeymoon Room. The canopy bed in the back Lavender Room, named for its flowered wallpaper and the hillside of lilacs and wildflowers outside its windows, has a lovely decorator coverlet; the towels and shower curtain in the bathroom are a striking lavender.

Three rooms on the ground floor and seven upstairs, including two suites, have private baths. Four rooms in the annex share two baths.

Hot popovers are Doug Clickenger's specialty at breakfast, which also includes seven kinds of juices, scrambled eggs, waffles, bacon and sausage. A fire blazes in the brick fireplace. Old china and glassware line the shelves of this living antiques shop and, to complete the experience, Brenda wears a long country dress and mobcap as she serves. Dinners for groups may be arranged in advance.

Doubles, $35 to $60.

The Horse and Hound Inn, Wells Road, Franconia 03580. (603) 823-5501.

A secluded farmhouse converted into an inn in the 1940s, the Horse and Hound has 12 guest rooms, six with private bath.

Rooms vary in size and decor — the tiny Honeymoon Room is so named because "it's all bed," according to Heidi Larson, who with her husband Eric and his parents Betty and Bob Larson took over the inn in 1985. The Meditation Room, with a view onto the rear yard and hillside, is done up in shades of blue, with blue velvet chairs and a blue-tiled bathroom.

The rear lounge is called the library because of its ample collection of books and magazines, plus games and stereo. There's an outside terrace in back for summer brunches and barbecues. Three fireplaces in the lobby and dining rooms warm things up in winter.

Breakfast and dinner are served in two rustic beamed dining room made attractive by tall white candles, white linen, brown carpeting and beige napkins intricately folded on white and green floral china.

Appetizers are standard, from chilled juice with sherbet to shrimp cocktail ($1.25 to $5.50). Entrees ($9.50 to $17.95, most in the mid-teens) are more ambitious, with three versions of roast Long Island duckling (l'orange, Normandy and Bombay), scampi a la francaise or steak au poivre.

Petite English trifle, kahlua cheesecake, homemade double strawberry ice cream and liqueur parfaits are among the desserts. Two dozen wines are priced from $7.50 to $24, with the house Partager at $1.75 a glass or $8 a bottle.

Dinner nightly, 5:30 to 9:30, closed Wednesday off-season. Sunday brunch.

Doubles, $50 to $65.

Rabbit Hill Inn, off Route 18, Lower Waterford, Vt. 05848. (802) 748-5168.

Just over the Connecticut River from Littleton and easily accessible to Franconia is this comfortable old inn across from the village church in the much-photographed hamlet of Lower Waterford. Part of the reason it has prospered for so long is the reputation of its fine dining room (see below).

The pillared, three-story main building surrounded by flower gardens dates back to 1825 and has served as an inn on the Portland-to-Montreal route most of that time. Many of the more popular rooms are in a two-story wing converted in the 1950s from a ballroom and carriage house. They were typical motel units, but new innkeepers Beryl and Eric Charlton have quite effectively covered up or replaced the plasticity with country touches.

The Charltons, originally from Great Britain, had settled in York, Pa., where he worked as a chemical engineer and she as a nurse. In 1980 they left their jobs, hopped in the car and looked around for something to do, landing, as so many do, at an inn. Their son Paul, having graduated from college, is now assistant innkeeper. A father of newborn twins, he is an enthusiastic spokesman for the inn and the area.

British touches are seen here and there, in the hunting horns and horse brasses in the public areas, old English prints in some of the rooms, and other family treasures. You can order by mail Beryl's authentic Scottish shortbread or plum pudding to add to your Christmas festivities.

Upstairs in the main building is a cozy reading nook, crammed with books and replicas of rabbits given to the Charltons by various guests. A big stuffed rabbit sits in a hall chair, and small china rabbits rest on bureaus in some of the rooms. A few rooms have fireplaces and canopied beds. Hooked rugs and antiques like an old cradle abound.

Table d'hote breakfasts are $3.75 to $4.75, including juice or cereal and coffee. Pancakes come in short stacks (three) or tall stacks (six) and, of course, are served with Vermont maple syrup. The oatmeal bread served at dinner makes equally good toast at breakfast, and is also used for French toast. Those who enjoy British bangers are pleased to find them on the menu.

Doubles, $35 to $65, EP.

Dining Spots

Tim-Bir Alley, 28 Main St., Littleton. (603) 444-6142.

Tim and Biruta Carr, who both worked for the Sheraton Corporation and were transferred all over the place, met when both landed in Oklahoma City at the same time. When they decided to open a restaurant of their own in 1984, they settled in, of all places, Littleton, N.H.

Their teeny place is really down an alley and hard to find, but their menu is outstanding, if somewhat sophisticated for the area at dinner time (they do a good weekend breakfast and daily lunch business, when the fare is more what you might expect).

With seven tables, seating 22 lucky people (plus a small counter with several stools), theirs is a simple but pleasant place. White linens, a votive candle in a crystal bowl and peach-colored carnations are on each table. The cafe curtains are trimmed with eyelet embroidery, walls are hung with posters and macrame, and classical music plays at night.

The menu changes weekly, with usually one soup, two appetizers, a pasta dish and four or five other entrees. Cream of spinach and almond, or cream of mushroom, leek and brie are a couple of the soups; shrimp with vodka-orange cream, terrine of three smoked seafoods, chilled fresh asparagus with smoked salmon mayonnaise or, our choice, an absolutely outstanding scallop mousse with fresh dill and Dijon vinaigrette, more than enough for two to share, are in the $4 to $4.50 range. The house salad was an interesting mix of greens, mushrooms, red peppers and Swiss cheese, served on glass plates with piquant vinaigrette or blue cheese dressings.

At $14.95, the mixed grill was the most expensive entree — an unusual mix of lamb chop with rosemary and feta, veal scaloppine with banana, rum and cream (a bit too sweet) and tournedo of beef with choron sauce; it was beautifully presented around asparagus spears, red caviar on sour cream over roast potatoes, and bits of asparagus and zucchini in the middle. A

Lovett's By Lafayette Brook in winter.

smoky flavor pervaded the linguini with duck, scallions, tomato and smoked Swiss cream ($10.25), an unusual and memorable combination.

Desserts are limited — a pound cake with peach-blueberry sauce, a double chocolate cake and two ice creams when we visited. A carafe of the house Pierre Dourthe wine for $8 accompanied.

Breakfast, Saturday 8 to 11, Sunday 8 to 1; lunch, Tuesday-Saturday 11 to 2; dinner, Wednesday-Saturday 6 to 9. No credit cards.

Lovett's By Lafayette Brook, Profile Road, Franconia. (603) 823-7761.

Before dinner, guests usually gather in the inn's small lounge (where the marble bar is from a Newport mansion) for socializing. Then they're seated in one of the three beamed-ceilinged dining rooms where each receives a service plate on which a round piece of paper details the surprisingly extensive menu. Table d'hote dinners are priced from $14 to $17.50, according to choice of entree.

A plate of pates and cocktail spreads with crackers makes a good appetizer, as do things like fresh salmon mousse, tabbouleh or calamari Genovese. Unusual soups include such summer offerings as cold bisque of fresh watercress with chervil, cold black bean soup with Demarara rum, wild White Mountain blueberry soup or strong mutton broth with fresh vegetables and barley.

Among the 17 entrees might be curried turkey or lamb with Lovett's chutney, sauteed Colorado trout, broiled Eastern tilefish, veal marengo, chicken in apples and calvados or brandy and herbs, or such standbys as chicken livers, ham steak with pineapple and broiled scrod.

The wine list, limited but serviceable, is pleasantly priced from $6 to $12 except for two bottles at $14 and $19.50 (for DeLas chateauneuf du pape).

Desserts are extravagant, from hot Indian pudding with ice cream to meringue glace with strawberries, macaroon crumble pie and butterscotch ice cream puff. We remember with gusto the chocolatey Aspen crud from 15 years ago and, yes, it's still on the menu. Some things, like Lovett's, don't change much over the years. And that's rather reassuring.

Dinner nightly, 6:30 to 7:45. Reservations and jackets required.

Franconia Inn, Easton Road, Franconia. (603) 823-5542.

The large dining room with well-spaced tables and small-paned windows looking out toward the mountains is quite handsome with gold linens, gold walls, cane back chairs and crewel-like curtains. The limited menu offered by Culinary Institute-trained chef Murray Noyes is somewhat creative and considered locally a bit pricey.

A typical dinner might begin with a choice between escargots pernod or herring and sour cream ($4.25 and $3.95). Entrees ($10.95 to $17.95) might be bouillabaisse, duckling with an orange brandy and gruyere cheese sauce, veal cordon bleu, rack of lamb with mint sauce, fresh vegetables sauteed and served in a pastry shell for the vegetarian, or the chef's special spicy ginger and soy sauce stir-fry of the day, the ingredients changing nightly among shrimp, scallops, beef, pork, lamb, veal and chicken.

The many fancy after-dinner drinks and coffees are an alternative to a rather limited dessert selection — cakes, pies and fruit melbas comprising most of them. The wine list has about 30 entries, priced from $9.95 for a Rosechatel special reserve 1980 white bordeaux to $18.95 for Jadot moulin a vent.

Dinner nightly, 6 to 9.

Sugar Hill Inn, Route 117, Franconia. (603) 823-5621.

Innkeepers Carolyn and Richard Bromberg change their five-course dinner menu seasonally. It's $18 and served on weekends only in summer and early fall; during foliage season and winter the inn is MAP, but some lucky outsiders can come for dinner after the inn guests are taken care of.

The dining room is country-pretty, with dark green and rose calico quilted mats on the polished tables, draperies to match, Hitchcock chairs, and spotlit theorem paintings on velvet. A white candle in a hurricane lamp and a small carafe of flowers are on each table.

"We do a lot of roasts in the fall and winter," says Richard. Beef and pork Wellington are favorites then. Tournedos with a sweet cream mustard or bordelaise sauce are often on the menu; veal chausseur, chicken Normandy stuffed with apples, sage and thyme or scallops baked in nests of crabmeat stuffing are possibilities. Carolyn's estafado, a Greek beef stew, won a prize in a Smucker's contest (she included a quarter cup of apricot preserves).

You might start with hot curried crab spread, shrimp mousse, or the aged cheddar cheese sold at John Harmon's country store up the road. One of the favorite soups is mushroom dill, and the salad could be mandarin orange.

In summer, blackberry or blueberry mousses are often on the dessert menu; chocolate or maple mousses at other times. Cherry cheese tarts, pecan pie, bananas Foster, apple crisp, an acclaimed praline and cream torte and what Richard thinks is the most wonderful summer dessert, a fruit tulip, round out the menu. Beer and wine are available. Smoking is banned in this inn.

Dinner, 6:30 to 7 in season.

Rabbit Hill Inn, Lower Waterford, Vt. (802) 748-5168.

The menu changes every day at Rabbit Hill, so that the innkeepers can offer the freshest of foods in the remotest of areas. If fresh salmon is available, they might serve it in a mousse, or poached with dill cream sauce.

Table d'hote dinners are a bargain $12.50 to $15.50, including an appetizer, salad (with the house mustard dill dressing) and dessert. The menu changes daily, but you could start with a chilled cantaloupe or fruit soup or clam chowder, and then tear into your small loaf of hot oatmeal bread (just the smell of it baking causes severe hunger pangs).

Entrees like fresh baked haddock, chicken curry with chutney and toasted almonds, roast loin of pork in a mustard crumb coat, boiled beef dinner with mustard sauce or broiled sirloin strip steak are complemented by a trio of colorful vegetables stir-fried in butter. They are also complemented by the area's most extensive wine list, well chosen and nicely priced.

Desserts might be fresh nectarine pie, raspberry Bavarian, Indian pudding, or British-born innkeeper Beryl Charlton's plum pudding with rum sauce.

The two dining rooms are very cheery: one with white cloths and red napkins, and one with red woven mats on polished tables. Pewter abounds, in the water glasses, service plates, salt and pepper shakers, vases and hurricane lamps. One room is carpeted; the other has the original wide-board floors, and a wood stove warms things up in winter.

Dinner nightly, 6 to 9.

Sunset Hill House, Sunset Road off Route 117, Sugar Hill 03585. (603) 823-5522.

There could be no more spectacular a setting for a restaurant/inn than the Sunset Hill ridge commanding nearly 180-degree vistas both east and west. The four adjoining dining rooms at Sunset Hill House take full advantage of the view to the east.

The printed menu changes nightly; table d'hote dinners including fruit cup, melon or juice, choice of dessert and beverages range from $12.95 to $14.50, according to entree. Typical offerings might be deep fried chicken with cranberry sauce, roast pork loin, chicken marsala, prime ribs or veal piccata. Desserts could be Indian pudding, pies, Harvey Wallbanger cake or creme de menthe parfait.

The inn, housed in what was once the annex of the original Sunset Hill House, has 35 guest rooms, most with private baths, available at $47.50 to $55 per person, MAP.

Lunch, noon to 2:30; dinner, 6:30 to 9.

Polly's Pancake Parlor, Hildex Maple Sugar Farm, Route 117, Sugar Hill. (603) 823-5575.

Polly and Wilfred "Sugar Hill" Dexter opened their pancake parlor in 1938, when they charged 50 cents for all you could eat, mainly to have a way to use up their maple syrup. Their daughter, Nancy Dexter Aldrich, and her husband Roger operate the farm and restaurant now; they charge considerably more than 50 cents, but it's still a bargain and a fun place to go for breakfast, lunch or early dinner and a slice of local life.

Bare tables sport red mats shaped like maple leaves, topped with wooden plates handpainted with maple leaves by Nancy Aldrich, who, in her red skirt and red bow, greets and seats diners. Red kitchen chairs and sheet music pasted to the ceiling add color to this 1820 building, once a carriage shed. Its most appealing feature is big louvred windows with a view of the awe-inspiring Mount Lafayette range beyond.

Pancakes are served with maple syrup, granulated maple sugar and maple spread; an order of six costs $3.10 or $3.30 for plain pancakes made with white flour, buckwheat, whole wheat or cornmeal. All of these are available with blueberries, walnuts or coconut for $4 or $4.20. The Aldriches grind their own organically grown grains and make their own breads, sausage and baked beans (with maple syrup, of course).

If, like us, you don't really crave pancakes in the middle of the day, try the homemade soups (lentil is especially good), quiche of the day (our ham and cheddar melted in the mouth) or a super good BLT with cob-smoked bacon ($2.95). Cereals, eggs, muffins made with pancake batter, salads and sandwiches like grilled cheese and cob smoked ham, croque monsieur, and even peanut butter with a maple spread are available.

The homemade pies ($2, add 50 cents for a la mode), are outstanding. Hurricane sauce, made from apples, butter and maple syrup, served over ice cream, is $2.05.

No liquor is served, but the coffee, made with spring water, is great and, as a matter of fact, a glass of the spring water really hits the spot.

In the shop, through which you pass to get to the dining room, you may purchase pancake packs, maple syrup and sugar, jams and jellies and even the maple-leaf painted plates. Polly's also does a big mail-order business.

Open from 7 a.m. to 7 p.m., mid-May to mid-October, and weekends in early May.

Diversions

Franconia Notch State Park, south of Franconia. The wonders of one of the nation's most spectacular parks are well-known. Thousands visit the Flume, a 700-foot-long gorge with cascades and pools, and the Basin, and gaze at the rock outcroppings, most notably the Old Man of the Mountains. Echo Lake at the foot of Cannon Mountain is fine for swimming. The Cannon ski area has retired its original 1938 aerial tramway but a modern replacement carries tourists to the summit for the views that skiers cherish — and gets them back down without the challenges which hardy skiers take for granted.

Cannon Mountain. In an era of plasticized, free-wheeling skiing, the serious ski areas with character are few and far between. One of the last and best is Cannon, which considers itself the first major ski mountain in the Northeast (1937). Operated as a state park, it remains virginal and free of commercialism. The setting is reminiscent of the Alps, when you view the sheer cliffs and avalanche country across Franconia Notch on Lafayette Mountain and the majestic peaks of the Presidential Range beyond. From the summit, much of the skiing varies from tough to frightening, as befits the site of America's first racing trail and the first World Cup competition. But there is plenty of intermediate and novice skiing as well. Lift prices are downright bargains: $19 on weekends, $17 on weekdays, with a $4 surcharge for use of the tram.

New England Ski Museum, next to the tram station at Cannon Mountain, Franconia. Skiers particularly will enjoy this small museum which opened in December 1982 with themed displays which change annually. The maroon parka belonging to the founder of the National Ski Patrol is shown, as is a photo of him taken at Pecketts-on-Sugar-Hill. One of the more fascinating exhibits traces the evolution of ski equipment. "Ski Tracks" is an informative and impressive 13-minute audio-visual show with 450 slides tracing the history of New England skiing. Open daily 10-4, Memorial Day-Columbus Day and Dec. 15-March 31. Adults $2.

Sugar Hill Historical Museum, Sugar Hill. Sugar Hill people say not to miss this choice small place, and they're right. It displays an excellent collection in a modern, uncluttered setting and gives a feel for the uncommon history of this small hilltop town, named for the sugar maples which still produce maple syrup ("everyone who can, taps the trees," reports museum director Mitchell Vincent). The life of the community is thoroughly chronicled in photographs and artifacts. The Cobleigh Room recreates a stagecoach tavern kitchen from nearby Lisbon, and the Carriage Barn contains mountain wagons and horse-drawn sleighs, including one from Bette Davis's former estate. Open July-October, Thursdays and Saturdays 1 to 4, Sundays 2 to 5. Adults $1.

Sugar Hill Sampler, Route 117, Sugar Hill. Commercialism gives way to personality and history in this place behind the Homestead Inn. The large dairy barn, with nooks and crannies full of New Englandiana for souvenir shoppers, is literally a working museum of Sugar Hill history. Owner Barbara Serafini Parker is the sixth-generation descendant of one of Sugar Hill's founders and takes great pride in sharing her thoughts and possessions, even giving handwritten descriptions on the beams. In one rear section full of family memorabilia, she displays her grandmother's wedding gown, which she wore in a pageant written by her father and presented for President Eisenhower on the occasion of the Old Man of the Mountain's birthday in 1955. Amid all the memorabilia is an interesting selection of quaint and unusual merchandise, including maple syrup made by the Stewart family on Sugar Hill, and a special spiced tea mixture called Heavenly Tea. Many New Hampshire foods are featured, and you can taste samples of several.

Shopping. In Sugar Hill, **Harman's Cheese and Country Store,** a tiny place with a large mail-order business, proclaims "the world's greatest cheddar cheese." Many of its food and local items are one-of-a-kind, according to owner Maxine Aldrich, who is carrying on the late Harman family tradition. The **League of New Hampshire Craftsmen Shop,** at the base of Cannon Mountain, is housed in a gray, contemporary Alpine chalet-style building between the foot of Gary's Slope, a Cannon ski trail, and Echo Lake. In Franconia, the **Garnet Hill** shop offers fine bed clothes (English flannel sheets, comforters and the like), as well as pricey children's clothing, all in natural fibers. Its main retail outlet is on Newbury Street in Boston — enough said.

Extra-Special

The Frost Place, Ridge Road off Route 116, Franconia. The farmhouse in which the poet lived from 1915 to 1920 and in which he summered through 1938 is a low-key attraction not to be missed. It was here that he wrote most of his best-known works, executive director Donald Sheehan said of the property opened by the town of Franconia as a Bicentennial project in 1976. The house remains essentially unchanged from the 1920s; most of it is occupied in summer by a visiting poet, but the front room and a rear barn are open with interesting Frost memorabilia, including his handwritten "Stopping by Woods on a Snowy Evening" and a rare, large photo of Frost at age 40 working at his desk in the room. Out back, a half-mile nature trail has plaques with Frost's poems appropriate to the site; in two cases, they are on the locations where he wrote them. As if the poetry and setting weren't enough, the stand of woods happens to contain every variety of wildflower indigenous to Northern New England. Open July and August, daily except Tuesday 1 to 5; weekends 1 to 5, Memorial Day-June and Labor Day-Columbus Day. Adults, $2.

Squam Lakes, N.H.
Midas Touches Golden Pond

The movie "On Golden Pond" has cast the largest private lake in the country quietly into the public eye.

"Before the movie, not that many people knew the lake was here," said Pierre Havre, who with his wife Jan restored a rundown resort into the Manor in 1983. They started something of a boom in year-round innkeeping in an area that long has been a low-key haven for homeowner-members of the influential Squam Lakes Association, whose membership reads like a Yankee who's who.

Now the Holderness area between Squam and Little Squam lakes has four inns in various stages of development and the surrounding area has three new bed and breakfast establishments. Just east of the Squam Lakes, Meredith, at the head of the closest part of Lake Winnepesaukee, is the site of the area's largest new inn as well as trendy new restaurants and shops.

"All of a sudden," notes Bill Webb of the new Inn on Golden Pond, "the Squams have 50 beds and, with skiing close by, we're hoping to make this a destination area year-round."

Passersby see the striking sign in front of his inn and "stop just to ask if this is the place where the movie was filmed," Bill Webb says. It isn't, but like most of the Squams' new entrepreneurs, he takes full advantage of the association.

Pierre Havre boards inn guests and public on his 28-foot pontoon craft for twice-daily cruises along the 50-mile shoreline of Squam Lake. Its water is so pure that the 1,000 or so homeowners drink straight from the lake and its setting is so quiet that it's a nesting place for loons, which are the lake's trademark. Other than by private boat, the Lady of the Manor is the only way visitors can see the sights that Katharine Hepburn and Henry Fonda made famous (the Thayer house, Purgatory Cove) and sample the changing moods of a very special lake.

Besides the lakes, the nearby historic town of Center Sandwich — a picturesque crafts colony which is everybody's idea of what an old New England village should be — and the new upscale pleasures of Meredith beckon visitors.

Now, thanks to the emergence of some good new inns, they have a home base from which to enjoy the charms of Golden Pond.

Inn Spots

The Manor, Route 3, Holderness 03245. (603) 968-3348.

Sometimes called the Manor on Golden Pond, this is the largest and most luxurious of Squam Lake's new inns. It is also the only one with lake frontage and access, which is a major plus.

Built from 1903-1907 by an Englishman who had made a fortune as a Florida land developer, the mansion, with its leaded windows, gigantic fireplaces and oak and mahogany paneling is a gem. High on Shepard Hill, commanding a panoramic view of the lake and mountains, the honey-colored stucco structure has a porte cochere guarded by a statue of a

Squam Lake is visible through porte cochere at the Manor.

German shepherd. Other bits of sculpture are dotted around the grounds. A large swimming pool off to one side, a clay tennis court in the pines and a lawn set up for croquet complete the picture.

An elegant living room done in shades of blue and apricot, a cozy library with a small TV and many games plus a deck off one side, a lounge and a piano bar are available for the use of guests. Innkeepers Pierre and Jan Havre, he a retired American Airlines pilot, have done a splendid job of restoring the formerly run-down Squam Lakes Resort. Jan, an artist, did the decorating with a California flair.

All 14 guest rooms (with English names) in the manor house and newer Mountain View wing are different, though they share the luxe wall-to-wall taupe carpeting. Most of the bathrooms are small but modern; a few have old-fashioned pedestal sinks. Some of the bedrooms have working fireplaces, and some have great views of the lake. Most are spacious, and all are pretty. We especially liked the Buckingham — a huge corner room with marble fireplace and kingsize bed. There are rooms in five cottages as well, and the Dover Cottage, which has two bedrooms and a living-kitchen room with fireplace, is smack beside the lake and available in season for $695 a week.

A European-style breakfast buffet, with fruits and juices, cereal, croissants and muffins, is served to inn guests. Canoes, a sailboat and a fishing boat are also provided.

The inn's elegant dining room (see below) is becoming renowned for lunch and dinner.

Doubles, $54 to $114.

Red Hill Inn, Route 25B, Box 99M, Center Harbor 03226. (603) 279-7001.

In the summer of 1985, the red brick summer estate which served as the administration building for the short-lived Belknap College was restored after 11 years of dormancy into a full-fledged inn and restaurant atop a rural hillside with a view of Squam Lake.

"From your room you can see where they filmed 'On Golden Pond,'" the inn's brochure proclaims. All ten guest rooms on the second and third floors of the mansion have private baths. They vary from double rooms with twin beds to five suites with sitting rooms and working fireplaces, two with private balconies and a pleasant view. A separate stone cottage contains another suite, and eight more guest rooms were scheduled for opening in 1986 in an out-building.

Room rates include a full country breakfast, with a choice of cereal, eggs, toast, muffins and such, served buffet style in a front dining room.

Dinner is served nightly in two other dining rooms (see below), one an airy sunporch with large windows capitalizing on the glimpse of Squam Lake and another with a fireplace for cool nights. Another large fireplace is in the comfortable living room, also with picture windows.

Co-owner Rick Miller, a Meredith native who returned to the area after 10 years of innkeeping in the Bahamas, said a pool and tennis court are in the works. So is a cocktail lounge in another side porch upon whose walls hang the extensive collection of auto license plates acquired by his partner, Don Leavitt.

Meanwhile, guests are invited to stroll along the path through the herb garden in which hardy varieties are grown for the kitchen. In winter, the paths through the inn's 50 acres of fields and forests are used for cross-country skiing.

Double rooms and suites, $55 to $75.

The Inn on Golden Pond, Route 3, Box 126, Holderness 03245. (603) 968-7269.

Franconia native Bonnie Webb and her Massachusetts-born husband Bill returned from three years in California in October 1984 to open this bed and breakfast inn in a 100-year-old residence with a rear section dating back 200 years.

No, the inn is not on Golden Pond (it's across the road from Little Squam, which you can't really see in summer) "and other than the fact that Jane Fonda once used the upstairs bathroom, we have no connection with the movie," the inn's lengthy fact sheet tells guests.

The Webbs have spruced up the place considerably, each of the eight guest rooms (six with private baths) handsomely appointed with twin or double beds, pretty curtains with matching cushions, hooked rugs and needlepoint handwork done by Bonnie. Each room, named for an animal (Bear's Den, Raccoon's Retreat), has its needlepointed sign with the appropriate animal thereon. Bonnie also makes the mints which are put on the pillows when the beds are turned down at night.

The spacious, comfortably furnished living room is particularly inviting with television set, stereo, fireplace, a small "cheater" organ, and numerous

96

books and magazines. The large rear window looks onto a treed lawn with garden chairs and a hillside of 55 acres for cross-country skiing. A 60-foot-long front porch is a relaxing spot in summer.

A full breakfast is served at individual tables in two attractive dining rooms. Bacon and eggs as well as another hot dish are among the daily offerings.

Doubles, $50 to $60.

The Penny Farthing Inn, Shepard Hill Road off Route 3, Holderness 03245. (603) 968-3012.

This century-old inn which had seen better days was in transition in late 1985, British-born Allan Crawford and his wife Janice having just purchased the former Normandie Farms Inn after spending nine years in Saudi Arabia.

The Crawfords were working with former chef Stephen Wells of St. Thomas to turn the well-regarded classic French restaurant, Cafe Normandie, into a place for nouvelle European cuisine. The old cafe bar was converted into a common room for inn guests, who will experience a British flavor with high tea in the afternoon.

Upstairs, the inn was undergoing extensive renovation to emerge with nine guest rooms, seven with private baths. The inn and restaurant are to be open year-round for breakfast, lunch and dinner daily.

The Crawfords relished the prospects. "This is an exciting area in that the zoning in Holderness is so strict," Allan said. "Ours is the last commercial property to be developed."

Doubles, $55.

The Inn at Mill Falls, Mill Falls Marketplace, Meredith 03253. (603) 279-7006.

This 55-room luxury hotel opened in 1985 after being erected in five months by a crew of 150 in what manager Kathy Cummings calls "a minor miracle."

With two Bostonians as partners, a 38-year-old local real estate broker, Edward "Rusty" McLear, developed the $2.5 million inn as the last phase of an ambitious shopping and restaurant complex fashioned from an old mill site at the western end of Lake Winnepesaukee, about eight miles southeast of Holderness. "We couldn't understand why a beautiful resort area like this had nothing more than a couple of cottages in which to stay," explained his wife, Linda McLear, proprietor of the Cupola bookstore in the marketplace.

A white frame structure on five levels, the inn has rooms of varying size and color schemes, decorated in contemporary French country style with matching draperies and bedspreads, plush chairs, television and spacious bathrooms, each with a basket of amenities. Samplers on the walls, framed pictures of 19th century Meredith, plants in an old sleigh and antique headboards lend a bit of history.

The inn has a small indoor swimming pool, jacuzzi and sauna, but no grounds to speak of. A bridge over the waterfall which gives the project its name connects it to the busy marketplace, in which inn guests and the public can dine at the Millworks restaurant and the Provisions delicatessen.

Doubles, $67 to $87; off-season, $45 to $60. Four luxury rooms with balconies, $105 and $110.

Dearborn Place, Route 25, Center Harbor 03226. (603) 253-6711.

An attractive white house with mustard trim on lawns sloping toward Center Harbor Bay across the road has been converted into a bed and breakfast by Peg Lamphrey, who runs a real estate agency in another part of the building.

Guests enter through the kitchen, pass through the dining room where a continental-plus (granola, yogurt) buffet breakfast is spread out each morning on a harvest table and through another room in which breakfast is eaten, and settle in an pleasant sitting room with a wood stove, small television set and some interesting antique pieces, particularly a very old Remington typewriter.

One of the five guest rooms (each with private though not necessarily adjoining bath) is downstairs. It has a kingsize bed with an old chest and hooked rug at its foot. An old school desk just outside the room serves as a table, and is topped appropriately with a bowl of polished apples. Upstairs, one room has fancy brass beds with white spreads; a brick chimney slants through the middle of the third-floor suite.

Tea and wine coolers are served in the afternoon.

Doubles, $50.

Dining Spots

The Corner House Inn, Center Sandwich. (603) 284-6219.

In five years, innkeeper Jane Kroeger and chef Don Brown have created one of the area's more popular restaurants in this delightful Victorian house in the center of town. Dinner is by candlelight in a rustic beamed dining room with blue and white tablecloths and red napkins, or in three smaller rooms off the other side of the entry. The striking handicrafts on the walls and shelves are for sale by Anne Made; the same for the art works from Surroundings gallery.

Lunches are bountiful and bargains; we saw some patrons sending half of theirs back for doggy bags. We, however, enjoyed every bite of the Downeaster ($3.95), two halves of an English muffin laden with fresh lobster salad (more than you'd ever get in a Maine lobster roll costing twice as much), sprouts and melted Swiss cheese. We also tried a refreshing cold fruit soup (peach, melon and yogurt, sparked with citrus rinds) and an interesting crepe filled with ground beef and veggies ($2.50). Lemon sole at $5.95 was the priciest entree; most people seemed sated with soup and half a sandwich, and possibly a dessert of frozen chocolate kahlua pie or pina colada sherbet.

For dinner, you might start with lobster salad in an avocado half or sesame chicken with honey dip (both $2.95). Entrees run from $8.95 for chicken cordon bleu to $13.95 for veal Oscar. One diner said the broiled lamb chops were the best she'd ever had. The limited wine list starts at $8.50 for Entre deux Mer or Portuguese Dao. "Sandwich was a dry town when we came here and they just granted us a beer and wine license," Jane Kroeger said, "so they must think we're all right."

Upstairs, she is gradually redecorating four guest rooms — one up a separate steep staircase with a private bath, the other three sharing one bath. Doubles are $40 to $50 and include a full breakfast.

Lunch, daily 11:30 to 2:30, dinner 5:30 to 9:30 in summer; shortened hours and closed Monday and Tuesday in winter.

Windowed alcove has view from small dining room at Corner House Inn.

The Common Man, Ashland Common, Ashland. (603) 968-7030.

Founded in 1971 by Alex Ray and hailed for food that is the most consistent in the area, the Common Man attracts enormous crowds — we faced a half-hour wait at 8:30 on a Wednesday evening — and has spawned many other restaurateurs, Jane Kroeger and Don Brown of the Corner House among them.

A jigsaw puzzle is at the ready on a table near the entrance; inside, old records, sheet music and Saturday Evening Post covers are for sale. Upstairs is a vast lounge with buckets and lobster traps hanging from the ceiling, a long pine counter set for Chinese checkers and chess, plush sofas in intimate groupings and an outside porch overlooking the shops of Ashland Common. The rustic, beamed main dining room, separated into sections by a divider topped with books, is crowded with tables sporting a variety of linens and mats, chairs and banquettes.

The dinner menu is plain but priced right, from $6.95 for London broil or baked stuffed sole to $10.95 for prime rib or veal Oscar. A "grate steak" serving "from one ridiculously hungry person to three very hungry people," complemented with a medley of fresh vegetables, is $19.95. The chef says he gets creative with specials, perhaps scrod with oyster sauce, duckling with kiwi fruit or bouillabaisse in winter.

Lunches are also pleasantly priced, with a raft of interesting sandwiches for $2.95 and eight more substantial entrees from $3.95 to $5.95. How about the great king crab feast, the crabmeat broiled and topped with broccoli and cheddar for $2.95? Desserts vary from hot Indian pudding to a creamy cheesecake and white chocolate mousse. The house wines are Craftsbury Creek, Californias bottled specially for the Common Man.

Lunch, Monday-Saturday 11:30 to 2:30; dinner, 5:30 to 9, Sunday 5 to 9.

Country Options, 27 N. Main St., Ashland. (603) 968-7958.

To our minds the most creative restaurant in the area, this former rooming house was renovated in 1983 by Sandy Ray, formerly of the Common Man, and partner Nancy Puglisi. They've given it a charming country look, with wreaths and baskets everywhere, and a special teddy bears' table in the dining room.

Upstairs are four freshly decorated guest rooms (all sharing two adjoining bathrooms marked for men or women), available for bed and breakfast (doubles, $30 to $40). Downstairs is Divine Desserts, a small bakery living up to its name and a dining room with a pretty enclosed porch where breakfast is served. The breakfast mat lists the menu, its items named after quilt patterns.

The gem of the operation, however, is the Friday and Saturday night dinners, five-course meals served for the astonishingly low fixed price of $15. "It's like an intimate dinner party in a private home," says Sandy Ray, who serves up to 40 people at pink-linened tables on the porch or in the interior dining room at one seating. Guests arrive at 6:30 for hors d'oeuvres and wine, tasting what Sandy suggests will go with the meal that night.

Dinner could start with fennel soup and feta cheese turnovers or leek timbales, go on to a mushroom and pine nut salad with raspberry vinaigrette or Sacramento salad, refresh the palate with a sorbet (cranberry wine, cantaloupe wine and minted pineapple are a few), present an entree like baked walnut shrimp, lamb with artichokes and lemon, roast duck with ginger and lime sauce — all garnished with such vegetables as garlic red jacket potatoes and tomato pesto tart — and end with a divine dessert of frozen lemon frost souffle, chocolate cloud roll or pecan pie. Wine and beer only are served.

Breakfast, 8 to noon daily except Monday; dinner, Friday and Saturday at 7.

The Manor, Route 3, Holderness. (603) 968-3348.
The area's most luxurious inn also contains its most sumptuous dining room, a picture of elegance from its leaded windows and tiled fireplaces to the crystal chandelier hanging from the beamed ceiling covered with rich floral wallpaper. Exotic lilies and beige napkins fanned in crystal wine glasses accent the tables dressed in white over burgundy linen. The brochure advertises romantic candlelight dining and believe us, it is so dark it's hard to read the menu — the waiter had to bring us a flashlight!

An excellent house salad of greens laced with peanuts and mandarin oranges preceded our entrees, nicely herbed lamb chops Dijonnaise and heavily sauced steak Diane. Dinner entrees range in price from $8.95 for chicken in mustard sauce to $14.95 for the steak Diane, veal with broccoli and lobster or filet and shrimp with linguini. A fine Torresella merlot for $16 accompanied; a mocha ice cream pie and Irish coffee made worthy endings.

Lunch, including fancy sandwiches, a smoked salmon plate or avocado stuffed with seafood salad ($3.95 to $6.25), is served in the main dining room or on a front terrace.

Lunch, Monday-Saturday 11:30 to 2:30; dinner 5:30 to 9 or 9:30; Sunday brunch, 11 to 2:30.

Red Hill Inn, Route 25B, Center Harbor. (603) 279-7001.
Colorful china with a pattern of morning glories, garden flowers and candles in hurricane lamps complement the pink-linened tables in the two dining rooms and airy sunporch of the Red Hill. The front dining room and the end of the porch offer a view of Squam Lake; a warming fireplace compensates for the lack of view in the inner dining room.

The dinner menu is somewhat unusual — heavy on chicken and vegetarian dishes, light on beef and devoid of veal, lamb or pork. Most of the appetizers ($2.75 to $3.95) sound interesting: escargot souffle, four-onion soup, shrimp and crab tartlet, and baked stuffed onion. The stuffed vegetable platter, ratatouille in pastry shells and fresh vegetable kabobs are specialties; other entrees ($9.25 to $14.10) include brandied chicken, broiled swordfish with orange sauce, coquilles St. Jacques and steak au poivre. A rich chocolate silk pie, amaretto cheesecake and berry pies are among the popular desserts.

Dinner nightly, 5 to 10.

Pine Shore, Route 3, Holderness. (603) 968-3003.

Seafood is the theme at the casual summer restaurant which gave Alex Ray of the Common Man his start. The menu language and prices are similar to those of the Common Man — you can dine very well for $6.95 on three scallop dishes, haddock, clams, scrod, fried oysters and fresh trout (bone not removed, the menu notes).

Imagine the Downeast Feast of chowder, lobster, clams, scallops, fish and chips, serving one to three people for $18.95. Baked lobster pie is $8.95; a minnow menu for youngsters has six offerings for $2.95. Desserts are primarily ice creams from Squam Lakeside Farm.

The older section of the Pine Shore is summer rustic; a newer, skylit greenhouse section is sprightly with butcherblock tables, cane chairs and handsome blue and white patterned tablecloths. A mannekin clad in a bathing suit with a television set as his head greets patrons at the entrance.

Dinner only, 5:30 to 9:30, May through Labor Day.

The Chef's Hat, Route 3, Holderness.

The locals gather for gossip and breakfast at this lunch counter and decorless dining room next to the Brick Village Shops. The service is fast (morning coffee poured on arrival), the portions ample and the prices from olden days.

The ham and mushroom omelet special with good homemade white toast and lackluster home fries set us up to skip lunch; the breakfast on a bun (the house version of an egg McMuffin) was a meal in itself for $2.25.

Open for breakfast and lunch.

The Millworks, Mill Falls Marketplace, Meredith. (603) 279-4116.

The outdoor patio and an upstairs greenhouse overlook the town docks and lake at this popular, multi-leveled restaurant which opened in 1984 in a central location in the Mill Falls Marketplace. There are intimate fieldstone alcoves, booths, tables with placemats or linen, an abundance of hanging greenery, exposed pipes on the ceilings, mill artifacts and local paintings on the arched brick walls.

The menu offers something for everyone as well and suffered as a result when we were there. For dinner, we skipped the special shrimp "novelle" on pasta in favor of baked stuffed shrimp and veal marsala ($10.95 and $8.95), the former adequate and the latter mediocre. Salads with poppyseed or buttermilk dill dressings came on clear glass plates; a bread board with two big Pepperidge Farms-style rolls was accompanied by pads of butter in aluminum wrap.

Lunch, daily 11:30 to 3, dinner 5 to 10.

Extra-Special

Ice Creams, Old and New. A trek to the ice-cream stand is an after-supper tradition at many a family resort area like Squam Lake. "The world's best ice creams" (according to the Pine Shore restaurant which serves them) have been dispensed for years at **Squam Lakeside Farm** on Route 3, across from Little Squam Lake. Banana oreo, black cherry, amaretto nut, rum raisin and banana strawberry are among the flavors of cones priced from $1 to $1.70, kiddie size 70 cents.

Ice cream becomes a work of art in a high-tech setting at **Nuage Ice Cream Gallery** in the Mill Falls Marketplace, Meredith. Hazelnut chocolate, amaretto, chocolate chip, rum raisin, blueberry and many more are served in cones, sundaes or what have you. "We try not to mask the flavors but to enhance them," the manager informed us. They do that very well.

Diversions

Squam Lake. The lake made famous in the movie "On Golden Pond" is so screened from public view that passersby get to see it only from a distance or up close at precious few points. But you can — and should — experience it via Pierre Havre's **Lady of the Manor,** a 28-foot covered pontoon boat with a 90-horsepower motor. Former airline pilot Pierre is a knowledgeable and talkative guide as he conducts two-hour tours of the lake twice a day from late May through October.

He tells the history, relates vignettes, stops to watch resting loons and visits the places made famous in the movie. "That's the Thayer cottage," he says from a distant vantage point before discreetly passing the house loaned for the summer's filming and so remote that many locals have yet to find it. Purgatory Cove with Norman's famous rock was as foreboding the stormy day we visited as it was during the climactic scene in the film. "On a sunny day," he relates, "you'll see no more than a dozen boats on the second biggest lake in New Hampshire."

Chocorua Island, also called Church Island, is a favorite stop. The site of the first boys' camp in America, it now has an inspiring outdoor chapel in which summer worship services, complete with crank organ, have been conducted continuously by area churches since 1903. At 10 a.m. Sunday, the dock area is said to resemble the approach of the Spanish armada as upwards of 250 churchgoers arrive in a variety of boats.

Boat tours leave from The Manor at 10 a.m. and 4 p.m. Monday-Friday and 11 and 4 on Sunday. Adults $8, children 12 and under $3.50.

Center Sandwich, an historic district, still looks much as it did two generations ago when Mary Hill Coolidge and the Sandwich Historical Society organized a display of hooked and braided rugs that led to the opening of a crafts shop. Known as **Sandwich Industries,** the shop became the first home for the League of New Hampshire Craftsmen. It is open daily from Memorial Day through mid-October with myriad craft and gift items. Free crafts demonstrations are given several days a week in summer, and an outdoor art exhibit is staged during Sandwich Old Home Week in mid-August.

"On Golden Pond" sights are seen from Lady of the Manor boat tour.

The **Sandwich Fair,** one of New England's outstanding country fairs scheduled in mid-October, marked its 75th anniversary in 1985. Summer residents may go home after Labor Day, but they usually return for the Sandwich Fair.

The main roads and byways of this picturesque village lead to any number of interesting crafts and antiques shops. **Surroundings,** a gallery in the center of town, is known for fine art. We were intrigued by the handweaving done by Roberta and Robert Ayotte, on display and for sale at **Ayotte's Designery,** their fascinating shop and studio in the former high school, open Thursday-Saturday 10 to 5. We also admired the wonderful pillows, especially those with cat portraits, done by Anne Perkins of **Anne Made** at **Hill Country Antiques.** Her wall hangings, quilts and pillows decorate the walls of the nearby Corner House Inn and are snapped up by purchasers as fast as she puts them up.

Shopping. Local items — many with a loon motif — are available in the boutiques of **Brick Village Square,** billed as a mini-mall in the center of Holderness with 10 small, open shops and the office of the Squam Lakes Association, which has maps and books as well as handouts on Squam Lake history and water research.

Other than the art and crafts shops of Center Sandwich, the best place for shopping is the new **Mill Falls Marketplace** in Meredith, with 20 enterprises from **Irish Tweeds** to the expansive **Leighton Tracy Gallery. Provisions Ltd.** is a large gourmet food shop par excellence, open daily from 7 a.m. to 9 p.m. for breakfast, lunch and dinner. Absent are the souvenir shops indigenous to much of the Lakes Region. At Linda McLear's **Cupola,** one customer asked if there were any T-shirts with "Meredith" printed on the front. No, was the reply — you have to go to Weirs Beach to find that kind of thing. Lamented the customer: "But then it won't say 'Meredith.'" Similarly, the loon items in Holderness signify, but do not say, Squam Lakes.

103

Cross-country skiing is great on trails throughout Jackson.

Jackson, N.H.
A Rugged Mountain World

Drive through the old red covered bridge into Jackson and you enter another world.

It's a world isolated from the hubbub of the lower Mount Washington Valley and enveloped by mountains of the Presidential Range, tiptoeing toward the East's highest peak (6,288 feet). It's a highland valley of pristine air, scenic beauty, and peace and quiet. It's a European-style mountain village of 600 residents and often a greater number of visitors.

Jackson is one of the nation's earliest year-round destination resorts, dating to pre-Civil War days (and not all that changed since its heyday around the turn of the century). It's a village of spirited tradition and pride, from the book of recipes used in Jackson's early lodges to the Jackson Resort Association's claim that "nowhere else in the world will you find a more concentrated area of diverse recreational opportunities."

Today, skiing is the big deal in Jackson and its sister village of Glen. There are two downhill ski areas, Wildcat and Black Mountain; a world-class cross-country center in the Jackson Ski Touring Foundation, and fabled Tuckerman Ravine, where the diehards climb to the headwall of Mount Washington for one last run in June.

The two worlds of skiing — alpine and nordic — co-exist in friendly tension. Explained Betty Whitney, who was staffing the village information center the last time we stopped: "Thom wanted to advertise 'Ski Tour Jackson' and I wanted to stress alpine, so we ended up simply 'Ski Jackson.'" Betty Whitney and her husband came to Jackson in 1936 to establish Black Mountain and Whitneys Inn; Thom Perkins is the energetic executive director of the prestigious Jackson Ski Touring Foundation.

There are modern-day amenities, two golf courses among them. But this is a rugged area, better epitomized by the Appalachian Mountain Club hiking camp at Pinkham Notch than the Mount Washington Auto Road (its bumper stickers boasting "This Car Climbed Mount Washington"), better experienced from a secluded mountain inn than from one of the chock-a-block motels down the valley in North Conway.

Inn Spots

Dana Place Inn, Pinkham Notch, Route 16, Jackson 03846. (603) 383-6822.

Harris and Mary Lou Levine never expected to own an inn, but they went to lunch with a broker and somehow got talked into buying Dana Place Inn in 1985. They've been so busy upgrading the inn that, said Harris on our fall visit six months later, "we haven't even read a newspaper since April." Anyway, he added, Dana Place is a spot for escape and total relaxation.

The out-of-the-way location of this Colonial farmhouse which carries the name of the original owners, who became innkeepers in the 1890s, is special. It's up in the mountains some 2,000 feet above North Conway, just before you reach Pinkham Notch in the midst of the White Mountain National Forest, and right beside the Ellis River.

The Ellis River cross-country ski trail, one of the most skied trails in the country, ends at the inn, and skiers often come inside for lunch (featuring hearty soups and chili) in the lounge. In summer, inn guests cool off in a scenic swimming hole in the rushing river, and in all seasons, picture taking is in order, with Mount Washington rising behind the birch trees.

Besides the lounge with its grand piano, there are two dining rooms (see below) and, for gathering, the Lodge Room, a rustic high-ceilinged expanse with fireplace, television (only one Maine channel comes in because Dana Place is too remote for cable) and games.

A small patio outside the Lodge Room faces the lawn leading to the river, and a hammock strung between the trees is a great place for relaxing. A swimming pool, tennis courts, volleyball and health spa with indoor hot tub are other amenities. Crab apple trees on the property burst into color in the spring and the inn gardens outside the dining rooms are spotlit at night.

The sixteen guest rooms, nine with private bath, vary in size and decor from rustic to contemporary. All had been or were being redone with pretty floral wallpaper and white spreads when we stayed. Some can be turned into suites for families; groups and families also can be accommodated in condominiums which the Levines manage nearby. Our large room with sitting area had a view over the gardens toward Mount Washington, a most comfortable kingsize platform bed and a large modern bathroom with tub and shower.

The serenity of the Dana Place Inn, the Levines say, makes you calm down even against your will. Perhaps the night we joined some anniversary celebrants and other guests to close the bar while singing around the piano (played with pizzazz by a young woman guest from Los Angeles, who was in show biz) was a little out of keeping. At any rate, we heard about it from two British couples who were trying to sleep on the third floor!

Doubles, $55 to $85, including full breakfast; $80 to $110, MAP.

Christmas Farm Inn, Route 16B, Box 176, Jackson 03846. (603) 383-4313.

A basket of bright red buttons proclaiming "We Make Memories" is beside an arrangement of garden flowers inside the entrance to this historic, ever-expanding property where Christmas is reflected, if not celebrated, all year long. The buttons are part of Sydna and Bill Zeliff's promotion effort for their lively inn (he was in marketing with duPont and handles this venture accordingly). The flowers are from the pretty grounds, which won the valley's annual garden competition in 1985.

Few inns have such a fragmented history: part jail, part church, part inn, part farmhouse, part sugarhouse. The property was given by a Philadelphian as a Christmas present in the 1940s to his daughter, who tried and failed at farming on the rocky hillside before the place was revived as an inn. Hence the name, and whence all nicely detailed on the back of the dinner menu.

"We'd never stayed in an inn before we bought this one in 1976," says Bill Zeliff, and they're obviously making up for lost time. Located off by itself above Jackson Village, the entire place has a real inn feeling. The Zeliffs aim to bring people together for an inn-family experience, putting on everything from lobster bakes in summer to cross-country trail lunches in winter. They publish the North Pole Ledger, a fancy newsletter for guests, and keep a scrapbook for every year in the bar "so that the guest experience becomes part of the memory," says Bill. Patrons reciprocate; many of the wreaths, samplers and such on the walls are gifts from guests.

Two living rooms at the front of the 200-year-old main inn contain a library, a piano, a chess game, and Santa and Mrs. Claus beside the fireplace. Bingo, games and movies on the VCR are nightly features. The rear barn has a huge game room with ping-pong, bumper pool, large-screen TV, an enormous fireplace and a sauna. Across the road are a swimming pool with cabana, a putting green, shuffleboard and volleyball court. Everywhere you look are paths, brick walls and gardens with flowers identified by labels.

Oh yes, about the guest rooms, of which there are 35, most with private baths. Twelve in the main inn have Christmasy names like Three Wise Men or those of Santa's reindeer, and are traditionally furnished in what Sydna terms early-attic Colonial style. The red and green 1777 saltbox out back has nine deluxe rooms, and most luxurious of all are the four new suites in the barn, each with a living area with sofa and velvet chair, television, high sloped ceilings, large baths and loft bedrooms. Three cottages, each with two bedrooms and private baths, large sundecks, TV and fireplace, are first to be rented in the winter. Other accommodations are in the Log Cabin, the Sugar House and a bunk room for four.

Breakfast and dinner are served daily (see Dining Spots).

Doubles, $96 to $136, MAP; many package plans.

The Inn at Thorn Hill, Thorn Hill Road, Jackson 03846. (603) 383-4242.

Quite possibly Jackson's best view of the Presidential Range is from the front porch of this neat yellow inn, built as a private residence in 1895 and converted into an inn in 1955. All the mountains are labeled for identification purposes on the 45-year-old painting at the end.

An even broader view, wide enough to encompass even the weather

Lush flowers greet summer guests of Christmas Farm Inn.

station atop Mount Washington, opens through the picture windows in the long, lovely living room. The near end, with yellow and white area rugs, has a handsome dining table; the far end, in yellows and blues, has comfortable sofas around a fireplace. Between the living room and the entry hall is a more casual parlor with television, a basket of yarns and bobbins, stuffed animals collected from across the world on an armoire, and a teddybear in a chair.

Some of the valley's best meals are served in an attractive dining rooms at the rear (see below). Before and after, Bob Guindon, new innkeeper with his wife Pattie, keeps patrons entertained with tales from his 11 years as a baseball player with the Boston Red Sox organization while he pours drinks in a pub called "The Snug."

The Guindons renovated 19 of the 22 rooms in the inn, a carriage house and three cottages in the first few months after they took over in 1985.

The best rooms are the five with private baths on the second floor. They are richly furnished with period antiques, colorful floral wallpapers and oriental rugs; some have sinks in the rooms, as well as large bathrooms. Rooms on the third floor share baths and may be rented as suites.

The carriage house at the side, which skiers would consider more like a chalet, has seven large carpeted bedrooms with modern baths off a pine-paneled living room with plump sofas and a large stuffed bear by the raised fireplace. Also available are three cottages of varying sizes sleeping up to seven. A pleasant swimming pool is screened by a hedge.

Doubles, $110 to $120, MAP.

Whitney's Village Inn, Route 16B, Jackson 03846. (603) 383-6886.

Why this is now called the Village Inn we (and the previous owners) don't know. It's not in the village, but rather up in the mountains at the foot of Black Mountain, with ski trails in the rear and a somewhat Bavarian feeling to a rambling complex of inn, outbuilding, barn and cottages totaling 36 guest rooms.

Although primarily a winter place (with the family-oriented Black Mountain ski area out back, a lighted skating rink, sledding and tobogganing), summer fun is not overlooked. The skating rink turns out to be a natural spring-fed pond for swimming and lazing tucked away in the trees across the street. The inn has a tennis court and volleyball, croquet and other lawn games. Once you're here, you're away from everything else but nature. No wonder it's popular for an old-fashioned country vacation.

Fifteen guest rooms in the main inn have private baths and four on the third floor share. Rooms are carpeted, nicely furnished with antiques, and have good-looking quilts. Some at the rear have two upholstered chairs by a table with a floor lamp for reading and a magnificent view onto the ski slopes. Some have desks and large bureaus. Two two-bedroom cottages have fireplaces. Eight family suites with bedroom and living room are in an out-building, and Brookside cottage has two deluxe and two standard units.

The inn has a front parlor with jigsaw puzzles in various stages of completion, a formal parlor with piano, the Greenery lounge with a flagstone floor and sliding glass doors opening onto a patio, and downstairs, a recreation room with ping-pong table, games and television. In winter, there's the rustic Shovel Handle Pub in the barn for lunch and apres-ski.

Breakfast and dinner are served in a country dining room, which has stenciled wallpaper above pine paneling, beige linen cloths, rose napkins and green carpeting. Dinner entrees run from $10.95 for chicken champignon or broiled scrod with a hint of paprika to $14.95 for charbroiled Delmonico steak. More unusual items are smoked mackerel and mushroom fritters for appetizers, veal bourguignon and roast duckling au poivre for main courses.

Doubles, $98 to $128, MAP.

The Wentworth Resort Hotel, Route 16A, Jackson Village 03846. (603) 383-9700.

The Wentworth was the "grand hotel" of Jackson at the turn of the century when Jackson had 24 lodging establishments. Abandoned for a time, it was grandly restored in 1983 into a luxury resort with modern conveniences but retaining much of the style and charm from its golden era.

The 18-hole golf course behind the hotel is part of the Jackson Ski Touring Center layout in the winter. Other facilities include clay tennis courts, swimming pool, cocktail lounge and elegant restaurant (see below).

In the turreted, yellow and green Victorian structure plus annexes and out-buildings (some with great views of the golf course) are a total of 55 guest rooms.

In the main inn, plushly carpeted halls lead to 20 spacious guest rooms on the second and third floors. All are beautifully restored in different shapes and sizes, with French Provincial furnishings, private baths (most have refinished, old-fashioned Victorian claw tubs with showers), an upholstered chair under a reading lamp, and color television. Beige patterned draperies and bedspreads are coordinated with restful cream walls and rust carpeting.

The large, formal lobby is richly furnished in French Provincial as well. Sofas and arm chairs are scattered across the green carpeting, and a wood stove is at the ready in the brick fireplace.

Doubles, $80 to $110, EP.

Wildcat Inn and Tavern, Route 16A, Box T, Jackson Village 03846. (603) 383-4245.

If the Wentworth is the deluxe renovation, the Wildcat exemplifies Jackson's timeless past. Looking like something out of yesteryear, it exudes a sense of history in fifteen upstairs guest rooms, nine with private baths, as well as in a two-bedroom cottage. Rooms vary but are furnished with antiques and hooked rugs. We liked the corner room in peach and green with quilted bedspread. One homey twin-bedded room has a sitting room as well.

With two fireplaces and a large-screen TV, the huge Tavern is a popular gathering place for apres-skiers and others. Folksingers perform on weekends.

A full breakfast featuring pastries baked on the premises is served guests. Innkeepers Pam and Marty Sweeney are proud of their birchemusli, a European dish of chilled oatmeal mixed with fruit and nuts and topped with fresh whipped cream, and sometimes spike their hot chocolate with schnappes.

Doubles, $48 to $54.

The Village House, Route 16A, Jackson Village 03846. (603) 383-6666.

A new greenhouse-style porch in which breakfast is served and a swimming pool out front are attractions at this cheery yellow and white bed-and-breakfast establishment on seven peaceful acres at the edge of Jackson Village. A small gazebo atop a hill and a wicker-filled front porch provide fine views of the mountains. "It's very quiet — so quiet that even my watch stopped," quipped Ron DeCamp, innkeeper with his wife Jackie.

A cozy parlor has rustic furniture and a wood stove. In winter, the DeCamps serve popcorn to guests who gather after skiing at the BYOB bar in the greenhouse. All around are baskets collected by Jackie, who always seems to find a place for one more. Muffins and fruit breads are served for continental breakfast.

The second and third floors contain ten guest rooms, eight with private baths. Some have hooked rugs and homemade afghans. One room has wicker chairs and loveseat; another a double and a single bed. Decor is mixed Victorian.

Doubles, $39 to $54.

Dining Spots

L'Auberge Madeleine, Route 302, Glen. (603) 383-6772.

After leaving the Modern Gourmet in Newton, Mass., for four years back in her native France, famed chef-instructor-writer Madeleine Kamman settled in Glen in 1984 to be near her family and opened a small personal restaurant and cooking school that's the essence of France and the essence of Madeleine Kamman.

The place is a reflection of her tastes and efforts (she was washing the walls as her students prepped when we returned to chat the morning after we enjoyed an exeptional dinner). From January to May the cooking is her own; the rest of the year the students take over, under her tutelage.

In two small dining rooms, the lower half of the walls are pine paneled and the upper half a dusty rose in one, a pretty blue in the other (the larger room is for non-smokers). They're outfitted with Hitchcock chairs (the stenciling picks up the pastel pinks and blues of the decor), bordered cloths and overcloths made in Provence on tables that are rather close to each other (and there's no music to muffle conversations). French crystal and such becoming accents as beautiful wreaths with birds she made herself plus an interesting collection of plates on the walls (Sevres, Quimper, a handpainted wedding plate and a set of 1790 china from Vienna) add to the French country feel.

But, as you can imagine, the food is the focus. In season (July-October), prix-fixe dinners ($18.50 to $19.50) are served weeknights and more expensive a la carte dinners on weekends (as they are Saturday nights most of the rest of the year). We found the former extraordinary, from soup to dessert, and Madeleine said of the masterpiece prepared by student Holly Beermink "I rated that perfect — I couldn't have done better myself." What more could student or patron want?

Madeleine Kamman at her restaurant.

Our dinner began with an elegant vegetable puree in a clear glass bowl, containing fall vegetables from turnips to red peppers to parsnips, and garnished with baby limas and corn. A plain green salad in the French style preceded the entrees: a gutsy peasant chicken dish, the house offering of the night, and a tenderloin steak, the only alternative. With our entrees came a julienne of carrots and snap peas and a gratin of potatoes garnished with parsley and oregano. No salt and pepper shakers were on the table, and we found that such perfectly seasoned food had no need for them. Desserts were a baked apple (it sounds plain, but was divine) and an intensely rich chocolate ganache. With a $16 bottle of St. Emilion, this was a feast to remember.

"We do women's food — la cuisine de femme," asserts Madeleine. "It's not chef's food and there's a big difference." Much of it is simple provincial fare, but she says her secret is in the execution — "not creative ideas that fall flat."

On the weekend menu, you might find appetizers such as cream of spinach soup with smoked mussels, tartlet of mushroom hash topped with melting raclette, terrine of rabbit and hazelnuts with mixed vegetable salad, or grilled Belon oysters in pouilly fuisse butter. Entrees could be boneless medallion of salmon with sea urchin cream, or braised quails with grapes and chartreuse sauce. Frozen sambucca sabayon, two-lemon tart with blueberry puree, grapefruit ice cream with red berry puree, and dark chocolate genoise soaked with Mozart liqueur and filled with butter ganache are among the changing desserts.

When we visited, Madeleine was talking of retiring after the 1986 season; at age 55, she said, 18-hour days of classes and food preparation were proving too much. But Madeleine has a mind of her own (and a way of changing it). Whatever, she had plans to stay in Glen, perhaps open a B&B and serve dinner on Saturday nights.

Dinner, Monday-Saturday 6 to 9, July-October; Saturday only in winter. No credit cards.

The Inn at Thorn Hill, Thorn Hill Road, Jackson. (603) 383-4242.

The exceptionally pretty dining room here is long and narrow with pressed oak high-backed chairs at well-spaced tables set with white linen, red fringed napkins, white china, candles in hurricane lamps and baskets of flowers from the gardens. Dark green floral wallpaper, white wainscoting, stained glass and a multitude of baskets complete the setting.

Head chef Greg Bartlett and an assistant from Ireland are known for traditional New England cuisine at reasonable prices. Entrees like lobster pie (with puff pastry for the crust), an inn standby for 12 years; chicken Thorn Hill baked with honey and bacon; veal dishes, and nightly specials like beef Wellington or vegetable stir-fry are priced from $8.75 to $14.95, but half are under $10.

Appetizers are straightforward as well: marinated mushrooms, liver pate, shrimp cocktail, scallops wrapped in bacon. The dessert tray changes nightly. The house dessert is a chocolate pate covered with strawberry cream sauce, a dish which innkeepers Bob and Pattie Guindon first sampled in France; the "outrageous" brownie a la mode is served in a huge goblet, $4.50 for two.

When we visited, the Guindons were planning to expand the wine list with additional California vintages.

Dinner nightly, 6 to 9.

Dana Place Inn, Route 16, Jackson. (603) 383-6822.

The dining rooms here are country elegant with an accent of Danish contemporary. There's a cozy center room with Scandinavian teak chairs; the skylit and airy lower level has large windows for viewing the spotlit gardens, crab apple trees and bird feeders outside. Pink linen, burgundy napkins and pink candles provide a romantic atmosphere.

Swiss chef William Rudd, who formerly was at the Bernerhof restaurant, adds a Swiss touch to the changing menu with specialties like wiener schnitzel and Swiss custard pie. Other entrees ($12.95 to $16.95) include veal marsala, chicken Veronique, pork tenderloin calvados, duckling a l'orange, braised fillet of salmon pommery, rack of lamb persille and New York sirloin.

Dinner begins with a complimentary relish tray of cottage cheese, cranberry-orange conserve and a good chick pea concoction. Fresh rolls and an excellent small salad follow. We liked the wiener schnitzel and the frog's legs provencale (imported from India, because the chef doesn't like domestic), served with red Bliss potatoes and zucchini, yellow squash and tomatoes sauteed in bacon fat. A special chocolate cake with a delicious almond-flavored icing and chocolate mousse pie with a walnut crust were winners among desserts.

Harris Levine takes great pride in his temperature-controlled wine cellar

Old wagon is filled with autumn bounty at entrance to Dana Place Inn.

and the wine list, with labels posted and varieties explained. Prices are reasonable.

Dinner nightly, 6 to 9.

Wildcat Inn and Tavern, Route 16A, Jackson Village. (603) 383-4245.

Food is what the Wildcat Inn is known for. The old front porch had to be converted into a dining room to handle the overflow from the original two dining rooms, as ancient, cozy and homey as can be.

Sitting beneath a portrait of Abraham Lincoln, we enjoyed an autumn lunch in a small, dark inner dining room with bare floors, mismatched chairs and green linen. An exceptional cream of vegetable soup was chock full of fresh vegetables; that and half a Reuben sandwich made a hearty meal for $4.25. We also liked the delicate spinach and onion quiche, served with a garden salad dressed with creamy dill.

Dinner entrees run from $8.50 for lasagna to $15.95 for filet of beef Oscar. Wildcat chicken is served like cordon bleu but wrapped in puff pastry and topped with mustard sauce; bulgogi is a dish of thinly sliced beef with Wildcat sauce over a bed of rice. You also can get shrimp and vegetable tempura, beef Wellington for two and "the extravaganza" — shrimp, lobster and scallops sauteed with vegetables and rice.

The wine list is limited; the desserts slathered with whipped cream are memorable. Chocolate silk pie, mocha ice cream pie, blueberry cheesecake, frozen lemon pie and the Mount Washington brownie topped with vanilla ice cream, hot fudge sauce, whipped cream and creme de menthe are tempters.

In summer, you can dine out back at white, umbrella-covered tables in the attractive new tavern gardens, which won the garden club award for 1984. In winter, the historic tavern is a popular watering hole for skiers.

Breakfast daily, 7:30 to 9:30; lunch, 11:30 to 3; dinner, 6 to 9 or 10.

Christmas Farm Inn, Route 16B, Jackson. (603) 383-4313.

With everything else going for it, the Christmas Farm Inn also tries to be "an MAP experience," says innkeeper Sydna Zeliff. "We've tried to make the food the focal point."

The large candlelit country dining room is Christmasy, of course, what with the red, white and green color scheme, plates with red bows, wreaths over the fireplace and the hutch filled with Christmas plates.

Appetizers and desserts are standard (shrimp cocktail, creme de menthe sundae), but entrees are a bit more adventurous. Medallions of pork McIntosh, lamb shish kabob, wiener schnitzel, chicken Kiev, filet of sole Marguery and soft-shell crabs provencale are among them. Prices range from $11.25 to $13.75 and include salad, vegetable, potato and homemade breads. One night's specials were a cheddar cheese and chive soup, London broil and seafood newburg. The Christmas Farm sundae combines vanilla ice cream and maple syrup.

Dinner nightly, 6 to 9.

The Plum Room, Wentworth Resort Hotel, Jackson Village. (603) 383-9700.

A huge calico wreath in plum shades sets the stage for dining in the Plum Room, aptly named and pretty as a picture with dark rose carpeting, upholstered French Provincial chairs with plum backs and seats, and tables set with pink napkins on white cloths over plum undercloths reaching to the floor. The flowers are apt to be pink carnations, the wine glasses have pink stems and the white china is bordered in plum.

New American cuisine is offered by chef John Palughi, who trained at the Culinary Institute of America. Among his creations on the ambitious dinner menu are braccioli, two sauteed rolls of prime sirloin stuffed with proscuitto, and tenderloin tips in Bock beer sauce. The large choice also includes such entrees ($15 to $19) as burgundy rack of lamb, veal Tuscany, Wentworth garden scampi, pork calvados, and Danish haddock or trout served with a sauce of stilton, cream and lemon. Entrees come with marinated mushrooms, choice of potato or wild rice, and homemade bread; vegetables and salads are extra.

Seafood pate, smoked fish plate, scallops seviche and brie en croute are among appetizers, $4 to $7.50. Favorite desserts include almond amaretto cake, chocolate truffle cake, linzer or hazelnut torte, Italian lemon cake and the chef's own orange or peach sorbet.

Dinner, nightly 6 to 10.

Thompson House Eatery (T.H.E.), Route 16A at 16, Jackson Village. (603) 383-9341.

An old red farmhouse dating from the early 1800s holds a rustic restaurant renowned for salads and sandwiches, a soda fountain, and the adjacent **Soft Touch Shop** featuring quilts and appealing sweaters, especially some for children with animal buttons.

In the decade since he opened, chef-owner Larry Thompson has created so many unusual dishes that, hearsay has it, he had no room for hamburgers or french fries. Instead, sandwiches have flair: turkey with asparagus spears, red onions, melted Swiss and Russian dressing; ham with sliced apples and sharp cheddar; knockwurst marinated in beer and grilled with tomatoes, bacon, cheese and mustard. Salads are creations: marinated artichoke hearts and mushrooms atop a bed of greens, garnished with salami, cheese, eggs, tomatoes and more; scallops on a bed of greens with tomatoes and vegetables; half an orange filled with turkey salad. At both lunch and dinner, such items are $4 to $5.

Dinner entrees ($8.25 to $11.50) include "Baked Popeye," a notable spinach casserole with fresh mushrooms, bacon and cheese, with an option of scallops. Other artful combinations are chicken and sausage parmigiana, filet of sole crowned with crabmeat and artichoke hearts, seafood Francesci, veal cacciatore and several stir-fries. Beer and wine are available.

Patrons eat in several small, rustic rooms and alcoves at tables covered with pastel floral cloths, or outside on a canopied rear deck. It's the kind of down-home place that tourists love and — wouldn't you know? — it was so jammed from a tour bus that we couldn't get in for lunch.

Open daily from 11:30 to 10, Memorial Day-October.

The Bernerhof, Route 302, Glen. (603) 383-4414.

A turreted Victorian inn with sloping greenhouse addition is home for Swiss cuisine in an old world setting, nine upstairs guest rooms with shared and private baths, plus the noted cooking school, A Taste of the Mountains. It is here that Steven Raichlen, the Boston food and restaurant writer, teaches five-day and weekend courses in spring and fall, assisted by chef-owner Ted Wroblewski.

Meals are served in three dining rooms amidst pine paneling, beamed ceilings, crisp white linens, a piano and a Swiss stove. The greenhouse addition goes off the Zumstein Room cocktail lounge with oak-paneled bar.

The house specialty is fresh Delft blue provimi veal, deboned by the chef and used in wiener schnitzel, emince de veau au vin blanc, piccata a la Suisse and schnitzel cordon bleu. Other entrees ($10.95 to $14.95) are a veal steak persillade and veal ragout, fish of the day and scallops provencale. Delices de gruyere and shrimp remoulade are favored among appetizers ($4 to $5.95). A delectable array of desserts (most $2.75 to $3.25) include a concoction of vanilla ice cream and kirsch in a meringue topped with bing cherries and whipped cream, profiteroles aux chocolat, chocolate silk pie made with Myers dark rum, and chocolate fondue for two. (Cheese and beef fondues are available in the bar and dining room as well.)

At lunch, try the Swiss ploughman's lunch, with wedges of emmenthal and gruyere, dark bread, pickled onions and cabbage salad, or a Grenoble sandwich, cured ham on dark bread with an herbed yogurt dressing. Caesar salad and bratwurst with onions are other choices, in the $3.95 to $7.95 range.

Lunch, noon to 3, dinner nightly 6 to 9:30, Sunday brunch 10:30 to 2:30.

Red Parka Pub, Route 302, Glen. (603) 383-4344.

This is the perfect place for apres-ski, from the "wild and crazy bar" with a wall of license plates from across the country (the more outrageous the better) to the "Skiboose," a 1914 flanger car that pushed snow off the railroad tracks and now is a cozy dining area. Somehow the rest of this vast place remains dark and intimate, done up in red and blue colors, red candles and wood ice-cream parlor chairs.

The menu, which comes inside the Red Parka Pub Table Times, features hearty steaks, barbecued ribs, teriyakis and combinations thereof ($7.95 to $13.95), a salad bar with 30 items and breads, a children's menu and basic desserts.

Dinner nightly, 5 to 10.

Diversions

Downhill Skiing. Wildcat, looming across Pinkham Notch from Mount Washington, is a big mountain with plenty of challenge, a 2,100-foot vertical drop from its 4,100-foot summit, top-to-bottom snowmaking, four chairlifts and a gondola (adult lift tickets, $18 weekends, $15 weekdays). **Black Mountain** is half its height and far smaller in scope, but its sunny southerly exposure and low-key, self-contained nature make it particularly good for families (adult tickets, $14 and $10). Nearby are **Attitash** in Bartlett and **Mount Cranmore** in North Conway. **Tuckerman Ravine** on Mount Washington is the place where the hardy ski when the snows elsewhere have long since melted, if they're up to the climb (a 1,500-foot vertical rise for a half-mile run down).

Extra-Special

Cross-Country Skiing. Jackson was rated by Esquire magazine as one of the four best places in the world for ski touring. That's due in large part to the efforts of the non-profit Jackson Ski Touring Foundation, founded in 1972 and now with 91 miles of well groomed and marked trails starting in the village of Jackson and heading across public and private lands into the White Mountain National Forest. They interlace the village and link restaurants and inns, as well as connecting with 40 miles of Appalachian Mountain Club trails in Pinkham Notch. It's possible for cross-country skiers to take the gondola to the summit of Wildcat and tour downhill via a 12-mile trail to the village of Jackson 3,200 feet below.

Hikes and Drives. The Jackson Resort Association publishes a handy guide to nine walks and hikes, from the "Village Mile" stroll to Thorn Mountain trails. A good overview is offered by the **Five-Mile Circuit Drive** up Route 16B into the mountains east of Jackson, a loop worth driving both directions for different perspectives. Look for spectacular glimpses of Mount Washington, and stop for a picnic, a swim or a stroll through the cascades called Jackson Falls, part of the Wildcat River just above the village. The Appalachian Mountain Club has a guide for tougher hikes in the White Mountains.

Shopping. It's no surprise that the biggest store is the **Jack Frost Shop,** a distinctive landmark that's a serious ski shop as well as a fine apparel store with a few gift items plus a Nordic rental shop and ski school. Other than a couple of small galleries and antique shops, "downtown" Jackson consists of a post office, town hall, the Jackson Community Church and the tiny red 1901 Jackson Library, open Tuesdays and Thursdays from 11 to 4 and 7 to 9. For a more rigorous shopping foray, head down valley to the boutiques of North Conway and the ever-expanding Conway factory outlet centers.

Sherburne House (circa 1695) is one of oldest structures at Strawbery Banke.

Portsmouth, N.H.
A Lively Past and Present

Settled in 1623, the Portsmouth area ranks as the third oldest in the country after Jamestown and Plymouth. In many ways it looks it, the early Colonial houses hugging the narrow streets and the busy riverfront conceding little to modernity.

This is no Jamestown or Plymouth, nor is it Newport, a similarly sized and situated community with which it occasionally is compared. The city has no large hotels, its downtown blessedly few chain stores or trendy boutiques, its residents little sense of elitism. What it does have is a patina of living and working history, a pride in its past and present, a noticeable joie de vivre.

The sense of history is everywhere, from the famed restoration called Strawbery Banke to the ancient structures dating back to the 17th century tucked here and there across town. Named for the profusion of wild berries found on the shores by the English settlers, Strawbery Banke after 25 years of restoration efforts is a living museum of 37 historic buildings at the edge of downtown.

Portsmouth's pride in past and present evidences itself in the six museum homes of the Historic Portsmouth Trail, the creative reuse of old buildings around Market Square and on the Hill, and the pending renovation by the General Electric and Marriott interests of the magnificent old Wentworth-by-the-Sea resort hotel out in Newcastle.

You can sense Portsmouth's joie de vivre in its flourishing restaurants (good new ones seem to pop up every month), the number and scope of which are far beyond the resources of most cities of 26,000. You can see it in its lively Theatre by the Sea and its newly opened Music Hall. You can feel it in its Prescott Park Arts Festival, the Ceres Street Crafts Fair, the Seacoast Jazz Festival.

Happily, Portsmouth retains its historic sense of scale, an enclave of antiquity along the Piscataqua River, four miles inland from the Atlantic. The Portsmouth Navy Yard is across the river in Kittery, Me. The Pease Air Force Base is west toward Dover. The shopping centers and fast-food strips are out in Newington. The beach action is down in Rye and Hampton. All but a few tourists stay at motels at the Portsmouth Circle.

While travelers pass by on the New Hampshire Turnpike, Air Force jets stream overhead, and tugboats and ocean vessels ply the river to and from the sea, Portsmouth goes its merry, historic way.

Inn Spots

Martin Hill Inn, 404 Islington St., Portsmouth 03801. (603) 436-2287.

The first bed-and-breakfast inn in Portsmouth (1978), the Martin Hill was acquired in 1983 by Jane and Paul Harnden, who with another couple were visiting their favorite town from Nashua, where they lived. "We had hardly heard of bed and breakfast," says Jane, "but during breakfast at the inn the owners said they would like to sell in about three years and, I thought, this is me."

It turned out that medical problems forced the owners to sell that summer, and now the Harndens are the friendly innkeepers who dispense gobs of information about the many restaurants in town, historic attractions and whatnot, as well as cooking delicious breakfasts that usually include a marinated thin steak or pork chop.

The handsome yellow house, built in 1820, is within a long walk of downtown. Although it is on a commercial street, it's quiet because of air-conditioning and one can escape in summer to a nicely landscaped back yard where flower beds thrive and where tea is served at 4 p.m.

The three bedrooms in the inn (two more, done in a more casual country style, are in the next-door annex and are available in summer) are elegantly decorated. The downstairs room, called the Library, is in shades of rose and has a twin and a double pineapple poster bed. Upstairs, the Master Bedroom, mostly blue, has a queensize canopy bed and oriental rugs on the wide board floors. The smaller Guest Room has a double bed. All rooms have modern baths, loveseats and a comfortable chair, leather-topped writing desks, armoires, and nice touches like potpourri in china teacups and a decanter of cream sherry with two crystal sherry glasses. Fluffy comforters are folded on each bed.

Breakfast is served on a long, gleaming mahogany table in the antiques-filled dining room. Orange juice might be followed by Jane's scrumptious baked apple, the core filled with brown sugar. For French toast, the Harndens use Italian sourdough bread. Our scrambled eggs were served with a pork chop and sliced cranberry bread, and the coffee pot was bottomless. It's a great time to compare notes on the restaurants of the night before and to plan the day, with the help of Paul, who, he says, can plot you out a trip up to Quebec and back. Clearly the Harndens love their role as innkeepers and go out of their way to be helpful.

Doubles, $50 to $60.

Martin Hill Inn is decked out for Christmas.

The Inn at Christian Shore, 335 Maplewood Ave., Portsmouth 03801. (603) 431-6770.

An abundance of antiques, an inviting dining room with fireplace, and quite lavishly decorated air-conditioned guest rooms with television are attractions in this 1800 Federal house, located in the historic Christian Shore area.

Across from the Jackson House, Portsmouth's oldest, the structure was renovated and redecorated in 1979 by three antiques dealers, Charles Litchfield, Louis Sochia and Tom Towey. "It was a neighborhood eyesore," Tom says, but you'd never know it today.

In the main entry hall is a desk with baskets of candies and nuts, a grandfather clock and an etched glass light. The richly furnished sitting room crammed with antiques is used as a sixth guest room in summer.

Upstairs are five guest rooms, several with canopy or four-poster beds and one a tiny single. Three rooms have private baths (including one with peach towels resting on a leather couch), another with a double and single bed has a half bath, and two share. All have handsome furnishings like crocheted afghans.

A long harvest table dominates the beamed breakfast room, with its large brick fireplace and an organ in the corner. Three smaller dining tables with upholstered wing chairs are around the sides. The innkeepers' collection of rabbits covers every shelf in the room, some in a 1900 lacquered Japanese cabinet, some on the floor — some ceramic, some cement.

A full breakfast including ham or perhaps steak is cooked by any of the three innkeepers, with the other two waiting on tables.

Doubles, $45 to $50; single $30.

The Inn at Strawberry Banke, 314 Court St., Portsmouth 03801. (603) 436-7242.

You can't stay much closer to Strawbery Banke than here, so you may wonder why young innkeepers Mark and Kerrianne Constant add the extra "r" to the attraction upon which they capitalize. Perhaps it reflects the updating they have done to the 1800 ship captain's house situated almost up against the street, as so many in Portsmouth are.

In 1985, the couple added a cheery skylit sunroom and breakfast room at the rear of the main floor. In early 1986, they added another guest room on the side, and planned for 1987 a larger addition in the rear to raise the total number of guest rooms to eight.

A curving staircase leads to two of the nicest front-corner rooms. The spacious Blue Room with blue stenciling on white walls has a double and single bed, and the antique white desk, nightstand and dresser with which Kerrianne grew up. Indian shutters inside the windows are a feature of the adjacent Yellow Room. Both share a bathroom made colorful by matching floral window and shower curtains and curtains enclosing the wash basin. They also share a pleasant upstairs common room with the Brown Room, its beamed ceiling contrasting with a modern sink and vanity along one side and a half bath off the other.

The third-floor attic has a mini-suite with sitting room, twin beds and private bath.

The new sunroom looks out onto the rear yard and the trellised rose garden of the historic Governor Langdon House just behind. Kerrianne sets out a continental breakfast buffet with homemade breads and muffins on the old cookstove at the side.

Doubles, $45.

The Inn at Strawberry Banke.

Sheafe Street Inn, 3 Sheafe St., Portsmouth 03801. (603) 436-9104.

An in-town location also very much in the midst of things draws people to this 1815 center-staircase Federal rowhouse, formerly the Petrie-Clemons Inn. "My guests like to be right in town and leave their cars," reports innkeeper Kevin Finnegan, who's on call a few minutes away from his home across the river in Kittery. "They feel it's like living in old Portsmouth."

Kevin comes in mornings to put out a health-food buffet breakfast — including granola, yogurt, fruit, nuts and such, as well as baked goods from the excellent Ceres Street Bakery next door — in the small, fireplaced common room with tables, service bar, refrigerator and stove, which are at guests' disposal. "They can eat whenever they want, come and go as they please — we don't even have an official checkout time," Kevin says.

The most prized room is across the tiny hall on the main floor, its Indian-shuttered windows opening right onto Sheath and Penhallow streets. It has a private bath ingeniously tucked into a limited space, four-poster bed, old settee, oriental rug over the pine floor, two chandeliers, a candle in a brass holder and ivy on the fireplace mantel — no wonder you think you're back in old Portsmouth, although today's street noise might bother some.

119

Two rooms and a shared bath are on each of the second and third floors. They vary from one with a single and double bed to another with two singles joined together "because we couldn't get a double bed up the stairs," acknowledges Kevin. Stenciling, brick walls, white curtains trimmed with chenille balls, painted headboards, area rug, and a window seat with cushions are among the decorative touches.

Doubles, $50.

Inn at Cafe Petronella, 115 State St., Portsmouth 03801. (603) 431-2209.

The art deco rooms above the Cafe Petronella restaurant are not to everyone's taste and may be noisy (you can hear the lively and arty restaurant below and, in summer, the motorcyclists who congregate at a bar next door). It appeals to those who enjoy artistic flair and communal living (one of the two shared baths has what Dutch innkeeper Marjen Redfield-Frank calls a co-ed shower with shower heads at different levels).

The Flamingo Room in which friends once stayed has a working fireplace, an old chenille spread on the bed and pictures of flamingos all around. The Chicago Limelight Room, described as "soft and green, Bogart's dream," has a sink in the corner and furniture of the 1930s, which Marjen found in an Ogunquit antiques shop. On the third floor, Caribbean blue and white walls form the loft of the Bahama Room, which has a bright red bureau and shares a tiny w/c with the Wallis Sands Room "so you don't have to go downstairs in the middle of the night," our guide informed.

An enormous painting by Marjen's brother accents the airy second-floor common room, as art deco as the rest. A continental breakfast is served in the cafe downstairs.

For 1986, Marjen planned to add two or three suites in a turquoise house behind the cafe along Sheath Street.

Doubles, $45 and up.

Dining Spots

Strawbery Court, 20 Atkinson St., Portsmouth. (603) 431-7722.

In this city of restaurants, most discriminating diners consider Strawbery Court the leader in consistently fine dining.

It certainly is the most elegant and subdued: Eleven well-spaced tables in the large dining room of a brick 1815 Federal house that is home to talented young chef Douglas Johnson and his dentist partner, Dr. Frank Manchester. The platinum-colored walls and carpet seem to turn a restful dark gray at night. A few spotlit oil paintings and a large bouquet of gladioli on the service table provide accents. A perfect long-stemmed pink rose is in a vase on each white-linened table. A tall white candle is lit on each; the rest of the lighting comes from candles on a sideboard, a crystal chandelier and discreet ceiling track lights. Even the restrooms are lit by candles, as is the small upstairs lounge with pretty rust velvet sofa, two printed chairs and warming fireplace.

Service is solicitous and formal, the menu being explained knowledgeably if a bit by rote, and the silver and china place settings being changed with each serving.

Dinner can be ordered prix-fixe for $28 or a la carte. Among appetizers ($4.75 for duck liver mousse to $5.95 for Norwegian smoked salmon), we

Dining room at Strawbery Court is elegant and subdued.

sampled the latter, thinly sliced pieces garnished with capers, onion and caviar. Good, crunchy and hot French wholewheat bread slices were served from an enormous basket; the ice water was flavored by lemon slices. The colorful house salad ($3.75) was composed like a painting: Boston lettuce and radicchio topped with a fan of mushrooms, shredded radish, beets, carrots and snow peas.

Entrees run from $14.50 for medallions of pork Dijon to $17.95 for tournedos sauteed with Madeira, shallots, roquefort cheese, walnuts and veal glace. We liked the sweetbreads in a dark Milan sauce and the thick and rosy medallions of lamb, served with pimento (red) and pesto (green) sauces. Between them was a ribbon of whipped potatoes; on the side, a bundle of crisp white asparagus tied with red pepper.

The desserts ($3.95) are triumphs. The popular gateau au fromage is a delicate cheesecake laced with armagnac and grand marnier on a layer of genoise. A real wow of a dessert was a pear poached in red wine, cored and stuffed with frangelico and hazelnut ice cream, the top dipped in a caramel glaze, the bottom in a fresh red raspberry glaze, and served on a bed of semi-sweet chocolate sauce.

A specially offered 1985 beaujolais nouvelle at $12 was excellent and also the best bargain on the expensive wine list.

Doug Johnson, a native Rhode Islander and Culinary Institute of America grad, cooks in the classical French style with a nouvelle presentation. He does it all himself, assisted occasionally by some of the staff of five who accompanied him to Strawbery Court in 1983 from his acclaimed restaurant, L'Armagnac, in Columbus, Ohio.

Dinner Tuesday-Sunday, 6 to 9.

The Tavern at Strawbery Banke, 38 Marcy St., Portsmouth. (603) 431-2816.

The white Georgian structure dating to 1709 was moved to its site next to Strawbery Banke in 1937, was operated briefly as the Oracle House

121

restaurant, and was reopened as a fine restaurant with assertive cooking in 1984 by Ian MacKenzie. The tavern has three fireplaced dining rooms, an intimate upstairs lounge and an outdoor courtyard that might make you feel you are in Europe. It's screened by a high fence, shaded by Norway maples and enlivened by a trickling fountain.

For lunch in summer, we'd choose the courtyard, or possibly the cozy, eat-around bar upstairs with a view onto Prescott Park. Our winter dinner was in the small right front room, rather spare in the Colonial style with Windsor chairs at four tables, white linens, a fire blazing in the hearth and a tad too brightly lit for our tastes. Unforgettable was the view out the window across the river to the Portsmouth Navy Yard, its lights shimmering on the water.

Nor will we forget the powerful and inventive fare offered on the limited dinner menu. The spinach and bell pepper soup was a stunner, as was the smoked seafood plate ($4.95) presented fanned out in nouvelle style with mussels, scallops and a strong coriander vinaigrette.

Changing entrees range from $11 for ragout of beef tenderloin with roasted chestnuts, pearl onions and burgundy to $19 for lobster baked with cognac cream and brie cheese. The smoky taste of the appetizer was repeated in the night's pasta with smoked salmon and goat's cheese ($13.95) as well as the breast of chicken stuffed with mussels and shrimp ($14.50). Herb Dijon and creamy dill dressings were among the choices for the salads, and our Robert Mondavi fume blanc ($15) was nicely served in a marble bucket. A slice from a terrine of Bavarian cream and genoise, studded with strawberries and kiwi fruit that looked like shiny jewels, was appropriate for the holiday season.

Lunches are creative as well, from chicken salad with apples, walnuts and pesto ($3.95) to sauteed Swiss chard on an English muffin with poached eggs and chive hollandaise ($4.95).

Lunch, 11:30 to 2; dinner, 5:30 to 10; Sunday brunch, 11 to 3; closed Mondays.

Seventy Two Restaurant, 45 Pearl St., Portsmouth. (603) 436-5666.

The name comes from young chef James J. Miceli's original success, 72 Islington, a small and highly rated restaurant he opened in 1982 on Islington Street. In November 1984, he moved around the corner into what was formerly a Baptist church, a smashing site to be converted into a restaurant.

From the front entrance you ascend stairways on either side to what was once the airy sanctuary. It's an incredible space, with high rusty red ceiling, tall arched windows and well-spaced tables for 75. At the far end over the kitchen is a balcony which must have been the choir loft. It's now a cocktail lounge with ornate metal banister, tables, piano and a sofa seating a family of stuffed bears from Jim Miceli's collection in his bachelor pad downstairs.

Tiny lamps are on each table, crisply set with white linen, pink napkins folded in porcelain rings and white china. The setting could not be more regal, if a bit intimidating, especially when the dining room is not filled.

Locals fault the service while applauding the dinner fare. "French food with a New England flair" is how self-taught chef Miceli describes it. The ambitious menu lists octopus, Maryland soft-shell crabs and chilled lobster remoulade among 13 appetizers ($5.25 to $7.95). Soups might be French brie with sherry or fresh oyster stew.

122

Lion statues greet diners outside the Library restaurant.

Entrees ($11.50 to $18.95) include lobster-stuffed haddock, swordfish pecan, veal Oscar, Long Island duckling, beef Wellington and rack of lamb. They're served with fresh breads, seasonal vegetables and a baked stuffed potato.

The dessert cart might contain hazelnut torte, poppyseed and frangelica cheesecake, a midnight layer cake and a linzer torte. The rather pricey wine list comes in a little wine-colored book.

Dinner nightly, 6 to 10; Sunday brunch, noon to 3.

The Library at the Rockingham House, 401 State St., Portsmouth. (603) 431-5202.

The old Rockingham Hotel has been converted to apartments, but Michael Hallinan restored part of the ground floor into an extravagant restaurant in 1975. Its ornate carved wood ceiling, mahogany paneling, fireplaces, huge mirrors and bright blue napkins set the stage for books, books and more books on shelves in three rooms. Some bookshelves enclose booths for intimate dining.

The appealing menu is reasonably priced and the specials interesting (sweet and sour chicken, veal amandine, tournedos Oscar and cream of eggplant soup the last time we were there). For lunch, we tried a fennel and gruyere quiche ($4.25) that was as tasty as it was generous, accompanied by a super-good spinach salad with a mustard dressing and homemade croutons. The mussels mariniere ($5.25) arrived in a large glass bowl abrim with garlicky broth in which to dip chunks of the homemade rolls. The strawberry cheesecake for dessert was at least three inches high.

For dinner, Thailandese beef salad and broiled pork with peanut curry sauce are among provocative appetizers ($2.75 to $5.25). Entrees run the gamut from the aforementioned mussels mariniere ($7.50) to carpetbagger steak ($14.95); fried squid, vegetable Alfredo and duckling with raspberry sauce are a few.

Lunch, 11 to 3; dinner, 5 to 11; Sunday brunch.

123

The Toucan, 174 Fleet St., Portsmouth. (603) 431-5443.

How could you not like a restaurant where the focal point is a toucan named Piwi in her own glassed-in cage, and the restrooms are labeled "He Can" and "She Can?" The food is fine, and the atmosphere upbeat, at this new cafe brought to you by the folks who operate the somewhat more sedate and established Library at the Rockingham.

Up a flight of stairs beside a waterfall flowing over a stone wall, you can see, on high, an enormous mechanical toucan on a perch, head bobbing from side to side. Toucan is divided by curved glass brick walls into a lounge with green marble bar, above which is written, in neon, "grab a beakful," and a bistro-like restaurant with green and white tile floor, tables covered with shelf paper (crayons are provided for doodling), bentwood chairs, colored theatrical lights on a track and framed posters on the walls. Gracefully curved windows provide glimpses of downtown Portsmouth. Cactus plants in clay pots are here and there; toucans in stained glass and other guises are colorful accessories.

Served all day, Toucan's menu is basically Mexican, with a smattering of American, South American and, after 5 and for lunch specials, Cajun dishes like blackened snapper. Crisp homemade tortilla chips and a snappy salsa are served as soon as you sit down. The tortilla soup ($2.50) is a meal in itself, loaded with cheese and spicy enough to bring out the Kleenex. Calamari salad ($4.95) is served with artichoke hearts and pimentos in a terrific marinade.

The oyster shot is one of the most requested appetizers; it's a blue-point oyster in a shot glass with a bit of champagne, spicy sauce and chopped coriander. A real hangover cure!

Mexican pizza, nachos various ways, big red chili burger, taco salad, barbecued ribs or chicken are other treats. With the barbecued dishes you get whirley bird fries, cole slaw and jalapeno corn bread. Roasted duckling with orange chili chutney, Cajun blackened sirloin, jumbo shrimp gumbo and grilled mustard shrimp are some "down by the bayou" entrees. For dessert, try an apple burrito or deep fried ice cream.

Sangria is $10 a liter; the wines are inexpensive (but beer is better with many of these dishes) and you can get Cajun steak and eggs, French toast bayou or huevos rancheros at Aunt Chilada's brunch on Sunday.

Open daily, 11:30 to 11.

L'Auberge, 96 Bridge St., Portsmouth. (603) 436-2377.

A one-room, very personal restaurant in the French provincial style is run rather casually by Francois Rolland and his wife Kathy — he in the kitchen and she out front, and neither crosses the line. It's of the old school and open at the chef's whim; "when I make enough money I close the doors and take off to France," he says.

A sign inside the canopied entrance to the out-of-the-way house warns "this is not a diner," intending to convey that the meal will take some time. The decor is unpretentious: hurricane candles and brown linens, pretty beveled windows and stained glass.

All the French classics are offered, from $9 for five chicken dishes to $16 for beef Wellington or chateaubriand. Dinners include crusty French bread, potato or rice pilaf, vegetable and salad. The French wines are a bargain, and the crepes Suzette and cherries jubilee outstanding.

Lunch is locally popular; how could it not be with entrees priced from $3.95 for fettuccine Alfredo to $6.50 for scallops sauteed with mushrooms and shallots? Luncheon specials are offered, and coffee, tea or milk are 50 cents.

Lunch, 11:30 to 1:30; dinner, 5:30 to 10; closed Sunday and Monday, plus June and part of July.

The Grill, 37 Bow St., Portsmouth. (603) 431-6700.

One of Portsmouth's best waterfront views is from the upstairs dining room of the Grill or, in summer, outside from its lower True Blue Cafe and Deck. The view isn't everything, of course, since this location has gone through several incarnations as restaurants which haven't made it. But new owners who run a popular restaurant near Harper's Ferry, W. Va., have changed everything since they took over in 1985.

The two upstairs dining rooms divided by a peach wall and mirrors are quite stunning; the gray carpet and green linens are perfect foils for the huge pink and red amaryllis blossoms in red vases on each table. The dinner menu is billed as "fanciful American," featuring mesquite-grilled lamb and seafood ($13 to $18).

The "fanciful" extends from some of the appetizers (smoked eel with dilled cream cheese and roasted red peppers, grilled squid and Cuban black bean soup) through entrees (prime rib of veal baked with ground allspice or cod cheeks and monkfish tails sauteed in wine).

The downstairs cafe, its posts hung with lantern lights, is more casual. Appetizers, pastas, sandwiches and salads are offered day and night in the $3 to $7 range ($8 for steamed lobster). The same fare is available on the deck beside the water.

Lunch daily from 11:30, dinner from 5 to 10; Sunday brunch, 10:30 to 3.

The Blue Strawbery, 29 Ceres St., Portsmouth. (603) 431-6420.

Portsmouth's restaurant renaissance was inspired by chef James Haller and the Blue Strawbery, which opened in a narrow 1797 restored ship's chandlery across from the waterfront in 1970. It's known far and wide, better regarded nationally than locally, especially since a spate of letters in the daily newspaper in 1985 revealed a consensus that the restaurant was resting on its laurels.

His priorities reported to have changed, the author of "The Blue Strawbery Cookbook" now spends much time traveling and on television, expounding on how to cook brilliantly without recipes. When he's at the restaurant, his inspired dinners are considered to be better than ever. When he's not, which was said to be increasingly frequently, many have been disappointed to the point of outrage.

Prix-fixe dinners of six courses ($28.50 to $30) are served at two seatings nightly. The choice of entree includes one each from land, sea or air.

125

Waiters serve the meals family style from huge platters, sometimes offering seconds.

Dinner by confirmed reservation only, 6 and 9 p.m., Sunday 3 and 6 p.m.; closed on Monday and Tuesday from mid-October to Memorial Day.

The Metro, 20 High St., Portsmouth. (603) 436-0521.

Very popular locally is this art nouveau bar and cafe, pleasantly decked out with brass rails, stained glass, old gas lights, mirrors and dark wood, leather banquettes, bentwood chairs and nifty Vanity Fair posters.

The Metro's award-winning clam chowder (first prize in the New England competition at Newport) is a popular starter. Salads, sandwiches, fettuccine Alfredo, baked spanakopita and several entrees are offered at lunch ($4.50 to $7.95). Dinner is a mix between regional and continental (Long Island duckling, chicken Athenian), $10.95 to $14.95. Desserts, attractively displayed on a fancy old baker's rack, include baklava, walnut pie and caramel custard.

Lunch daily, 11:30 to 3; dinner, 5:30 to 9:30 or 10; brunch Saturday and Sunday.

Anthony's Al Dente, 59 Penhallow St., Portsmouth. (603) 436-2527.

Also popular locally, usually jammed and considered rather expensive is this institution in the Custom House Cellar, dark and grotto-like with stone and brick walls and slate floors, accented with paintings and oriental scatter rugs.

The six-page menu combines both northern and southern Italian specialties. After the usual antipasti, soups and salads come 12 pastas, made on the premises. Listed as "first main courses," they make a meal in themselves (at prices from $8.50 to $14.50, they should). Ten second main courses of veal, chicken and scampi ($10.75 to $14.50) are supplemented with daily Italian specialties featuring beef, lamb or game.

Dinner nightly, 6 to 10, Sunday 5 to 9.

The Dolphin Striker and Spring Hill Tavern, 15 Bow St., Portsmouth. (603) 431-5222.

Fresh seafood and a few entrees with a creative flair are the hallmarks of the Dolphin Striker, a plain but historic restaurant upstairs with cozy stone-walled Spring Hill Tavern beneath.

Natives rave about the seafood, from the simple broiled haddock served with lemon butter ($9.25) to seafood provencale ($14.75). Lobster is an accent to the sole Andrea and Hannah Mariner's pie, filled with seafood in a rich sherry and sour cream sauce ($12.85). Noisettes of veal Madeira, rack of lamb Dijon and steaks also are available. French silk and key lime pies, fruit sorbets, black magic chocolate cake and a "strawberry bazaar" are among the scrumptious desserts ($2.50 to $4.25).

Lunch, 11:30 to 2; dinner, 5:30 to 9:30.

The Oar House, 55 Ceres St., Portsmouth. (603) 436-4025.

Located in an old grain warehouse dating from the early 1800s, this casual restaurant has quadrupled in size since its opening in 1975. But the ancient aura remains: rough brick and stone walls hung with nautical photos, dark beams, bare floors, a jolly bar and two dining rooms — one upstairs,

Historic structures are visitor attractions at Strawbery Banke.

with a glimpse of the waterfront. One table in the other dining room is enclosed in a brass bedstead.

Tiny oil candles flickered as we lunched in a booth in the tavern after sipping a very good bloody mary made with clamato juice. Thick clam chowder studded with clams, potatoes and corn was fine; the accompanying turkey and avocado sandwich a bit dry. Shrimp marinara crepe ($4.95) and a green salad loaded with carrot strips, bean sprouts, sunflower seeds and a creamy dill dressing made a great lunch combination.

Dinner entrees tend toward the traditional seafood, chicken, veal and beef dishes, priced in the $11 to $15 range.

Lunch and dinner daily, Sunday brunch.

Diversions

Portsmouth offers much for anyone with an interest in history. The Greater Porstmouth Chamber of Commerce publishes an excellent "Walking Tour of Downtown Portsmouth's Waterfront," which also can be driven (although directions get confusing because of one-way streets). The 2.3-mile tour takes in most of the city's attractions, including some we had passed for years unknowingly — such is the charm of an area crammed with discoveries at every turn.

Strawbery Banke. Billed as "an American original," this walk-through museum is the careful restoration of one of the nation's oldest neighborhoods, its 37 structures dating from 1695 to 1945 and depicting four centuries of cultural and architectural change. Some have simply been preserved; some are used by working artisans (independent of the museum, they are earning their living rather than merely re-enacting history); others are used for educational exhibits including archaeology, architectural styles and construction techniques and, on the outside, historic gardens. The collection of local arts and furnitrue is shown in five historic houses. Significantly, these are not all homes of the rich or famous, but rather of ordinary people. As the museum's 25th anniversary program noted, "This is the real story of history — the dreams and aspirations, the disappointments and frustrations of common people." That is the glory of Strawbery Banke, and of much of Portsmouth. Open daily 10 to 5, May-October; adults $5.50.

The Portsmouth Trail. Six of Portsmouth's finest house museums are

127

open individually and linked by a walking tour and common ticket ($6). Considered the one not to miss is the 1763 **Moffatt-Ladd House,** a replica of an English manor house located just above Ceres Street restaurants and shops. The yellow 1758 **John Paul Jones House** and the imposing **Governor John Langdon House** (1784) are others.

Prescott Park. This waterfront park with gardens and amphitheater offers a good vantage point for watching river activity, as well as an arts festival and almost daily noon-hour goings-on. You can visit the hot dog vendor and join the locals on lunchtime picnics. Or you can drive or walk across a short bridge from Marcy Street to Pierce Island and then to Four Tree Island where picnic tables are in the midst of river activity.

Entertainment. The Theatre by the Sea, launched in 1964, now offers year-round entertainment in the 1894 red-brick Portsmouth Brewery building at 125 Bow St., part of a complex including the Warehouse restaurant and Theatre Inn Bed and Breakfast (its handful of motel-type rooms, used by actors in winter, are offered to the public in summer). While "Godspell" was playing at the theater, the **Portsmouth Music Hall** opened with fanfare at 28 Chestnut St. at Christmas 1985 with a two-week run of "Peter Pan." Portsmouth Magazine, a tabloid newsweekly, noted the combination of music hall and restaurants makes Portsmouth "New Hampshire's liveliest city" and promptly launched publication of a Portsmouth Nightlife Guide.

Shopping. Most of the traditional tourist shopping attractions have passed Portsmouth by, heading for the upscale outlet strip along Route 1 north of Kittery or the shopping malls of Newington. In town, the most interesting shops are around Market Square. **Salamandra Glass** has colorful, exquisite hanging glass pieces and vases with fluted edges among items made in the adjacent studio. **Macro Polo, Wholly Macro and Tai-Pan Alley Gifts** offer women's clothing, gourmet items and such. Nearby are **Country Tweed, Bowl and Board, Paper Patch, Pappagallo,** and **Bow Street Candle and Mug. Kingsbury House** at 93 State St. is the gift shop run by the Guild of Strawbery Banke. Also on the periphery of the Banke are the **Red Sled Christmas Shop** and the **Marcy Street Doll Co.** Strawbery Banke has working crafts shops offering the wares of potters, a cabinetmaker, a weaver, and dories made in the boat shed.

Extra-Special

Newcastle. Drive or bicycle out Newcastle Avenue (Route 1B) through the quaint islands of Newcastle, the original settlement in 1623, dotted with prosperous historic (and new) homes. The meandering roads and treed residential properties, many with water views, mix contemporary-style houses with those of days gone by. You can view Fort Constitution, visit the new seacoast park at Great Island Common (parking $2), and take a gander at the soon to be restored Wentworth-by-the-Sea, a majestic resort hotel if ever there was one.

The ocean is just beyond guest rooms at Stage Neck Inn.

The Yorks
Great Gateway to Maine

The visitor quickly agrees with what the Chamber of Commerce directory proudly proclaims: "The Yorks are a perfect introduction to Maine. They have everything for which the Great State is famous: rocky coast, sandy beaches, a lighthouse, a mountain, rivers,...lobsters, folks who really do say 'ayuh.'"

The focal point of the Yorks is, of course, the water — specifically, the harbor where the river confronts the sea. From fashionable York Harbor, whose waters are as protected as its seaside homes, it's barely a mile inland along the York River to historic York Village, the oldest surviving English settlement in Maine. From the harbor, it's also barely a mile along the shore to York Beach. Abruptly, the rocky coast yields to sand; the trailer parks symbolize the transition from tree-shaded affluence to honky-tonk strand. Beyond are Nubble Light, one of America's most photographed lighthouses, and Cape Neddick Harbor, a quieter and quainter fishing site. Sand gives way again to rocks as Bald Head Cliff rises off the forested Shore Road near the Ogunquit town line.

Yes, the Yorks provide a good introduction to Maine, from the Cape Neddick fishermen to the amusement areas at crowded York Beach.

But much of the appeal of the Yorks is elsewhere. It's in York Village, where a national historic district embraces both private structures and eight house museums. It's in York Harbor, a verdant enclave of Colonial homesteads and gracious estates whose occupants in 1892 formed the York Harbor Reading Room men's club, an offshoot of which was the York Harbor Village Corporation. It established the first zoning laws in Maine and prevented the hordes and development of York Beach from spilling into York Harbor.

129

It is here where the Yorks' inns are concentrated, allowing visitors to partake of a private place in which past melds into present.

Inn Spots

Stage Neck Inn, Off Route 1A, Box 97, York Harbor 03911. (207) 363-3850.

Once an island and now a promontory where the York River becomes a harbor, Stage Neck was the site of the Marshall House, the first of the area's resort hotels. It was razed and rebuilt in 1973 as the Stage Neck Inn, a low-profile contemporary resort whose understated luxury fits the setting.

A disproportionate number of Cadillacs is in the parking lot, giving a hint of the clientele for whom Stage Neck is designed. There are tennis courts, a swimming pool and private beach, golf privileges, posh public rooms with water views, and a gorgeous dining room in which jackets are required for dinner.

There also are water views from the private patios or balconies of 86 guest rooms on three floors, the sprawling building having been designed into the landscape and opening on three sides to ocean, river and beach. Guest rooms are comfortably furnished in a restful deep rose and moss green, with twins or kingsize beds, two comfortable chairs and a table, color TV and phone, rates varying with the view. The most choice are corner rooms with wrap-around porches and views in two directions.

Meals in the elegant, chandeliered dining room with floor-to-ceiling water views from windows on three sides are what natives consider special-occasion deals. Fancy wallpaper, blue velvet chairs with round backs, blue and white draperies, and pewter service plates atop blue and white linens add to the setting.

The large dinner menu embraces American and continental fare. Appetizers range from $4.50 for mussels vinaigrette to $6.75 for lobster cocktail; the lobster bisque for $5.25 is a house specialty. The 23 entrees ($11.25 to $17.75) run the gamut from boiled lobster to tournedos Rossini. The innkeeper's dinner is half a baked stuffed lobster and a broiled sirloin ($15.95).

Sandwiches, salads and entrees like seafood omelet and beef tips bourguignonne ($6.50 to $8.50) are offered at lunch in the airy, dark blue and white Tap Room, also with water views. Light lunches also are available at the Pool Club.

Breakfast, 7:30 to 10; lunch, noon to 2; dinner, 6 to 9 or 10.

Doubles, $90 to $125. Closed December-April.

Dockside Guest Quarters, Harris Island, Box 205, York 03909. (207) 363-2868.

Just across the river from Stage Neck on an island unto itself is the Dockside, which 30 years ago began taking in boaters in the handsome late 19th cenury white homestead. Owners David and Harriette Lusty enjoyed innkeeping so much they added the Crow's Nest with an apartment and two studios on the water, then built the Quarterdeck cottages, and finally added the contemporary Lookout on the hill. They retain the name "guest quarters" (which is something of a misnomer), such is the tradition of this place.

The lovely grounds, very homelike, lead to water's edge and are spotted with lawn chairs, flower gardens and picket fences.

The day's tides are posted on the blackboard in the Maine House, where the dining room and parlor are furnished with antiques, marine paintings and ship models, and the rambling wrap-around porch opens to sea views. The house has five guest rooms, ranging from a twin room without private bath to a studio sleeping two to four. The front corner room is the choice of many.

The three multi-unit cottage buildings have twins or double bedrooms, studios, an efficiency and apartment suites for two to four. Each has use of a porch or deck with view out the harbor entrance to the ocean. All told, there are 18 units.

A continental breakfast buffet featuring just-baked muffins is served in the dining room for $1.75. Lunch and dinner are available next door at the Dockside Dining Room (see below).

Doubles, $51 to $55.50; studios, $53 to $59.50; apartment suites, $86; doubles with shared bath, $35. Two-night minimum in season. Closed mid-October to Memorial Day.

York Harbor Inn, Route 1A, Box 573, York Harbor 03911. (207) 363-5119.

A history dating back to 1637 and a family's labor of love. That's the story of this busy turn-of-the-century inn restored and reopened in 1981 by twin brothers Joe and George Dominguez, their younger brother Garry and Joe's wife Jean.

Listed in the National Register of Historic Places and built around a 1637 post-and-beam sail loft which was moved to the site and now is used as a central room, the inn once served as headquarters for the York Harbor Reading Club, which continues to this day. The Dominguez brothers, all graduates of Colgate University, spent a year and a half restoring the inn, and are still adding to it (in 1985 they opened the adjacent 1785 Yorkshire House, with nine more rooms and private baths).

This is an old-fashioned, full-service inn with a character you sense immediately when you enter the main Cabin Lounge, its pitched ceiling (the former sail loft) now covered with tiny white Christmas bulbs lit all year. The dark English-style Cellar Pub with a solid cherry bar and furniture clustered around the corner fireplace has weekend entertainment, and the dining rooms serve three meals a day (see below).

All 12 guest rooms in the rambling main inn share baths but plans were to convert them to private. They are nicely furnished with touches like white wicker headboards and rocking chairs, pink puffy quilts, and perhaps a writing desk. One room has a four-poster bed, white frilly curtains, oriental rug and towels stashed in an antique crib. A decanter of sherry is put out in the upstairs hallway each evening.

In the newly opened Yorkshire House, a large front room has an oak bed, a working fireplace and a case full of books. From most rooms you can hear the ocean rolling up against the inn's semi-private beach across the street beneath the Marginal Way.

Guests are served a continental breakfast of fresh fruit, juice, and blueberry or bran muffins.

Doubles, $75 with private bath, $60 to $70 shared.

Edwards' Harborside Inn has own wharf where harbor meets ocean.

Edwards' Harborside Inn, Stage Neck Road, Box 631, York Harbor
03911. (207) 363-3037.

An inn for five years with a grand location at the entrance to Stage Neck,
"where harbor and ocean meet," this three-story turn-of-the-century private
residence was renovated in 1985 by new innkeeper Jay Edwards. A Portsmouth auto dealer and third-generation innkeeper, he says he jumped at
the chance of acquiring what he thinks is "the prettiest place in the world."

The property faces water on three sides, has its own long wharf (from
which Jay likes to take guests in his boat for whale-watching or moonlight
cruises) and a small beach beyond the lawn.

Each of the 10 rooms has one or two double beds, television, air-
conditioning and view of river or harbor — or both. Friends who stayed
in the second-floor York Suite ($120) with water views on three sides felt
as if they were on a yacht. The suite is indeed a beauty: a sofa against one
picture window, two comfy velvet upholstered rockers, two double beds,
green carpet, colorful floral wallpaper and an enormous blue bathroom with
what Jay says is "the only potted bidet on the East Coast" (a plant sprouts
from inside).

Other rooms are different sizes and shapes, individually decorated, and
four have private baths.

In the off-season, the Bay View queensize bedroom becomes a welcoming
parlor. It's richly furnished with a plush white sofa, chairs and red patterned
rugs, and sherry is available for guests on the sideboard. A small lobby area
has books and games. Coffee and Danish pastries are served for breakfast in
the sun porch.

Doubles, $55 to $85.

Cliff House, Bald Head Cliff, Shore Road, Box 2274, Ogunquit 03907.
(207) 646-5124.

One of the nation's grand old resorts, operating nearly continuously for
114 years, is the venerable but up-to-date Cliff House. Located on the

Ogunquit-York line, it seems more allied in feeling and tradition with York than with its Ogunquit address and orientation.

Spectacularly situated on 75 forested acres of oceanside headland atop Bald Head Cliff, the Cliff House has been operated by four generations of the Weare family since 1872. Once catering to the Cabots and Lodges of Boston, the Havemeyers of New York and the Biddles of Philadelphia, the area's first hotel gradually added annexes (the latter with the first private baths in the area). In 1960, it built the area's first swimming pool and in 1963, the first motel to be incorporated into a resort setting. The top two floors of the inn were razed, motel wings and the Cliffscape conference facility were added, and now the sign at the entrance reads more accurately, "Cliff House and Motel."

The mystique and tradition of the Cliff House remain. Regulars still come for a week (or weeks) at a time, enjoying modern resort amenities and three meals a day. The accommodations are in motel-type units (except for an old-fashioned guest house with three efficiencies), and you can get rooms without meals.

Each of the 105 motel rooms has seaview balcony, color television, phones, two beds and chairs grouped around a table. The trolley parked in front of the main inn transports guests back and forth to Ogunquit and the beach. Victorian furniture decorates the lobby and adjacent library.

The spacious dining room, its windows overlooking the ocean, has tables set primarily for four with white linen, pale blue napkins, hurricane lamps and bentwood chairs. Beyond is a modern lounge and a great outdoor patio sporting orange deck chairs above the ocean. A small dining room with fireplace is inviting in the off-season.

The continental dinner menu is more interesting than many, including Cajun shrimp, seafood rotini, filet of sole with a lime hollandaise sauce, chicken in champagne-pineapple sauce, beef tips glazed in a zesty Dijon-caper sauce and lobster sauteed in sherry. Entree prices range from $8.95 for chicken jardiniere to $17.95 for lobster in cognac cream sauce en croute. Baked oysters Remick ($4.95) is an appealing appetizer.

Tuna, shrimp and lobster salads and sandwiches are featured at lunch, priced from $4.25 to $7.95.

Breakfast, 8 to 10:30; lunch in lounge or on patio noon to 3 (July and August only); dinner 5:30 to 9:30; Sunday breakfast buffet, 8 to noon.

Doubles, $84 to $90, EP; three-day minimum in season. Closed December-March.

Lighthouse Inn, Nubble Road, Box 795, York Beach 03910. (207) 363-6072.

Recently built on a hilltop with a commanding view the length of Long Sands Beach, this would more accurately be called a motel, and so it was named until 1985. But the hospitality of Ann and John Flentje from Luxembourg, the lawns and private balconies, the picnic area in the back yard and the continental breakfast with muffins baked by Ann qualify it as more than a motel.

John Flentje, a general contractor, did much of the construction himself. He opened in 1982 with eight units, then added four luxury suites and twelve more units in 1984. Rooms are in three buildings on different levels, those on the highest with a view of Mount Agamenticus and those on the lowest with a view of the gardens. Wine barrels full of flowers are all around.

All rooms have modern baths, TV and air-conditioning. Luxury suites have one or two bedrooms, a sofabed and refrigerator.

Ann Flentje is up at 5:30 in the morning to bake apple or cinnamon muffins and grind the beans for coffee (the complimentary breakfast is served in a corner of the office). Then she tends to her flowers, including 30 rose bushes beside their cottage.

Doubles, $75 to $95; suites $95 to $105.

Dining Spots

Cape Neddick Inn, Route 1 at Route 1A, Cape Neddick. (207) 363-2899.
This interesting combination of innovative restaurant and Walt Kuhn art gallery burned to the ground in May 1985. Undaunted, owners Robbie Wells, Pamela Wallis and Glenn Gobeille had the place rebuilt to the original plans, with a 20 percent expansion in size, and celebrated a grand reopening at Thanksgiving.

That's fortunate, for this is one of the more artistic settings and one of the more creative menus for dining along the southern Maine coast. On two levels, the dining room has Windsor chairs at nicely spaced tables covered with beige cloths, mismatched china and candle holders, rose napkins and cobalt blue glasses. Potted palms, flowers in vases, fancy screens, paintings and sculptures emphasize the feeling of dining in a gallery.

The limited menu changes every six weeks. Nightly specials revolve around duck, fish, chicken, veal and tournedos — the varying preparations not decided until that afternoon.

Soups ($1.75) might be roasted garlic, cauliflower-fennel or potato, leek and cream. Appetizers ($4.50 to $5) when we visited were goose liver and veal pate, shrimp dahomienne, oysters Florentine, and oysters on the half shell with sambucca and tomato horseradish dip ($1.25 per).

Entrees are $12.50 for sauteed chicken with black bean sauce and tomato, mushroom and risotto to $17.50 for chateaubriand on a crouton with goose liver pate and green peppercorn mustard sauce. Among the choices: rabbit fricassee wrapped in phyllo leaves, Hunan stir-fried pork, beef, vegetables and nuts, and shrimp and mussel scampi on fresh pasta. Specials could be paella or breast of capon with cranberry-orange cointreau sauce and chestnut stuffing.

"Don't forget Glenn's desserts," the menu correctly urges. They range widely from tortes and tarts to chocolate confections from a repertoire of more than 500 developed over the years. The wine list is appealing and fairly priced.

A huge fieldstone fireplace, a collection of baskets, art books to read and a cherry bar enhance the inviting, tomato-colored cocktail lounge.

Dinner nightly in summer, 6 to 9; closed Mondays and Tuesdays rest of year; Sunday brunch.

Pipers Grill & Oyster Bar, Route 1, York Corner. (207) 363-8196.
A small, one-story house opened as a restaurant in 1985 with a busy cocktail lounge and a spare dining room of bare wood tables on pedestals, a few baskets on the rafters, Laura Ashley print wallpaper and curtains, a

Rebuilt Cape Neddick Inn offers dining in art gallery setting.

large picture of an artichoke on one wall and not much else. The emphasis is not on decor but rather on eclectic food at reasonable prices.

The dinner menu includes mesquite-grilled burgers and all kinds of pizzas, one of them topped with shrimp, sun-dried tomatoes and pesto, chicken nachos and barbecued ribs as well as some attractive entrees priced from $7.95 for grilled chicken with bacon and mushrooms and a riesling sauce to $14.95 for T-bone steak. Grilled lamb chops with rosemary and zinfandel sauce are a bargain $9.95. The tenderloin of pork is done with Granny Smith apples and black current sauce, the daily pasta might be with scallops and prosciutto, and the grilled tuna marinated with artichokes and bell peppers (all about $11). Seasonal vegetables could be sauteed green beans, shredded beets and yams.

Steamed mussels in tomato and garlic and a beef sate with a spicy Szechwan peanut sauce are among appealing appetizers ($2.95 to $3.95). The wine list is limited but chosen with an eye to price, the house Partager going for $7.50 a carafe and muscadet available for $9.50.

Lunch, Monday-Saturday 11:30 to 2:30; dinner, 5 to 10, to midnight Friday-Sunday; Sunday brunch, noon to 3.

York Harbor Inn, Route 1A, York Harbor. (207) 363-5119.

From their hilltop perch, three of the four charming dining rooms here look onto (and catch the salty breeze from) the ocean across the street. One room, the main Cabin Loft lobby with fireplace, is used in winter; another is an enclosed porch, and a third beamed room looks like a pub.

Mismatched chairs, small paned windows, blue and white plates displayed below the beamed ceiling, overcloths of varying colors over white with pink napkins, small oil lamps and sloping floors convey an old-fashioned feeling. Red geraniums in the window boxes are a colorful accent; the table flowers are, unfortunately, fake.

Chef Gerry Bonsey's dinner menu features Yankee seafood with contemporary accents. Among appetizers ($3.75 to $4.50) are mussels provencale, smoked salmon, broiled oysters covered with crabmeat and bearnaise sauce, and a dish called Tatnic Bay Treasure — scallops, shrimp and crabmeat in a creamy veloute sauce. Brie cheese soup, a concoction with mushrooms, cream, julienned vegetables and white wine, is a popular starter.

Entrees run from $10.75 for chicken stuffed with broccoli and cheddar cheese to $15.75 for filet mignon. The recipe for veal Swiss was requested by Gourmet magazine; pasta with shrimp and scallops, and chicken stuffed with lobster and boursin cheese are other specialties. The innkeeper's clambake is priced daily.

Special desserts are the Toblerone Swiss chocolate walnut confection and chocolate sundae, plus a chilled lemon and caramel souffle.

Six salads, croissant creations and Mexican dishes are among offerings on an extensive luncheon menu.

Lunch, Monday-Friday 11:30 to 2:30; dinner nightly, 5:30 to 10:30; Sunday brunch, 11:30 to 2:30.

The Spice of Life, Route 1A at Village Square, York Village. (207) 363-4902.

A pub-like pine-paneled bar and a dining room with walls covered with plates and whatnot comprise the Spice of Life, where the chairs are mismatched, the glasses and service plates are all different, and a vat of soup (something like lamb and lentil) often simmers on the old stove by the back wall. Frank Hamory, who owns it with wife Dorothy, is Hungarian, but the only Hungarian offerings are a few bottles of wine like Egri Bikaver.

Starters (most $3.25) include soused shrimp, herring in wine sauce, marinated squid and smoked bluefish salad (the family has its own smokehouse). Among entrees ($9.95 to $12.95) are haddock done several ways, scallops, shrimp, veal with prosciutto and provolone, duckling with a honey and apricot glaze, and a chicken breast stuffed with crabmeat. Partager wines are $7.25 a liter, and a great selection of beers is offered.

Cajun bread pudding with rum sauce, chocolate amaretto pie and chocolate pecan praline pie are $2. In the bar-lounge, you can get chili, soup, or quiche of the day at very moderate cost.

For lunch (not served in summer), mussels vinaigrette, chunky chicken sandwich, quiche with salad and baby beef liver sauteed with onions are some of the choices ($2.50 to $5.50).

Dinner, 5 to 9 or 9:30; closed Sunday.

Dockside Dining Room, Harris Island, York. (207) 363-4800.

Overlooking the harbor next to the Dockside Guest Quarters, this gray-shingled structure houses an airy dining room on two levels, several round tables on the porch screened from floor to ceiling, and a small gift shop.

The decor is slightly more "au courant" than that of the inn next door, with white bentwood ice-cream parlor chairs, flowers in beer or Perrier bottles, green mats with paper napkins on Formica tables, green carpet and blue walls, and everywhere a water view.

It's an especially fine setting for a nautical lunch. For $4.75 to $7.95, you can get broiled scrod, fried or baked scallops, shrimp salad in a croissant, lobster salad in a tomato, roast duckling and a few other items. Most are accompanied by cheese and crackers, cheese bread and the "salad deck" — items from the salad bar set in half of an old boat.

The same appetizers are offered at lunch and dinner: marinated mushrooms, baked onion soup, herring and sour cream, seafood chowder and

Waterfront activity is on view from Dockside Guest Quarters.

shrimp cocktail ($4.50). Dinner entrees run from $7.95 for broiled scrod to $12.50 for strip sirloin. Favorites are the roast stuffed duckling (from Hickory Stick Farm in Laconia, N.H.), baked scallops and boiled lobster.

The wine list bears bargains: Graves for $7.50, Mirassou cabernet sauvignon for $10 and Monterey chardonnay for $11.

For 16 years Steve and Sue Roeder have been managing the restaurant. Their formula obviously works too well to change much.

Lunch, noon to 2; dinner, 5:30 to 9, Sunday noon to 2:30 and 5:30 to 8:30. Closed Mondays, also mid-October to Memorial Day.

Kevin's Village Restaurant, 226 York St., York. (207) 363-2952.
Nothing could be more down home than this five-year-old restaurant which looks as if it's been there forever (the shingled building dating back 60 years was well-known as a bake shop and then as Cox's Store). Historically a local gathering spot, it still is.

The counter with five stools, cash register, a service bar in the corner and books for sale in front, hides the kitchen. On either side are two dining rooms which resemble those of 30 years ago. The windowed room to the left is a mishmash of tables and booths, covered with oilcloth that looks like lace, dripping candles in Chianti bottles, fake flowers, Metaxa dolls, family pictures, ruffled curtains, an old radio on the shelf and stained-glass pieces hanging in the windows — all rather endearing. Prices are endearing as well.

Water (on request) arrives in plastic glasses, and the waitress arrives when she pleases (we waited almost an hour for breakfast one morning). But what arrives is great. For lunch, we had an excellent eggs Florentine ($4.95) and a garden pouch of veggies with chicken ($3.50), while our son had a burger with Village fries in chunks, skins and all, and a Coke served in a large Mason jar.

Most of the cooking is done by Kevin Fortier, who is 29 and from "way up Maine," according to our waitress. His lengthy dinner menu embraces everything from beer-batter haddock to shrimp cacciatore, chicken Hawaii

137

to liver grilled with onions and bacon. If the more than thirty menu entrees aren't enough, he's got a dozen nightly specials — perhaps steak and crab claws, Cornish hen or lobster stew. Almost everything is under $7.95; steak, veal and fried seafood platter are most expensive at $10.95. Kevin's has a full liquor license; Principato wines are $4.95 a bottle.

Interesting breakfasts run from chocolate chip pancakes to chili with meat. We thoroughly enjoyed our apple-spice pancakes and apple and cheddar cheese omelet when they finally arrived.

Open daily, 9 to 8, to 9 p.m. on weekends.

Las Cimas, Varrell Lane at Route 1A, York Harbor. (207) 363-4130.

Just up from the harbor, in the restored gray wood Lancaster Building, is this tiny and colorful Mexican restaurant and boutique, opened in 1984 by Minerva Gonzales, who hails from Torreon, Mexico, and her husband.

She makes the delicious salsa; it's fairly mild but crushed hot peppers are served on the side. Guacamole, nachos with different toppings, tacos, enchiladas, burritos, chalupas, chili and combination plates thereof are in the $2.50 to $7 range. Soft drinks are served in Mason jars (Las Cimas was expecting to receive a liquor license when we visited). Actor Noel Harrison, who has a place down the street, drops in for a mug of coffee and hot chocolate combined, topped with whipped cream. Hot dogs and salads are also available, and a special dessert consists of two lightly fried flour tortillas with sugar, cinnamon and ice cream.

Open for lunch and dinner; closed in winter.

Cape Neddick Lobster Pound, Route 1A, Cape Neddick. (207) 728-6777.

A gray shingled building practically over the water, the Cape Neddick cries out for an outdoor deck. However, there are glorious views (especially at sunset) from every window inside the two-level bar and dining area, which has free-form wooden tables, deck chairs and paper mats decorated with lobsters. Loud music plays in the background — live on weekends — and it's all very picturesque and casual.

Offering more than just lobster, the menu lists things like bouillabaisse and teriyaki steak. Boiled lobster and the Cape Neddick Down East shore dinner are priced daily; lobster stew is $5.25. Broiled haddock or scallops and shrimp scampi are $9.25 to $12.75; the "Fisherman's Luck" special could be charbroiled tuna. Fried clams, lobster salad, fish and chips and lobster roll and fries complete the selection.

Open from 5 p.m., summer only.

Diversions

Beaches. Inn guests probably will be grateful for the peace and quiet of the inn grounds and sheltered beaches. Or you may be as lucky as we were and find a parking spot and place at **Harbor Beach,** next to a private club. But if you want surf, join the throngs on **Long Sands Beach,** one of Maine's sandiest and deservedly crowded. It was a refreshing oasis on one unforgettable 100-degree day when we and everyone else placed our sand chairs in the ocean and lounged in the water trying to keep cool. If there's not enough action on the beach, surely there is in the amusement area of downtown York Beach. On past **Short Sands Beach** at Cape Neddick Harbor is a sheltered beach good for children.

Marginal Way. A three-mile walk along the ocean between shore and homes begins at Harbor Beach and extends to Nubble Light. It's more rugged than Ogunquit's better known Marginal Way, but well worth the effort for the views and the natural landscaping (wild roses, bayberry, blueberries and ground juniper).

Cape Neddick Park. Off River Road are 100 acres of woods preserved by Brenda Kuhn as a memorial to her parents. The park contains the **Walt Kuhn Gallery,** which has the late artist's Maine landscapes and circus drawings as well as works of other local artists, the **Vera Spier Kuhn Sculpture Garden** of contemporary sculpture (including a colorful one that looks like a jigsaw puzzle atop a chariot and another that's all pink dots on posts), and a performing arts amphitheater for summer entertainment. Picnic tables are scattered about.

The York Historic District. The history of the first chartered English city in North America (a refuge for early Puritan settlers from Massachusetts) is on display in York Village. The Chamber of Commerce has an excellent brochure detailing walking and driving tours. The **Old Gaol Museum,** once the King's Prison, is the oldest surviving public building of the British Colonies in this country; on view are the dungeon, cells, jailer's quarters and household effects. The **Emerson-Wilcox House** (1740), the enormous **Elizabeth Perkins House** (1730) beside the river and the rambling **Sayward-Wheeler Mansion** (1720) are open, as are **Jefferd's Tavern** (1750), the 1745 **Old School House,** the **George Marshall Store** and the **John Hancock Wharf,** with old tools and antique ship models in a warehouse owned by a signer of the Declaration of Independence. Most are concentrated along Lindsay Road, which leads to **Sewall's Bridge,** a replica of the first pile drawbridge in America. Nearby, Route 103 passes an intriguing looking mini-suspension bridge for pedestrians (called the "wiggly bridge," for good reason), which leads to a pathway along the river from York Harbor to Sewall's Bridge. Out Route 91 is a small stone memorial next to the trickling **Maud Muller Spring,** which inspired John Greenleaf Whittier's poem.

Extra-Special

Factory Outlet Shopping. Anyone who rejoiced when Dansk opened its first large factory outlet at Kittery is probably ecstatic about the several miles of outlets along Route 1 from Kittery to York. Although some are the same kinds of clothing outlets that you find in Freeport, the specialty here seems to be china, glass and kitchenware. We have found tremendous bargains at **Villeroy & Boch** (place settings and oversized dinner plates at up to 75 percent off), **Mikasa, Royal Doulton** and **Waterford-Aynsley.** You can admire the river view from benches outside the **Corning Designs** store at the Maine Gate Outlets. There are **Lenox, Oneida, Scandinavian Design, Georges Briard, Van Heusen** and **Samuel Roberts** (ultrasuede at 50 percent off) in various malls and small plazas on both sides of the highway. New ones pop up all the time, and it takes policemen to untangle the bumper-to-bumper shopper traffic on summer weekends.

The Kennebunks, Me.
The Most and Best of Everything

For many, the small coastal area known as the Kennebunk Region has the most or best of everything in Maine: the best beaches, the most inns, the best shops, the most eating places, the best scenery, the most tourist attractions, the best galleries, the most diversity.

All have combined to produce what oldtimers like gift shop owners Henry and Priscilla Pasco see as overkill. Concerned over a gradual deterioriation in the century-old traditions of one of Maine's earliest summer havens for the wealthy, they were instrumental in Kennebunkport's hosting of a 1985 conference on "Preserving Town Character," sponsored by Maine Citizens for Historic Preservation and Kennebunkport's business and historical associations, among others.

The Kennebunks offer a case study in town character. Actually, there are at least three Kennebunks. One is the town of Kennebunk and its inland commercial center, historic Kennebunk. The second is Kennebunkport, the changing coastal resort community which most tourists mean when they think of the Kennebunks. A third represents Cape Arundel, Cape Porpoise and Goose Rocks Beach, their rugged coastal aspects largely unchanged by development in recent years.

Kennebunkport and its Dock Square and Lower Village shopping areas have become so congested that a shuttle bus runs from vast parking areas on the edge of town. The streets teem on summer nights with strollers who have spent the day at the beach.

And yet you can escape: walk along Parson's Way; drive out Ocean Avenue past Spouting Rock and Vice President George Bush's mansion and around Cape Arundel to Cape Porpoise, a working fishing village; bicycle out Beach Avenue to Lord's Point or Strawberry Island; visit the Rachel Carson Wildlife Preserve; savor times gone by among the historic homes of Summer Street in Kennebunk or along the beach at Goose Rocks.

One of the charms of the Kennebunks is that the crowded restaurants and galleries co-exist with the annual Unitarian Church blueberry festival, the Rotary chicken barbecue and the solitude of Parson's Way.

Watercolorist Edgar Whitney proclaimed the Kennebunks "the best 10 square miles of painting areas in the nation." Explore and you'll see why.

Inn Spots

Old Fort Inn. Old Fort Avenue, Kennebunkport 04046. (207) 967-5353.

The main lodge in a converted barn is the heart of the Old Fort Inn. You enter through the reception area and Sheila Aldrich's antiques shop. Inside is a large rustic room with enormous beams, weathered pine walls and a massive brick fireplace, the perfect setting for some of Sheila's antiques.

Old Fort Inn

Greek Revival Nott House is a Kennebunkport historic attraction.

That's where she and husband David, transplanted Californians, set out the continental buffet breakfast each morning — guests pick up wicker trays with calico linings, help themselves to the buffet and sit around the lodge or outside on the sun-dappled deck beside the large swimming pool. Sheila bakes the sweet breads (blueberry, zucchini, banana, oatmeal and pumpkin are some); the croissants are David's forte.

The stone and brick carriage house out back has, up a spiral staircase, 10 large and luxurious guest rooms off a central corridor on the second floor. All are decorated in different colors, all have private bathrooms (shower only), plush carpeting, color television and kitchenettes, plus such nice touches as velvet wing chairs, stenciling on the walls and handmade wreaths over the beds. "My wife agonizes over every intricate detail," says David. "I call her Miss Mix and Match." Her decorating flair shows; even the towels are color-coordinated.

The inn is a quiet retreat away from the tourist hubbub but within walking distance of the ocean; at night, David says, the silence is deafening. The inn boasts a well-maintained tennis court, as well as the pool. Most guests are repeat, long-term customers, and it's easy to see why.

Doubles, $70 to $92; three-night minimum in summer; closed November-April.

The Captain Lord Mansion, Pleasant Street, Box 527, Kennebunkport 04046. (207) 967-3141.

For starters, consider the architectural features of this beautifully restored 1812 mansion: an octagonal cupola, a suspended elliptical staircase, blown glass windows, trompe l'oeil hand-painted doors, 18-foot bay window, a hand-pulled working elevator.

The inn is so full of historic interest that public tours are given in summer for a nominal fee. You'd never know that it was converted from a boarding house for senior citizens only in 1978.

The Captain Lord Mansion.

Guests can savor all the heritage that makes this a National Historic Register listing by staying overnight in any of the 16 sumptuous guest rooms and enjoying hot or iced tea in the parlor or games beside the fire in the Gathering Room. Each of the guest rooms on three floors has been carefully decorated by Bev Davis and her husband Rick Litchfield. Eleven rooms have working fireplaces; all have private baths (though some created from closets are rather small), and the corner rooms are especially spacious. All have nice touches like sewing kits and a tray with wine glass and corkscrew.

Since their young daughters were born, Bev has busied herself with making pin cushions and needlecraft "Do Not Disturb" signs for the rooms as well as opening a gift shop on the main floor. Breakfast is served family-style at large tables in the kitchen. It includes soft-boiled eggs plus fresh muffins and breads — Bev's zucchini bread is renowned, as are some of the hors d'oeuvres she prepares for wine gatherings for guests at New Year's and Halloween.

Doubles, $89 to $119, lower January-May.

Kennebunkport Inn, Dock Square, Kennebunkport 04046. (207) 967-2621.

In a nicely landscaped setting just off busy Dock Square, with a view of the river, is the graceful 19th-century mansion housing the Kennebunkport Inn, plus a 1930 motel-style annex in the rear. A small octagonal swimming pool with a large wooden deck fits snugly in between.

Excellent meals can be sampled in the inn's lovely dining rooms (see below). Drinks are served in the cocktail lounge or by the pool.

Young innkeepers Rick and Martha Griffin have furnished the 20 guest rooms in the annex with period pieces, Laura Ashley wallpapers and different stenciling everywhere. One of the larger rooms has a four-poster bed, sofa and velvet chair. All rooms have private baths and color television.

Five more bedrooms are in the main inn, which also has a fireplaced cocktail lounge and a game room.

Doubles, $62 to $72; suites $78 to $92; lower off-season.

The Captain Jefferds Inn, Pearl Street, Box 691, Kennebunkport 04046. (207) 967-2311.

If you like antiques and pets, you'll love the Captain Jefferds, which has an abundance of both. Ambrose the orange cat was snoozing on the porch chair when we came through the ornate white iron fence and up the brick walk.

Innkeepers Warren Fitzsimmons and Don Kelly, antiques dealers from Long Island, bought the inn in 1980 and moved their collection in; decorators and antiquarians, they have made the 1804 sea captain's mansion into a stunningly colorful and comfortable spot.

Warren cooks breakfast in the small but efficient kitchen; Don serves it formally in the handsome dining room. Guests may eat at 8 or 9 o'clock seatings. Eggs Benedict, blueberry crepes, quiche, frittata with seasonal vegetables and flannel (hash with poached egg) are in Warren's repertoire and he never repeats a breakfast in seven days.

A living room with an amazing collection of majolica, a sunlit solarium, a brick terrace and an expansive lawn with comfortable loungers are places where guests can relax with a book or whatever.

Nine of the eleven guest rooms have private full-tiled baths; the one on the main floor and three upstairs have fireplaces. All are luxurious, with chaise lounges, Laura Ashley linens, firm mattresses, woolen blankets and four pillows on each bed. The partners collect antique white cotton spreads and quilts; they have such an extensive collection that they change them around from time to time.

Most of the rooms have Victorian wicker pieces. "I hate plastic," says Don — we defy anyone to find a bit of it in this enchanting place.

Doubles with breakfast, $65 to $85. Two-night minimum, July-October.

Dock Square Inn, Temple Street, Box 1123, Kennebunkport 04046. (207) 967-5773.

"I make people feel at home," says Bernice Shoby, who with her husband Frank operates this six-bedroom inn which is the epitome of Victoriana, "and most of them come back."

They have run the inn for 17 years, for many years just in summer when Frank was on vacation from his industrial arts teaching job; in 1982 they

White fence surrounds spacious grounds at Captain Jefferds Inn.

143

moved from Connecticut and now it's open from March through November.

The common rooms and bedrooms are filled with the Shobys' collections of antiques. They were planning a small shop to house the overflow.

The house originally belonged to David Clark, Kennebunkport's most prolific shipbuilder, and the bedrooms are named after his ships. Most have private baths, some ingeniously built into small spaces, and color cable TV; some are air-conditioned.

We stayed in the spacious upstairs corner room with carved walnut bed, a chaise lounge and Laura Ashley wallpaper. Though the inn is near Dock Square, the street noise didn't bother us as after we closed the street-side window and put on the fan.

The Sobys provide a bicycle built for two, free beach passes, and bowls of fruit and candy to nibble on. A ring on the old school bell summons guests to the kitchen at 9 a.m. to feast on fresh fruit cups (which could include mango and papaya), choice of cereals with a big bowl of blueberries, and maybe a cheese omelet with sausages, or blueberry pancakes with Bernice's own blueberry syrup (she bakes all her own breads, puts up her own preserves, and politely declines requests for her recipe for the best blueberry muffins ever).

Doubles, $55 to $68, lower off-season; closed December-February.

The 1802 House, Locke Street (off North Street), Box 646A, Kennebunkport 04046. (207) 967-5632.

A quiet location on an out-of-the-way residential street is offered by Charlotte and Bob Houle in their attractive small bed-and-breakfast inn.

Sitting on the chairs on the side deck, you'd think you were out in the country. Inside, all is comfortable and up-to-date despite the structure's heritage. Guests gather in an open common room, where a fire in a cast-iron potbelly stove on a brick platform warms the air on chilly days and there are couches and magazines for reading.

Adjacent is the breakfast room with a long table lined with captain's chairs and topped by pretty flower arrangements. Charlotte Houle's blueberry pancakes one morning we were there still linger in the memory; walnut pancakes are a specialty in winter. We also liked Bob's eggs Benedict on another morning. Other entrees might be French toast or sour-cream scrambled eggs.

All six guest rooms on the first and second floors have private baths and are tastefully furnished in a Colonial motif that fits the house. We enjoyed our stay in the Camden Room in the downstairs lower front corner with a striped velvet chair and modern bath (shower only). Across from it is the Arundel, with two double beds and a working fireplace. Upstairs are three more rooms, one with fireplace. "Hearthside specials" are offered from November through April.

Doubles, $64 to $74; two-night minimum in season.

Port Gallery Inn, Route 9, Dock Square, Kennebunkport 04046. (207) 967-3728 or 967-5451.

Colorful geraniums and large wooden swans mark the entrance to the Port Gallery Inn, a classic white Victorian house converted into an inn and gallery in 1984. A large painting of a swan hangs over the living room mantel ("painted for my grandmother, who loved swans, when she was

89,'') says one of the owners. Relatives of the innkeepers or guests often play the grand piano in the parlor.

Although breakfast is not served, the innkeepers will prepare lobster or steak dinners ($18.95 to $22.50) for guests by reservation in the chandeliered dining room or on the charming side porch with black wicker and wrought-iron furniture and lovely stained-glass pieces.

Not for nothing is "gallery" part of the inn's name. The Marine Art Gallery features paintings by Lawrence E. Donnison of England, whose art is on view throughout the first floor.

Upstairs are four guest rooms and a honeymoon suite, each with private bath and color television hidden away in a hutch.

Doubles, $69 to $89.

Harbor Inn, Ocean Avenue, Box 538A, Kennebunkport 04046. (207) 967-2074.

The large, wrap-around front porch with river view is appropriate at the Harbor Inn. Texans Charlotte and Bill Massmann find themselves right at home on the wicker rocking chairs on the Southern-style veranda of the 1903 Victorian summer house they converted into an inn in 1985. A decanter of sherry awaits guests in the large front parlor.

To the rear is the lace-curtained dining room with wallpaper patterned with pretty iris, where Charlotte serves a breakfast of seasonal fruits, cereals, croissants and pastries prepared in a Texas-size kitchen created from four downstairs rooms.

The eight guest rooms (two of them suites, all with private baths) on the second and third floors are handsomely decorated with canopy or four-poster beds, comfortable chairs and fresh flowers.

Doubles, $70 to $85; two-night minimum on ?ummer weekends; no credit cards; closed mid-December to May.

The Inn at Harbor Head, Cape Porpoise, RD 2, Box 875, Kennebunkport 04046. (207) 967-5564 or 967-4873.

The location of the rambling shingled home of David and Jean Sutter on a rocky knoll right above the picturesque Cape Porpoise harbor is the special attraction at this small new B&B. Out front are exquisite gardens with a sundial; a private rear terrace and lawns lead down to the shore for swimming from the floats or watching the lobster boats go by.

The country kitchen is the central feature — it has to be when you must pass through it to get to the guest rooms. From it emanates a full breakfast that might include blueberry pancakes or scrambled eggs, served in a stenciled dining room warmed by a wood stove. Afternoon tea is served in the sitting room.

The best room (with private bath) is on the ground floor in front with brass bed, frilly white coverlets and curtains (and a big parrot perched on one of the curtains). Upstairs, two guest rooms share a bath.

Doubles, up to $73.50.

Dining Spots

The Glass Menagerie, Route 1, Kennebunk. (207) 985-6886.

It's a far cry from its former status as a pizza parlor, this colorful storefront restaurant at the end of a shopping plaza north of Kennebunk. It also happens to be home of some of the more inventive food we've had in a long time.

Chef-owner Virginia Gearan transformed the former pizza parlor into a rainbow of colors reflecting the large Glass Menagerie mural she acquired at an auction and installed on one wall. Black canopied curtains cover the two windows, plush beige sofas are around the bar, modern blond cane-seat chairs are at tables covered with floor-length blue patterned cloths, votive candles flicker in tall stemmed glasses, and prints of exotic animals like zebras and gnus adorn the raspberry-colored walls. The Christmas wreaths hung in 1983, the year they opened, fit into the decor so well "that we left them up," Ginny reports.

Delicious escargots in edible shells made a perfect appetizer, accompanied with toasted bread for mopping up the garlic sauce. The night's house salad — three triangles of aspic amid black olives, cucumber slices and sour cream on a bed of iceberg lettuce — proved curiously refreshing. So was the complimentary wine sorbet which followed.

For entrees, we happened to choose the extremes in price. The pasta of the day ($6.95) was mixed with spinach with cheese and vegetables, baked in a casserole and served with grapes and iceberg lettuce. The seafood strudel ($15.95) was a knockout, studded with pieces of lobster and accompanied by potatoes that resembled ribbons of toothpaste, decorated with red caviar, and a ratatouille with boursin cheese.

The trio of fresh fruit sorbets ($3.25) turned out to be four: honey-lemon, kiwi, watermelon and grapefruit, doused in a tart raspberry sauce.

The specials vary daily, as do salads (the previous night's was spinach with strawberries and a sweet and sour dressing). Fish might be sole with raspberries and almonds in a hollandaise sauce, the chicken sliced in a mix of herbs and drambuie, the filet mignon served in a salad with mustard vinaigrette, and the dessert, brandied strawberries.

Dinner, 6 to 9 or 10; closed Monday.

The Tides Inn By-the-Sea, Goose Rocks Beach, Kennebunkport. (207) 967-3757.

The area's other most intriguing menu comes from an unlikely place as well, at an inn with a somewhat down-at-the-heels facade. Old metal chairs line the front porch facing the ocean, a pot-bellied stove is in the pub, the cluttered dining room is partitioned by a screen from the entrance to the kitchen, and there's a rustic dining porch.

John and Marie Cameron, who run what she calls "a casual, crazy place with a true Maine air," have upgraded the inn gradually over the last 14 years, and the restaurant stresses regional, new American and French cuisine.

The decor is fairly nondescript with bentwood chairs, tables covered with paisley cloths and blue napkins, and fake flowers. Taped classical music plays in the background. The food is assertive: grape leaves stuffed with lamb, spinach and walnuts, and a spicy orange curried chicken among appetizers, grilled salmon with fresh salsa and mixed seafood grill among entrees, and, for dessert, fruit tuilles or a chocolate bombe that one addict called unreal. The price is right: appetizers, $3.50 to $4.50; entrees, $8.25 to $14.75; desserts, $2.95 to $4.25, and wines starting at $8.50 for one of our favorites, a Bandiera cabernet sauvignon.

We ordered the grilled lamb and vegetables ($10.75), a large plate bearing chunks of nicely-seared lamb, tender new potatoes, zucchini and red peppers, plus a side portion of salsa laced with coriander as well as the regular minted pear chutney. Also good was the fettuccine Alfredo with a side dish of crisp cauliflower, broccoli and carrots. For dessert we split an extraordinary almond cake, dense, moist and covered with a fresh peach sauce.

Twenty-two guest rooms upstairs and in a new annex range in age and decor from extra-plain and old-fashioned to modern, and are $42 to $95 a night. The annex rooms, with kingsize beds and modern baths, are the more expensive.

Dinner nightly, 6 to 9, closed November-April.

Windows on the Water, Chase Hill, Kennebunkport. (207) 967-3313.

The windows are architecturally interesting at this sleek new restaurant opened in 1985 on a hilltop above the harbor; they also offer one of Kennebunkport's better water views. So the name was a natural, as is the attractive two-level outdoor deck, which may be the best place in town for a summer lunch.

At lunch, you design your own meal, ticking off the ingredients for a sandwich or salad from a menu that serves as the order form, as in a railroad dining car or private club. Except that here you literally create your own, down to the last garnish of carrots or green pepper. It's slightly confusing, but novel and fun. Salads and sandwiches go for $4.50, no matter how many items you choose to add on. We were a bit disappointed in the small size of one chef's salad, mostly turkey and ham; for some reason the shrimp-based salad with cheese was much more ample. The poppyseed vinaigrette dressing was excellent, and the Whitbread's ale so cooling on a hot summer day that we had two.

Inside, the main dining room has a cathedral ceiling, track lighting, and a green color scheme accented by vases of black-eyed susans. A smaller room beyond is even nicer with a bowed front window and, when we were there, a fantastic arrangement of Queen Anne's lace and lilies. Upstairs is an attractive lounge with plaid sofas, wingback chairs and more bouquets of flowers.

The dinner menu reminds us of a Chart House; as a matter of fact, we were told that the owner was formerly with that chain. Shrimp teriyaki, Hawaiian chicken, kabobs and prime rib and all kinds of steaks are priced from $8.95 to $15.95. Mud pie and a fruit compote are a couple of the desserts. For brunch, you might order huevos rancheros or a lobster-stuffed potato.

Open daily for lunch, dinner and Sunday brunch.

Kennebunkport Inn, Dock Square, Kennebunkport. (207) 967-2621.

The dining rooms on either side of the inn's entry are extra pretty, with fringed valences, lace curtains, Laura Ashley wallpaper and stenciling, hurricane lamps, jars of fresh field flowers on the fireplace mantels and well-spaced tables done up in white over beige.

Innkeepers Martha and Rick Griffin have garnered quite a culinary reputation and go to France frequently to learn new dishes, with which to dazzle their frequent repeat customers. Smoked trout mousse with rye toast, baked mussels in herb and garlic butter, and marinated shrimp, charbroiled and served with hollandaise sauce, are among appetizers in the $4 to $5 range.

The dozen or so entrees ($13.95 to $16.95) on the changing menu might be sauteed lobster with watercress puree and tarragon sauce, a mustard-ginger rack of lamb or king crab pie in a rich mornay sauce.

Breakfast, 7:30 to 10; dinner, 6 to 9; dining room closed November-March.

White Barn Inn, Beach Street, Kennebunkport. (207) 967-2321.

Runners at breakfast, lovers at dinner — that's the impression we got after sampling one of each meal at the White Barn Inn.

Breakfast is something of a local tradition in a Colonial room notable for pretty stenciling on the walls. We thought every shorts-clad jogger in town must have been there, stoking up on such carbohydrate-laden goodies as pancakes chock full of blueberries, thick French toast and fantastic pecan muffins, huge and gooey. Of course, you can get the usual egg dishes; slivers of fresh melon garnish every plate, and the coffee cup is refilled endlessly.

For dinner, the barn soaring up to three stories with all kinds of farming artifacts hanging from beams and pulleys is almost too atmospheric for words. The convivial gather around the gorgeous solid brass bar, and the truly jovial perch around the baby grand and sing along with the pianist. Tables are set with silver and linen, and the colorful impatiens on the deck are spotlit at night.

White Barn Inn.

The fairly extensive menu contains few surprises, although gingered and sherried sirloin slices are one of the appetizers ($3.95 to $6.50). For entrees ($9.95 to $16.95), you can get coquilles St. Jacques, veal roast or steak au poivre. Included are a fine house salad with a creamy cucumber dressing and some heavenly hot rolls.

We shared the escargots baked in mushroom caps, heady with garlic, and enjoyed a fine filet mignon and marinated lamb. The hot fudge puff and strawberries with cointreau were delightful desserts.

The inn also has 21 rooms and suites ranging from simple to elegant, most with private baths. Doubles, $50 to $85.

Breakfast, 8 to noon in season; dinner, 6 to 9:30; Sunday brunch, 11:30 to 1:30. Closed Mondays off-season, also January to mid-March.

Cafe Topher, Western Avenue, Kennebunkport. (207) 987-5009.

The smart-looking cafe opened by Christopher Riley in 1983 was such a success that he and his wife Hylah added Topher's Tavern underneath. The dining room with latticed room dividers, abundant plants and art works, and fanned pink napkins perched in wine glasses is most attractive and intimate.

The menu is a mixed bag from the nachos, potato skins and artichoke hearts for "munchins" to marinated beef kabob or scallops and shrimp hunter style. Topher's chicken stuffed with green beans, wrapped in bacon and served with a bearnaise sauce appeals, and baked stuffed haddock with newburg sauce is a favorite.

Dinners are priced from $7.82 for sauteed sirloin tips on rice to $12.91 for scallops provencale (none of the prices is rounded off).

At lunch, salads, shrimp or lobster rolls, burgers and sandwiches are available; a fine setting is the nicely landscaped outdoor patio, all decked out with deep rose linens and white molded chairs.

Lunch daily, ll:30 to 2:30; dinner, 5:30 to 9:30; Sunday brunch.

The Breakwater Restaurant and Inn, Ocean Avenue, Kennebunkport. (207) 967-3118.

For years, the dining room in this antiques-filled inn with a big wrap-around porch has been touted for its food and for its view across the mouth of the Kennebunk River toward the open Atlantic; sunsets here are spectacular. Red linen overcloths, candles in hurricane lamps, hanging plants and framed Saturday Evening Post covers add to the dining scene.

An unusual feature of the menu is that entrees are grouped by price, with three each from $8.50 through $9.50, $10.50 and so on up to $13.50. Chilled cucumber soup is one of the appetizers; we might lean to the Maine shrimp bisque ($2.60) and scallops seviche ($3.95). The baked stuffed sole with lobster sauce ($9.50) is always popular; so are the seafood scampi and the combination filet and lobster tail (both $13.50). A tossed salad or a spinach and mushroom salad with Caesar dressing comes with the meal.

The pleasant prices go right through dessert ($1.40 to $2.50) for grasshopper pie, strawberry rum cake, honey walnut torte and, sometimes, bananas Foster.

The Breakwater and its newer companion, the Riverside, offer 20 rooms with private bath. Doubles, $40 to $70, include continental breakfast.

Dinner, 5:30 to 9:30 or 10; closed November to mid-May.

Samuel Hill Tavern, Route 1 north, Arundel. (207) 985-3316.

Some locals refer to this newly restored 1790 house and barn as "the poor man's White Barn." Despite the beamed ceilings and tin wall sconces, the soaring main dining room feels new, the prices are reasonable, and the weekend night we dined the place was packed and so hot we were grateful to be seated next to an open door. A pianist played quietly in the background, and the ambience proved quite elegant.

The menu is fairly straightforward: appetizers from $2.95 for fruit compote to $5.25 for jumbo shrimp cocktail; entrees from $8.95 for broiled haddock to $13.95 for lamb chops with mint jelly.

The muffins were hearty and the house salad an interesting mix of greens, cucumber slices and cherry tomatoes with choice of six dressings; both the creamy garlic and creamy horseradish were excellent. Entrees of fettuccine with white clam sauce and haddock Florentine (both $9.95) were fine, the former a heaping bowl that was too much and the latter served in a gratin dish atop a platter of tomatoes, mushrooms, snow peas and onions. A

149

Fetzer fume blanc for $11, a good choice from the severely limited wine list, was served in a marble ice bucket. Desserts were standard and we were sufficiently sated to pass.

Lunch daily, 11:30 to 2:30; dinner, 5:30 to 9:30 or 10.

Olde Grist Mill, Mill Lane, Kennebunkport. (207) 967-4781.

Beside the Kennebunk River, this mill on the National Register of Historic Places dates to 1749 and has been little changed since, but for the addition in 1985 of a piano bar with wing chairs and oriental-type rugs that purists think mars the front. Owner David Lombard's father was the miller here in the 1930s; the mill has been in his family since it was built.

The restaurant is decidedly popular with the tour-bus set as well as families (there's a children's menu) and locals who like to browse in its good country store and gift shop across the lawn, away from the madding crowds of Kennebunkport's Dock Square.

Dinner entrees are $10.50 to $17.50 for steak au poivre; a shore dinner for $27.50 brings steamers, lobster and all the trimmings. Johnny cake, baked Indian pudding and other traditional New England dishes are offered in a Colonial atmosphere. Among desserts are a frozen strawberry mousse with grand marnier and a cappuccino sundae.

Lunch, noon to 2; dinner, 5:30 to 9; closed Monday, also November-April.

The Chef's Whim, Lower Village, Kennebunkport. (207) 967-3491.

Beverly Jaccoma, housewife turned chef, worked as a pastry chef at the White Barn for two months in 1985 before opening her small restaurant with a view of the river behind Meserve's Market. From a tiny kitchen emerge "chef's whims" for cafe-style dining inside at glass-topped tables or outside under blue and white checked umbrellas.

Lunch on vegetable soup or haddock chowder and half a chicken salad sandwich ($3.95), chicken oriental or crab Louisiana salads with a croissant, a roast beef and boursin sandwich, and for dessert a frozen lemon pie, mandarin chocolate mousse or blueberry coupe with vanilla sauce. The bacon and tomato quiche is $3.95 and the salad plates $3.95 to $5.95.

If the whim hits, Beverly will serve a hot entree at night such as seafood medley, deviled crab or ham Wellington. You can bring your own wine, and passersby like to stop in for coffee or lemonade and a dessert.

Hours vary with the season. Summer: Tuesday-Saturday 11:30 to 8, Sunday and Monday 11:30 to 3.

Kennebunk Inn, 45 Main St., Kennebunk. (207) 985-3351.

This cheerful looking 1799 inn facing Kennebunk's main street was a "classic flophouse" in the words of Angela and Art LeBlanc when they bought it in 1978. Now it has 30 guest rooms, 12 with private baths, and an esteemed hotel-style dining room with high upholstered chairs, pink and white linen, candles in hurricane lamps and Tiffany-style stained-glass windows.

The food is consistent — considered a major virtue in the area — and reasonably priced. Dinners range from $7.95 for baked haddock in casserole or broiled scrod to $13.95 for veal Oscar. Chicken comes five ways: Alaina, parmigiana, Atlantis (with a crabmeat stuffing), Florentine or Mirabella. The

150

LeBlanc family are proud of their specialties, many of them bearing their names: among them shrimp en croute, Angela's veal under glass and Alan's royal scallops with peaches; a Saturday evening feature is duckling flambeed at tableside for $12.95. An almost hidden outdoor patio off to the side of the inn looks attractive for lunching.

Breakfast, lunch and dinner daily.

Mabel's Lobster Claw, Ocean Avenue, Kennebunkport. (207) 967-2562.

Somehow, this place is fancier than you expect from the name or the exterior. You sit at booths or tables with leather chairs, there's linen and carpeting, and citronella candles flicker at night. For 16 years, Mabel Hanson has presided in what is a small, personal place which some innkeepers call their favorite. She does all her cooking and baking, quite a feat considering the size of her menu.

Seafood and lobster reign, of course; you can get fried haddock or gulf shrimp for $9.50, seafood newburg for $12.50, a complete shore dinner for $18.95 or lobster Savannah for $19.95. When we were there, the twin lobster special was $11.95.

Start with Mabel's homemade soup or chowder, $2 a cup, and finish with an ice cream parfait, pie a la mode or Mabel's famous peanut butter ice cream pie ($2.50). The menu is extensive enough that you don't have to be a seafood lover — or even want a full dinner — to eat here; there are salad, lobster rolls and children's plates.

Lunch, 11:30 to 3; dinner, 5 to 10.

Extra-Special

Tilly's Shanty, Cape Porpoise. If you prefer your Maine lobster in an informal outdoor setting, shun the better known Nunan's Lobster Hut or Spicer's Gallery nearby, which are deservedly popular in their own right. Head right onto the pier at Cape Porpoise. Behind Spicer's is a shanty where you place your order and then sit at a battered picnic table beside the water. When we were last there, lobster dinners ranged from $6.95 to $11.95, depending on size. Steamers were $4.90, a lobster roll, $4.95, and lobster stew, $3.25 a cup and $5.95 a bowl. Tilly's is open daily until 8 p.m. BYOB.

Diversions

Beaches. Gooch's and **Kennebunk** are two sandy strands with surf west of town (parking by permit, often provided by innkeepers). The fine silvery sand at **Goose Rocks Beach** looks almost tropical and the waters are protected. The beaches are at their uncrowded best at non-peak periods and early or late in the day.

Parson's Way. A marker opposite the landmark Colony Hotel notes the land given to the people of Kennebunkport so that "everyone may enjoy its natural beauty." Sit on the benches, spread a blanket on a rock beside the ocean, or walk out to the serene little chapel of St. Ann's Episcopal Church by the sea.

Ocean Avenue. Continue past Parson's Way to Spouting Rock, where the incoming tide creates a spurting fountain as waves crash between two ragged cliffs, and Blowing Cave, another roaring phenomenon within view of Walker Point and the impressive George Bush summer compound. Go on to Cape Porpoise, the closest thing to a fishing village hereabouts, with a working lobster pier and a picturesque harbor full of islands.

History. The Kennebunkport Historical Society has its attractions: the 1853 Greek Revival Nott House called **White Columns** and the 1899 **Town House School** with exhibits of local and maritime heritage. But inland Kennebunk is more obviously historic: The 1825 **Brick Store Museum** has an excellent collection of decorative and fine arts and offers walking tours of Kennebunk's historic district. Summer Street (Route 35) running south of downtown toward Kennebunkport is considered one of the architecturally outstanding residential streets in the nation; the 1803 **Taylor-Barry House** is open for tours, and the aptly named yellow-with-white-frosting "Wedding Cake House" (1826) is a sight to behold (though not open to the public).

Seashore Trolley Museum, Log Cabin Road, Kennebunkport. A two-mile-long, 20-minute trolley car ride is a featured attraction at the oldest and largest electric railway museum in the country. On view in three exhibition barns are more than two dozen trolley cars spanning seven decades from the horse-drawn cars of the late 1800s to the streamlined models of the 1950s. Visitors can watch craftsmen restoring vehicles in the workshop and climb aboard the extravagantly restored cars, which range from British double-deckers to a car from Montreal that one of us remembers taking for trips downtown in the '40s.

Arts and Crafts. Its scenery has turned Kennebunkport into a mecca for artisans. The Art Guild of the Kennebunks numbers more than 52 resident professionals as members and claims the Kennebunks are the largest collective community of fine art on the East Coast. Art and galleries are everywhere, but the largest concentration is around Kennebunkport's Dock Square and the wharves to the south. Fine crafts are shown at **The Pascos,** the shop and home of civic boosters Henry and Priscilla Pasco, a brother-sister team whose 45-year tenure makes theirs "by far the oldest shop around." Nearby in the new Wharf Lane Shops are the **Priscilla Hartley Gallery,** in its 25th season and the oldest in Maine, the **Van Sinderen Furniture** and woodworking shop, and out over the water, Lou and Bob Lipkin's distinctive **Goose Rocks Pottery.** For a change of pace, visit the grounds of the **Franciscan Monastery** (where, as some savvy travelers know, spare and inexpensive bedrooms are available) and St. Anthony's Shrine; the shrines and sculpture include the towering piece which adorned the facade of the Vatican pavilion at the 1964 New York World's Fair.

Shopping. Dock Square and, increasingly, the Lower Village across the river are full of interesting stores, everything from the **Tipsy Mouse** with gourmet foods and wines to the **Port Canvas Co.,** with all kinds of handsome canvas products. **Zamboanga** has a fine array of gifts, home furnishings, tiles and many kites. The splendid **Kennebunk Book Port,** the **Paper Patch,** the **Haberdashery** and the **Zoo Apparel** (clothing), **Plum Dandy** (crafts), **Once a Knight** (games), **Port Folio** ("paper with panache"), the **Whimsy Shop,** the **Mole Hole** and the cute shops at new Union Square and the new Schooners complex are some.

Fine Camden Harbor view is offered from porch at Smiling Cow shop.

Camden, Me.
Where Mountains Meet Sea

From where she stood in 1910, all that native poet Edna St. Vincent Millay could see were "three long mountains and a wood" in one direction and "three islands in a bay" the other way. Her poem, written at age 18 and first recited publicly at Camden's Whitehall Inn, captures the physical beauty of this coastal area known as the place where the mountains meet the sea.

Today, the late poet might not recognize her beloved Camden, so changed is the community now teeming with tourists in summer. The scenery remains as gorgeous as ever, and perhaps no street in Maine is more majestic than High Street, its forested properties lined with the sparkling white homes one associates with the Maine coast a generation ago. Back then, when you finally reached Camden after the slow, tortuous drive up Route 1, you had unofficially arrived Down East.

Those were the days, and visitors in ever-increasing numbers still try to recapture them in a town undergoing a bed-and-breakfast inn boom and a proliferation of smart, distinctive shops.

A small-scale cultural life attracts some; others like the outdoors activities of Camden Hills State Park. But the focus for most is Camden Harbor, with its famed fleet of windjammers setting forth under full sail each Monday morning and returning to port each Saturday morning.

Camden has an almost mystical appeal that draws people back time and again. Sometimes, amid all those people, you just wish that appeal weren't quite so universal.

Inn Spots

Norumbega, High Street, Camden 04843. (207) 236-4646.

Imagine having the run of a grand Victorian castle overlooking Penobscot Bay, one of the great late-19th-century villas along the Maine coast.

It's possible, thanks to the vision and work of V. Mark Boland, a former private school administrator who scoured the South and East from Mississippi to Bar Harbor looking for the perfect house in which to open a bed-and-breakfast inn.

He found it in the 1886 cobblestone and slate-roofed mansion built for Joseph B. Stearns. inventor of the duplex system of telegraphy, and for a few years the summer home of journalist Hodding Carter. After renovations costing more than half a million dollars, Norumbega opened in 1984 with seven sumptuous guest rooms on the second and third floors and a main floor with public rooms like those in the finest estates.

Indeed, this is a mini-Newport-style mansion, from its graceful entry with oriental carpets and ornate staircase (complete with a cozy retreat for two beside a fireplace on the landing) to the smallest of the guest rooms on the third floor. Even it has two Victorian rocking chairs around a skirted table, a queensize bed, hooked rugs on pine floors, oak dresser with pieces of Blue Hill's Rackcliffe Pottery on top, a bathroom with an old clawfoot tub and separate shower stall, and costs a cool $100 a night.

Mark Boland, who greets guests, pours tea or wine in the afternoon and prepares a breakfast worthy of royalty, says that staying at Norumbega is almost like being a guest in a museum, and we agree. The parlors, the library, the second-floor reading room, the flower-laden rear porches on all three floor and the expansive lawns are available for guests. Interestingly, the front door is locked at all times, probably to discourage sightseers.

In the morning, guests gather at the large damask-covered table in the formal dining room at 8 or 9:15 for what truly is a breakfast feast for the eyes as well as the palate: platters of local and exotic fruits, three kinds of juices, sweet breads and, the piece de resistance, the main course — in our case, French toast topped with a dollop of pink sherbet and sliced peaches, which all eight at our table agreed was the best we'd ever had. Being thrown together with strangers somehow works here — there's enough room for togetherness and also for escape, if you like.

The price is steep, but the value is received. All seven rooms have private baths and most have fireplaces and canopied beds. The best (and quietest) are those away from the road in the rear with views of the water.

Doubles, $100 to $130.

Edgecombe-Coles House, 64 High St., Camden 04843. (207) 236-2336. Another substantial summer home, on a hilltop almost across the street from Norumbega, also opened for bed and breakfast in 1984.

Innkeepers Terry and Louise Price named it for their fathers and furnished it rather spectacularly with antiques, oriental rugs, original art, stenciling which Louise did herself (she also loves to wallpaper), and interesting touches like draperies around the showers (and English soaps and herb shampoos for guests).

Each of the five guest rooms is different, but most have quilts and bedspreads made by Louise's mother. By far the most elegant is the huge front room with kingsize bed, fireplace and picture window framing a grand ocean view.

In the luxurious living room are a leather sofa, piano and many books.

Breakfast is served in the rear dining room or outside in the garden. Strawberry waffles and giant sweet popovers are among the specialties.

Doubles, $60 to $85; lower off-season.

Norumbega is a grand Victorian mansion overlooking Penobscot Bay.

Hawthorn Inn, 9 High St., Camden 04843. (207) 236-8842.

The exterior of this pale yellow Victorian house with corner turret and rocking chairs out front perhaps deceives.

Inside, the atmosphere seems more contempory and the airy common rooms are a mass of plants and ficus trees. The seven guest rooms vary from three upstairs which share one of the world's largest bathrooms to what we must say is a rather strange new room in the basement, furnished in contemporary style and having a freestanding tub and semi-partitioned toilet right in the room.

A rear deck offers a glimpse of Camden Harbor. On the sloping back lawn, guests can play croquet or listen to the Shakespeare Company plays just a short path away.

Cactus plants are in the window of the dining room, where a full breakfast — homemade muffins plus ham and cheese quiche when we visited — is served at three tables.

Doubles, $50 to $65.

The Whitehall Inn, 52 High St., Camden 04843. (207) 236-3391.

This rambling inn (built in 1834, an inn since 1901) is a fixture on the Camden scene, generations of families returning annually for vacations to partake of the hospitality offered by the Dewing family and their offspring. The front porch is supplied with the obligatory rocking chairs, and youngsters play lawn games alongside the inn.

Edna St. Vincent Millay of nearby Rockland gave the first recitation of her lyric poem, "Renascence," in 1912 in the inn. Her sister was on the dining room staff and one of the guests, recognizing her talent, arranged for her acceptance at Vassar College. Her pictures and high school diploma hang over the piano.

Forty-one guest rooms, all but three with private baths, are entered from meandering corridors on the second and third floors. Each is furnished simply and contains an old-fashioned, in-house telephone.

Breakfast and dinner are served in the large, old-fashioned and pleasant dining room with paned windows overlooking the side lawns. The changing dinner menu might range from $10 for smoked chicken and fruit plate to $14 for sauteed medallions of tenderloin. House specialties include boiled lobster, poached salmon and crabmeat Florentine, and local blueberries show up in everything from pancakes to bread puddings.

Doubles, $95 to $110, MAP. Closed mid-October to Memorial Day.

Lord Camden Inn, 24 Main St., Camden 04843. (207) 236-4325.

If the Whitehall is Camden's grand dowager, the Lord Camden is the new kid on the block — and feels it. An 1893 brick storefront and the Masonic Temple in the heart of downtown Camden were restored in 1984 into a modern, rather impersonal 27-room inn with elevator, private baths and in-room television.

Most rooms on the second, third and fourth floors are ersatz Colonial with original brick walls, and brass or mahogany four-poster beds. Coveted rooms with balconies overlook the harbor beyond the stores across the street (the higher the floor, the higher the price).

Continental breakfast is delivered to rooms; chocolates are put out when the covers are turned down at night.

Doubles, $80 to $120; lower off-season.

Camden Harbour Inn, 83 Bay View St., Camden 04843. (207) 236-4200.

Four large new ground-floor guest rooms were added in 1984 to this Victorian inn atop a hill overlooking the harbor. One is a suite with fireplace and two have outdoor decks.

Otherwise the 18 guest rooms in the original structure are of 19th-century vintage, with clawfoot bathtubs and antique furnishings. Ten rooms have private baths; the rest share.

A full breakfast is included in the room rates. Dinners in the new solarium dining room, which is considered to have one of the best restaurant views in town, are open to the public, as are the acclaimed Sunday brunch and the crowded Thirsty Whale Tavern with live folk music. "Maine Courses" on the dinner menu lean heavily to seafood; they range in price from $9.95 for haddock broiled in a wine and butter sauce to $18.95 for baked stuffed lobster.

Doubles, $65 to $115; lower off-season.

Aubergine, 6 Belmont Ave., Camden 04843. (207) 236-8053.

Widely known for their French cuisine (see below), David and Kerlin Grant have refurbished the upstairs guest rooms in a pleasant house built in 1886 along a side street that remains residential.

All are nicely decorated with antique furnishings, floral wallpapers and a light, sunny quality in keeping with the yellow exterior. The two third-floor rooms we once shared with our sons have been converted into one extra-large room in what Kerlin explains is a continuing effort to recreate the French-style farmhouse inn from which it takes its name. Four of the six rooms have private baths; the other two share.

The old-fashioned swing on the front porch and the living-room-type bar just inside the entrance invite dalliance for a pre-dinner drink.

The complimentary continental breakfast served in the country-pretty dining room or enclosed porch features fresh berries and wonderful hot croissants with berry preserves. You may book for dinner and the night, or for a two-night minimum stay.

Doubles, $65 to $75.

Extra-Special

The Owl and the Turtle, 8 Bay View St., Camden 04843. (207) 236-4769 or 236-2302.

Ever want to stay in a library? Here you can pretend.

Most people know this as a good bookstore and, more recently, as an appealing tea room with a balcony overlooking the harbor. But it also has three comfortable motel-style guest rooms with television, air-conditioning, wall-to-wall carpeting even in the bathrooms, and each with an outdoor balcony.

Continental breakfast is served in the rooms, and a complimentary cream tea is offered afternoons in the tea room. The scones are a specialty and owner Rebecca Conrad says that visitors from England tell her the cream here is better than that in Devon.

Light lunches, cool drinks and coffees also are served in the paneled tearoom, where one wall is covered with pictures of Maine writers. Check the four tiny tables which the Conrads' son built into the railing of the narrow outdoor balcony.

Doubles, $60. No smoking permitted.

Dining Spots

Youngtown Inn, Route 52, Lincolnville 04849. (207) 763-3037.

New and immensely popular locally and with guests referred by several Camden innkeepers is the Youngtown Inn, a scenic four miles inland from Camden past pretty Lake Megunticook. Bright geraniums in pots and an enormous portico distinguish the facade of the black-shuttered, pure white Federal-style New England farmhouse built in 1810.

Inside, owner James Rutland, a Delta Airlines pilot, and manager Karen Ruth have put together a charming country restaurant. Red velvet-seat bentwood chairs on wide pumpkin-pine floors, huge brick fireplaces, wreaths, quilts, plants, wood stove, piano, local pottery and art — it's all quite a mishmash, but it works. An airy porch off the main dining room is most pleasant for dinner on summer nights, and the tavern is inviting anytime.

Augmented by a blackboard listing daily specials, the smallish menu (five appetizers, eleven entrees) is creative and the cooking assertive.

Smoked bluefish pate ($3) served in a ramekin topped with almonds sticking up like little waves was certainly powerful. Crisp toast rounds and julienned zucchini, carrots and cucumbers on ruby lettuce accompanied. Herbed shrimp brochettes, mussels Mexicana and baked mushrooms stuffed with spinach, walnuts and feta cheese are other appetizer choices.

Large salads containing many vegetables were topped with delicious honey

Youngtown Inn has charming country atmosphere for dining.

tarragon or strong vinaigrette dressings. A basket of rolls and sweet breads was served piping hot.

Entrees (from $6.75 for pasta primavera to $12.75 for roast duck with chutney lime glaze) include a crabmeat enchilada, chicken in phyllo and the ubiquitous, but always good, Maine haddock done several ways (beer battered is one). Both the fettuccine and scallops in a mushroom, Dijon and cream sauce, and the Tex-Mex tenderloin of pork were excellent, the former garnished with flowers. The pork was roasted with green chiles and lime and layered with tortillas — we wished the salsa had been hotter (as in spicy), however.

Specials at our visit were shrimp scampi for an incredible $9 (we often ask ourselves how most Maine restaurants manage to keep their prices so low), haddock stuffed with lobster and crab and topped with mornay sauce, and stir-fried pork and vegetables. Soup was a mushroom and chive bisque. Lemon souffle, chocolate kahlua mousse, blueberry cobbler a la mode and a hearty lime cheesecake were $2 or $2.50.

The wine list offers bargains as well, with a Fetzer chardonnay and Sebastiani cabernet sauvignon for $10 and Chateau Ste. Michelle fume blanc for $12. House wines are Partager or Mondavi, $2 or $2.25 a glass.

Upstairs are six plain but attractive guest rooms sharing three baths and furnished with colorful quilts. Guests have use of a spacious porch above the portico, and can walk to a nearby beach on the lake. A continental breakfast featuring Maine products is served. Doubles are $35 or $45.

Dinner nightly, 5:30 to 9:30.

Aubergine, 6 Belmont Ave., Camden. (207) 236-8053.

The first fine French restaurant in the Camden area (indeed, a pioneer in nouvelle cuisine on the Maine coast), Aubergine is known for inspired food. Innkeeper David Grant, who trained in France, is chef and his wife Kerlin is a horticulturist who fills the public rooms with lavish bouquets of flowers from her cutting gardens outside.

An aubergine carpet, pictures of eggplants, pale yellow walls trimmed in gray, frilly white curtains, white wood chairs, white-linened tables topped with flowers in flute-like vases, and some fine antique pieces make the airy dining room and adjacent porch pretty as a picture.

The food presentation is pretty as a picture as well, and the menu, which changes monthly, takes advantage of the freshest and most colorful ingredients available.

Appetizers are $5 to $8.95 (for feuillete of lobster with truffles or smoked salmon). We thought the wild game pate garnished with several cornichons, toast triangles and homemade chutney superb.

Entrees range from $12.95 for pasta with saffron, red pepper and crab to $17.95 for filet of beef with five peppercorns. Salmon with lobster sabayon, ragout of chicken, sweetbreads and wild mushrooms, and lamb with roasted garlic and sage were offered when we last visited. We remember fondly a ragout of scallops and snails, the perfect French bread and a superb tart with buttercream and fresh raspberries for dessert. Other summer desserts ($3.75) include chocolate mint charlotte, lemon Bavarian cake and a plate of sorbets and cookies.

Dinner, Tuesday-Sunday 6:30 to 9; reservations required.

Swan's Way, 51 Bay View St., Camden. (207) 236-2171.

It's billed as "international down-home" cuisine, but whatever is served in this casual coffeehouse-style restaurant, it's certainly interesting and good.

The basic menu lists exotic hot and cold drinks — how about tea with grand marnier and whipped cream or cafe Brazil (banana, dark rum, coffee and milk)? — platters, sandwiches, salads and a host of coffees and teas. The smoked mussel sandwich with mozzarella and tomatoes on toasted garlic bread, the toasted crab sandwich and the Tuscan salad with salami, chicken, cheese and who-knows-what-all are $4.25 to $6.25

The changing entrees and desserts pack the crowds in. One night's entrees ($6.95 to $10.25) might be Andalusian shellfish stew, chicken Veneto, swordfish on a bed of garlic, new potatoes and zucchini topped with a basil cream sauce, caponata rolls and Creole crab crepe tortes.

Desserts ($2.95 to $3.50) range from triple chocolate almond gateau and frozen chocolate mousse to peaches baked with an almond filling and served in a caramel souffle, and apricot roulade. The timbale filled with fresh strawberries and strawberry mousse sounds enticing. Many people stroll down to Swan's Way in the evening just for dessert and coffee.

The dining areas in this old house with masses of flowers out front have bare floors, mismatched chairs at pedestal tables, lace curtains, good-looking posters on the walls, candles in old glass vases plus gladioli in a large pottery vase here, a faded oriental rug there.

Dinner nightly, 5 to 11:30.

The Secret Garden, 31 Elm St., Camden. (207) 236-8911.

New in the summer of 1985 was this small, creative restaurant with dining garden out back. It's the most colorful place around, all decorated with green or pink overcloths atop wild floral cloths, cream colored walls, green chairs, moss green carpeting and tall napkins of every hue in the rainbow. With fresh flowers in clay pots, white china, silver side plates and huge wine glasses, the setting could be straight out of Neiman-Marcus.

Texas owners Dan and Charlotte Holly continue the flair outside in the small garden courtyard they developed with redwood bar, pastel-colored stools with flowered seats, deck chairs of pinks and greens, flowers in all manner of pots and brass lanterns on the side. Casual fare like nachos is served out there.

Charlotte Holly's menu features American regional cuisine. Appetizers ($3.50 for vegetable soup to $6.50 for lobster fiesta) include a rustic pate served with cornichons and homemade red-pepper jelly and a spicy crab Avery, laced with a creamy Louisiana Avery Island sauce.

The six entrees run from $11.95 for chicken stuffed with cheeses, basil, spinach, nuts and mangos to $18.50 for double stuffed tenderloin (prime beef wrapped in veal and stuffed with foie gras and truffles). Lamb chops are marinated in petite sirah and served with lemony choron sauce and asparagus; sea scallops and filet of sole are married with fresh herbs, lemon, mustard and Italian sun-dried tomatoes.

Mango cheesecake, chocolate marquese in strawberry sauce and homemade blueberry ice cream are among the desserts. The California wine list is well-chosen and pricey, from the high teens to $70.

Dinner nightly, 6 to 11; closed mid-September through May.

The Waterfront Restaurant, Harborside Square off Bay View Street, Camden. (207) 236-3747.

There's no better waterside setting in Camden than this appropriately named establishment with a large outdoor deck shaded by a striking white canopy that resembles a boat's sails.

You can watch the busy harbor as you lunch on fried clams (the most expensive entree at $7.95 and including a good gazpacho and french fries), a California salad or lobster roll. Other interesting selections include lemon chicken salad, smoked salmon with toasted bagel, seafood on a toasted roll with remoulade sauce, crabmeat rarebit, mussels mariniere and enchiladas.

Many of the luncheon salads also are available as dinner entrees, and the homemade sweet and sour bacon, lemon parmesan and tomato-pesto dressings are outstanding.

The accent is on seafood among dinner entrees ($8.95 to $12.95). Swordfish grilled over applewood, seafood Florentine, cioppino, shrimp with feta cheese, and poached salmon with avocado butter are popular choices.

For appetizers, the smoked fish sampler with the local Ducktrap River Trout Farm smoked salmon, mussels and trout appeals, and all kinds of shellfish are available at the raw bar.

Lunch daily, 11:30 to 2:30; dinner, 5 to 10.

Walker's Harvest, 69 Elm St., Camden. (207) 236-4823.

A bit away from the mainstream is this attractive new restaurant with large downstairs bar, a contemporary upstairs dining room with interesting art and crisp blue and white napkins and mats, and a small rear outdoor deck sporting white tables shaded by yellow and white umbrellas.

Even without a view, we found the deck a pleasant spot for lunch: a special of monkfish in a simple butter sauce with homemade coleslaw and garnish of cantaloupe, and a not-so-special crab salad in a wooden tomato on a bed of lettuce. Peach trifle was a fine dessert.

Dinner entrees run from $7.25 for stir-fried vegetables to $12.25 for something called, we know not why, "the kiwi's choice," medallions of

Outdoor dining is popular at the Waterfront Restaurant.

veal in a creamy mustard and orange sauce. The menu also includes chicken marsala, chicken sauteed with vermouth and ginger and topped with a shrimp, and a basket of fresh seafood fried in beer batter. Clam puffs with sour cream dip are most novel among appetizers, and "chowdah" is $1.95 a cup.

Lunch daily, 11:30 to 2; dinner, 6 to 9.

Blueberry Puffin, Public Landing, Camden. (207) 236-9660.

The sign says "No Puffin, Please" at this gourmet foods shop par excellence, which has four tables outside for enjoying the bounty prepared within.

Croissants, blueberry muffins and a souffle or egg baked in cheese are among breakfast offerings, served from 10 to noon. Beautiful salads, interesting sandwiches and fanciful desserts are available all day. A delectable fruit salad with brie and French bread is $3.50, and box lunches can be ordered to go. Open daily in season.

Round Top and Galley Takeout, Bay View Street, Camden.

Twenty-four flavors of ice cream are available at this old-fashioned ice cream counter and take-out restaurant, which has a few tables on the wharf.

A lobster roll is $4.95 (in a box with french fries, $5.45) and a hot dog, 95 cents. But it's the ice cream that's the main attraction: everything from bubblegum, ginger and cappuccino to rum raisin and Brand X (vanilla with M&Ms) available in cones (75 cents to $1.35), frappes and sherbet freezes.

Diversions

Water pursuits. Any number of boat cruises on Penobscot Bay leave from the Camden landing, where there are benches for good viewing of the passing boat parade. For a longer cruise or ferry rides to the islands, go to Lincolnville Beach or Rockland (a favorite excursion is the ferry trip to Islesboro for lunch at the Islesboro Inn). The Lincolnville Beach is popular for swimming; a more secluded, picturesque setting is the little-known Laite Memorial Beach with treed lawns sloping down to the water, a small beach, picnic tables and old-fashioned fireplaces off Bay View Street.

Inland pursuits. Some of the East Coast's most scenic hiking is available on trails in Camden Hills State Park. Mount Megunticook is the highest of the three mountains that make up the park and the second highest point on the Eastern Seaboard. If you're not up to hiking, be sure to drive the toll road up Mount Battie, an easy one-mile ride and the view is worth the $1 toll. A scenic drive is out Route 52 to Megunticook Lake, an island-studded lake that emerged eerily from the clouds the first foggy afternoon we saw it. A walking tour of Camden and a bicycle or car tour of Camden and adjacent Rockport are available through the Camden-Rockport Historical Society.

Cultural pursuits. Founded in 1978, the **Camden Shakespeare Company** gives three plays in repertory from June 21 to Sept. 1 in the natural, stone-tiered Bok Amphitheater behind the Camden Public Library. The sylvan setting adds much to matinee or evening performances of the likes of "Macbeth," "Much Ado About Nothing" and "The Glass Menagerie" (1985 season). Each play takes place on a different "stage" on each side of the 200 seats set up and taken down for each performance. The **Farnsworth Museum** in the center of Rockland ranks among the finer regional art museums in the nation. The collection focuses on American art from the 18th century to the present, with prized works by the Wyeth family. The **Farnsworth Homestead** next door, open for a fee, is considered one of the most beautiful Victorian houses in the country. Nearby in Rockland is the **Shore Village Museum,** locally called the lighthouse museum because of its intriguing collection of lighthouse and Coast Guard memorabilia.

Shopping pursuits. Camden is a mecca for sophisticated shopping, and all kinds of interesting specialty stores and boutiques pop up every year. Among our favorites: **The Smiling Cow,** a large and venerable gift shop with a myriad of Maine items, has a great view from its rear porch over a river that ripples down the rocks toward the harbor; you can take in the picturesque scene while sipping complimentary coffee or tea between shopping forays. **Unique 1** specializes in natural fiber sweaters, but also has pottery, baskets, gifts and even a wind socket with a moose on it. **Heather Harland** offers interesting kitchen items and cards. A large carved gull wearing a windjammer tie attracted us into the **Ducktrap Bay Trading Co.,** a gallery of wildlife from decoys to paintings. **The Admiral's Buttons** has preppy clothing and sailing attire. We bought a handmade Maine wooden bucket for use as a planter from **Once a Tree,** which also had great clocks, toys, bracelets and everything else made from wood. **Perspectives,** a cooperative gallery representing 14 "artisans in cahoots," is a highlight of the new Harbor Square Shops. **The Winemporium,** with excellent Maine food products including local goat cheese, Ducktrap River Trout Farm smoked fish and fine wines, is our favorite place in the Highland Mill Mall. Among traditional favorites are **Haskell & Corthell** and the **House of Logan,** both fine apparel stores, and **Margo Moore,** for distinctive clothing and gifts.

Rowantrees Pottery put Blue Hill on the map.

Blue Hill, Me.
Treasure of Tranquility

Between the chic of Camden and the bustle of Bar Harbor lies a largely unspoiled area jutting into East Penobscot Bay. Its focal point is the tranquil treasure known as Blue Hill.

So small that the unknowing tourist almost could miss it, the village lies between the 940-foot-high hill from which it takes its name and an inlet of Blue Hill Bay. A few roads and streets converge from different directions and, suddenly, here it is: Blue Hill, Maine, population 1,644.

This is the center of an area long known for fine handicrafts, especially pottery. Indeed, Rowantrees Pottery owner Sheila Varnum says it is the pottery which "put Blue Hill on the map." Founded 50 years ago, the pottery has inspired a number of smaller crafts ventures by craftspeople who cherish the simplicity of the area.

Not for water or resort pursuits do visitors come to Blue Hill. It's the kind of place where the sign over the pay phone warns, "this phone doesn't work the way you're used to. Dial your number, wait for the loud tone and after your party answers, deposit 20 cents." We managed to get through the second time around.

There are no town beaches nor marinas, no shopping emporiums to speak of, and only one motel. What there are, instead, are world-famous potteries and crafts cooperatives, a handful of fine inns and restaurants, rural byways that remain much the way they were a generation ago and invite aimless exploration, and a sense of serenity that draws the knowing few back time after time for the utter peace and quiet of it all.

Go, but don't tell too many other people about your find.

Arcady Down East is imposing brown-shingled Victorian mansion.

Inn Spots

Arcady Down East, South Street, Blue Hill 04614. (207) 374-5576.

An enormous, brown-shingled Victorian mansion on a hilltop south of town was converted into an elegant bed and breakfast inn in 1984 by Floridians Tommie and Andy Duncan, who dole out Southern hospitality in an atmosphere of turn-of-the-century splendor. One hundred years old and listed on the National Register, the structure offers on its main floor a library, a game room, a dining room and porches looking out onto the distant bay.

A lovely staircase from the foyer splits in two directions to the second-floor guest rooms. Of the eight rooms, three have private baths, two are semi-private and three share.

The Duncans have furnished the rooms with items collected from their travels: The Juan Carlos master suite has a kingsize bed, fireplace, lamps and rugs from Mexico and Spain; the Victoria and Albert rooms have twin beds, antique furniture and pretty quilts, and share a dear bathroom with original columns that look like wood but really are tin. Three rooms at the rear share a vast skylit bathroom containing what's said to be the oldest bathtub in Blue Hill.

Tommie Duncan serves continental breakfast plus — fresh juices, home-made breads like lemon bread, and perhaps a bacon quiche or sausage cheese balls — in the formal, dark-paneled dining room complete with needlepoint chairs, fireplace, piano and a knight in armor, or outside on the porch at tables fashioned from the bases of old sewing machines.

Doubles, $45 to $65. Open Memorial Day to mid-October.

Blue Hill Inn, Route 177, Blue Hill 04614. (207) 374-2844.

Its flag flying out front, this trim white Colonial inn with Wedgwood blue shutters — a landmark in the heart of Blue Hill for nearly 150 years

— has been considerably spiffed up since Rita and Ted Boytos of Connecticut assumed ownership in 1984. Plush carpeting, modernized bathrooms and new wallpaper eliminate the slightly rundown atmosphere we experienced when we stayed here in 1982.

All 10 guest rooms have private baths and are furnished with comfortable, traditional pieces that Rita Boytos says reflect "a homey Down East style." The large front parlor is full of reading materials and has a television set.

Rita Boytos serves complete, one-entree dinners by reservation (if the reservation numbers are sufficient). The meal was cream of celery soup, spinach salad, popovers, broiled halibut with cauliflower and carrots, and French silk pie for $12 the night we visited. She usually puts out pate or cheese and crackers for the BYOB cocktail hour in the front parlor.

Guests order breakfast a la carte ($1.50 to $3.50) in the refurbished dining room with maple tables, blue and white wallpaper and dusty rose carpet, or on the rear pine-paneled porch with frilly blue curtains.

Doubles, $48.

Altenhofen House, Peters Point, Blue Hill 04614. (207) 374-2116.

Looking somewhat like a Southern plantation house, this white pillared and red brick structure commands a hilltop location on its own peninsula just outside Blue Hill and is surrounded by water on three sides. German owners Brigitte and Peter Altenhofen have restored the 1815 house with furnishings from the 19th century.

The six guest rooms, all with private baths, are named for the New England states. Three have fireplaces, the Massachusetts is especially spacious, and the Maine is a three-room suite suitable for four.

The Altenhofens' horses, stabled in a rear barn, are available for rides. Peter, a Lufthansa pilot, takes guests up in his seaplane anchored out front. You can swim in a small pool or watch television in the cozy parlor.

A full breakfast includes eggs in various styles. Homemade pastries and tea or coffee are served in the late afternoon.

Doubles, $70 to $180 (for a three-room suite); three-night minimum in July and August.

Surry Inn, Route 172, Box 25, Surry 04684. (207) 667-5091.

The lawns outside this out-of-the-way inn atop a hill about eight miles northeast of Blue Hill slope down to Contention Cove, which has "the warmest ocean water in Maine," according to Sarah Krinsky, innkeeper with her husband Peter. They restored the sprawling 1834 house in 1982 after stints at the Blue Hill Inn and the Barrows House in Dorset, Vt.

Sarah did the stenciling in the unusually pretty public sitting rooms and eight guest rooms (six with private baths), most of which have beautiful old quilts, and antique furnishings collected by Peter. A stenciled tree covers a pipe in one bedroom; another has its own private staircase. A very large porch alongside is a great place to relax and gaze at the cove.

In 1984, Peter constructed five more modern rooms, all with private baths, in an outbuilding behind the inn.

Full breakfasts include eggs any style, French toast or pancakes, and the bran muffins with raspberry jam are memorable. Excellent dinners from a limited, changing menu are served in the attractive dining room (see below).

Doubles, $42 to $48.

The Pilgrim's Inn, Deer Isle 04627. (207) 348-6615.

Another young couple, Jean and Dud Hendrick, run this handsome Colonial inn south of Blue Hill in Deer Isle. The striking, dark red 1793 house is on a spit of land with harbor in front and mill pond in back.

Listed on the National Register of Historic Places, the inn exudes an aura of history, from its pumpkin pine wide-paneled floors to its formal Victorian parlor.

Jean Hendrick has redecorated the rooms in sprightly Laura Ashley style; oriental rugs and quilts lend elegance to the prevailing simplicity. Each of the 11 guest rooms has a wood stove and six have private baths.

Dud Hendrick, a former Dartmouth College lacrosse coach, tends to an extensive herb and vegetable garden behind the inn during the day; at night he tends bar in the paneled tap room, serving drinks to guests (he even made a fresh raspberry daiquiri for one when we were there), who gather at 6 o'clock in the comfortable downstairs common room for abundant and delicious hor d'oeuvres.

The Pilgrim's Inn at Deer Isle.

A single-entree, prix-fixe dinner is served at 7 in the charming dining room (a former goat barn), simply decorated with farm utensils and quilts on the walls, mismatched chairs, tables with fresh flowers and dark-green overcloths, and 10 outside doors that open to let in the breeze.

If there is room, the public is welcome by reservation for dinner ($17.50, prix-fixe). We'll never forget a Sunday night dinner: Jean Hendrick's salad with goat cheese, homemade peasant bread, her heavenly paella topped with nasturtiums (such a pretty dish it should have been photographed for House Beautiful) or her sensational raspberry chocolate pie on a shortbread crust. Beef Wellington is served Saturday night, pork with fruit on Thursday and the bay's bounty on Friday. Wines are exceedingly inexpensive.

Homemade granola, scones, fresh melon and omelets are featured at breakfast.

The inn has several bicycles for guests' use; the lawns sloping down to the mill pond in back are great for lounging. The Hendricks do not allow smoking in bedrooms or the dining room.

Doubles, $110 to $130, MAP only. Three-night minimum in August. Closed November to mid-May.

The Manor, Battle Avenue, Box 276, Castine 04421. (207) 326-4861.

Due west of Blue Hill via roundabout roads lies Castine, the most sophisticated resort town in the East Penobscot Bay region, and the Manor. A dramatic summer cottage designed in 1895 by Mead, McKim and White for the commodore of the New York Yacht Club, this hilltop inn overlooking the water was condemned and about to be torn down when Paul Brouillard saved it for restoration purposes.

He and his wife Sara, who grew up in the house while her parents ran it as an inn, have done a fine job with renovations, which are still in progress. Some of the 14 large rooms and suites have a view of Castine's harbor. One suite has a huge brass bed, purple furniture and many window seats.

We stayed in a suite across from the main entrance (connected to the main house by an archway). The large bedroom is in what had been the billiard room with side porch beyond. The dark, fireplaced living room in the old hunting room would have been more inviting in winter than on a sunny July day.

Front porches in the main building have been glassed-in to produce a striking marble and mahogany Oyster Bar, in which cocktails, wines and hors d'oeuvres are served. The small dining room was redecorated in 1985 and is the setting for some inventive dinners (see below).

Guests are served a substantial continental breakfast in the dining room or outside on the front porch. Sara decorates the items on the buffet — brie and apple slices with tiny violets, fresh fruits with nasturtiums — and offers three kinds of pastries or lemon loaf. In season, she serves peaches picked from a friend's tree.

Doubles, $45 to $55; suites with sitting area, $65 to $85.

Dining Spots

Firepond, Main Street, Blue Hill. (207) 374-2135.

It's hard to imagine a more enchanting setting than the dining porch beside the stream at Firepond. The screened porch, which wraps around the small bar and interior dining room, is the place to be on a summer evening, its garden-type glass tables topped by woven mats and lit by candles, the sounds of water rippling below and spotlights illuminating the gleaming rocks. It's almost magical, and usually must be booked well in advance.

The food is almost magical as well. We like to start with the selection of pates ($4.50) — country pork, chicken liver and vegetable on one visit — with croutons, cornichons, mustard and cumberland sauce. Other recent choices included gallantine of pheasant, timbale of salmon and scallops and ravioli primina, and hot or cold soups (cream of red bell pepper and gazpacho the last time we were there).

Entrees range from $9.75 for a sensational chicken with walnuts, plum sauce and ginger to $14.75 for tournedos Dijonnaise. On various visits, we've enjoyed a fine salmon with hollandaise sauce, an interesting dish of lamb, spinach and feta cheese baked in puff pastry, duckling roasted with ginger and lime glaze, and fettuccine with mussels and pesto. Rice pilaf and crisp vegetables accompany, as do a variety of breads like Swedish rye, pumpkin and dill herb.

Desserts are few but select, among them a silken praline cheesecake, grand marnier chocolate mousse and ginger ice cream.

Austrian owners John and Beth Hikade have put together a hefty wine list showing labels, ranging from good values to expensive vintages.

Dinner nightly, 5 to 9:30, Memorial Day to Columbus Day.

Porch dining beside the brook at Fire Pond.

Jonathan's, Main Street, Blue Hill. (207) 374-5226.

A rear addition in 1985 doubled the size of this cheery, informal spot where some creative fare is turned out by Jonathan Chase. In contrast with the front's somewhat close and intimate quarters, the new section with bar, bow windows and pitched ceiling is airy and open.

Interesting specials supplement the printed menu. An appetizer of smoked Atlantic salmon from the nearby Ducktrap River Trout Farm was served with Bremner wafers, carrot slices and onions.

Among dinner entrees ($8.75 to $13.50), we enjoyed a special of scallops nicely sauteed with mint and tomatoes, and shrimp flamed in ouzo served on linguini. A tasty Greek lemon soup and a fish provencale soup with cumin, included in the price of the entree and served in clear glass bowls, preceded. A chocolate cointreau mousse and frangelico cheesecake are among the worthy endings. The wine list is exceptional and reasonably priced.

Lunch daily, 11 to 2:30; dinner, 5 to 9:30.

Surry Inn, Route 172, Surry. (207) 667-5091.

Dinner in a simple nouvelle style attracts patrons to this handsome dining room with its black-beamed ceiling, bentwood chairs, pale pink cloths on well-spaced tables and a view of Contention Cove.

Complete dinners range from $11 to $15, depending on choice of entree — the list of six or seven is printed daily.

On a typical night, you might begin with a zippy cheese spread on wheat thins served with drinks, then a choice of soups (gazpacho, cream of summer vegetable or sweet and sour cabbage at our visit), a plain green salad and homemade French bread. We had a fantastic shrimp Sambucca, eight huge shrimp in a spicy tomato sauce, and fresh halibut broiled with sour cream and herbs. Other choices included veal with mustard cream sauce, medallions of pork, Viennese chicken, a garlicky scallops Nicoise, and crabmeat with almonds and cream.

The strawberry Bavarian and a rich chocolate grand marnier mousse were exceptional desserts, and we'd gladly return in August to try the inn's most special dessert, frozen lemon mousse with fresh blueberries and whipped cream. The wine list is small but choice.

Dinner nightly except Tuesday, 5:30 to 9.

The Manor, Battle Avenue, Castine. (207) 326-4861.

Trained as a chef in France, innkeeper Paul Brouillard serves acclaimed dinners at the Manor, when he's not down at the Castine harbor overseeing **Dennett's Wharf,** a busy and most casual (long picnic tables) seafood restauraunt which he also owns, with Maine's longest oyster bar and a deck over the water.

The Manor's dinner menu changes daily. A typical spring dinner began with smoked eel with salmon roe, terrine of rabbit with game sauce, poached Belon oysters with periwinkle sauce, and wild mushrooms in puff pastry (on some nights, Paul will make sushi). The soups were shrimp bisque with blue shrimp and caviar or partridge consomme en croute. Entrees ($12 to $17.50) that night were duck breasts in armagnac, roast saddle of veal with porcini mushrooms, roast pheasant with champagne and truffles, rack of lamb with pommery mint sauce, and lobster basilique with steamed shellfish.

Whew! Until Paul acquired a pastry and sauce chef to assist, it was little wonder that the dinner schedule tended to be erratic.

Dinner, nightly 5 to 9. Reservations advised.

Sarah's Shoppe, Main Street, Blue Hill.

Named for its owner's granddaughter who was born just before he opened it in 1980, this ice cream parlor and cafe with screened porch and beer-wine license is popular with locals for breakfast, lunch and dinner.

Blueberry pancakes, a ham and cheese omelet with generous amounts of sliced ham, and Sarah's egg McMuffin are among breakfast choices in the $3 to $4 range. Country-style dinners are priced from $3.95 to $8.95, and a lobster dinner with choice of salad and potato is $10.95. Among the homemade ice creams are Swiss almond, orange-pineapple, M&M and grapenut.

Open daily, 7 a.m. to 10 p.m., mid-May to October.

Blue Hill Lunch, Water Street, Blue Hill.

All the quiches, soups, breakfast pastries and desserts are made by Merle Bisberg at home and trucked to her small family restaurant with side porch behind the drug store.

Anadama bread is served with breakfasts; you can get a bagel with cream cheese and lox for $3.75. The fish chowder is renowned, and the fresh crabmeat roll ("with just a touch of mayonnaise — no fillers") is a bargain $3.75. A few daily specials supplement the sandwich and salad menu; for dessert, the deep-dish blueberry pie comes with real whipped cream.

Breakfast and lunch, Monday-Friday 7 to 2:30, Saturday breakfasts in summer, 7:30 to 11:30.

Diversions

Crafts. Pottery and handicrafts abound in Blue Hill and indeed, all across the East Penobscot Bay peninsula and onto Deer Isle and Stonington. The **Brooklin Crafts Cooperative** in Brooklin, the **Eastern Bay Cooperative Gallery** beside the water in Stonington and **North Country Textiles** in South Penobscot are within driving distance.

The world-famous **Haystack Mountain School of Crafts** at Sunshine on Deer Isle, which often has shows, is worth the drive simply for the breathtaking view from its unsurpassed setting on a steep, forested slope with stairs down to East Penobscot Bay. Visitors are welcome from Thursday to Sunday, 10 to 4.

Rowantrees Pottery, the institution inspired in 1934 by Adelaide Pearson through her friend Mahatma Gandhi, is still going strong in a rambling house and barn reached by a pretty brick path through gardens at the edge of Blue Hill. Inside, you may be able to see potters at work; veteran employees like Grace Lymburner in the upstairs shop might recall for you the days when as children they joined the story hours and pottery classes run by Miss Pearson and her protege, Laura Paddock. Sheila Varnum, who was associated with the founders since she was 3, has owned the pottery since 1976 and has continued its tradition. Named for the mountain ash trees above its green gate along Union Street and one of the few production potteries in the country, Rowantrees is especially known for its jam jar with a flat white lid covered with blueberries, as well as for unique glazes. Items are attractively displayed for sale. Summer hours: weekdays 7 to 5, Saturday 8:30 to 5, Sunday noon to 5.

Rackliffe Pottery at the other end of town is an offshoot of Rowantrees, Phil Rackliffe having worked there for 20 years. He and his family make all kinds of handsome and useful kitchenware in a work area next to their small shop on Route 172. The soup tureens with blueberry, strawberry or cranberry covers are especially nice.

Kneisel Hall Chamber Music Series. Concerts by well-known faculty members are given Wednesday evenings and Sunday afternoons from late June to early August in a rustic concert hall off upper Pleasant Street. The series is part of the summer session of the Kneisel Hall School of Music, founded by Dr. Franz Kneisel. Innkeepers say a summer tradition for many of their guests is to arrive on Wednesday and stay through Sunday, taking in two concerts, visiting the potteries and dining at Firepond.

Meadow House Herb Shop and Gardens, Old Cart Road off upper Union Street. A special treat are the gardens and herb shop run since 1971 by Rosanne and Joe Dombek. The yard outside their house is a veritable showplace of gardens that would be the envy of many a municipal park — and they do it all themselves. Strolling through 12 herb gardens, a rose garden, vegetable garden and gardens for cutting flowers is heaven for the amateur gardener; the more than 200 varieties of herbs plus many other plants are noted by types and dates hand-painted on small rocks. A grape arbor, mint, hops, woodruff, heather and elderberries are features of the Libation Garden, "which we planted as a lark," says Rosanne Dombek. A path through woods with animal statuary and rustic bench emerges into the gray-green garden. While her husband tends to the gardens, she minds

Stairs lead to ocean from Haystack Mountain School of Crafts.

the shop and over the winter makes most of the wreaths, hot pads, sachet bags and such for sale. Open Tuesday-Saturday in season, daily in August.

Blue Hill Farmer's Market, Route 172 at the Blue Hill Fairgrounds. Each Saturday in July and August from 9 to 11:30 a.m., local farmers and artisans gather here for a real downhome event. Horse-drawn wagons give the youngsters hayrides, while residents and visitors mix through a small but interesting display of everything from local produce to goat's cheese, jellies, handmade gifts, lamb's wool and patterned ski sweaters.

Shopping. Other than the aforementioned places, the best shopping is in Castine. One of the more unusual stores we've found is that of **The Water Witch** on Main Street in Castine. Tall, dark and striking Jean de Raat, the water witch herself, sells in her small shop a variety of beautiful clothes made of cotton Dutch wax batiks and Java prints, as well as British Viyellas. Wrap skirts, long and short dresses, quilted jackets, purses, place-mats, pillows, even tea cozies are made from these vibrant prints. At the foot of Main Street is **Treworgy's,** a neat ship's chandlery that is a local institution with gifts from around the world.

Extra-Special

Palmer Day III Excursions, Stonington (207) 367-2207. Capt. Reginald Greenlaw conducts daily cruises on his 45-passenger boat in the waters off Stonington. He is as entertaining as his excursion, a 16-mile trip that goes near Isle au Haut, offering closeup views of untold varieties of birds, deer and a small island covered with seals, one of which jumps up beside the boat for the raw fish the captain brings along. It's the most interesting nature cruise we've taken. Daily, July 4 to Sept. 1, 2 p.m.; adults $7, children under 10, $4; reservations advised.

Mount Desert Island, Me.
The Other Harbors

Mount Desert Island has long held a special appeal, first as a summer resort for society and later as the site of a national park beloved by campers and naturalists.

Its focus for us, as well as for increasing numbers of others, has always been Bar Harbor and the eastern part of Acadia National Park. Since our first vacation there 25 years ago, we've witnessed the changes — for better and worse — as tourism impacted relentlessly, and still Bar Harbor remains dear to our hearts.

Be advised, however, that there are other harbors and another side to Mount Desert Island. The other side is the quieter side, one which its devotees call "the right side" of this fabulously varied island.

Even the right side is wonderfully diverse. Northeast Harbor and Southwest Harbor are barely two miles across Somes Sound from each other, but far apart in spirit and character.

Northeast Harbor is the yachting harbor, a haven for Rockefellers and some of the world's great boats, a moneyed place where yachting is the seasonal preoccupation. Southwest Harbor is the working harbor, where fishing and boat-building are the year-round occupation. Here and in Bass Harbor, the native flavor of coastal Maine remains.

Some of the choice parts of Acadia National Park are close at hand: Seawall, Wonderland, Beech Mountain, Echo Lake and Eagle Cliff. Thuya and Asticou gardens are treats, and we know of few better views than those up and down Somes Sound, the only natural fjord in North America.

For a different perspective than most visitors get of Mount Desert, try the other harbors on the "right side."

Inn Spots

Asticou Inn, Route 3, Northeast Harbor 04662. (207) 276-3344.

Majestically situated at the head of Northeast Harbor on a hillside where the mountains slope to the sea, Asticou has been a bastion of elegance since 1883.

The fireplace in the lobby is always ablaze — "to take the chill off foggy mornings or late afternoons," our friendly guide informed. The lobby with its huge oriental rug and wing chairs gives way to a parlor decorated in blues, beiges and a cheery rust. Beyond is a bright and breezy cocktail lounge with sliding doors onto the outdoor deck, a great place from which to view the goings-on in the harbor amid white furniture, yellow umbrellas and petunias in planters. The enclosed each porch is used for games and television viewing. The spacious dining room (see below) serves three meals a day and a Thursday evening buffet that draws people from all over the island.

A carpeted staircase or an 85-year-old Otis elevator lead to 46 guest rooms on the second and third floors. Rooms vary from those with twin beds, rose carpeting and frilly white curtains framing views onto the harbor to a suite with a sofa, two peach chintz chairs and a desk in a sitting room plus two twins in the bedroom. Four have private balconies viewing the water. Seventeen more rooms are available in the Cranberry

Rear deck and grounds of Asticou Inn overlook Northeast Harbor.

Lodge, Bird Bank and Blue Spruce guest houses and the Topsider cottages. The most striking are the contemporary, circular Topsiders with decks, full-length windows, attractive parlors and kitchenettes.

The perfectly landscaped grounds offer a swimming pool, tennis, gardens and, all the while, changing vistas of the harbor. Guests have privileges at the Northeast Harbor Golf Club.

Rates are MAP in season (June 22 to Sept. 15), EP with continental breakfast in the off-season when only the guest houses and cottages are open.

Doubles, $122 to $132, MAP; off-season, $46 to $68, EP. Two-night minimum in season. Open May-October.

The Claremont, Clark Point Road, Southwest Harbor 04679. (207) 244-5036.

The other grand dowager of Mount Desert, the Claremont marked its 100th anniversary in 1984 (a year later than the Asticou, but it's the island's oldest continuously operating inn, with only three owners in its first century).

Entered in the National Register of Historic Places in 1978 as a reminder of the "prosperous, relaxed and seasonal way of life" of Maine's early summer resort era, the original light yellow structure has been considerably spiffed up of late and the name has been shortened from the Claremont Hotel and Cottages. But the inn's wrap-around veranda and the heavy white wood slant-back chairs lined up side by side on the rear lawn still provide a relaxing view of Somes Sound, and croquet is the sport of note, the annual Claremont Croquet Classic recognized as the home of nine wicket croquet.

The main inn building contains lobby and living rooms full of wicker and sofas, a handsome dining room addition (see below) and 21 guest

173

rooms (singles, doubles and suites) on the second and third floors, all with private baths. Also available for longer stays are eight cottages (with living rooms, fireplaces and decks) and two guest houses (the Phillips with a massive fieldstone fireplace in the parlor is particularly inviting).

Besides croquet, boating and tennis are offered here, and the hardy can swim off the dock in chilly Somes Sound. The Boathouse is a fine spot for a light lunch or cocktails.

Doubles, $100 to $114, MAP. Cottages and rooms in Clark guest house available EP or MAP. Inn open mid-June to mid-September, cottages and guest houses mid-May to mid-October.

Harbourside Inn, Harbourside Road (Route 198), Northeast Harbor 04662. (207) 276-3272.

Built in 1888 in the style of the Seal Harbor Club, this 18-room shingled hilltop mansion is run very much their way by the Sweet family (take it or leave it, and most people take it). "We're old-fashioned and intend to keep it that way," Mrs. Sweet explains. She and her husband, who formerly managed the Jordan Pond House, acquired the mansion in 1977 from a woman who would sell only to Maine residents who would maintain the heritage.

The heritage indeed remains, from the nasturtiums nurtured from the original seeds still brightening the entry circle to the original carpets from China, somewhat worn but too prized to be discarded. Guests gather in a pleasant parlor with wing chairs in shades of blue or on the front sunporch, all done up with bright cushions and curtains in appropriate Northeast Harbor colors, preppy pink and green.

Nine guest rooms on the first and second floors have working fireplaces, and three have their own porches. All 14 have private baths and are furnished in 19th century style. "We had great fun with the wallpapers," Mrs. Sweet said; one bathroom's paper has small red hearts with big hearts on the borders, and a bedroom is papered with irises. The honeymoon suite has kingsize bed and a porch with cathedral ceiling, wicker rockers and a lounger. A first-floor suite offers a sitting room with comfortable chairs grouped in front of the fireplace and a kitchenette in an alcove, a a room with a kingsize bed, and an old-fashioned tub in the bathroom.

A complimentary breakfast of homemade blueberry muffins and coffee or tea is served on the sun porch or in the office each morning.

Lest the inn's name mislead, the Sweets stress that the once-sweeping view of the harbor from their hilltop is now obstructed by a century's growth of trees.

Doubles, $50 to $80; suites, $90 to $150. Open June-September.

Grey Rock Inn, Harbourside Road, Northeast Harbor 04662. (207) 276-9360.

Remarkable gardens and a prolific hanging begonia at the door greet visitors to this little-known inn, said to have been a gathering place for socialite Northeast Harbor families after it was built in the 1890s as a private residence.

Inside the inviting large fieldstone and shingled mansion with yellow trim is a veritable showcase for British innkeeper Janet Millet's decorating tastes: an array of wicker like you've never seen, fans and paintings from the

Lush plantings and hanging begonia grace entrance to Grey Rock Inn.

Orient, fringed lamps, masses of exotic flowers — far too much and too overwhelming to describe, particularly since Janet shunned publicity, saying she had all the business she wanted.

People who stay at Grey Rock must like eclectic elegance, for that's what they get. The two fireplaces in the living room and parlor are kept aglow, even in mid-summer, because the innkeeper finds her guests want it that way. Wicker serves as furniture and art, from table lamps to loveseats, from desk to plant stand.

The 12 guest rooms are equally exotic. The huge corner room with canopied four-poster bed, oriental screen and private balcony could not be more romantic. Some of the rooms have fireplaces, and all have views of the trees or gardens atop this wooded hilltop set high above and back from the road.

Janet serves an exemplary continental breakfast, including all kinds of fresh fruit, baked goods and what she states is "a good cup of coffee for a British lady."

Doubles, $85 to $110. Open spring through October.

The Moorings, Shore Road, Southwest Harbor 04679. (207) 244-5523 or 244-3210.

Betty and Leslie King have run this delightfully informal, old-fashioned place for 25 years in a location they call the "Little Norway of America" and one we find the most appealing on the island, smack on the shore at the start of Somes Sound in Manset.

The rambling white house with dark shutters in the Maine style contains nine guest rooms, all with private baths. There also are five motel units (one with two exposures billed as having "probably the finest view on the coast") and six units in four cottages. The Kings have upgraded their rooms with cheery new wallpapers and furnishings, and the five on the inn's second floor now sport delightful decks and balconies to take advantage of the view.

We dubbed our corner bedroom the Agatha Christie Room because several of her paperbacks were on the bureau (Betty makes the rounds of all the lawn sales to pick up the books, her son volunteered). It's the only one without a water view but, as with the other rooms, the towels were large and fluffy, the beds had colorfully patterned sheets, and a candle was in a ceramic holder beside the bed.

The fireplace glows on cool mornings in the living room, which has a television set in a windowed alcove and enough books and magazines to start a library. The coffee pot is kept filled all day in the adjacent office, where complimentary orange juice and donuts are served every morning.

Outside, two rowboats filled with geraniums brighten the path to the front door. In back are canoes, bicycles and a stony shoreline for swimming, beachcombing and clamming. The Kings provide charcoal for the grills beside the shore, a memorable spot to barbecue a steak for dinner as you watch the sun set.

Doubles, $40 to $45 (two small singles, $30); motel units, $40; cottages, $50 to $60.

Lindenwood Inn, Clark Point Road, Box 1328, Southwest Harbor 04679. (207) 244-5335.

Towering linden trees shade this turn-of-the-century sea captain's home converted into a stylish bed and breakfast inn in 1984 by Don Johnson. The front porches on both the first and second floors have nice old rocking chairs and the entry parlor and living room are decorated with distinction.

Upstairs are six guest rooms, four with private baths and two sharing. One room has rattan furniture and a peacock chair, the original bathtub and a view of the harbor; another has a bed covered with a comforter, chairs in an olive color and an oriental rug. The smallest room is quite spiffy in cane and chrome.

Behind the house is a cottage with a newly added deck, a super water view through the front picture windows of the living room, a small kitchen and two bedrooms, offered for $75 a night.

Don serves a full breakfast in the cheery, flower-filled dining room warmed by a fireplace on cool mornings. Among his specialties are baked grapefruit, blueberry pancakes, French toast, and spinach and cheddar quiche.

Doubles, $35 to $50, two-night minimum mid-June through Labor Day; lower rates rest of year.

Bass Harbor Inn, Shore Road, Bass Harbor 04653. (207) 244-5157 or 244-7432.

This striking structure with high peaked roofs occupying a treeless site would seem more at home in Mendocino than in what the manager says is the area's oldest fishing village, "the place where the fishing action is." It looks and smells new, but actually only the interior of an 1832 house was gutted and restored in 1985 into a sleek bed and breakfast inn by Kim Strauss and Carl Taplin.

Nine modern rooms with white walls and shared or half baths are nicely decorated with hooked and throw rugs, colorful quilts, vases of wildflowers and paintings collected in his world travels by the grandfather of one of the owners. One room with a half bath retains the original brick fireplace;

the front corner room opens onto a small deck. The third-floor suite with cathedral ceiling sleeps six, has a kitchenette and a bathroom with a triangular mirror, available for $80 a night.

A continental breakfast of muffins and fruits is served in the office-common room. The innkeepers sometimes take guests out on their boat to Gott's Island.

Doubles, $35 to $45; open June-November.

Dining Spots

The Claremont, Clark Point Road, Southwest Harbor. (207) 244-5036.
The new dining room addition with views on three sides, excellent service and the food of longtime chef Billie McIntire make this popular with residents on the quiet side of the island.

They like to have drinks at the boathouse (which now also serves sandwiches and salads for lunch) and then head into the high-ceilinged dining room, a picture of elegance with fancy china on white over pink linens, pink napkins, moss green carpet and pink and green wallpaper. It's almost as pretty as the view across the lawns onto scenic Somes Sound.

The appetizer du jour is often the best choice on the limited menu; otherwise, go for the iced Maine crabmeat cocktail ($3.95). Native crabmeat also heads the dinner entrees, baked in a ramekin with artichoke hearts, sherry sauce and gruyere cheese. Other entrees ($10.95 to $13.95) include baked shrimp stuffed with scallops or crabmeat, coquilles St. Jacques duglere, shrimp and sole baked in parchment, chicken baked with a spiced fruit glaze and three steak dishes.

The produce comes from the inn's gardens and the baked goods from its bakery. The chef's homemade desserts include cheesecake, a daily special and either ice cream or lemon ice with Claremont cookies.

Lunch at the boathouse, noon to 2, mid-July through August; dinner, 6 to 9, late June through Labor Day, jackets required. Cocktails at the boathouse, 5 to 9. No credit cards.

Asticou Inn, Northeast Harbor. (207) 276-3344.
The $29 buffet every Thursday night draws people by the hundreds — up to 300 people in mid-August — to the posh dining room of the Asticou Inn. Thursday happens to be maid's night off hereabouts, so summer residents join inn guests for the extravagant spread followed by live music and an evening of socializing.

The pillared dining room is decorated with handpainted murals of trees and flowers on the deep yellow walls, brass chandelier, small oriental rugs, lovely flowered china and tiny plants in clay pots. Most coveted seating is in the adjacent enclosed porch, with great views through picture windows onto the harbor beyond.

Dinners are $19.50 prix-fixe, the mimeographed typewritten menu changing daily. A typical dinner offers eight entrees from broiled native scallops in casserole with tartar sauce, fried butterfly fantail shrimp with cocktail sauce or prime ribs to a choice of omelets, cold sliced meats and cheeses with potato salad or spaghetti with meatballs. Meals begin with chilled juices, assorted relishes and breads and perhaps smoked salmon with cream cheese, continue with tossed or hearts of palm salads, and finish with desserts like frozen chocolate mousse, creme de menthe parfait, macaroons or a cheese tray.

Lunch, 12:30 to 2; dinner, 7 to 8:30, mid-June to mid-September. Jackets required at dinner.

Clark Point Cafe, Clark Point Road, Southwest Harbor. (207) 244-5816. Right up against the street in "downtown" Southwest Harbor, this storefront cafe opened in 1985 and was just what the area needed: something between the formality of the aforementioned inns and the rustic seafood houses all around.

Proprietors Carole and Vance O'Donnell, who also own the Act II deli on Main Street and the Parkview Inn at Otter Creek, serve breakfast, lunch and dinner in this restaurant divided into two sections with pine paneling, a small bar, and tables sporting yellow mats and white napkins.

The extensive dinner menu ranges widely: entrees like chicken fettuccine, teriyaki, "almost" Oscar and cordon bleu, beef from tenderloin tips to steak Diane, seafood from broiled swordfish to shrimp and-or scallops scampi, pleasantly priced from $7.95 to $11.95. Among appetizers, a seafood cocktail for two with shrimp, lobster and crab, on the other hand, is a rather staggering $19.95, and half a dozen oysters on the half shell go for $7.50.

The same appetizers are available at lunch, along with sandwiches, salads, pastas and such, $2.75 to $7.95 (for tuna, shrimp and crab salad). Best bargain is the three-egg omelet du jour, $2.95 at lunch or breakfast.

Breakfast daily, 7 to 10:30; lunch, 11:30 to 3; dinner, 5 to 10; May-October.

The Moorings, Shore Road, Manset. (207) 244-7070. New owners Susan and Peter Boisvert have expanded the Moorings restaurant, the old deck now an enclosed addition to the spacious dining room and a large new deck jutting over the water. As is the case with the inn of the same name next door, we know of no better up-close water view than this, looking up Somes Sound from water level with Acadia's mountains rising in the background.

Seafood is featured on the menu, which runs the gamut from steak to pork chops ($7.95 to $14.95). Nightly specials when we last visited were broiled salmon, swordfish and shrimp scampi. The Moorings feast for $19.95 includes a 50-item salad bar, chowder, steamers, lobster and apple pie.

A lobster roll is $7.95 at lunch, and tourists pour in for the early lobster bake (lobster, steamers, mussels, corn on the cob, salad bar and berry pie for $12.95), served at 1 and 4 p.m. on the deck or inside.

The Moorings also offers a basic to fancy breakfast menu and even — shades of the Jordan Pond House — English tea, served with cinnamon toast or popovers from 2 to 4 for $2.95.

Breakfast, lunch and dinner daily in season.

Tea on the lawn is a tradition at the Jordan Pond House.

Jordan Pond House, Park Loop Road, Acadia National Park. (207) 276-3316.

Rebuilt following a disastrous fire in 1980, the new Jordan Pond House is a large, strikingly contemporary complex with cathedral ceilings, two levels, outdoor decks, huge windows and one of the good Acadia Gift Shops. The majestic setting remains the same, with lawns sloping down to Jordan Pond and mountains rising beyond.

Lobster stew ($8) or soup and a Jordan Pond popover served with strawberry preserves and butter ($6) are popular luncheon items. Dinners get more formal, featuring steaks and lobster (boiled, stuffed, saute, stew and salad) as well as baked chicken and sole, priced from $8.95 to $18. The fresh fruit ice creams are made on the premises from original recipes dating back to the late 19th century.

Even if you don't eat here, do stop for tea on the lawn, an island tradition. You sit on old-fashioned chairs and sip tea or drinks with popovers ($2 each).

Lunch, 11:30 to 2:30; tea, 2:30 to 5:30; dinner, 6:30 to 9:30, June-October.

Seafood Ketch, On the Harbor, Bass Harbor. (207) 244-7463.

"Please, no fishing from the dining room windows or deck," begs the sign at this shanty beside the harbor. Here is the real thing, a delightful, family-style place run by Ed and Eileen Branch with lots of fresh seafood and everything homemade, down to the loaf of crusty French bread served with dinner. Except for twin club steaks for $10.95, nothing on the extensive menu is over $9.95, including the baked lobster-seafood casserole, the recipe for which Ed is proud to have been asked to share with Gourmet magazine. The day's catch is $6.95, the Maine scallops $8.95 and nightly specials might be steak au poivre, shrimp with julienned vegetables or veal medallions.

The menu also includes light or luncheon fare, $1.95 for a BLT to $5.95 for a lobster roll. Among desserts are Ed's secret mocha pie and, according to the menu, "the world's best carrot cake — Ed says so." The decor is simple, but fresh flowers grace the tables in both dining room and deck. There's a full liquor license.

179

These folks do have fun with their meals, as attested by their motto, "What foods these morsels be." The fun continues non-stop from 7 a.m. to 9:30 p.m. daily, May to November.

Popplestone, Harbor Drive, Northeast Harbor. (207) 276-3208.

Housed in a handsome contemporary wood structure, Popplestone capitalizes on its view of the busy yachting harbor through huge windows on two levels.

It's a great place for lunch, especially on a sunny day on the outdoor terrace. Lobster comes in a newburg crepe ($7.95), a lobster salad roll ($6.25) and a salad plate ($9.50), the last also available in combination with crabmeat. A cold shellfish plate with half a Maine lobster, crabmeat and shrimp is $13.95.

At night, seafood entrees start at $8.95 for poached haddock and go to $14.95 for the cold shellfish plate. You also can get chateaubriand or rack of lamb for two, and Maine's Ducktrap River Trout Farm smoked salmon as an appetizer ($4.50). Desserts choices change daily.

Lunch, 11:30 to 5; dinner, 5 to 9:30.

A sampling of other, more casual eating spots, particularly good for seafood or sea atmosphere:

Beal's Lobster Pier, Clark Point Road, Southwest Harbor. Beside the Coast Guard Station, Beal's offers lobsters to go as well as to eat at picnic tables on the working dock. The last time we visited, they were priced at $5.10 a pound boiled (boiling ends between 6:30 and 7:30). A lobster roll (all lobster meat with a dab of mayonnaise in a toasted hot dog bun, $4.75) makes a fine lunch, supplemented by great french fries and lemonade from the **Captain's Galley** next door (open 9 a.m. to sunset). For dessert, try the galley's blueberry cake or a butter pecan ice cream cone.

Abel's Lobster Pound, Route 198, Somes Sound. This Mount Desert institution has vastly changed since we started going there 25 years ago when everyone sat family-style at picnic tables under the pines above the shore and the lobsters were boiled in front of you. Now, the dining is inside a rustic restaurant serving an expanded menu and even cocktails, but you also can take out lobsters and clams from noon to 9.

Head of the Harbor, Route 102, Southwest Harbor. A lobster dinner was $8.95 and a fried clam dinner $6.95 when we stopped at this rustic indoor-outdoor restaurant which opened in 1984 on a hill above Somes Sound. You can eat on an outdoor deck or on a screened porch overlooking the water. Beer and wine are available. Open 11 a.m. to 10 p.m. daily, Memorial Day to Labor Day.

Diversions

Acadia National Park. The most famous sites are along Ocean Drive and the Park Loop Road out of Bar Harbor, but don't miss the park's other attractions on this side of the island. The Beech Mountain area offers Echo Lake, with a fine beach, changing rooms and fresh water far warmer than the ocean. Hike up Beech Cliff for a great view of the lake below (yes, you may hear your echo). Past Southwest Harbor and Manset are Seawall, created naturally by the sea, and the Wonderland and Ship's Harbor nature trails.

Somes Sound and Somesville. Follow Sargent Drive out of Northeast Harbor along the fjord-like Somes Sound for some of the island's most spectacular views (it's the closest thing we know of to the more remote areas around Lake Tahoe). At the head of the sound is Somesville, a classic New England village and a joy to behold: the whites of the houses brightened patriotically by geraniums, petunias and morning glories in flowerboxes that line the street. The entire town is listed on the National Register of Historic Places, and the **Mount Desert Historical Society** buildings chronicle the history of the island's earliest settlement. The Masonic Hall in Somesville is home of the **Acadia Repertory Theatre,** which stages a full summer season.

Boat cruises. Untold numbers of cruises — public, private and park-sponsored — leave from Northeast Harbor and Bass Harbor. You can take a naturalist tour to Baker Island, a lobster boat or a ferry ride to Swans Island or the Cranberry Islands, and the park's cruises are particularly informative. If you'd rather observe than ride, poke around one of the ten or more boat-building yards in Southwest Harbor.

Museums. Southwest Harbor is nationally known for its variety of birds (many consider it the warbler capital of the country), so fittingly this is the home of the **Wendall Gilley Museum,** a monument to the memory of one of the nation's outstanding bird carvers. Opened in 1981 in a solar-heated building, it shows birds and decoys, special exhibitions, and daily films and programs on woodcarving and natural history (admission is $2.50). Also in Southwest Harbor is the **Mount Desert Oceanarium,** a building full of sea life and lobster lore, with a touch tank, whale exhibit, fishing boats and more (adults, $3).

Shopping. The area's best shopping is in Northeast Harbor. **The Kimball Shop** is one of the snazziest gift shops we've seen, a pageant of bright colors and room after room of zippy clothes, pretty china, furniture, kitchenware and almost anything else that's in. Another nice gift shop is the **Shorebird.** The **Holmes Store** is the place for adult clothing, **Animal Crackers** for children's clothing, the **Northeast Harbor Store** for a rainbow of teen and sports apparel. **Provisions** market has an excellent deli and bakery, and the **Cask and Wedge** offers gourmet foods and wines.

Extra-Special

Asticou Terrace and Thuya Gardens, Route 3, Northeast Harbor.
You can drive up, but we recommend the 10-minute hike nearly straight up a scenic, well-maintained switchback path and stairs to the prized gardens above Northeast Harbor. A plaque relates that landscape architect Joseph H. Curtis left this "for the quiet recreation of the people of this town and their summer guests." Who would not enjoy the showy hilltop spread combining formal English flower beds with informal natural Japanese effects, some common and uncommon annuals plus hardy rhododendron and laurel that appear as a surprise so far north. As you might find on a private estate, which this once was, there are a gazebo, a free-form clear-water pond, and a shelter with pillowed seats and deck chairs for relaxing in the shade. Open daily, free.

Kingfield-Sugarloaf, Me.
Sophistication, Wilderness Style

You can't get much farther north and east in the United States and still be in the vicinity of civilization. That's one of the appeals of the Victorian town of Kingfield and its large northern neighbor, Sugarloaf USA.

This is rugged, backwoods, outdoors country, a place where moose-watching is a common pastime and where lumberjacks and logging trucks share trails and roads with cross-country skiers and jeeps topped with rafts and canoes. Maine's second highest mountain, Sugarloaf, is surrounded by 900 square miles of wilderness and lakes, a few settlements with names like West Carry Camp and Portage, the whitewater rapids of the Kennebec and Penobscot rivers, and beyond, Mount Katahdin, the Allagash and French Quebec.

Against this backdrop are two clusters of civilization — a sort of sophistication, wilderness style.

Kingfield (population 1,000) is a 19th-century mill town which gave birth to the inventive Stanley family of Stanley Steamer fame and where three mills still produce rolling pins, pepper mills and drum sticks. It also has three inns with restaurants of note.

Sixteen miles northwest is Sugarloaf USA, a rapidly emerging four-season resort area with snowfield skiing, a tough new wooded golf course designed by Robert Trent Jones Jr., a growing summer performing arts program and all the amenities of a self-contained resort village, including a new seven-story hotel. Sugarloaf's current expansion from a well-known but isolated ski area into what it calls "a mountain of things to do all year long" represents the largest investment ever in a resort in Maine.

A worthy counterpoint for the tasteful chic of the new Sugarloaf is Kingfield, which retains its Victorian look. A small band of restorationists have recreated period inns in which history resides and have saved the 1903 schoolhouse from the wrecker's ball to become the Stanley Museum.

Inn Spots

The Winter's Inn, Box 44, Kingfield 04947. (207) 265-5421.

A wealthy merchant named A.G. Winter, whose son Amos began the Sugarloaf development, and his inventor friends, the Stanley twins, built this Georgian Colonial Revival country mansion on a hilltop at the edge of Kingfield for his new bride from New York in 1898. The deep mustard gold structure with white trim and curved facade is listed on the National Register of Historic Places and open for tours, such is the mark of Michael Thom, architect turned innkeeper.

But rather than tour you'd have more fun staying, as we did during a skiing expedition to Sugarloaf, in one of the 10 elegantly furnished guest rooms, dining on excellent French fare in Le Papillon restaurant (see Dining Spots) and savoring the treasures of some extraordinary public rooms.

A velvet sofa in front of a grand piano is a focal point of the Grand Hall, with a lounge and bar off to one side and two dining rooms off the other. The main focal point, however, is the flowing Georgian oak staircase which ascends past a Palladian window at the midway landing to a com-

Winter's Inn is housed in landmark Victorian structure.

fortable sitting area with sofa, wood stove and chess set for the use of guests in the luxurious rooms on the second floor. Another sitting area serves the third floor.

A Canadian from Toronto, Michael Thom had admired the house for years on his way to Sugarloaf from Boston, where he worked as an architect. He stopped on impulse one day, soon acquired the structure, and set to work restoring it into an inn. When he uncovered the original Stanley blueprints, he realized the magnitude of his treasure. He and his old cat Balthazar share it with overnight guests and lend it for some of Kingfield's more gala parties.

Michael's skill as an architect, designer and collector is evident throughout, from the gladioli in oriental vases and the stuffed armadillo over the fireplace in the Grand Hall to the small bedrooms fashioned from attic-type crannies on the third floor. The five second-floor bedrooms, each smashingly decorated in vivid colors and Victorian furnishings, are sumptuous. One has an old curved iron bedstead; another is all in blues and purples with velvet chairs and sofa beside the window, a kingsize bed, a lamp with a base sculpted like a jade tree, and a sunny yellow bathroom. The four guest rooms on the third floor include a single and a suite converted from the bunkroom in which our family once stayed. The upstairs rooms share two baths.

The exterior facilities are as luxurious as the interior. Sunday brunch is served in season on the deck around the large swimming pool in the rear yard, looking up toward Sugarloaf. There's also a tennis court.

Doubles, $110 to $130, MAP.

The Herbert, Main Street, Box 67, Kingfield 04947. (207) 265-2000.

The handsome exterior of this three-story hotel, described in its history as located at "Main Street on the Corner," is grandly lit by spotlights at dusk — an inviting oasis in the wilderness on a dark evening. Built in 1918 by a Maine legislator and judge, it had been abandoned for several years and was "a mess" when chef Peter Freyer first saw it. But it was carefully restored and reopened in 1982 as an inn bearing the first name of its original owner, Herbert Wing.

Novel historic touches abound: the exposed sink on the dining room wall, just inside the entrance, where diners arriving by stagecoach could wash up before eating; the old Western Electric phones in each room, by which guests can call the front desk (when they work); the brass fixtures, light switches and outlet covers from the first electrified building in Kingfield.

A moose head stands guard over the marble fireplace in the large lobby, with much Victorian furniture and two plush sofas of deep plum velvet. Downstairs is the Woodworks, a vast brick bar and lounge full of video games and a pool table. A steam room with sauna and hot tub is popular with skiers.

The 32 guest rooms, including two two-room and one three-room suites, but mostly small doubles, are pleasantly furnished with double or twin beds, white bedspreads, and fresh wallpaper. Each has a private bath with steambath and sauna. The original glass windows above the doors in each room open to the hallway, letting light and noise in or out.

Doubles, $50, EP; $84, MAP.

Three Stanley Avenue, 3 Stanley Ave., Kingfield 04947. (207) 265-5541.

One of two Stanley homes which still stand on Stanley Avenue, this Queen Anne-style late Victorian house is run as a bed and breakfast by Sue and Dan Davis, owners of the esteemed One Stanley Avenue restaurant next door.

Located on a residential street across the Carrabassett River from the center of Kingfield, it's simple and quiet, almost eerily so, at least the time we were the only guests there and slept right through the 7:30 to 9 breakfast service next door. No matter; Dan Davis gets up at 5:30 every day to get the kids off to school and start dinner preparations, "so I'm here anyway," he said as he served up juice, blueberry pancakes and superior coffee at the indecent weekday breakfast hour of 10.

The six guest rooms, three each on the first and second floors, are simply furnished and decorated with a number of Victorian pieces. Some are small and share a bath; one has two beds and a sofa. Our room, the downstairs front opening onto a large porch, was the largest and had a spacious and modern bathroom. Arriving after dark, however, we were on our own since Dan was cooking at the restaurant and we missed not having any common room or place to sit and read before dinner. (Many guests sit in the parlor with a small bar at One Stanley Avenue as they peruse the dinner menu.)

Doubles, $35 to $40.

Sugarloaf Inn Resort, Carrabassett Valley 04947. (207) 237-2701 or (800) 343-4075.

This pleasantly alpine-contemporary inn off to one side of the foot of Sugarloaf ski area is a cut above many of its ski-area genre, thanks to the touch of local skier-entrepreneur Peter Webber.

A full-service inn with the Sugartree indoor sports complex nearby, it offers 40 deluxe rooms on the upper three floors, plus more than 100 rooms in surrounding condominiums, ranging from studios to five bedrooms. The inn's large parlor with velvet sofas arranged in groupings before fireplace and television set is especially comfortable.

Doubles, $65 to $150 in winter, lower off-season. Package and family plans.

Dining Spots

One Stanley Avenue, 1 Stanley Ave., Kingfield. (207) 265-5541.

Native Mainers Dan and Sue Davis were looking for a home and a restaurant site in 1971 when they spotted a for-sale sign on a tree outside an unimposing house at the head of Stanley Avenue, a residential street named for Kingfield's best known family. Skiers both (he'd been cooking at Vail), they painted the exterior an attractive white, restored the interior and scrounged enough furnishings to open a restaurant in December 1972.

The Queen Anne-style Victorian was listed on the National Register of Historic Places in 1982 and is a trove of elegant Victoriana. Be sure to

check out the old oak reach-in refrigerator that keeps the wine collection at the right temperature in the front hall and the Chickering square piano in the small parlor with a bar. That's where the Davises have presented concerts from a classical pianist to a mime, as well as displaying some of the Stanley family collections which Sue has been instrumental in preserving through the new Stanley Museum.

It is the food, however, for which One Stanley Avenue is famous, and justly so. Dan is basically self-taught, though in 1976 he studied with Louis Szathmary at the Bakery in Chicago; it was he who advised Dan to start cooking with the foods of Maine, applying classic techniques to indigenous products. That accounts for the interesting local specialties that outnumber the continental entrees on the menu which changes seasonally. Amazingly, Dan does all of the cooking, with assistance from 13-year-old daughter Sarah, serving an ambitious menu to up to 65 people in two small dining rooms and an enclosed porch on a busy night. Another unusual touch: several entrees and appetizers carry two prices, the lower a smaller portion for lighter eaters.

On the autumn night we dined, entrees included a maple cider chicken, dilled lobster on zucchini, roast duck with rhubarb glaze, and pork loin with juniper berry and port wine sauce. We delighted in the alluvial chicken, served with fiddlehead ferns and two-rice pilaf, plus side dishes of glazed carrots and sweet and sour cabbage. Even more memorable was the succulent mound of sweetbreads with applejack and chive cream sauce. A loaf of good wholewheat bread with sweet butter, green salads, coffee and orange sherbet desserts came with the price of entree ($9.50 to $18). With a $10.50 bottle of Sutter Home zinfandel, two of us feasted for less than $40.

For appetizers, Dan Davis serves things like smoked Maine salmon and mussels, rumakis, or cream soups (lovage, chard, beets or beet greens). He obtained the recipe for his chocolate Maine guide cake from a man in his 80s, who got it from a man in his 80s who cooked it over a fire with a reflector oven. His mignonettes Mercurio, named for his next-door neighbor, are two noisettes of beef tenderloin, sauteed with mushrooms and garlic, and served with a burgundy and cream sauce. Such are some of the endearing and enduring Maine touches of an outstanding restaurant.

Dinner nightly except Monday, 5 to 9; closed Oct. 20-Dec. 22 and Easter to July 4.

Le Papillon at the Winter's Inn, Kingfield. (207) 265-5421.

The two dining rooms are as elaborate as the rest of the house, except for the comfortable brown canvas directors' chairs to sit on. Gold over white tablecloths, draperies over lace curtains, ferns in the windows, oil paintings on fancy wallpaper, fireplaces, mirrors and candlelight make for romantic dining. From every window are views of the rugged countryside, a contrast to the poshness within.

The new chef is Susan Foster, who studied with Dennis Gilbert of the late: lamented Vinyard restaurant in Portland. Her menu is small but choice, with entrees of veal, duck, steak, salmon, chicken and scallops, done with different sauces at different times of the year. The duck might have a raspberry port glaze; the veal, apples and calvados cream. Each night there is a chef's evening special for $13.95 — an entree of perhaps chicken, pasta or sometimes a roast, with soup, salad and dessert. You might begin with mussels in puff pastry, smoked trout with chervil cream, or pasta with marinated goat cheese and fresh herbs ($4.25 to $5.95) and then enjoy a chilled blueberry soup in summer, or curried butternut squash, scallop bisque or tomato vermouth in winter.

The walnut blue cheese vinaigrette is a winner among the three salad dressings. Three desserts are always offered, usually a fruit tart, something chocolate and homemade ice cream. On our latest visit, Susan was making a dobos torte with thin layers of sponge cake, chocolate butter cream and caramel — we wished we were staying again for dinner! The house wine is Partager, $2.50 a glass, and the wine list is most reasonable, with Fetzer cabernet sauvignon at $11 and vouvray at $15.

Dinner nightly, 6 to 9; Sunday, brunch 11 to 3, dinner 5 to 8.

The Herbert, Main Street, Kingfield. (207) 265-2000.

His wife was our informative waitress at One Stanley Avenue, but chef Peter Freyer gets the accolades at the Herbert. After some years of apprenticing at Vermont restaurants, he was ready for the challenge of managing the reopened Herbert Hotel's main dining room. "To me it seemed this area could use something between real fancy and basic," he said.

He started with family basic and slowly upgraded to what he now calls an "international menu and white tablecloth dining — selecting a wine, enjoying appetizers, taking time." Make that blue over white and white over blue tablecloths, blue chairs, peach-colored walls, lace curtains, candles in brass holders and pillared columns in this airy, high-ceilinged dining room of the old hotel school (the open sink along the wall inside the dining room entrance — in which stagecoach passengers washed up for dinner — adds an historic if not especially attractive note).

Among appetizers are pate de cognac, smoked salmon with dill cream sauce, and chicken breast marinated in an herbed yogurt sauce. The four poultry entrees give an idea of Peter's range: chicken Rosallia with grand marnier and strawberries, chicken tandoori, Chang Kung duckling and his favorite, Napa chicken with a Napa grape stuffing and topped with apricot brandy sauce. Other entrees run the gamut from haddock Olympia and seafood Savannah to steak au poivre and Herbert ribs (with a secret sauce).

The menu suggests wines to go with each entree, right down to the last vegetarian casserole. They come from a list of 90 nicely chosen selections at wallet-pleasing prices (many in the single digits and only four above the teens).

Entree prices ($8.95 to $15.95, except for vegetarian dishes and salads) include cheese spread and crackers, salad, homemade breads and vegetables. For dessert, you can get bananas Foster ($3.50 for two), Black Forest crepes (with a chocolate kirsch butter) or Peter's prized maple marble cheesecake.

Dinner nightly, 5:30 to 9:30; Sunday brunch.

The Truffle Hound, Village West at Sugarloaf. (207) 237-2355.

Considered the fanciest restaurant at Sugarloaf, this small place established a year before One Stanley Avenue and Winter's Inn enticed skiing gourmets off the mountain down to Kingfield is open in winter only.

The continental menu ranges from $10 for baked sole stuffed with lobster sauce to $13.50 for veal Oscar and steak au poivre. Roast duckling a l'orange and broiled lamb chops rosemary are other choices. The wine list is extensive, and the dessert menu lists such goodies as English trifle, baked Alaska, chocolate hazelnut cake and walnut fudge ice cream bombe.

Lunchtime brings eggs Benedict, chicken divan and fettuccine carbonara ($3.50 to $4.50) in addition to soups, salads and sandwiches. After a long morning on the ski slopes, we had a great curried carrot soup, a hearty cheeseburger topped with Swiss cheese, and a not-so-successful open-faced fresh haddock sandwich with a supposed hollandaise sauce on a toasted hot dog bun.

The restaurant, with three rooms done up in beige and blue and lit by tiny candles at night, is a peaceful respite from the crowds at the nearby base lodge.

Lunch, 11:30 to 3; dinner 5:30 to 9:30, winter only.

Gepetto's, Village West at Sugarloaf. (207) 237-2192.

Casual and always crowded, and considered to be the place where the action is, Gepetto's serves up breakfast, lunch, dinner, and apres-ski and evening entertainment in a greenhouse with butcherblock tables or a tavern with a loud bar and large-screen television.

This is not for tete-a-tete dining. The fare tends to be basic chicken, pork chops, steaks and fried or baked fish, from $4.25 for a chopped sirloin plate to $12.95 for an oversized porterhouse with onion rings. One wintry night we tried the last, which was quite adequate. The others in our party had an interesting chicken dish with mushrooms and sour cream ($8.50) and a ham pizza ($4.50), washed down with a carafe of the house Sebastiani red ($7.50).

Gepetto's, which also operates a restaurant year-round in Boothbay Harbor, is open daily in summer from 11 to 8 with a limited menu.

Open daily in winter for breakfast, lunch and dinner.

Sugarloaf ski trails are backdrop for new Lodge and base village.

Longfellow's, Main Street, Kingfield. (207) 265-4394.

Established in 1980, Longfellow's restaurant and Riverside Lounge is a rustic, casual affair with polished wood tables, beamed ceiling, homespun curtains, old glass lamps and plenty of local color coming and going at the bar.

We thought it a find for an inexpensive lunch, as we enjoyed a cup of soup du jour (hearty vegetable) with a tabbouleh salad and a vegetable quiche with garden salad for a bargain $6.30 plus tip.

At night, the extensive menu is divided into Italian, Mexican, seafood and "some of our favorites" sections, priced from $3.75 for spaghetti to $9.95 for shrimp scampi or bay scallops and beef teriyaki. Quite a list of desserts and liqueured coffees concludes both lunch and dinner menus. The Lounge opens at 4:30 for darts, pool and other games.

Open daily, lunch 11 to 5, dinner 5 to 9 or 9:30.

Diversions

Skiing. Starting in 1950, **Sugarloaf USA** is what put Kingfield on the map. Its isolated site made it a destination resort, its distance from population centers made it uncrowded and a relative bargain, and its wilderness location gave it a character all its own. The south-face, above-the-treeline snowfields are known for open European-style spring skiing — a Down East version of Mount Washington's Tuckerman Ravine with lifts. The 2,637-foot vertical drop, one of the greatest in the East, is steep at the top, intermediate in the middle and easy at the bottom, and the extensive lift system follows suit so that skiers can ski the level which suits them. The rapidly growing base area has several village clusters with numerous restaurants and pubs, boutiques, condominiums and the new seven-story Lodge and conference center, complete with auditorium and stage for performing arts festivals. Adult lift tickets: $25 weekends, $22 weekdays.

Ski touring. The Carrabassett Valley Touring Center, just south of Route 27 near the Sugarloaf access road, is considered Maine's premiere cross-country facility. Sixty-three miles of marked trails, most former logging roads, slice through the semi-wilderness with varying degrees of difficulty. Moonlight tours and spring cookouts are popular.

White-water rafting. Since a group of bear hunters first rafted down the Kennebec River in 1976, rafting has been a boom sport in these parts from May into October. The Kennebec, the Penobscot, the Dead, the Rolling

Thunder and the Carrabassett rivers each has its own fans. Outfitters like Downeast Whitewater, Northern Outdoors and Rolling Thunder River Co. guide trips and package tours through swift rapids and calm pools, usually stopping for a steak cookout at lunch and often ending up in a hot tub or bar.

Golfing. Since September 1985, golfers have enjoyed the new 18-hole Sugarloaf golf course designed by Robert Trent Jones Jr. at the foot of the mountain. From what was once impenetrable woodland, he created a course that's scenic, bold and, in his words, "really in the wilderness and that's unusual." It's a heavily wooded course, which gives golfers a sense of isolation, like walking through a forest.

Summer arts. Sugarloaf has become something of a center for performing arts. **The Hartford Ballet** is in residence for three weeks in late July and early August; free outdoor rehearsals daily in the Village Courtyard and a finale review are among the public attractions. **The Portland String Quartet** is in residence about the same time, with students giving three public concerts. The Portland Symphony Orchestra also gives a Boston Pops-style program in early August on the Birches Slope. The biggest draw of all is the annual art show, featuring two dozen painters and sculptors during Homecoming Weekend each October.

Shopping. In season, the Sugarloaf area has boutiques one normally associates with ski resorts. Kingfield's tiny Main Street has three places of interest: **Patricia Buck Designs** is full of custom-knit sweaters, hats, legwarmers and such which she designs, plus works by Maine artists and craftsmen, antiques, quilt squares, potpourri, coffees, spices, and Maine mustards. **The 1850 House** has an excellent collection of antiques and art, gift items, baked goods, specialty foods and fine wines. The biggest store in town is **Keenan Auction Co.,** a factory outlet with good bargains on clothing, ski apparel, shoes, Woolrich knits and the like.

Extra-Special ─────────────────────────

The Stanley Museum, Kingfield. Founded in 1981 in the former Stanley School which was slated to be razed, this fledgling museum has an ambitious $1 million plan to preserve and show the Stanley tradition of painting, photography, music and steam transportation. Sue Davis of One Stanley Avenue, the museum's executive director, calls herself the museum's "guiding force" — "she *is* the museum," corrects husband Dan. The inventive Stanley twins — Francis Edgar and Freelan Oscar — and their American Renaissance family are inextricably woven into the fabric of old Kingfield; their legacy is gradually being collected and exhibited at the museum. A Stanley Steamer car was on loan inside the entrance when Dan Davis led us through, and Sue Davis was about to travel to Michigan to escort another one back. Air-brush portraits by F.E. Stanley, photographs by Chansonetta Stanley Emmons (sister of the twins), their photographic dry-plate coating equipment and the violins they made, family scrapbooks and other memorabilia are fascinating. Still in the developmental stage, the museum is open at varying times from 1 to 4 p.m. daily except Monday, summer through foliage, and weekends at other times.

Oxford Hills and Lakes, Me.
Not Where It's At — Yet

The famous — some locals call it infamous — milepost sign out in the middle of nowhere giving distances to nearby places like Norway, Denmark, Mexico, Poland, Paris and Naples would fool no one.

This is anything but the center of the universe. It's more like the name on the school bus we passed, "State of Maine, Unorganized Territory."

The Oxford Hills region is an unspoiled land of sparkling lakes, hills that back up to the mighty White Mountains and tiny hamlets with English-sounding names like Center Lovell and Lower Waterford. It's an area of great beauty — we hear that the National Geographic called Kezar Lake one of the nation's ten most beautiful (its other claim to fame is that Bridgton native Stephen King has a summer home along its forested shore). There's a fortuitous concentration of small country inns that epitomize the genre.

Unusual as a time capsule from the past, the area offers little in the way of formal activity or tourist trappings. "You are on your own," the Westways inn brochure advises.

"More and more people seek the serenity of this inland area," reports Lynn Baker, proprietor of the Artemus Ward House, a bed and breakfast establishment where a real English tea may be served.

"We're really out in the country," adds Barbara Vanderzanden of the Waterford Inne. "But we have a central location not far from North Conway or the Maine coast."

The charms of this rural retreat have yet to be discovered by the crowds. But each year visitors find a new attraction. The latest is the Lake House, a fine restaurant that also offers bed and breakfast. Says co-owner Suzanne Uhl-Myers: "Western Maine is where it's going to be at."

Happily, it's not there yet. That remains its special joy.

Inn Spots

Westways on Kezar Lake, Route 5, Center Lovell 04016. (207) 928-2663.

Each of the inns in this area has its distinctive appeal. At Westways, it's the great location right on the east shore of upper Kezar Lake, plus its heritage as a small, private luxury lodge from the past.

Built in the 1920s by the owner of the Diamond Match Company as a corporate retreat, it was opened to the public in 1975 with its original furnishings, from the books in the guest rooms to the 1925 billiards table and vintage bowling alley in the recreation hall. "We're unique as a time capsule," says Nancy C. Tripp, manager for the four owners from Boston. "It has been left as it was in the '20s."

The main floor contains a large kitchen and an immense living room, with many Italian antiques, a huge stone fireplace and, at either end, hand-carved oak tables that can each seat 12 for dining. Beyond is a long dining porch running the width of the lodge with windows right above the water, and a grand old boathouse where cocktails and nibbles are served on the screened porch as the sun sets over the White Mountains (see Dining Spots).

Dock and boathouse at Westways on Kezar Lake.

A small interior dining room, with many Japanese prints on the wall, is used for winter dining. The downstairs also has a restroom with an ornate wrap-around needle shower which invigorates the entire body and compensates for the lack of showers upstairs.

One of the seven guest rooms has full private bath, while two have half-baths and four share four baths in the hallways. Nicest is the Matriarch's Room with private bath, two double beds, hand-carved furniture and windows on two sides. Both the Maple Room with handmade maple furniture and the Blue Room with spacious seating area and twin beds have half-baths and lake views. Many think the Horses Room, named for the series of Fox Hunt prints on the walls, has the best view in the house. Only one of the three smaller rooms in the former servant's quarters lacks a water view.

Westways also rents out a former stableman's cottage by the day and five houses on the grounds (two brand new), accommodating up to 14 at weekly rates of $475 to $1,000.

Lodge guests are served full breakfasts, with choice of pancakes, French toast, eggs any style or omelets. They also have the run of the 100-acre forest, which includes a dock at the boathouse with a swimming area in the crystal-clear waters of what is a quiet, almost private lake and a sand beach a quarter-mile down the shore. And if you're into handball, try the fives court in another outbuilding (tournaments are sometimes held here).

Doubles, $76 to $104, EP; $104 to $132, MAP. Closed April and November.

The Waterford Inne, Box 49, East Waterford 04233. (207) 583-4037.
This handsome inn and antiques shop really is out in the country — half a mile up a rural lane, its pale yellow and mustard exterior commanding a hilltop view and containing nine well-furnished guest rooms, a comfortable and charming folk-art-filled living room, and a semi-public dining room of note.

Former New Jersey school teachers Rosalie and Barbara Vanderzanden, a mother and daughter team, carefully restored and furnished the 1825 farmhouse in 1978, eventually augmenting the original five bedrooms with four more in the old woodshed leading to the red barn out back.

Special touches abound in each room, six of which have private baths. Duck pillows, duck wallpaper and a duck lamp grace the deluxe Chesapeake Room, which has kingsize bed, a working fireplace and a super second-story porch overlooking the farm pond and mountains. A quilted whale hangs behind the bed in the Nantucket Room, complete with map of the island and a bathroom almost as large as the bedroom itself. The Strawberry Room in the woodshed has strawberries on the lamp, rug, quilts, pillow and sheets, and even strawberry-scented potpourri in a strawberry-shaped dish.

Full breakfasts for $5 ("we'll cook whatever you want," says Rosalie) are served in the beamed dining room or in good weather on the porch.

Dinners for $18 are served to guests and, by reservation, to the public in the dining room filled with the women's pewter collection. Up to 20 can be served, when the front parlor and porch are used as well. Although there is no choice, Rosalie will work around diets such as vegetarian and when a large party makes a reservation, will ask for their preference.

A typical dinner might start with cream of broccoli soup, go on to dilled scallops over angel hair pasta with vegetables and salad not long out of the garden, and end with an angel food cake with whipped cream and peaches. Chilled cucumber soup and veal marsala might make up another dinner. Leg of lamb often appears, as do game hens, duckling, sole, and pork or beef tenderloin. Grand marnier souffle and deep-dish apple pie are frequent desserts, and guests may bring their own wine.

Doubles, $40 to $65, EP.

The Artemus Ward House, Routes 35-37, Waterford 04088. (207) 583-4106.

Bed and breakfast, antiques, English tea, horses and history are the claim to fame of Lynn Baker's delightful spot.

Built in 1805 and later the home of Charles Farrar Browne, the noted humorist known as Artemus Ward, who was a favorite of Abraham Lincoln's, the attractive white clapboard house is the area's only inn with beach frontage on Keoka Lake out back. Lynn's daughter breeds Welsh cobs and gives instruction in dressage and jumping at the adjoining Waterford Stud and Equestrian Center; she also stenciled the pretty canvas floor cloth decorating the stairs. Says Lynn: "You can sit either on the side porch and watch the horses, or out front and watch people go by."

The Waterford Inne and barn occupy rural setting.

Having lived several years in England, she returns frequently, picking up more antiques for her inn (from time to time she has run an antiques shop here). For several years she served high tea from Wednesday to Sunday; now it is served by prior arrangement only, from 3 to 5, for $4.50. Proper tea sandwiches of cucumber, egg, tomato and cheese, homemade scones and crumpets, and tarts of plums or apricots accompany Tetley tea or Fortnum & Mason's royal blend.

Guests have use of a pink and green sitting room with fireplace, a "courting hole" cut in its door. A small television set is available in the large room just inside the entrance, where a big bowl of yellow daisies sits on an oak table and there's a wood stove.

The attractive dining room has hooked rugs on painted floors, candles in tin sconces and a collection of English blue and white china. The harvest table is made from wainscoting salvaged from a bathroom that was being remodeled. Here guests are served full breakfasts of fresh orange juice, apple cider, berries in the summer, stewed fruits at other times, hot or cold cereal, sweet rolls, blueberry muffins, and bacon and eggs or fruit pancakes.

One bedroom is downstairs; its bathroom has a clawfoot tub with hand-held shower. Three more are upstairs, one with private bath and two sharing. They are cozy, with eaves and nooks and hooked rugs; most have portraits of Artemus Ward. Bottles of Poland Spring mineral water are placed in each room. Don't miss the carved rabbit from an old merry-go-round, with the biggest ears you ever saw, guarding the stairs.

Lynn Baker, an accomplished cook, may serve dinner to house guests on request.

Doubles, $35 to $40, including full breakfast. Closed Jan. 15 to May 15.

Olde Rowley Inn, Route 35, North Waterford 04267. (207) 583-4143.

History fairly oozes from every nook and cranny of this rambling red building with the sagging roof smack up against the road atop the hill that is North Waterford. Built in 1790 and opened as a stagecoach inn in 1825, it had been abandoned when two young sisters and their husbands found it in 1980 and restored it with care as to its history. Pamela and Peter Leja and Debra and Michael Lennon share the innkeeping duties.

Dried herbs hang over the massive open hearth in the keeping room, where inn guests gather under a low-beamed ceiling. A rocking chair and a high-backed bench surround the fireplace, and atop the mantel is a needlepoint picture of a Colonial lady done by Pamela's mother. There are pumpkin pine floors and wainscoting made of 14-foot-long boards that had been hidden under 15 coats of paint.

A "tightwinder" staircase ascends to the second floor and the five guest rooms, one with private bath and four sharing. Authentic pierced tin lanterns cast light on the uneven floors of the hallways. The cozy beamed bedrooms, named after local dignitaries, are furnished with period wallpaper and furniture, white bedspreads, colored towels, hooked rugs, and perhaps a half bath or washstand.

A full country breakfast is included in the rates. In winter, Irish oatmeal is popular with skiers. Guests also have a choice of eggs, sometimes there are blueberry pancakes, and the homemade oatmeal bread tastes terrific as toast.

A 1779 stage ticket found by an elderly lady in her attic across the street is in the frame of a picture of the old inn in the bar. Debra Lennon has a great reputation as dinner chef (see Dining Spots).

Doubles, $45.

Kedarburn Inn, Route 35, Box A-1, Waterford 04088. (207) 583-6182.

Built in 1858, this handsome white Colonial house with dark green shutters and broad lawns brightened with flower beds has been made thoroughly up to date by new owners Bill Ritchie, a horse trainer, and Edmond Rocheleau, a hair dresser, who has a salon in a corner of the house. They brought with them their striking furnishings and antique collections, some paradise finches with 15-inch-long tails and a prized canary who sings most of the day.

The dining room (see below) and the breakfast room are unusually attractive, as is the guest living room with a television set, comfortable sofas and many books. An outdoor patio is within earshot of Kedar Brook.

Upstairs are five comfortable guest rooms, two with private baths and two that share a large bathroom, plus a two-room suite. Another room with private bath and kingsize bed was being added in late 1985. One, with kingsize bed, is called the Honeymoon Suite and plans are to add a little deck off it. Towels are color coordinated in each room, and interesting pictures are everywhere. A huge quilt hangs on the stairs.

A full breakfast is served to inn guests and the public in the sunny breakfast room brightened by quilted mats, Phaltzgraf china and a collection of baskets and hammered brass trays. Blueberry pancakes, cheese omelets, homemade muffins and oatmeal honey toast are some of the fare.

Doubles, $50 to $60.

Center Lovell Inn, Route 5, Center Lovell 04016. (207) 925-1575.

The screened porch that wraps around this 1805 homestead appeals to guests as much as it did to Susie and Bill Mosca from Connecticut, who first saw the abandoned farmhouse in 1974. "We sat on the front porch and admired the view and that was it," Susie recalls. The view, with a glimpse of Kezar Lake down a long hillside and the White Mountains etched against the western sky, is indeed special.

The Moscas have renovated room by room the three-story structure, which has something of a Mississippi steamboat appearance thanks to the Floridian who added a mansard roof topped by cupola in the 1860s. The 1835 Norton House, a former barber shop, was moved to the site from Lovell and now adds five more guest rooms at the side.

The annex has large rooms with country furnishings and the rear room with double bed and a settee has a modern bathroom. Some of the guest rooms in the homestead have neat old chests for storing extra blankets. A large painting of pansies in an ornate frame graces one room, and all have country curtains. Six of the 10 rooms have private baths.

The common living room with a hooked rug has a wood stove and small organ. Glowing fireplaces, lit even on fairly warm days, cheer the dining rooms, where Bill Mosca's cooking is highly regarded (see below).

Doubles, $50 to $60, EP; $78 to $116, MAP. Closed November to Christmas and mid-March to May 1.

Lake House offers fine dining in Waterford.

Dining Spots

Lake House, Routes 35-37, Waterford. (207) 583-4182.

A landmark structure that had been Waterford's first inn (operating until the 1940s) was reopened late in 1984 as the Lake House, with a well-regarded restaurant on the main floor and three guest rooms sharing one bath upstairs.

Each dining room is pretty as a picture. The small front room has burgundy wallpaper above pale green woodwork, green carpeting and different china on each table. The larger rear dining room has dark burgundy napkins on top of pink linens, tables set with two large wine glasses at each setting and oriental rugs on the floor. Patrons can enjoy the antics of birds at feeders behind a couple of one-way mirrors. A classical guitarist plays on Thursday evenings.

A changing menu of regional nouvelle cuisine is offered by Suzanne and Michael Uhl-Myers, the young proprietors. A sorbet clears the palate before the main course; a mixed salad follows.

The wine list with more than 100 selections is one of western Maine's most extensive and most reasonably priced, reflecting Suzanne's former career as a wine consultant. Monthly wine-tasting dinners are scheduled October through May.

Appetizers range from $1.95 for nachos with "a hot sauce for the brave" to $5.25 for smoked seafood from Maine's Duck Trap River Farm. Suzanne's duck liver mousse pate is made with grand marnier. The changing soups might be a creamy red onion with a shot of sherry on the side, curried carrot or a smoked salmon soup.

Entrees start at $8.95 for pasta with fresh vegetables and go to $16.95 for the house specialty, double breast of duck, presented with the sauce of the month. A sloe gin and orange sauce might glaze the grilled tuna, lobster might be served out of the shell with a fennel, vermouth and cream sauce, the veal could be sauteed in lime and white wine, and the shrimp sauteed in garlic and presented in a reduced cream sauce of basil and fresh tomatoes. Vegetables the night we visited were carrots with anisette dressing and julienned strips of butternut squash with red peppers.

Some people come just for the homemade desserts, which include mocha mousse, pies, German chocolate cake with coconut-pecan topping, "Cloud Nine" (puff pastry mounded with fresh cream whipped with a cordial of one's choice) and "Waterford Kiss" (equal parts of cream, amaretto and Waterford cream topped with whipped cream and a chocolate morsel), priced from $2.25 to $3.25. Crepes Suzette may be flambeed tableside, $12.95 for two. Desserts, coffee and cordials are available separately after 8 p.m.

Dinner, Tuesday-Sunday 5 to 10.

Olde Rowley Inn, Route 35, North Waterford. (207) 583-4143.

Three candlelit dining rooms in a 1790 roadside stagecoach inn couldn't be more historic or romantic; that the food is so good is a bonus.

Stenciled reproduction wallpaper and a handful of tables with assorted overcloths are in one small dining room. Beyond and down a few stairs is the 1825 carriage house connecting inn to barn. In one dining room here, the exposed-beam ceiling is hung with old baskets and dried herbs; frilly white curtains surround the small windows. Copper wall lanterns illuminate the hand-stenciled wallpaper in the third room.

Chef Debra Lennon's continental menu starts with deep fried Monterey Jack cheese with dill sauce, a trio of mushroom, celery and carrot pates, a scallop tart or wonderful cream soups — the carrot bisque and mushroom laced with cognac being standouts.

Fresh homemade breads and a mixed salad of greens, vegetables and fruits with house dressings come with the meal. Entrees ($8.95 to $14.50) include hunter's chicken, Dijon veal, sole stuffed with salmon mousse topped with bearnaise sauce, shrimp amandine, lobster pie and pepper steak. Wild rice pilaf and seasonal vegetables accompany.

Desserts are to groan over: trifles with raspberries and peaches or chocolate, strawberries and bananas, walnut bourbon pie, bread pudding with butter bourbon sauce, French silk pie and a four-layer French chocolate cake filled with rum mousse, priced from $1.95 to $3.25.

Dinner nightly, 5 to 10; sometimes closed one or two nights a week in winter.

Center Lovell Inn, Route 5, Center Lovell. (207) 925-1575.

The heritage of five generations of Italian cooks, whose recipes chef-owner Bill Mosca grew up with along the Connecticut shore, is the dining attraction at this abandoned farmhouse-turned-inn overlooking Kezar Lake. The tables in two small, plain dining rooms have peach cloths and red napkins; in summer, there's outdoor dining on the wrap-around porch as the sun sets over the Presidential Range.

Dining is taken seriously here, Bill Mosca going so far as to prepare special feasts of six or seven courses for holidays and other occasions. Roast suckling pig and baby leg of lamb stuffed with prosciutto are featured main courses; a Mediterranean fish course of pastry shells filled with lobster, oysters, scallops and eggplant in a cream sauce is a treat.

Regular dinners might begin with one of six appetizers ($2.25 to $3.95). Favorites are fresh fruit chilled in champagne, artichoke hearts and steamed mussels. Among entrees ($8.95 to $14.50), the milk-fed veal marsala and veal Margarita are outstanding. Shrimp is baked and stuffed with crabmeat or sauteed in olive oil with spices and wine. Baked filet of sole is stuffed with shrimp and flavored with sherry. Entrees are served with Italian bread, salad with Italian dressing (an acclaimed homemade blue cheese dressing is $2.50 extra), vegetable and pasta. Six pasta dishes are listed after the entrees for $5.50 to $8.75, and a house specialty — lobster fra diavolo — can be ordered with two days' notice.

Susie Mosca makes the desserts: a rich Italian cheesecake, spumoni and parfait de menthe, ice cream Nero and occasionally a trifle, $2.50 to $2.95. A demitasse of espresso for two is $1.75, or you may order French roast coffee with anisette. The wine list is reasonably priced, with the emphasis on Italian and French vintages.

Dinner, nightly from 5; reservations required.

Westways on Kezar Lake, Route 5, Center Lovell. (207) 928-2663.

The theatrical background and cooking (with a tendency toward macrobiotic) of chef Jack Kavanagh make for some interesting, surprising combinations at this rustic lodge beside the lake. From cocktails in the boathouse through dessert, visitors are in for an unusual experience.

The changing menu features three entrees nightly, priced from $11 to $17 a la carte; prix-fixe dinners are $16 to $19. Chef Kavanagh says his main effort is to use foods indigenous to the area, paying attention to cholesterol and salt content.

Raw vegetables with a curry dip and a plate of cheese, grapes and crackers might be served with cocktails. Soup choices could be a chilled cantaloupe, hot cream of parsnip or mushroom consomme with Japanese noodles. The chef is especially fond of his maple pecan salad dressing, atop salads he makes colorful with seasonal lettuce and vegetables. His basket of homemade breads always includes one made with cheese, and sometimes his rum-pumpkin bread, served with rosettes of butter.

Among the entrees you might find sirloin steak with bordelaise sauce, a curried leg of lamb and veal moutarde. Fresh tuna, sturgeon, mako shark, marlin and sea bass are sometimes on the list. Roast duck might be served with amaretto sauce; the fresh trout stuffed with a combination of spiced crumbs, green grapes and nuts. Baked restuffed potatoes, rice pilaf with peanuts or zucchini, red pepper and onions sauteed in tamari sauce are possible accompaniments.

Kiwi cheesecake, rum chocolate mousse, Aunt Effa's sour cream raisin pie, and always a dessert of fruit (such as poached pears with blueberry compote) are among sweet endings. And, says the chef, "we always have to have our Swiss chocolate cake for our decadent patrons." The wine list is reasonably priced, with Ridge zinfandel, for instance, at $12.50.

Tables are set with white linens, dark rose napkins and interesting floral arrangements on the porch, where dinner is served with a water view on summer nights, inside the main room at hand-carved oak tables warmed by a fieldstone fireplace, or in the small winter dining room. All are fitting settings for a distinctive meal.

Dinner, nightly 6 to 8:30; reservations requested.

Kedarburn Inn, Route 35, Waterford. (207) 583-6182.

The antiques in the corner cabinets are illuminated at night in the candlelit dining room of the 1858 Colonial house, which looks the way a formal dining room of the period did (except perhaps for the prized paradise finches near the rear window). The innkeepers' collections of copper,

Bed, breakfast and dinner are available at Kedarburn Inn.

hammered brass and baskets are on display here and in the sunny breakfast room, popular for the Sunday brunch and also used when dinner time gets busy.

Bill Ritchie is chef, while partner Ed Rocheleau does the baking and waits on tables. Bill will vary his menu on request for house guests, and takes great pride in the Irish potatoes he prepares from his mother's recipe.

Prices are so low that guests wonder how they can do it: appetizers like stuffed mushrooms for $2 and shrimp cocktail for $3.95; entrees from $7.95 to $9.95, and desserts under $2. Marinated chicken or steak barbecued on the inn's charcoal grill, sole Florentine and seafood newburg are popular. Downeast lobster dinners are served on Friday and Saturday nights in summer, the price varying depending on lobster size. Ice cream puff and mud pie are among desserts. The wine list was limited (only Paul Masson) when we visited, but Bill said he was building it up.

Dinner, Thursday-Saturday 5 to 9; Sunday brunch, 10 to 3; breakfast daily for public, 7 to 11.

The Oxford House Inn, 105 Main St., Fryeburg. (207) 935-3442.

Opened in August 1985, this attractive 1913 country house is very personally run by John and Phyllis Morris, formerly of North Conway. Their creative cuisine has quickly gained a wide reputation.

Tables are set with delicate pink crystal, heavy silver and Sango Mystique peach china, with candles in clay pots and fresh daisies on our visit.

The menu, which changes seasonally, comes inside sheet music from the 1920s. Dinner begins with complimentary homemade crackers and cheese spread, a salad of fresh greens and fruits (berries and melons), perhaps with a tomato tarragon dressing, and fresh nut and corn breads. Appetizers ($2.75 to $6.95) are Maine crab chowder, a house pate, hot smoked Atlantic salmon, baked camembert in puff pastry with fruit and smoked seafood plate.

The 10 entrees ($11.95 to $15.95) include such creations as turkey Waldorf splashed with applejack, poached salmon pommery, pork with pears and port, scallops in puff pastry and Canadian steak pie. John does most of the cooking, but the desserts are Phyllis's: fresh fruit trifles, amaretto chocolate cheesecake, fresh fruit flans and tarts, and an acclaimed bread pudding with peaches and blueberries.

Thirty wines are offered, and the downstairs was being renovated for a tavern. Upstairs are five guest rooms, three with private baths, $50 to $65 double with breakfast.

Dinner nightly, 6 to 9.

Diversions

The area's attributes tend to be quiet and personal. As the Westways brochure states: "Whether you prefer browsing through local antique shops, visiting the country fairs, watching the sun rise over the misty lake as you fish from your canoe at dawn or spending a quiet evening around the fieldstone fireplace, you are on your own." Some ideas:

The villages. General stores and the odd antiques or crafts shop are about the only merchandising in places like Waterford, North Waterford, Center Lovell and Lovell. But do not underestimate their charms. As Artemus Ward wrote of Waterford: "The village from which I write to you is small. It does not contain over forty houses, all told; but they are milk white, with the greenest of blinds, and for the most part are shaded with beautiful elms and willows. To the right of us is a mountain — to the left a lake. The village nestles between. Of course it does. I never read a novel in my life in which the villages didn't nestle. It is a kind of way they have." Waterford hasn't changed much since, nor have its surrounding towns. For action, you have to go up north to Bethel, east to Bridgton or southwest to Fryeberg and North Conway.

The lakes. Kezar, peaceful and quiet and somewhat inaccessible, lies beneath the mighty White Mountain range, its waters reflecting the changing seasons and spectacular sunsets. The lake is relatively undeveloped and private, with access only from the marina at the Narrows, the beach at the end of Pleasant Point Road and a point in North Lovell. The rest of the time you can rarely even see it (much to our dismay, for we got lost trying). Keoka Lake, at Waterford, has a small, pleasant public beach just east of the village on Route 118. Hidden lakes and ponds abound, and not far distant are more accessible Long Lake and Sebago Lake.

Extra-Special

Bonnema Pottery on Main Street in Bethel is a studio and showroom where Garret and Melody Bonnema craft and display their pottery in a barn beside their house. Seldom have we seen such appealing colors; according to the Bonnemas, their glazing is influenced by the colors in the mountains and valleys surrounding Bethel. Tankards, tiles, candelabras, casseroles, teapots and much more are their wares. We fell for some small and inexpensive rectangular vases they call "extrusions," just right for a few wildflowers, and bought several for gifts and for ourselves. Open daily.

Hard to find but worth the trip is the **Jones Gallery of Glass & Ceramics** off Route 107 in Sebago. Here are more than 3,000 works of art, everything from Chinese porcelain and Egyptian glass to Wedgwood teapots and Sandwich lamps displayed in brilliant profusion (admission $2.50). The Gallery Shop has original glass and ceramics, plus books, slides and gifts. Open daily, May to mid-November.

Rockport, Mass.
Old-Time Values and Virtues

They certainly don't need more crowds, the habituees of Bearskin Neck, Pigeon Cove and Marmion Way. Nor do those who cater to them.

But bargain-conscious travelers can seldom do better than in Rockport, the seaside Cape Ann resort town where the costs of food and lodging consistently remain five years behind the times.

Last we knew, lobster dinners were going for $7.95 at Ellen's Harborside. Rooms in the finest inns and motels cost $50 to $80, about one-third less than they'd command in equivalent locations elsewhere.

Why such bargains? Because Rockport was developed earlier, when costs were lower, than many such coastal resorts. "We were bed and breakfast long before the craze started," notes Leighton Saville, co-innkeeper at Seacrest Manor. Adds William Balzarini, owner of the Old Farm Inn: "The inns here keep their prices down because they don't have new mortgages with high rates." Rockport's century-old ban on the sale of liquor may have influenced prices, if only in lowering restaurant tabs when patrons BYOB.

The bargains help swell Rockport's year-round population of 7,000 to 35,000 in summer. Most, it seems, are on the streets near Dock Square and Bearskin Neck. Parking is usually a problem (arrive early or expect to park on distant side streets and walk).

Visitors are drawn by the rocky coast more typical of Maine, the atmosphere of an old fishing village now crammed with shops and art galleries, the quaintness of a "dry" town in which Sunday evening band concerts are the major entertainment, and the lively arts colony inspired by a picturesque harbor listed by Walt Disney Productions as one of the nation's most scenic. In fact, Motif No. 1, the red fishing shack on Bradley Wharf, is outranked as an artist's image only by the Mona Lisa. When it collapsed in the Blizzard of 1978, villagers quickly rebuilt it — such is the place of art (and tourism) in Rockport.

All around Rockport are the varied assets of the rest of Cape Ann. They range from the English look of quiet Annisquam, which is New England at its quaintest, to the working fishing flavor of busy Gloucester.

The allure of Rockport is so strong that its devotees return time and again. Crowded it may be, but it's hard to beat the prices.

Inn Spots

Eden Pines Inn, Eden Road, Rockport 01966. (617) 546-2505.

You can't get much closer to the ocean than from the rear deck that hovers over the rocks — or, for that matter, from five of the upstairs guest rooms — at this delightfully secluded inn by the sea.

The setting in what was formerly a summer home could not be more appealing. The lodge-like front parlor with fieldstone fireplace, the California-style side breakfast porch, the rear porch with brick deck below, even a couple of bathroom windows take full advantage of the water view across to Thatchers Island and its twin lighthouses. Although the shore here is rocky, the inn is within walking distance of two beaches.

The six upstairs guest rooms, all with private baths, are unusually spacious.

Ocean lies just behind Eden Pines Inn.

Most have two double beds (Room 6 has striking white seersucker and lace curtains enclosing a canopied bed) and private balconies over the water. We'd choose Room 4, all beige and blue in decorator fabrics with thick carpeting, a comfortable sitting area and an enormous bathroom done in Italian marble with a bathtub, a separate shower and a large window onto the ocean, next to the marble vanity.

Innkeeper Inge Sullivan, a blonde dynamo who is partial to marble and California fabrics, was redecorating the rooms one by one and had two more to go when we last visited in August 1985.

She and her husband serve a continental breakfast which includes Scandinavian pastries, midafternoon tea and setups for drinks. We know of few more picturesque places for the last than the lounge chairs on the rear deck smack beside the ocean.

Doubles, $54 to $79, summer two-night minimum. Open May-November.

Seacrest Manor, 131 Marmion Way, Rockport 01966. (617) 546-2211.

If Eden Pines has the ocean setting and decorator's flair, Seacrest has the lawns and gardens and a breakfast to remember. It also has a sweeping view of the ocean beyond the trees from its second-story deck above the living room.

Leighton T. Saville and Dwight B. MacCormack Jr. have been running their inn since 1972, so personally that many of the repeat guests have left gifts — their own watercolors of the inn, crocheted pillows and countless knickknacks, including a collection of rabbits "which just keep multiplying, as rabbits are prone to do," according to Leighton.

The main-floor library displays many British magazines ("our English guests tell us it feels like home"). The airy living room where afternoon tea is served has a distinctly masculine feel with leather chairs and dark colors.

The formal dining room is decked out in fancy red linen, Wedgwood china and crystal glasses at five tables for a breakfast which Town &

Country magazine called one of the 50 best in America. It begins with fresh fruit cup and fresh orange juice, continues with oatmeal and bacon and eggs, and ends with a specialty like blueberry or apple pancakes, French toast or corn fritters.

Guests have the run of the grounds, which include prolific gardens and a rope hammock strung between trees in a rear corner. The flower beds supply the small bouquets scattered through the inn.

Four of the eight guest rooms have private baths; the others share two. Rooms are comfortable if plain; each has kingsize or twin beds, color television, a couple of chairs and a desk rather like the kind you'd expect to see in a motel. The inn touch comes with mints on the bed table with nightly turndown service, soaps and shampoos, and a complimentary Boston Globe at the door in the morning.

Seacrest Manor is a special place which measures up to its motto, "decidedly small, intentionally quiet."

Doubles, $54 to $72, slightly less off-season; closed January.

Yankee Clipper Inn, Route 127, Box 2399, Rockport 01966. (617) 546-3407.

One of Rockport's larger and older inns, the Yankee Clipper has been run since 1946 by Fred and Lydia Wemyss and lately by their daughter and son-in-law, Barbara and Bob Ellis.

It began with nine rooms in the main inn, a Georgian mansion situated amid beautifully landscaped lawns on a bit of a point jutting into the ocean. More were added in the 1840 Bulfinch-designed neo-classic mansion across the road, and more contemporary rooms are in the Quarterdeck built in 1960 beside the water. The last has a third-floor penthouse suite with ruffled pillows on two double beds, a sofabed, and two velvet chairs facing floor-to-ceiling windows onto the ocean.

In the inn, Fred Wemyss sometimes shows movies on the VCR in the downstairs television room. There's a grandly furnished living room on the main floor.

The L-shaped dining porch takes advantage of the ocean view. It's for non-smokers only; the inner dining room is for smokers. A buffet lunch is served on the patio in good weather.

The food is down-home Yankee with one side of the dinner menu changing daily to provide what it calls "A Taste of New England" — roast turkey with sausage stuffing and baked scrod the night we visited (table d'hote for the public, $16).

Guests like to check the blackboard on the dining porch for announcements and Fred Wemyss's latest limericks, which he composes as the mood or situation strikes.

The heated saltwater pool is unusually attractive and hidden from the public eye.

Doubles, full American plan in summer, $114 to $174; MAP in spring and fall, $95 to $171; bed and breakfast in Bulfinch House, $60 to $80.

Addison Choate Inn, 49 Broadway, Rockport 01966. (617) 546-7543.

An in-town location, a prized antiques collection, a rear swimming pool and some of the best-furnished rooms around draw guests to this attractive, flower-bedecked house built in 1851 and boasting Rockport's first bathtub — in the kitchen, no less.

Motif No. 1 is a must-see attraction for visitors to Rockport.

That bathtub has been replaced, of course, but all six guest rooms and a two-room suite have large and modern hand-tiled bathrooms with pewter faucets. Each is furnished with rare antiques; the lamps in the blue room with a stunning canopied pine bed are intriguing. The third-floor suite has Laura Ashley fabrics and a stained-glass skylight in the bathroom. Mints are left on the pillows as beds are turned down at night.

Innkeepers Margot and Brad Sweet serve what she calls a "continental-plus" breakfast of fruits, muffins and soft-boiled eggs at intimate tables for two on the narrow side porch or in the dining room; "choatemeal" is the cereal in winter.

The rear Stable House with a sofabed on the main floor and a queensize bed in the loft is available for parties of four. Beyond is the small, tree-shaded pool area, so secluded in heart-of-Rockport terms "that you think you're up in the mountains," says Margot.

Doubles, $58 to $68; suite and Stable House, $85 to $95.

The Inn on Cove Hill, 37 Mount Pleasant St., Rockport 01966. (617) 546-2701.

Close to the heart of town and with a fine view of Motif No. 1 and the harbor from its rear third-floor deck is this Federal-style mansion built in 1791 and operated as a guest house the last 30 years.

Young innkeepers Marjorie and John Pratt have been redecorating it gradually. Nine of the 11 guest rooms have private baths; two on the third floor share. Each is nicely decorated in Laura Ashley fabrics and wallpapers, and each has a small black and white television set. Most rooms have handmade quilts and afghans and crocheted coverlets as well as oriental-style rugs.

The Pratts like to point out the structure's architectural features — such as the spiral staircase with 13 steps in the entry hall — and the antique furnishings in the small common room.

They serve a continental breakfast with muffins at outdoor tables topped by yellow and white umbrellas in the side garden or on trays in the bedrooms in cool weather.

Recipes for eight of their popular muffins (oatmeal, orange buttermilk and pumpkin, among them) have been printed for guests. A note is appended to the end: "If you find that your muffins are failing, we have conspired to leave out one essential ingredient from each of the recipes; that is umbrella tables in the summer and breakfast in bed in the winter. For access to both, come see us."

Doubles, $29 to $57; lower off-season; closed November to mid-February.

Dining Spots

Old Farm Inn, 291 Granite St. (Pigeon Cove), Rockport. (617) 546-3237.
Tops on everyone's list of favorite eating spots on Cape Ann is the Old Farm Inn, run with tender loving care since 1964 by the Balzarini family.

Housed in a red structure with white trim built in 1799 and once part of a dairy farm (the Balzarini grandchildren's ponies still graze in the meadow), the original dining rooms (and the newer garden room) are unabashedly early American, from the 80-year-old cast-iron stove near the entry to the old pieces of china in the corner cabinets.

Dinners start with complimentary crackers and a nippy cheese spread, a tray of crisp relishes (changing weekly), a loaf of delicious oatmeal bread, and a salad of mixed greens with good house dressing loaded with cheese. You might begin with the clam chowder, thick with clams and piping hot, for a bargain $1.75, or fresh lobster cocktail for $5.50.

Among entrees ($8.95 to $14.50), we loved the inn's special crabmeat mushroom pie, with plump whole mushrooms and abundant crabmeat topped with buttery bread crumbs, and the crabmeat Rockefeller, huge chunks of crabmeat in a mornay sauce. We also enjoyed another specialty, the roast duckling flambe, served with choice of orange or wine sauce.

The nightly blackboard specials — perhaps the Cracow cheese soup of cabbage and cauliflower pureed with chicken stock and blue cheese ("I made it up," says Bill Balzarini) or broiled haddock with a sweet red pepper sauce — get more creative.

Desserts are old-fashioned standard, except for a luscious Indian pudding slowly baked in a cast-iron stove and served steaming hot with ice cream melting over it.

Upstairs are three guest rooms with fireplaces, including a two-bedroom suite sharing a bath. The barn out back has four guest rooms, all with private bath and television, recently upgraded, comfortable and rather motel-like. Doubles, $48 to $59.

Dinner, Monday-Saturday 5 to 9, Sunday 4 to 9. No credit cards.

My Place, 72 Bearskin Neck, Rockport. (617) 546-9667.
When Cristull and Robert Sheath decided to open a restaurant in 1982 in an old black and yellow tea house at the very end of Bearskin Neck, they didn't know what to call it, Christull said, "so we called it My Place."

It's our kind of place, too, blessed with an unbelievable location on the rocks at water's edge and decidedly romantic with an un-Rockport-like rose and aqua color scheme and, at night, flaming torches and pink and blue spotlights on the rocks. As flute music plays while the sun sets, the setting is magical for diners on the two flower-lined outdoor decks and, indeed, for the people across Sandy Bay who say the nighttime sight enchants them as well.

Inside, the small restaurant evokes memories of the 1950s, with old

Dining on deck at water's edge is feature of My Place.

magazine covers embedded under glass on the linen-covered tables, floral napkin rings, a fireplace to take the chill out of the nights and a single rose on every table. (Check out the restroom with a bathtub filled with flowers, the aroma of eucalyptus and bright pink shower curtains hiding the hot water tank.)

Chef Charles Kreis's food is distinctive, especially such specials as Otsego Lake bass stuffed with clams or "stuffed ocean wolf fish."

Dinner prices range from $5.95 for soup and salad with homemade bread to $12.95 for baked sole stuffed with shrimp, scallops, crabmeat and lobster and served with a brandied bechamel sauce. Other possibilities include baked scrod or halibut with lime butter, ham steak and prime ribs, all but the last for under $10. Several lobster feasts are priced daily. The homemade cheesecake, mint ice cream pie and fresh fruit parfaits are worthy desserts.

Silver ice buckets are provided for those who bring their own beverages (setups, $1 per table). Or you can try one of Crystull's concoctions such as "sunset on the rocks," a refreshing blend of cranberry, lime and sherbet.

Brunch-lunch daily, 11 to 3; dinner, 5 to 9:30, mid-May through October.

The Galley, Bearskin Neck, Rockport. (617) 546-3721.

For 25 years Mike Parillo has been running this no-nonsense restaurant his way, with little in the way of decor beyond some stained-glass, hanging plants and the sensational harbor view outside.

The simple menu is augmented by many blackboard specials. "I've had hundreds of dishes," Mike explains, saying he never could have lasted 25 years "without making it interesting, if only for me to maintain enthusiasm for what I do."

When we visited, the appetizers were asparagus spears vinaigrette and clish chowder (you guessed it, for clams and fish), both $2.50. Atlantic chowder — "all good things from the Atlantic," from haddock to lobster — is served in three-size portions ($1.75 to $3.75). Entrees included lobster stew, an avocado, lobster and crabmeat salad plate, baked shrimp Michel and chicken marsala, all for $9.95. Listed among "delicious, delicious decisions" for dessert were cheesecake with brandied fruits, lime cream pie and a fresh peach pie with real whipped cream.

The Galley sells its Atlantic chowder and pecan pies for takeout.

Lunch 11 to 5, dinner 5 to 8:30; closed Tuesday; cash only.

Greenery Creamery, 15 Dock Square, Rockport. (617) 546-9593.

The name bespeaks the theme of this casual place, but nothing prepares one for the view of Motif No. 1 across the harbor from the butcherblock tables at the rear of the L-shaped dining room.

Seafood and vegetable salads ($4.95 to $7.95) are featured, as is a salad bar and an ice cream and pastry bar out front. Otherwise the fare runs from what co-owners Deborah Lyons and Midge Zarling call gourmet sandwiches to dinner entrees like seafood casserole, seafood linguini, chicken Milano and pesto pizza ($6.95 to $12.25).

For sandwiches, how about the Sproutwich — muenster and cheddar cheeses, mushrooms and sunflower seeds, crammed with sprouts and served with choice of dressing ($3.95). You can get a lobster or crab roll, or a peanut butter and honey sandwich.

Apple pie with streusel topping and cheesecake with fresh strawberries are popular desserts ($2.50 to $2.95).

Open daily, 9 a.m. to 9 p.m., May-October.

Ellen's Harborside, 1 T-Wharf, Rockport. (617) 546-2512.

Wholesome food, reasonably priced, is the attraction at this plain, local institution with a front counter and tables and a rear dining room overlooking the water.

The breakfast special could be eggs Benedict for $2.75; you can get a clam roll for $3.95 along with more mundane fare for lunch, and dinners run from $3.95 for fried squid to $9.95 for lazy lobster or Delmonico steak. For dessert, assorted pastries are 45 cents, chocolate pudding 95 cents and the most expensive item when we visited was vanilla ice cream with rhubarb sauce, $1.30.

Open daily from 5:30 a.m., early spring through late fall.

The Hannah Jumper, Tuna Wharf, Bearskin Neck, Rockport. (617) 546-3600.

The sign outside advises "ocean view from all tables — like having your meal on a boat," and the tourists respond accordingly. The menu is straightforward if uninspired; 10 dinner entrees run from $7.95 for chicken Kiev to $9.25 for fisherman's platter.

There's no doubting the popularity of the canopied outdoor Harbor Deck upstairs. You can savor the view and feast on light fare like a crabmeat quiche with salad for $4.50 or "lobster in the ruff" for $7.25.

Open from 11:30 to 8:30; closed November-March.

Helmut's Strudel, 49 Bearskin Neck, Rockport.

Not a restaurant as such (although you may share a small rear deck with a seagull or two on a couple of weathered captain's chairs), this small bakery makes a good stop for strudels (apple, cherry, cheese, almond and apricot, 85 cents a slice), blueberry croissants (95 cents), coffee, tea and "the best hot chocolate in town."

Diversions

The Seashore. Rockport is aptly named — it has the rocky look of the Maine coast, in contrast with the sand dunes associated with the rest of the Massachusetts shore. Country lanes lined with wild flowers interspersed between interesting homes hug the rockbound coast and criss-cross the headlands in the area south of town known as Land's End. We like the California look of Cape Hedge Beach from the heights at the end of South Street, the twin lighthouses on Thatchers Island as viewed from Marmion Way, and the glimpses of yachts from the verdant, narrow streets along the water in quaint Annisquam (stop for a lobster roll on the deck right over the water at the Lobster Cove).

Swimming is fine at Front and Back beaches in the center of town, the expansive Good Harbor Beach near the Gloucester line, the relatively unknown Cape Hedge and Pebble beaches at Land's End, and the Lanesville beach north of town. Parking can be a problem, but we've always managed.

Bearskin Neck. The rocky peninsula which juts into the harbor was the original fishing and commercial center of the town. Today, most of the weatherbeaten shacks have been converted into shops of every description. Glimpses of Sandy Bay and the Inner Harbor pop up like a changing slide show between buildings and through shop doors and windows. The rocky point at the end of the neck provides a panoramic view, or you can rest on a couple of benches off T Wharf and admire Motif No. 1 — the Rockport Rotary Club sign beckons, "This little park is just for you, come sit awhile and enjoy the view."

Shopping. Most of Bearskin Neck's enterprises cater more to tourists than residents. Main Street and the Dock Square area generally have better stores. **The Cormorant Shop** sells traditional sportswear for men and women. **The Madras Shop** has nifty sportswear, **Sand Castles** contemporary clothing and accessories, and **Kids & Company** everything for children. You can watch saltwater taffy being made at **Tuck's Candies.** Proceeds from the well-stocked **Toad Hall Bookstore** further environmental causes.

The Art Galleries. For many, art is Rockport's chief attraction. More than 200 artists make the town their home, and 37 galleries are listed in the Rockport Fine Arts Gallery Guide. **The Rockport Art Association,** with exhibitions and demonstrations in its large headquarters at 12 Main St., is a leader in its field. John Manship, a past president of the art association and son of Paul Manship, Rockport's famed sculptor whose Prometheus stands in New York's Rockefeller Center, has a gallery at Main and School streets. You could wander for hours through places like Paul Strisik's slick gallery next to the art association or Geraci Galleries in a 1725 complex of buildings at 6 South St.

Band Concerts. The summer Sunday evening concerts presented by the Rockport Legion Band at the outdoor bandstand near the water at Back Beach have been a Cape Ann tradition since 1932. Some of the original members are still active today, providing stirring concert marches, overtures and selections from Broadway musicals under the stars. Other than these, the best entertainment in town may well be, as a couple of guests at Eden Pines put it, "sitting on Dock Square and watching the world go by."

Museums. The **Sandy Bay Historical Society and Museum,** 40 King St., has early furnishings and exhibits on shipping, fishing and the local granite industry in the 1832 Sewall-Scripture House built of granite (open 2 to 6 daily in summer, free). The **James Babson Cooperage Shop** (1658) on Route 127 just across the Gloucester line, a small one-story brick structure with early tools and furniture, may be the oldest building on Cape Ann (Tuesday-Sunday 2 to 5, free). The **Old Castle** (1678) at Granite and Curtis streets, Pigeon Cove, offers early architecture, period furniture and clothing, artifacts and handicrafts, most of local origin (summer weekends, 1 to 4, free). Also at Pigeon Cove at 52 Pigeon Hill St. is the **Paper House,** built nearly 50 years ago of 215 thicknesses of specially treated newspapers; chairs, desks, tables, lamps and other furnishings also are made of paper (daily in summer, 10 to 5, 50 cents).

Extra-Special

Like the rest of Rockport, its museums are low-key. But you have only to go next door to Gloucester to see two of New England's outstanding showplaces.

Beauport, 75 Eastern Point Blvd. Interior designer Henry David Sleeper started building his summer home in 1907 to house his collection of decorative arts and furnishings. Most of the 40 rooms are small, but each is decorated in a different style or period with a priceless collection of objects. Sleeper designed several rooms to house specific treasures: the round, two-story Tower Library was built to acccommodate a set of carved wooden draperies from a hearse; the Octagon Room was built to match an eight-sided table. One of the breakfast tables in the Golden Step Room is right against a window that overlooks Gloucester Harbor; many visitors wish the place served lunch or tea. Guided tours Monday-Friday 10 to 4, mid-May to mid-October; also weekends 1 to 4 from mid-September to mid-October; adults, $4.

Hammond Castle Museum, Hesperus Avenue. Cross the drawbridge and stop for lunch or tea and castle-baked pastries at the Roof Top Cafe in this replica of a medieval castle, built in the late 1920s by John Hays Hammond Jr. to house his collection of Roman, **Medieval** and **Renaissance art and objects.** Concerts are given on the organ with 8,600 pipes rising eight stories above the cathedral-like Great Hall. Marbled columns and lush plantings watered by its own rain system are featured in the Courtyard. Guided tours, daily 10 to 4, May-October; Thursday-Saturday 10 to 4 and Sunday 1 to 4, November-April; adults $3.50.

Neoclassical white marble temple houses Sterling and Francine Clark Art Institute.

Williamstown, Mass.
Arts Town of the East

Blessed with an uncommonly scenic setting and the riches that prestigious Williams College attracts and returns, this small college town in the Berkshires has become an arts center of national significance.

Newsweek magazine called the annual Williamstown Theatre Festival "the best of all American summer theaters." Connoisseur magazine said its three leading museums make it "an unlikely but powerful little art capital." U.S. News and World Report found that educators consider Williams College tops among academic institutions in the country.

Williams, its associates and benefactors have inspired these superlatives. But they have geography and nature to thank for what some call "the Village Beautiful." Set in a verdant bowl, Williamstown is at the foot of Mount Greylock, the highest peak in Massachusetts, and surrounded by Vermont's Green and New York's Taconic mountains. Not only do these provide great outdoors activities (golf, hiking and skiing in particular). They also help Williamstown retain a charmed rural flavor that seems far more small-town than its population of 5,000 might suggest.

Williamstown is a sophisticated college town of great appeal, one that unfolds as you delve. The youthful dynamic of 2,000 college students is not readily apparent in the broader community. Besides natural and cultural attractions, there are fine restaurants and selective shops but distressingly few inns.

This is one place which has long been special, even without inns. If you simply drive around town, you'll miss the real Williamstown. Here you must stop and explore.

Inn Spots

The Orchards, 222 Adams Road (Route 2), Williamstown 01267. (413) 458-9611. (800) 231-2344.

Opened to the tune of many millions of dollars in the summer of 1985, the Orchards was designed to fill a conspicuous gap in terms of country

The Orchards is designed in the style of an English country hotel.

inn accommodations. It succeeds "along the lines of an English country hotel" (its words). But it's not the Berkshires' "most gracious country inn" nor "the finest inn in the Northeast," as its publicity hoopla claims. Rather, it's a spacious, spanking-new hotel-motor inn with telephones in bathrooms as well as bedrooms, in-room refrigerators and television controls at bedside.

The 49-room, three-story structure meanders around a small, open courtyard containing a little free-form, rock-bordered pool surrounded by outdoor dining deck, lawns and flowers.

The interior layout separates restaurant and shop from guest rooms; winding corridors expand into a drawing room with high ceiling. Polished antique English furniture of the Queen Anne period fills the living room, where complimentary scones and English tea are served on fine china in the afternoon and, perhaps, dessert and coffee or liqueurs after dinner. Coffee and breakfast pastries are offered there before the dining room opens in the morning.

The guest rooms are large, comfortable and colorful in the Orchards' pink and green theme (the site was long an orchard, but you'd never know it today from the shopping center across the street and the housing tracts behind on this, the most built-up side of Williamstown). Each room is different within the prevailing theme: marble bathrooms with terrycloth robes and Crabtree & Evelyn bath oils and soaps, separate dressing area, and small refrigerator. Some have working fireplaces, four-poster beds and bay windows. Cookies are served when the beds are turned down at night; the pillows are filled with feathers and down.

The inn has a sauna and jacuzzi, environmental chamber, four function rooms, an antiques shop, a cocktail lounge with fireplace and a beautiful dining room (see below).

Doubles, $85 to $130.

Le Jardin, 777 Cold Spring Road (Route 7), Williamstown 01267. (413) 458-8032.

A wooded hillside lush with pachysandra, a pond, a waterfall from the passing brook and, of course, gardens, welcome guests to this French-style restaurant and country inn converted from a 19th-century mansion two miles south of town.

A narrow stairway beside the entrance to the main dining room leads from the entry foyer to the four guest rooms, all with fireplaces and private baths. Most choice is the front corner room with the bed ensconced in a niche, stenciling and hooked rugs, and a tub with a jacuzzi in the large bathroom. The other rooms in country style are somewhat more plain.

The only television is in the front bar. Continental breakfast is served in the formal dining room (see below), where German chef-innkeeper Walter Hayn has achieved a good reputation.

Doubles, $45 to $75.

The Williams Inn, Junction of Routes 7 and 2, Williamstown 01267. (413) 458-9371.

After the old Williams Inn burned, the Treadway built a replacement (supposedly "on-the-green at Williams College," though not by our definition). We wish we could be more enthusiastic, but this is a three-story Colonial-modern motel rather than an inn.

The 104 air-conditioned rooms have full baths, color TV, oversize beds and early American furnishings. Facilities include an indoor pool, a whirlpool and sauna, elevators, lounge and dining room serving three meals a day. The inn's gift shop, the **Country Store,** is particularly good, featuring quilted bags, baskets, beveled glass ornaments, porcelain Christmas tree angels, appliqued denim jumpers, animal sculptures and such.

Doubles, $75 to $85.

Dining Spots

Capers, 412 Main St., Williamstown. (413) 458-9180.

Arguably the most popular eating and gathering spot in Williamstown, this has changed markedly since it evolved from the old British Maid across the street.

The Maid gave way to the Orchards and its founder, Penelope Corbin from England, now runs the inn's antiques shop. Her daughter Vicky is a partner in Capers with Tom Ralys, the Maid's maitre-d, and chef Win Rutledge out of Lenox.

The new Capers still serves breakfasts and only local eggs, breads and produce, but Williams grads would scarcely recognize the place — all done up in cafe chic with an angled oak bar, corner bandstand, track lighting from the beams, and dining on several levels with bentwood chairs, pink cloths, purple napkins, gray carpeting, framed posters of flowers on the dark wood walls and spotlights pinpointing the flowers on each table. It's all very colorful.

The British Maid's famous crepes are gone, but the remaining fare is eclectic and enticing. Consider the lunch menu: sandwiches and burgers in everything from English muffin to pita pocket, omelets and eggs Benedict, five kinds of pasta, three salad plates and an enormous array of mouth-watering desserts — chambord cake, lime meringue pie, double chocolate torte and blueberry cheesecake are a few. French onion soup, watercress and tomato salad, and a meringue chantilly would set you back $6.35.

The Sunday breakfasts are legendary, from the simple to the sublime. Eggs Benedict or kippered herrings on toast are both $5.50.

But for the eggs, many of the same dishes are available at night, the mix-and-match casual part of the menu listing hummus with tortilla chips, salad plates, a guacamole burger and four pastas, one of them linguini with steamed mussels. Among entrees ($12.95 to $17.95) are flounder Dijon with capers, duck bourguignon, steak au poivre and lamb provencale. And almost no one fails to succumb to one of those great desserts ($2.25 to $3), perhaps English trifle or strawberries Romanoff.

The classical background music ends on weekends at 9 when jazz or light rock musicians take to the bandstand. The wine list is limited; the house Papillion is $7 a carafe.

Open Tuesday-Saturday from 11, Sunday from 10.

The Mill on the Floss, Route 7, New Ashford. (413) 438-9123.

Genial Maurice Champagne, originally from Montreal, is the chef-owner at this established and well-regarded restaurant. He loves to socialize, so one reason he designed the blue and while tiled open kitchen was so that patrons could come up and talk with him as he cooked. The dark brown wood building, prettily landscaped, was once a mill; inside it is cozy, with beamed ceilings, paneled walls, a hutch filled with Quimper pottery, white linens and many hanging copper pots. Before dinner, complimentary Swiss cheese and crackers, and chicken liver pate with radishes and olives are served.

Chef Maurice Champagne in kitchen.

The menu is classical French. A bargain $12.50 prix-fixe dinner is served from Monday to Friday; Monday's dinner includes soup, salad, rolls, coq au vin with rice, creme caramel and coffee, and Wednesday's is antipasto, garlic bread, pasta with a choice of sauces and cold souffle grand marnier with raspberry sauce.

Otherwise, the regular menu lists appetizers from $1.50 for pate maison to $6.50 for coquilles St. Jacques; onion soup gratinee is $2.50. Entrees, including a green salad, are $9.50 for pasta to $17.50 for sweetbreads with black butter and capers or filet mignon bearnaise or au poivre. Duckling a l'orange, veal piccata, chicken breast amandine or provencale, and sliced tenderloin with bordelaise sauce are some, and the fish of the day might be halibut meuniere or swordfish.

For dessert (changing daily), you might find a nut torte, a chocolate roll cake filled with grand marnier souffle, or, for $7.50, have cafe diablo for two. Wines are quite reasonable; $2 brings a glass of the house valpolicello or Argentine chardonnay. In winter of 1986, M. Champagne took on an additional role as executive chef of **Drummond's,** to oversee the opening of the restaurant at the new **Country Inn** at the base of the Jiminy Peak ski area in nearby Hancock.

Dinner nightly from 5 p.m. (from 4 p.m. in July and August); Sunday, brunch 11 to 2, dinner from 2.

The 1896 House, Routes 2 and 7 south of Williamstown, (413) 458-8123.

An expansive red dairy barn structure with a pleasant new outdoor patio in front, this has been a restaurant known for beef dishes since its start in the 1920s. Under new ownership since late 1984, it stresses its Williams ties, ambitious expansion plans and regional nouvelle cuisine.

New owner E. Howland Swift, a development director at Williams, is the force behind the new partnership, which planned to build a 66-room New England-style inn and connecting Greenery restaurant behind the barn in 1986. Meanwhile, the existing restaurant is in the capable hands of Robin Lenz, wife of a Williams professor and a California-trained chef lately at the Brasserie in Bennington, Vt.

Dinner begins with crudities and crackers plus a basket of homemade breads (perhaps sourdough, Italian seeded white and banana) and two herbed vegetable pates (carrot-bacon and broccoli-fennel, the night we visited). Among appetizers ($2.75 to $4) are the locally grown Delf Tree mushrooms in a tart, smoked Norwegian trout mousse, and oysters sauteed with champagne, cream and pasta. Salads are extra (the local goat cheese baked with chives and garlic sounds interesting), and the green salad of four lettuces is dressed with a vinaigrette tinged with sherry.

Entrees range from $9.75 for scrod en papillotte to $15.50 for New York sirloin. Possibilities from the changing seasonal menu include bouillabaisse, duckling with homemade plum preserves, braised rabbit, local veal with Delf Tree mushrooms and creme fraiche, grilled shrimp with Cajun crab sauce, and such nightly specials as grilled albacore tuna with saffron tomato cream sauce or rainbow trout stuffed with trout mousse.

The wine list is reasonably priced (a Heitz barbera for $8.50), California wines are available by the glass and the house wine is a Spanish Olarra, rare for a New England restaurant. Desserts range from blueberry apple crumble or fresh fruit sorbet with Florentines to chocolate hazelnut torte with a chocolate rum filling and carrot cake with cream cheese frosting.

The dining room has an upscale barn interior of red carpeting, blue chairs with beige leather seats, floral tablecloths with blue napkins, candles in hurricane lamps, and brass lamps under antique paintings on the dark pine walls. A pianist plays 1950s tunes in the large cocktail lounge.

Lunch, 11:30 to 2:30; dinner, 5:30 to 9:30; closed Sundays.

The Orchards, 222 Adams Road, Williamstown. (413) 458-9611.

Upholstered reproduction Queen Anne chairs, rose and green carpeting, forest green walls and well-spaced tables set with soft rose linen, ribbed glassware, flowered German china, silver baskets for the rolls and antique teapots — what could be more elegant than the L-shaped, two-part dining room at the Orchards? We especially enjoyed a Saturday lunch, settled in the comfy high-backed rose velveteen chairs in an airy two-story greenhouse-like area at one end, looking onto the outdoor deck and courtyard. It was the next best thing to dining outside under striped umbrellas (it was too cool that day).

The inn's linen bill must be outrageous, based on the layers cautiously arranged by the young busboy (attired in formal maroon jacket and topsiders) as he changed the cloths. Each table bears intricate covered dishes for sugar and saccharin, pepper grinder and crystal salt shaker.

Poppyseed rolls were served as we sipped the Macon white house wine, a not particularly generous glass for $2.50. Sandwiches, salads and sandwiches are priced from $3.95 (for ham and cheese) to $6.25 for open-faced steak. Swordfish soup with vegetables was an interesting starter, as was the excellent chilled apple curry soup. The chicken salad with papaya slices, apples and pecans was a winner, and a beef bourgignon special was fine. Not so wonderful was the strawberry almond cake ($2), which tasted like a jelly roll; next time we'll try the peanut butter cheesecake or the pear flan.

The dinner menu features what is said to be New England cuisine with an old English flavor. That translates to regional cuisine with names like sauteed scallops Nantucket and supreme of chicken Greylock and, the only English touch we could find, prime ribs with popover and horseradish.

Among entrees ($10.50 for the chicken to $16.95 for lobster pie), we liked the sound of salmon poached in vermouth court-bouillion with leeks and baby shrimp, swordfish broiled with mustard butter sauce and served with dilled new potatoes, rock Cornish game hen with chanterelles and pecan wild rice, and domestic veal in a port wine sauce. Irish smoked salmon and smoked duck with blueberry sauce appealed among appetizers ($3.95 to $6.95), and for dessert, perhaps chestnut cake or frozen raspberry souffle.

Lunch daily, noon to 2; dinner, 5:30 to 9; Sunday brunch, noon to 2.

Le Country Restaurant, 101 North St. (Route 7), Williamstown. (413) 458-4000.

A country atmosphere and the personalities of chef-owner Raymond Canales, his wife Beverly and son Gregory pervade this long-established restaurant in the continental tradition. "We're sort of rustic," Beverly acknowledged as she showed the main dining room done up in beige and brown, with beamed ceiling, a mix of shaded lamps and candles on the tables, and a Franklin stove to ward off the chill in winter. The nicest of the three dining rooms with high ceiling and sunken area with fireplace is used for special occasions.

A striking antique piece from Brittany is decked out with wines, glasses and grapes; it's the sister to one behind the bar. "We want people to enjoy wines, so we don't have much of a markup," Beverly explained when we found some extraordinary bargains (carafes for $7.50, vouvray for $9, chardonnays from $11 to $18 and nothing over $20).

The extensive menu is supplemented by nightly specials, prime rib and veal curry the night we were there. Entrees from $9.95 for fettuccine carbonara to $16.95 for broiled lamb chops include chicken prepared four ways, shrimp three, and such standards as duckling bigarade, veal marsala and tournedos bordelaise. Southern pecan pie and baba au rhum are featured desserts.

Le Jardin offers country French dining and lodging.

Many of the appetizers and desserts are available at lunch, along with sandwiches, salad plates and entrees from $5.75 to $8.95 for items like chicken fricassee on toast, Spanish omelet and coquilles St. Jacques.
Lunch, Tuesday-Friday 11:30 to 1:30; dinner, Tuesday-Sunday 5 to 9.

Le Jardin, 777 Cold Spring Road, Williamstown. (413) 458-8032.
The large dining room is country French and quite elegant, with velvet striped seats, white linens and dark napkins placed sideways, hanging lamps with pierced tin panels, white draperies and plants in every window.
German chef Walter Hayn's blackboard menu is classic French, from the French onion soup for $2.50 to the herring in sour cream and escargots ($6). Dinner entrees ($12 for chicken Henry IV to $19 for steak au poivre flambe) run the gamut from Long Island duckling to veal steak Lyonnaise, all nicely prepared with fine cream sauces. The wine list struck us as strange, though there were Beaujolais Villages Jadot for $14 and Pere Patriarche for a bargain $8.50.
Desserts are $2.50 and tend to be very rich — chocolate truffle mousse cake, double fudge chocolate layer cake, hazelnut torte, kahlua cheesecake and pecan pie.
Dinner nightly, 5 to 10 (closed Tuesday in winter); Sunday brunch, 10:30 to 1:30.

The River House, 123 Water St., Williamstown. (413) 458-4820.
Popular with the college crowd, the expanding River House offers a large, varied menu of "New England country fare in an authentic 1870s setting," an original building with beamed ceilings, bare floors and candles in hurricane lamps, a large bar and newer additions where tables are covered by blue mats.
Soups, appetizers, salads, entrees, desserts, wines and bar selections are listed on the straightforward, five-page typewritten menu. The choices are numerous; suffice it to say that you can order almost anything you desire,

from artichoke hearts vinaigrette to deep fried eggplant with cheese to an open-faced reuben to Indian pudding with ice cream — nothing too trendy here. Entrees are $7.95 (manicotti, roast turkey) to $14.95 (steak, prime rib) and the homemade brownie is covered with the extraordinary fudge sauce of Mother Myrick's in Manchester, Vt. All ten wines are $9.50 or less (pina coladas and Guinness stout are more popular here).

Dinner, 5 to 10, late-night fare to midnight; Sundays and holidays, 1 to 9; closed Mondays.

Diversions

Williamstown's scenic beauty is apparent on all sides, but less known is the composite of its art and history collections. Art and history are best appreciated when viewed close up, away from the crowded settings of the great museums, according to Connoisseur magazine, which cites this intimacy as "the great gift" of Williamstown.

Extra-Special

Sterling and Francine Clark Art Institute, 225 South St. The most widely known of the town's museums chanced upon its Williamstown location through an old family connection with Williams and the fact that eccentric collector Sterling Clark, heir to the Singer sewing machine fortune, wanted his treasures housed far from a potential site of nuclear attack. Clark's neoclassical white marble temple opened in 1955 (he and his wife are buried under its front steps) and was expanded in 1973 by a red granite addition housing more galleries and one of the outstanding art research libraries in the country. The Clark's major strength lies in its holdings of French 19th-century paintings, English silver, prints and drawings (the Clark was the single largest source for the Renoir exhibition at Boston's Museum of Fine Arts in 1985-86). Shown mostly in small galleries the size of the rooms in which they once hung, the highly personalized collection of Monets, Turners and Winslow Homers quietly vie for attention with sculptures, porcelain and three centuries worth of silver (Clark liked good food and the silverware to go with it). All this is amidst an austere yet intimate setting of potted plants and vases of dried flowers, furniture and benches for relaxation. Amazingly, it's free, Tuesday-Sunday 10 to 5.

Williams College Museum of Art, Main Street. A $4.5 million extension to its original octagonal building in Lawrence Hall makes this museum, itself a work of art with "ironic" columns that are decorative rather than functional, a sleeper in art circles. It features traveling and special exhibitions as well as the college's holdings, notably the Cluett Collection of Spanish paintings and 19th and 20th century American works. Open free Monday-Saturday 10 to 5, Sunday 1 to 5. Nearby is the Hopkins Observatory, the oldest extant observatory in the United States (1836) and used as a planetarium and museum with twice-weekly free shows in the summer.

Chapin Library, Stetson Hall, Williams College. Nowhere else are the founding documents of the country — the Declaration of Independence, the Articles of Confederation, the Bill of Rights and drafts of the Constitution

— displayed together in a simple glass case on the second floor of a college hall. This remarkable library contains more than 25,000 rare books, first editions and manuscripts — you might ask to see James Madison's copy of Paine's "Common Sense." One floor below is the Williamsiana Collection of town and gown, while the lowest level of Stetson contains the archives of band leader Paul Whiteman, with 3,500 original scores and a complete library of music of the 1920s. Open Monday-Friday, 9 to noon and 1 to 5.

Williamstown Theatre Festival, Adams Memorial Theater, Williams College. Founded in 1955 (the year of the Clark Art Institute opening), the professional summer festival presents "some of the most ambitious theatre the U.S. has to offer," in the words of the Christian Science Monitor. Such luminaries as Christopher Reeve, Dick Cavett, Edward Herrmann and Marsha Mason return summer after summer to the festival they call home for productions of everything from Chekhov and Ibsen to Tennessee Williams and Broadway tryouts, all the while mingling with the townspeople. The festival uses the theater's main stage, but also includes the smaller Other Stage, emphasizing newer works in the 99-seat Extension added in 1982 to the same building. Leads from the main stage often join the festival's Caberet, which presents late-night revues at area restaurants. Festival performances Tuesday-Saturday, late June through August.

Nature. The prime spot — as well as the area's dominant feature — is the **Mount Greylock State Reservation,** a series of seven peaks with a 3,491-foot summit that is the highest in Massachusettts. You can drive, hike or bike to the summit for a spectacular five-state view. Other memorable views are obtained by driving the Taconic Trail through Petersburg Pass and the Mohawk Trail above North Adams. The vast **Hopkins Memorial Forest** northwest of the campus is an experimental forest operated by the Williams College Center for Environmental Studies, with nature and cross-country trails, plus the Barn Museum showing old photographs, farm machinery, implements and tools, and the Buxton Gardens, a farm garden designed to have certain flowers in bloom at all times. Williams College also recently reacquired **Mount Hope Park,** a former estate with extensive gardens and grounds.

Recreation. Golf is the summer pastime at the Taconic Golf Club, on the south edge of town and ranked as one of the tops in New England, and at Waubeeka Springs Golf Links in the valley at South Williamstown. In winter, there's skiing nearby at Jiminy Peak and Brodie Mountain ski resorts.

Shopping. The college-community stores are generally along Spring Street, running south off Main Street opposite the main campus and between campus appendages such as museum, science center and sports complex; the **House of Walsh** is an institution for traditional clothing. Water Street, an historic development which blossomed later, has distinctive shops including the **Cottage** and **Mole Hole** gift shops, **Phillips' General Store,** outdoors equipment at the **Mountain Goat** and stained glass at the **Glass Menagerie.** We always stop at the **Potter's Wheel,** an outstanding shop with stoneware, porcelain, glass, prints, woods, fibres and jewelry by top craftsmen, and last time came out with a nifty little acrylic sheep to hang in the dining room window.

Chesterwood was summer home and studio of sculptor Daniel Chester French.

Lenox, Mass.
The Good (and Cultured) Life

The gentle beauty of the Berkshires has attracted generations of artists, authors and musicians — as well as their patrons who appreciate the good life. At the center of the Berkshires in both location and spirit is Lenox, a small village whose cultural influence far exceeds its size.

In the 19th century, Lenox was home for Nathaniel Hawthorne, Edith Wharton, Henry Ward Beecher and Fannie Kemble. Herman Melville, Henry Adams, Oliver Wendell Holmes, Henry Wadsworth Longfellow, William Cullen Bryant, Daniel Chester French and Norman Rockwell lived and worked nearby.

Such was the allure of this tranquil mountain and lake country that many prominent Americans built palatial homes here. Lenox became an inland rival of Newport for such families as Westinghouse, Carnegie, Procter, Morgan and Vanderbilt (indeed, some of the 400 summered in Newport and spent the early autumn in the Berkshires).

The artists and the affluent helped make Lenox in the 20th century a center for the arts. Tanglewood, across from Hawthorne's home, is the summer home of the Boston Symphony, and Edith Wharton's Mount is the stage for Shakespeare & Company. Nearby are the Lenox Arts Center, the Berkshire Theater Festival, Jacob's Pillow Dance Festival, and South Mountain Concerts.

The Lenox area's cultural attractions are well known. Less so are some of its other treats; the picturesque Stockbridge Bowl (a lake), the Walker sculpture garden, the Pleasant Valley wildlife sanctuary, the Church on the Hill, and the mansions along Kemble and Cliffwood streets.

Staying in some of Lenox's inns is like being a house guest in a mansion. Many require a minimum three-day stay on summer weekends, and weekend prices often extend from Thursday through Sunday. Rates vary from weekend to midweek, from season to season.

Besides lodging in style, visitors may dine at some of New England's fanciest restaurants and enjoy $40 orchestra seats in the Shed at Tanglewood. The budget-conscious can find more reasonable places in which to stay and eat, and, while picnicking on the Tanglewood lawn, can hear the BSO almost as well as those in the Shed.

Except perhaps for the prices, we don't know anyone who doesn't enjoy the copious charms of Lenox.

Inn Spots

Apple Tree Inn, 224 West St., Lenox 01240. (413) 637-1477.

Imagine sitting by the pool, iced drink in hand, and listening to the music from Tanglewood waft up the hill. If you stay at the Apple Tree Inn, you don't even need to buy a lawn ticket.

We first met this inn, situated across from the main Tanglewood gate, a couple of incarnations ago, when it was Alice's at Avaloch (the original name of the estate) and Alice Brock of Alice's Restaurant fame was the chef. After that, it was the Portofino for a few years, and was taken over in 1983 by New Yorkers Greg and Aurora Smith, who have spent much energy and money to turn the handsome 100-year-old main house into a proper inn.

High on a hill amidst 22 acres covered with apple trees, the setting could not be more fortuitous. Greg, a keen gardener, has planted 7,000 bulbs and more than 300 varieties of roses, all labeled, in an effort to give the inn a fourth season — spring. The aforementioned pool, installed by the Smiths in 1985, is contoured to fit into the hillside beyond an old red barn; from it there is a commanding view of the countryside, including Tanglewood.

The inn includes a separate structure with 20 motel-like rooms, which the Smiths have upgraded.

Of more interest is the refurbishing done in the main house. Everywhere there is evidence of Greg's construction abilities and Aurora's decorating flair. Since the rooms had never been available to the public before, the Smiths had plenty to do, including replacing ceilings and putting in new bathrooms.

The sitting area is surrounded by walls with arches cut into them, outlined by Tiffany-type fixtures. It has velvet sofas and chairs for lounging in front of the fireplace, and a grand piano often played by visiting musicians.

All 11 new bedrooms on the second and third floors, many with working fireplaces, are picture-pretty with quilts and comforters, ruffled pillows and dust ruffles done by Aurora, a sculptor, who says she always has to have handwork to do while she is sitting down. Rooms either have new wallpaper or spiffy new paint jobs; they vary in size, some have twin beds, some have window seats, some on the third floor have skylights. Room 2 is the prize, with a high four-poster bed you have to use a step stool to get into. French doors covered with lace curtains open onto a private porch where you can sit and look at the waters of Stockbridge Bowl shimmering down below, if you are not inside enjoying the fireplace.

Blantyre is a Tudor-style replica of a castle in Scotland.

Several Raggedy Ann and Andy dolls peek through the staircase up to the second floor. They were made by Aurora, who also painted in wondrous colors the old shoe lasts that you'll find in each room.

Guests are served continental breakfast (usually muffins, sometimes popovers) and have use of the clay tennis court. Lunch, cocktails and dinner also are available (see Dining Spots).

Doubles, $80 to $185, suites $225 to $240 weekends; $70 to $150 and $175 to $195 midweek.

Blantyre, Route 20 and East St., Lenox 01240. (413) 637-3556 or 637-1728.

This rambling, Tudor-style brick manor was built in 1902 as a summer retreat for a millionaire in the turpentine business. A replica of the Hall of Blantyre in Scotland, it used to be called Blantyre Castle, and was a memorable place for dining in the baronial style. Today, "castle" has been dropped from the name, but the feeling remains in lodging as well as in dining.

In 1981 it was carefully restored even to the inside of the huge closets by Jane Fitzpatrick, whose Red Lion Inn in adjacent Stockbridge has welcomed guests in the old New England tradition for so many years. The result is worthy of a castle: a majestic foyer with staircase of black oak, public rooms with high beamed ceilings, rich and intricate carved paneling, crystal chandeliers and fireplaces with hand-carved mantels, and eight elegant suites and guest rooms, five with fireplaces.

The Peterson Suite has a fireplaced living room, large bedroom with kingsize bed and two baths. Victorian-style sofas and chairs make comfortable sitting areas at the foot of the ornate queensize four-poster beds in the Laurel and Cromwell suites. Even the smallest Bouquet and Ribbon rooms are fit for would-be barons and baronesses, if only for a night or two.

Twelve more contemporary rooms, several of them split-level loft suites, are available in the carriage house. Three cottages offer two-bedrooms suites with kitchenettes.

Four tennis courts, a swimming pool and competition croquet courts are available on 85 acres of woods and lawns.

Fruit, wine and cheese await guests on arrival. Cocktails and after-dinner coffee and cordials are served in the main foyer and crystal-chandeliered music room. A complimentary continental breakfast is served in the breakfast room or on the terrace.

A five-course, prix-fixe dinner is available for $50 for guests and the public by reservation. It is served at a long table in the formal paneled dining room or more intimately in one of the smaller dining rooms.

Doubles with continental breakfast, $150 to $200; suites, $175 to $350. Two-night minimum, weekends in summer and October. Open May-October.

25 Cliffwood Inn, 25 Cliffwood St., Lenox 01240. (413) 637-3330.

A magnificent classic Colonial built in Stanford White style in the early 1900s by the then-ambassador to France, this is almost a stage set for the furnishings of innkeepers Don Thompson and Hector Bellini, antiques dealers and restaurateurs who opened their inn in Lenox in 1984 after having restaurants in Texas and a catering service in San Francisco. Single-entree dinners served family style in the elegant dining room are an option for house guests.

The three-story mansion has ten fireplaces, one of them in the newly renovated bathroom off a third-floor guest room.

A large foyer gives access to all three main-floor public rooms, each of which has French doors opening to the full-length back porch. At one end of the house, the living room with 12-foot-high mirrors, white marble fireplace, grand piano and showy antiques is a decorator's dream. The music room in the center leads to the formal dining room, which has a black marble fireplace.

Dining here is "like having dinner in our home," says Don Thompson, the chef. A single-choice dinner for $30 (including wine) is served at 7:45 by Hector, who's the innkeeper and waiter. It usually begins with soup (cream of mushroom, or cabbage and leek), a green salad and homemade baguettes. The entree could be broiled sole in lemon butter or chicken breast with prosciutto and fontina cheese. Mocha rum raisin mousse, peach or raspberry ice cream and French silk pie with macaroon crust are some of the yummy desserts. Wines are "what's good at the wine store," says Don.

Up the stairs lined with wonderful Japanese woodprints are eight guest rooms, six with private baths and six with working fireplaces. Fine paintings, sculptures, and 18th century French antiques (many for sale) are evident throughout the house. Two of the larger rooms have sitting areas in front of the fireplaces; one with a bidet in the bathroom has a tiny balcony overlooking the rear gardens. A red comforter decorates the wall behind the kingsize bed in the other, the former library, which has two blue chintz chairs in front of the fireplace. A third double room has a private bath, while two smaller rooms share a large bath. On the third floor are three double rooms each with private bath and fireplace. One has the fireplace inside the entry to the bathroom and another converted from a small suite has two bathrooms — toilet in one, tub in the other.

A continental breakfast with homemade muffins and breads is served in the morning.

Doubles, $70 to $115 weekends, $50 to $90 midweek.

Whistler's Inn, 5 Greenwood St., Lenox 01240. (413) 637-0975.

Located across from the landmark Church on the Hill, this fine French-English Tudor mansion built in 1820 by Whistler's nephew was acquired in 1978 by Richard and Joan Mears from a member of his family. It has been upgraded gradually into a gracious inn with museum-like public rooms and 11 guest rooms of varying size, all with private baths. The Mearses call themselves "bi-coastals," since they run the inn eight months of the year and spend winters in Marin County, California, where they write novels and do photography (some of their output is evident throughout the inn).

Edith Wharton used the French salon with the grand piano, two fringed green velvet sofas and oriental carpets as the setting for a scene in "Ethan Frome." Beyond is a gracious porch above an Italian sunken garden and seven acres of land. A fireplace, comfortable chairs for reading and a decanter of sherry await guests in the library.

Blueberry muffins, cheeses, juices and occasionally hard-boiled eggs are served for breakfast in the formal dining room or on the sunporch and terrace.

Upstairs, guest rooms range in size from large to a tiny single with a small square bathtub. The bathrooms have been modernized and the colorful tiles in most are striking. One room has red velvet bedspreads, another Mrs. Whistler's original Chippendale armoire, and a third has antique paper on walls and ceiling. Original art works and the innkeepers' framed photographs decorate walls throughout the inn. Rooms are furnished with "as many antiques as possible," Joan Mears says.

Doubles, $60 to $150 weekends, $55 to $110 midweek. Closed January-April.

Walker House, 24 Walker St., Lenox 01240. (413) 637-1271.

It's clear that ex-Californians Peggy and Richard Houdek, who opened this bed-and-breakfast inn five years ago in the heart of Lenox, like music. A pecan Kimball grand piano in the living room has sometimes been used for recitals and often for singalongs, a pump organ is in the front hall and the guest rooms are named for composers, with appropriate memorabilia of the person and the period in each. Dick Houdek was a music critic and Peggy in administration at the San Francisco Opera, which is where they met.

It's clear also that the Houdeks like flowers, which are in profusion everywhere, inside and out, and cats (they have six live ones and uncounted inanimate replicas in the form of pictures, pillows and the like). Cats are the theme of **Los Gatos** — "the best little cathouse in Lenox" — a gift shop which Peggy runs at 30 Church St.

The result is an engaging clutter that shows the public rooms are clearly meant to be used. Ditto for the wide back veranda looking onto a landscaped yard and three acres of woods in back.

All eight guest rooms in the house, built in 1804 as the Walker Rockwell House, have private baths and five have working fireplaces. Some have clawfoot tubs, most have hooked rugs and comforters, and several have canopied beds with high oak headboards. The Verdi room with its wild green and white wallpaper, white iron bedsteads and wicker furniture is in airy contrast to the dark colors and period wallpapers in most of the rooms. The Puccini room downstairs has rose walls, brass bedstead, modern bathroom, fireplace and its own little porch.

Continental breakfast of fresh fruit or baked apples, muffins and croissants are served in the dining room, where a stuffed tiger, lion and lamb are seated at one table, and on warm mornings on the back porch.

Doubles, $75 to $110 weekends, $55 to $75 midweek.

Tudor facade of Whistler's Inn.   French salon at Whistler's Inn.

Brook Farm Inn, 15 Hawthorne St., Lenox 01240. (413) 637-3013.

The grand piano nestled in a bay window in the library of this Victorian house is likely to be played by innkeeper Frank Newton, a former bank president who with his wife opened this inn at the edge of town in 1981 and assumed ownership of the Gables Inn in the center of Lenox in September 1985. The Newtons, who restored brownstones in Brooklyn before moving to Lenox, are creative, high-energy types whose talented touch shows, from one of the world's smallest bathrooms in a third-floor guest room to the ledge full of little Victorian ceramic houses she collects in the dining room.

Furnished with elegance in Victorian style, Brook Farm is the equivalent of many a Lenox inn, but the Newtons aim for the mid-priced segment of the market with peak rates only half those of many others. They have a swimming pool and serve a full breakfast, to boot.

The most choice of the eight guest rooms with private baths are on the second floor, several with working fireplaces. One has a high canopy bed reached by a step stool, and pink and white upholstered chairs around a pink table. The Presidential suite has an ornate carved bed, a sofa angled into the corner, many pictures of presidents, and the only bath not in the room but around a corner in the hall. The third floor has smaller rooms, one with a kingsize bed under a skylight and another with dark blue wallpaper on walls and ceiling, brightened by white curtains behind the headboards and white ruffled pillows on the twin beds.

The dining room with beamed ceiling and a small adjacent porch are set for breakfast with white crocheted cloths, sterling silver, cut-glass crystal and fresh flowers. Mrs. Newton serves a full breakfast, which might be eggs, pancakes, French toast or quiche.

Doubles, $65 to $75 weekends, $50 to $60 midweek.

Wheatleigh, West Hawthorne Road, Lenox 01240. (413) 637-0610.

If you've ever dreamed of staying in an Italian palazzo, this place is for you. Built in 1893 by railroad tycoon Henry H. Cook as a wedding gift for his daughter who married a Spanish count, it was the scene of grand parties until the countess's death in 1946. An inn since the 1960s, it is opulent, dramatic, extravagant and romantic.

In 1981, Linfield and Susan Simon of Chicago purchased Wheatleigh with 22 acres of parkland designed by Frederick Law Olmsted. Their aim was to have a world-class restaurant (see Dining Spots), which they say now compares favorably with New York's greats, and luxury accommodations in the style of a small European hotel.

The imposing (some might consider it intimidating) entrance to the honey-colored brick building framed in wrought-iron leads into a Great Hall with stunning contemporary sofas grouped in front of windows offering a distant lake view at the far end. A majestic staircase leads to the second floor and 17 guest rooms with private baths, ranging in size from standard to enormous, or what the rate sheet calls "extraordinaire." Nine have fireplaces, some have balconies and all have newly acquired antiques; "we've been adding beautiful pieces every year," Susan Simon says.

The landscaped grounds include marble statues and fountains, a swimming pool and tennis court. Tanglewood is within walking distance.

Doubles, $145 to $275.

Birchwood Inn, 7 Hubbard St., Lenox 01240. (413) 637-2600.

The only inn among four Lenox structures listed in the National Register of Historic Places, the white 1840 house occupies the site of the home of one of Lenox's earliest settlers. Paul and Gail Macdonald acquired it in 1982 and restored it to its onetime status as an inn.

The spacious living room-library with shelves of books is fine for relaxing, with several conversation areas, red loveseats, oriental area rugs and a fireplace. Two sets of French doors open onto the inviting front porch. A smaller parlor, again with fireplace, has a television set. Hitchcock chairs and lace curtains grace the dining room, where fresh fruit and croissants are served for breakfast.

The five guest rooms on the second floor have private baths, while five on the third floor share two. Several of the larger rooms have canopied beds and comfortable chairs grouped around non-working fireplaces. Dormered rooms with sloping walls and alcoves on the third floor are notable for showy balloon curtains of diverse colors — "every inn seems to have white curtains and I wanted something different," Gail Macdonald explains.

Doubles, $50 to $135 weekends, $45 to $110 midweek. Closed December-April.

Underledge, 76 Cliffwood St., Lenox 01240. (413) 637-0236.

A large white house with corner turret and solarium atop a hill some distance out Cliffwood Street, known to Lenox residents as *the street* but one often missed by tourists, this estate built in 1900 by two sisters was converted into an inn in 1982 by Marcie Lanoue and her son Tom, a carpenter.

Six of the twelve guest rooms have private baths. One on the main floor has a kingsize bed, chintz sofa, working fireplace and a large walk-in shower, left over from the building's nursing home days. Otherwise you'd never know, for the transformation has been so deft. A large room off the stairway landing to the second floor has a new fireplace framed in oak, two loveseats and a kingsize brass bedstead; it leads out onto a pleasant porch. Another has a wicker chaise lounge and deep rose and black draperies. Smaller rooms on the third floor share one bathroom.

The entry foyer is richly paneled in stained oak. Contemporary off-white sofas surround the fireplace just off the lobby. In the living room are television, stereo, piano and games. A continental breakfast including muffins made by Tom's wife, Cheryl, is served in the solarium.

Doubles, $40 to $120 weekends, $40 to $90 midweek.

Gateways Inn and Restaurant, 71 Walker St., Lenox 01240. (413) 637-2532.

The landmark white, dark-shuttered mansion, built in 1912 by Harley Procter of Procter & Gamble and said to resemble a cake of Ivory soap, has long been a fixture in Lenox under the aegis of renowned chef-innkeeper Gerhard Schmidt.

Architect Stanford White inspired the two leaded windows by the main side entrance and the sweeping central staircase, which upon descending makes you feel you're floating into a ballroom. The nine guest rooms with private baths on the second floor are richly furnished in Colonial style with antiques and oriental rugs.

A front corner suite lined with books and containing a couch and two fireplaces was home for Arthur Fiedler during his Boston Pops concerts at Tanglewood. A semi-suite has a pillar in the middle with the bed at an angle, while a third room has heavy furniture carved in Austria.

Continental breakfast is served in one of the formal dining rooms (see below).

Guests may use the pool and tennis court at **Haus Andreas,** five minutes away on the Stockbridge Road in Lee. It's the elegant country home of Gerhard and Lilliane Schmidt and their son Andreas, which they share with overnight guests in six rooms (doubles, $80 to $145, four-night weekend minimum in summer).

Doubles, $80 to $110 weekends, $55 to $75 weekdays; Fiedler Suite, $200 and $120.

Dining Spots

Wheatleigh, West Hawthorne Road, Lenox. (413) 637-0610.

The aim of innkeepers Susan and Linwood Simon is to have the best restaurant in the Northeast, one that's the match "of any three-star restaurant in New York." Reports are that they're on their way with the acquisition in 1985 of chef Bill Holbert, who had been at Parker's at the historic Parker House in Boston, training ground lately for many a nouvelle chef.

The Minneapolis-born chef is Irish-Dutch, his wife is German and his three young daughters bear French names. But his cuisine is regional nouvelle, the emphasis on local and fresh — from morels to asparagus, shad roe to baby quails.

The menu changes weekly and is inventive, to say the least. Aforementioned quails might turn up as an appetizer in a terrine of duck foie gras and quail with champagne grapes ($8.50), as a soup in a quail consomme with quail eggs and truffles ($6.50) or as an entree in quail poached with Madeira stock and stuffed with veal sweetbread mousse on a nest of Anna potatoes ($24).

Wheatleigh offers dining and lodging in an Italian palazzo.

Otherwise, appetizers ($7 to $16) might be Malpeque oysters on the half shell with salmon roe mignonnette, squash blossoms stuffed with scallop mousse, warm squab and truffle salad, or crayfish bisque. Five to eight entrees are offered from $18 to $27, varying seasonally from shad roe sauteed with ginger and green peppercorns in spring, to lobster and sea scallops in sauterne with sweet corn and kale in summer, to loin of venison grilled with chestnut puree in autumn.

Inn-made desserts ($4.50 to $5) are exotic as well: sour cherry or grapefruit-vermouth sorbets in tulip pastry, pumpkin and fig ice creams, gateau Banchet or tart of starfruit and wild blueberries.

The Simons have doubled the size of their wine list, priced from $14 to $185, with a number available in half-bottles. "At the high end," says Linwood, "our wines become very reasonable. If you're of a mind to drink Chateau Lafite, this is the place to do it."

The main dining room has been refurbished with Chippendale armchairs imported from England. Three tile murals, each weighing 500 pounds, were found in England and put up on the walls; they acquire a luminescent quality in candlelight. The adjacent Library is notable for Empire chairs and old English stoneware from 1830.

Dinner nightly except Monday, 6 to 11 in summer, 6:30 to 9:30 rest of year; Sunday brunch, 8 to 2. Reservations required.

Church Street Cafe, 69 Church St., Lenox. (413) 637-2745.

This is the casual, creative kind of place of which we never tire, the one we keep returning to for a quick but interesting meal whenever we're in Lenox. We're not alone, for the place which opened in 1981 as an American bistro doubled in size in 1984 with a second dining room and expanded outdoor deck.

Owners Linda Forman and Clayton Hendrick have furnished their place simply but tastefully. On our last visit we admired all the amusing paintings of zebras on the walls, part of the changing art exhibits and all for sale. We also like the bar stools painted like black and white cows, udders hanging below, as well as the ficus trees lit with tiny white lights, the white pottery with colorful pink and blue flowers, the flute music playing in the background, and the reasonably priced wines.

Once Ethel Kennedy's chef, Clayton also worked in a Creole restaurant in Washington and that background shows. Blackened redfish might be a dinner special; a Cajun duck and sausage gumbo was an entree when we last were there.

The menu is wisely limited, with four appetizers and eight entrees at dinner. Start with a duck pate with orange and cognac sauce or the black bean nachos with two salsas (both $3.95). Spicy shrimp stir-fry, charcoal-grilled oriental chicken and eggplant rolatini are among entrees, $9.95 to $13.50.

Our latest lunch included a super black bean tostada and the Church Street salad, a colorful array with strips of smoked cheese, chick peas, sprouts, eggs and red pepper, with a zippy Dijon vinaigrette dressing on the side and wholewheat sunflower seed rolls, so good that we accepted seconds. Both were $4.95, which is the price of most of the eight offerings.

Among desserts, we recommend the chilled cranberry souffle, topped with whipped cream, and the Hungarian chocolate cake.

Open daily, 11:30 to 11, to midnight on weekends.

Gateways Inn and Restaurant, 71 Walker St., Lenox. (413) 637-2532.

Noted chef Gerhard Schmid, who prepared lunch for Queen Elizabeth during her 1976 visit to Boston, has presided over his inn's distinguished restaurant longer than any other chef in Lenox.

The gracious white mansion has three formal and rather austere high-ceilinged dining rooms. We'd choose the small and intimate Rockwell Room, named for the late artist who dined there regularly.

The menu, which rarely changes but is supplemented by fresh seafood and game in season, is a blend of classic American, French and German. All entrees are a fixed price of $21.50, including salad and rolls. House specialties are shrimp Andreas (stuffed with crabmeat and mushrooms), rack of lamb, and Norwegian salmon topped with shrimp and lobster meat and finished in a dill-champagne sauce, garnished with hollandaise and toasted almonds. Veal sweetbreads (mood of the day), duckling with mandarin sauce and medallions of beef with choron sauce are other possibilities.

The dozen appetizers run from $3.75 for fresh fruit with sherbet to $6.50 for lobster cocktail, escargots, or smoked trout or venison. Among desserts are Viennese apple strudel, sabayon torte and grasshopper pie.

Dinner, Monday-Thursday 5:30 to 9; Friday-Sunday, 4:30 to 9:30. Closed Mondays in winter.

Paolo's Auberge, Route 7, Lenox. (413) 637-2711.

Swiss-born chef Paolo Eugster, who arrived in the Berkshires by way of Hilton hotels in Hartford and Bangor, left Wheatleigh in 1985 to open his own restaurant in one of the area's oldest structures on the Pittsfield-Lenox Road.

Here, in a beautifully restored house, meals are served in a variety of small, elegantly appointed dining rooms. The lunch menu changes daily, with pastas, salads and light entrees in the $4.50 to $7 range.

Paolo's dinner menu is considerably fancier. Entrees start at $13.50 for a vegetarian plate and rise to $20.50 for baby lamb chops provencale and oven-roasted pheasant, hunter style. Other offerings include veak steak with morels, sweetbreads in black butter, calves liver with garlic and herbs in a red wine sauce, turbot with fennel and pernod, and shrimp in curry sauce with grilled banana.

A lobster bisque with caviar, duck galantine with Cumberland sauce and salmon quenelles in lobster sauce are $5.50 to $7.50. A watercress salad with poached egg is $4.50 and the sorbet to clear the palate between courses is $3. The 15 percent gratuity is added to the check; a small line at the bottom of the menu notes this, but some otherwise happy diners regret having missed it.

Lunch in summer, dinner nightly.

Cafe Lucia, 90 Church St., Lenox. (413) 637-2640.

Jim and Dianne Lucie have transformed the former Ganesh, which was an art gallery cum cafe, into an expanded cafe with art as a sideline. "We're a restaurant that shows and sells art," explains Jim, who opened up the kitchen so patrons can glimpse the goings-on.

Jim's Italian cuisine is favored by locals, who praise his pasta creations, chicken saltimbocca and homemade sausage with imported wild mushrooms. Other entrees ($10.95 to $14.95) include baked lasagna, braised veal with sweet peppers and mushrooms, and osso buco risotto, served with rolls and salad. Among desserts are gorgonzola and fresh pears, chocolate almond macaroon torte, chocolate-filled Italian rum cake, and a sauteed apple, cinnamon and sour cream pie.

Lunch and dinner daily in summer; dinner from 5:30, Tuesday-Saturday rest of year.

Apple Tree Inn, 224 West St., Lenox. (413) 637-1477.

The round dining room still has the spectacular panoramic view and carousel ceiling with ribs of bulb lights that it had when it was Alice's at Avaloch — Alice's upscale restaurant after she moved from Housatonic to the inn across from Tanglewood. It is all pink and white, with Austrian-type curtains.

In cooler months, meals are served in the McIntosh Tavern, a cheery haunt in winter, with red and white checked curtains, red tablecloths, paneled walls, booths and big fireplace.

Of the four pasta dishes offered at dinner, linguini al Gustav ($12.50) sounds wonderful: jumbo shrimp in a sauce of tomato, basil, garlic, olive oil and wine. Other entrees ($7.50 to $16.50) include halibut Siciliana, New England pot roast, breast of chicken in crab etouffe, two versions of veal scaloppini and strip steak. Nightly specials might be poached salmon in a caper butter sauce or marinated Cornish game hens with wild rice. Chesapeake crab cakes served with a remoulade sauce are a popular appetizer.

There are sometimes as many as 14 desserts ("you'd think you were in a Viennese pastry shop," says owner Greg Smith), with fresh fruit tarts, profiteroles and chocolate mousse cake always popular.

Lunch, daily noon to 2 during Tanglewood season; dinner nightly, 5:30 to 9:30.

Beckets at the Gables, 103 Walker St., Lenox. (413) 637-3416.

Ex-banker-musician Frank Newton of the Brook Farm Inn acquired the venerable Gables Inn in September 1985 and refurbished the restaurant in one quick week, reopening to appeal to the mid-price market.

A piano is in the foyer, the better for Frank to sing and play upon request, and old sheet music is framed on the walls. Two small and pretty

Waters of Stockbridge Bowl are on view from porch at Apple Tree Inn.

dining rooms are furnished with brass chandeliers, etched glass, pink linens, burgundy napkins and Lenox Academy plates. A pleasant bar has a few tables for dining as well.

Dinner entrees run from $6.95 for fettuccine Alfredo or linguini with clam sauce to $11.95 for New York sirloin. Most are in the $9 range and include chicken amandine, chicken vegetable Wellington, veal marsala, and scallops in champagne with kiwi fruit.

Appetizers ($3.50 to $4.50) include mushroom caps stuffed with crabmeat, gourmet fried cheese and sauteed langoustinos. Desserts are deep dish apple pie, a pecan and coffee brandy tart and fix-your-own parfaits.

The Newtons were renovating the seven upstairs guest rooms, five with private baths. Edith Wharton lived here when she was building the Mount.

Dinner nightly.

The Restaurant, 15 Franklin St., Lenox. (413) 637-9894.

A real international cuisine is served in this dark, funky little storefront restaurant. That is, when they serve — a sign in the window said, "Gone fishing, back in early December," when we tried to lunch there in early November. We had longed for one of their curries, their fanciful omelets and crepes (pate and mackerel, among the offerings) or the smoked oyster salad. In fact, the salad for two ($11.95) with pate, smoked oysters, salami, provolone, marinated mushrooms, egg, ripe olives and who knows what else was mighty tempting.

Dinner entrees ($7.95 to $16.95) range widely: hot and sour shrimp, Maltese langoustino crepe, roast duckling apricot, tofu and vegetable curry, pork schnitzel and two filet mignons glazed with pate. Salad, rice or vermicelli and a small loaf of French bread come with. There's a full liquor license.

For dessert, how about an apricot ginger crepe, chocolate truffle cake, sabayon, fruitcake Alaska for two or Arabian pudding?

Lunch daily in season, noon to 2:30; dinner, 6 to 10; Sunday, brunch 11 to 2, dinner 5 to 9; closed Wednesdays rest of year.

Diversions

Tanglewood, West Street, Lenox. The name is synonymous with music and Lenox. The summer home of the Boston Symphony Orchestra since 1936, the 210-acre estate above the waters of Stockbridge Bowl in the distance is an idyllic spot for concerts and socializing at picnics. The 6,000 seats in the open-air shed sell for $9 to $40; up to 10,000 fans can be accommodated at $6.50 each on the lawn (bring your own chairs, blankets, picnics and wine, or pick something up from the cafeteria). Concerts are at 9 p.m. Friday, 8:30 p.m. Saturday and 2:30 p.m. Sunday, last weekend of June through August.

Shakespeare & Company, Plunkett Street, Lenox. Edith Wharton's former estate above Laurel Lake, **the Mount,** is the magnificent outdoor setting for two Shakespeare plays presented in repertory Tuesday through Sunday evenings in summer. The neo-Georgian home of the novelist is open for tours ($3) from noon to 4 Tuesday-Friday, 10 to 4 on weekends in July and August.

Lenox Arts Center, Citizens Hall, Interlaken. An improvisational music-theater group presents three new productions each summer, Wednesday-Sunday at 9 p.m. Some of its plays and playwrights have gone on to Broadway.

Shopping. Lenox offers some of the most exclusive shops in the Berkshires. Along Main Street, the **Lemon Tree** is a suave gift and apparel store, one in which we always find something to take home for ourselves or others. **Yamato House** has a fine collection of American crafts and Japanese art. **The Different Drummer** (at the Lenox House Country Shops) has all kinds of kitchen ware, contemporary crafts, cards and even a bath shop. As a women's specialty store for more than three decades, **Elise Farrar** at 361 Pittsfield Road is a classic of its kind. Along Church Street, **Mary Stuart Collections** has wonderful needlework, potpourris and fragrances, children's clothes and custom-designed hand-painted stools. **Walter Peterson, Too** offers fine pottery, crafts and "wearable art." Neat casual clothes are at **Glad Rags,** and contemporary crafts at the **Hoadley Gallery.** **Ormsby's** is another interesting gift and accessories shop. **Crosby's** has one of the best selections of specialty and take-out foods north of New York.

Extra-Special ⊞

Chesterwood, Route 183, Stockbridge. Lenox's next-door neighbor, Stockbridge, has so many attractions — from the Old Corner House with Norman Rockwell's art to the Berkshire Garden Center (as well as the Red Lion, the epitome of New England inns) — that it should not be missed. Our favorite is Chesterwood, the secluded estate of sculptor Daniel Chester French, who is famed for the Seated Lincoln in Washington. Visitors start at a gallery in the old cow barn, see the 30-foot-high studio in which the sculptor worked and tour the grand Colonial Revival home in which he spent six months a year until he died there in 1931. The period garden, nature trail and museum shop appeal as well. Open daily May-October, 10 to 5. Adults $3.50.

Pleasant Bay is backdrop for dining room at Wequassett Inn.

Chatham, Mass.
Serenity Beside the Sea

Of all Cape Cod's towns, we are fondest of Chatham, a sophisticated, sedate and serene enclave of affluence beside the sea. This is the elbow of the Cape, where the hubbub of much of the south shore yields to treed tranquility before the land veers north to face the open Atlantic and the dunes of the National Seashore.

Known locally as "The First Stop of the East Wind," Chatham is one of the Cape's oldest towns (settled in 1656) and one of its most residential. Hidden in the trees and along the meandering waterfront are large homes and estates.

Explore a bit and you may see the gorgeous hydrangea walk leading up to a Shore Road mansion. Across from a windmill in a field of yellow wildflowers against a backdrop of blue ocean, it's the essence of Cape Cod. Or you may follow Mooncusser's Lane and find that the road ends suddenly at the river. Admire the view from the drawbridge on Bridge Street as well as the classic views of the Chatham Light.

Because it's so residential, Chatham has escaped the overt commercialism and tourism of much of the Cape. This is not a place for transients; the few inns and motels encourage long stays, and the bulk of the accommodations are in cottages or house rentals.

The summer social scene revolves around parties and private clubs. But almost everyone turns out for the Friday evening band concerts in Kate Gould Park.

Although Main Street, which winds through the center of town, seems filled with pedestrians and shoppers, chances are they're residents or regulars. Perhaps its air of stability and tradition is what makes Chatham so special.

231

Inn Spots

The Queen Anne Inn, 70 Queen Anne Road, Chatham 02633. (617) 945-0394.

Chatham's most posh inn — in terms of accommodations and dining as well as prices — is the house built by a sea captain in the 1840s as a wedding gift for his daughter. Austrians Guenther and Nicole Weinkopf reclaimed it from near ruin in 1978. Their grandly renovated structure has 30 guest rooms, all with modern baths and telephones, several antiques-filled public rooms, including a lounge with television, and an acclaimed restaurant (see Dining Spots).

All the spacious guest rooms and suites are furnished in antiques, including pencil post beds (some canopied) and bentwood rockers. The prized rear rooms have private balconies overlooking the gardens and Oyster Pond.

Guests may swim in the pond or walk 10 minutes to the beach. They also may play tennis on three new private clay courts hidden away in a park-like setting. Guenther, a licensed skipper, offers guests day cruises to Nantucket as well as picnic and sightseeing excursions to the Monomoy Islands. The inn's Tuesday night clambakes in the gardens are popular.

Complimentary continental breakfasts with homemade muffins are served in the dining room, or on the sunny porch beside the garden.

Doubles, $86 to $116.

The Captain's House Inn of Chatham, 371 Old Harbor Road (Route 28), Chatham 02633. (617) 945-0127.

Captain Hiram Harding's 1839 home was taken over in 1983 by Philadelphians David and Cathy Eakin, who spruced it up for their first innkeeping venture and added the personal touches that make it a comfortable, inviting place.

Set on three acres of shaded lawns screened by high hedges in a quiet residential section north of the village and a pleasant 10-minute walk from the water, the Captain's House is refined and quiet. The entrance hall and living room retain the original pumpkin pine floors and are furnished with antiques, oriental rugs and period wallpapers.

The 10 guest rooms with private baths in the main Greek Revival house have a variety of furnishings, including four-poster beds wih pineapple finials, lacy white fishnet canopies, white eyelet-edged curtains, colorful sheets and towels and comforters, braided rugs and soft velvet wing chairs for reading. Two have working fireplaces.

The most coveted room is in the Captain's Cottage, which Dave Eakin renovated in 1984 into a sumptuous suite with dark wood paneling, a nice oriental rug on the wide-planked floor, working fireplace, sofa and four-poster bed.

Cathy Eakin's touch is evident in the gardens as well as in the kitchen. She sets up a fine continental breakfast buffet on the sunny dining porch; included are English muffins and delicious homemade nut breads, blueberry muffins and preserves. While we enjoyed an early-morning stroll along the shore road, Dave drove into town to pick up copies of the Boston Globe for guests to read with breakfast. He also takes guests out fishing or for a luncheon cruise on his 35-foot sloop.

Doubles, $79 to $105.

Captain's House Inn of Chatham occupies residential site north of village.

The Bradford Inn and Motel, 26 Cross St., Chatham 02633. (617) 945-1030.

An exceptionally attractive motel cum inn, this venerable establishment is well situated in a residential section just off Chatham's Main Street. For years we have admired its cheery exterior with yellow awnings and gardens with flowers of every hue; the interior, we found, is just as nice.

Innkeepers William and Audrey Gray live in the 1860 Captain Elijah Smith House, which also serves as the office and commons facility. There is a parlor-lounge, and the Garden Room at the rear is where a full complimentary breakfast is served buffet style. In season, many prefer to linger over coffee on the yellow and white lawn furniture on the garden patio beside the small pool, savoring the extravagant roses and watching the birds feed.

Five of the largest rooms are in the Bradford House in front, while four are in the Carriage House near the pool. The other eleven are in the L-shaped motel building in back. Five have kitchens and some are suites; all are individually decorated and have private baths, cable television, refrigerators, telephones and air-conditioning.

Doubles, $83 to 98; three-night minimum in summer and holidays.

Wequassett Inn, Pleasant Bay, Chatham 02633. (617) 432-5400.

Blessed with a fine location above its private beach and peninsula separating Round Cove from Pleasant Bay (Wequasset is the Indian name for "crescent on the water"), the new blends quite nicely with the old in this resort compound with structures dating back 200 years. Cape Cod-style cottages, motel units and condo-type structures totaling 103 rooms are scattered across 22 acres amid pines, waterfront and tennis courts.

Large guest rooms and suites are tastefully furnished for what the inn calls "gracious resort living." Rooms have cable TV, refrigerators, phones and air-conditioning. At the disposal of guests are five tennis courts with a resident pro, sailboats and canoes, and a swimming pool plus a half-mile-long beach.

Guests may take their meals in the historic "square top" Eben Ryder House, which is acclaimed for fine dining (see below).

Doubles, $130 to $150, suites $185. American Plan available. Open mid-May to mid-October.

The Town House Inn and Lodge, 11 Library Lane, Chatham 02633. (617) 945-2180.

This Victorian inn, facing Main Street, is often decked out in red, white and blue bunting, especially for the Fourth of July parade which passes its front porch.

Innkeepers Svea Peterson, who managed a hotel in Stockholm, Sweden, and husband Russell are patriotic to the core, going so far as to acquire a rare set of show plates and champagne glasses from the S.S. United States liner at an auction in 1984. The one-of-a-kind set of china is proudly displayed amid nautical decor in the inn's restaurant.

The expanding inn complex totals 21 guest rooms, all with private baths, air-conditioning, color television, room phones and small refrigerators.

Ten rooms are in the main inn, which was considered one of Chatham's finest homes when it was built for Capt. Daniel Nickerson. Some of the original carved moldings, wood trim and hemlock wide board floors remain. Seven more rooms, three with queensize waterbeds, are in a wing opened in 1977; four are in the recently renovated country lodge next door, and there's a two-room cottage.

The Petersons offer Scandinavian pastries for continental breakfast. Heartier fare, including Finnish pancakes with fresh fruit, also is available. Lunches are served under the canopy of the Captain's Deck.

Doubles, $105 to $125, including continental breakfast. Closed January.

Chatham Wayside Inn, 512 Main St., Chatham 02633. (617) 945-1800.

When we first vacationed in Chatham nearly three decades ago, the Wayside seemed the quintessential New England inn — located in the heart of town and containing a lively tavern that was perfect for an after-dinner drink. Today, with the proliferation of inns everywhere, it no longer seems quintessential, although we must say the six round tables out front with colorful little umbrellas shading the relish-ketchup-salt racks remain inviting, and the inn's pleasant grounds back up to the village band shell.

The elongated structure dating from the 18th century consists of 27 guest rooms, three apartments, two suites and one cottage. All have private baths, television and telephones, and there's an outdoor swimming pool.

The long, slate-floored dining room with beamed ceiling has round wood tables decked out in white and brown linen and surrounded by leather-backed, cushioned chairs. Prime ribs au jus are the featured item on the traditional dinner menu, which is priced from $8.95 to $14.95 and includes potato, vegetable, beverage and salad bar. Lunch runs from $3.95 for omelet du jour to $7.95 for baked stuffed lobster casserole.

Doubles, $60 in summer, $50 rest of year.

The Cranberry Inn at Chatham, 359 Main St., Chatham 02633. (617) 945-9232.

The long porch in front of this red frame structure with white trim leads into what the Droney family — brothers Tim and Shawn, with assistance from their parents from Connecticut — calls "a friendly, homelike guest house." Once named the Traveler's Home and later the Monomoy House, the inn dates from the 1830s.

Guest rooms are small and simple but spotlessly clean, furnished with nice quilts. Some rooms have double beds and some have twins; family

Creative dining is offered on porch at Christian's.

suites can accommodate up to four. All rooms have sinks; the family suites have private baths.

There are a cozy living room with television, a small bar and a paneled dining room with captain's chairs and ruffled white curtains.

Many folks stop at the Cranberry Inn for breakfast. Seated on a small dining porch, we enjoyed Tim Droney's delicious cranberry pancakes with country sausage, juice and coffee for a bargain $3.85. For $3.60 you can have juice, two eggs, bacon or sausage, toast or muffin and coffee. Dinner also is served nightly from 6.

Doubles with shared baths, $38 to $40; family suites with private baths, $65; open mid-May to mid-October.

Dining Spots

Christian's, 443 Main St., Chatham. (617) 945-3362.

For a fine meal, a raw bar, cocktails on an upper deck or nightly entertainment in the classic English bar, Christian's is a favorite choice among locals.

With the help of his brother and his parents, chef Christian Schultz offers a creative dinner menu in the airy, casual porch or the more formal dining room with white linen, beamed ceilings, oriental rugs and latticed dividers.

With drinks comes a complimentary liver pate served with melba toast. Appetizers range from $4.50 for littleneck clams to $6 for pepper shrimp flamed with brandy. We liked the crab beurrecks wrapped in phyllo dough and a special called "cockles and such," which happened to be four Monterey oysters in a choron sauce.

Entrees run from $10.50 for fish of the day to $17.95 for seafood pillows Florentine, a concoction of lobster, shrimp and spinach-filled pasta pillows served on a beurre rouge. Roast duck with a fresh fruit sauce is the house specialty, and filet mignon is prepared three ways — bearnaise, au poivre or stuffed with brie. We enjoyed fresh halibut heavily sauced with asparagus hollandaise, and a superb veal and shrimp saute. These came with side plates of green and yellow squash, carrots and rice, plus crusty French bread and a simple salad of leaf lettuce and tomatoes with a zesty herb and cheese dressing. A grand marnier torte topped by a chocolate shell filled with grand marnier was a good dessert.

After dinner, we adjourned to **Upstairs at Christian's** for cordials and special coffees. A laid-back, luxurious space, it has a handsome curved oak bar, African mahogany paneling, 60 linear feet of shelves filled with books, and in interesting mix of eaves and niches with leather sofas and loveseats. A banjo player, "proud to be a preppy from North Chatham," sang rousing ditties while one of Walter Schultz's collection of old movies was being shown in "The Critic's Corner."

Dinner nightly from 6, raw bar from 4.

The Impudent Oyster, 15 Chatham Bars Ave., Chatham. (617) 945-3545.

With a name like that and an innovative menu, how could this place miss? Run by Michele and Peter Barnard and always noisy and jammed, patrons crowd together at small glass-covered tables under a cathedral ceiling, plants in straw baskets balanced overhead on the beams.

The international menu, based on local seafoods, is an intriguing blend of regional, Chinese, Mexican, Indian, Greek and Italian cuisines, among others. For dinner, we couldn't resist starting with the drunken mussels ($3.75), shelled and served chilled in an intense marinade of tamari, fresh ginger, Szechwan peppercorns and sake, with a side portion of snowpeas and red peppers. The Mexican chicken, chile and lime soup, one of the best we've tasted, was spicy and full of interesting flavors. Also delicious were the spinach and mushroom salads with either creamy mustard or anchovy dressings.

Among entrees ($8.50 to $16), it was difficult to choose from such imaginative offerings as celestial oysters (poached in champagne, topped with hollandaise and served on pasta), East Indian haddock, shrimp Mykonos flamed in ouzo, and Hunan bluefish. We loved the feta and fennel scrod, a Greek dish touched with ouzo and topped with feta cheese, and the swordfish broiled with orange and pepper butter. A spicy pinot grigio for $9.50 was a good companion for such assertive fare. A plate of several ice creams made with fresh fruit was a cooling finale.

The menu changes frequently, and is supplemented by nightly specials. It's the kind of cuisine of which we never tire, although we might prefer to have it in a more peaceful setting. We also could do without being told by the hostess that "Mary Lou will be cocktailing you this evening."

Lunch, 11:30 to 3; dinner 5:30 to 10; dinner reservations essential.

The Queen Anne Inn, 70 Queen Anne Road, Chatham. (617) 945-0394.

The Earl of Chatham restaurant at the Queen Anne Inn has a scant 12 tables, a European feel with oriental rugs and dark oak wainscoting, pretty pink linens and elegant place settings. It also has one of the fanciest menus around, thanks to chef Thomas Pandiscio, who won first prize in the 1983 crab-cooking olympics in San Francisco and is known for his crab mousse with three sauces, watercress, sorrel and lobster.

Queen Anne Inn is known for fine dining as well as lodging.

The hand-written menu changes nightly and the pricetag is dear: a chilled cream of zucchini soup with fresh chives at $6.50 is par for the course. Appetizers run from $7 for a warm goat cheese salad on European lettuces and watercress to $8.50 for a cold salad of smoked salmon and marinated sea bass stuffed with crabmeat. Fresh crabmeat raviolis, seafood sausage, warm venison sausage, and ragout of scallops, shrimp and lobster in brioche are other starters.

Main courses begin at $22 for fresh striped bass and crabmeat in a dill-wine sauce and top off at $25 for medallions of veal and oyster mushrooms in a truffle sauce. Noisettes of lamb are served with fresh rosemary and imported goat cheese, and a combination of breast of duck and roasted quail is served with foie gras in a truffle sauce with homemade noodles.

Innkeeper Guenther Weinkopf is proud of the desserts, which he compares favorably with those of any pastry shop in Europe. We've heard great things about the sacher torte, and the fresh fruit mousses and homemade sorbets are said to be out of this world.

Dinner nightly except Tuesday (outdoor clambake night in summer), late spring through December.

Wequasset Inn, Pleasant Bay, Chatham. (617) 432-5400.
In this area, we can't think of a more majestic water view amid more elegant surroundings than from the restored 18th century sea captain's mansion that houses the Wequasset Inn's dining room. Light lunches and cocktails are served on the large outdoor terrace covered by a yellow and white canopy, with pink geraniums framing a view of the sea. Large windows in the main dining room and the bar also take full advantage of the view. Inside all is blue and white, except for colorful fuchsias and plants perched on latticed stands.

The wine list is distinguished and the menu ambitious. Appetizers run from $6.75 for baked camembert en croute to $10.75 for smoked salmon with three caviars, shrimp cocktail or mussel and lobster salad.

For entrees ($17.25 to $22), how about duckling au poivre, veal sauteed with spinach and morels, lobster flamed with brandy, sole stuffed with smoked salmon and scallop mousse, or escalope of swordfish, served between layers of puff pastry and chanterelle sauce, garnished with a julienne of leeks and crayfish?

The pastry chef from France is known for his Paris-Brest, milles-feuilles and chocolate charlotte. The pear poached in zinfandel and English cream, and french fried ice cream coated with graham crackers and served with raspberry-grand marnier sauce also entice.

Lunch ($6.25 to $12.50) is no less extravagant, from papaya stuffed with baby shrimp to duck salad with snowpeas, watercress, endive and raspberry walnut dressing.

Lunch daily, noon to 2; dinner, 6 to 9; mid-May to mid-October.

Northport Seafood House, Route 28, Chathamport. (617) 945-9217.

Owner Joseph Aucoin collects antique signs, many of which are on display alongside other local memorabilia in several rooms seating 175 diners inside this large white house with green shutters at the edge of a shopping complex north of Chatham. Small table lamps light the glass-covered tables, the emphasis is family-casual and a highlight is the salad bar.

There's something for everyone here: a children's dinner menu for $5.95, earlybird specials at $6.95, special house drinks ($3), a small but serviceable wine list ($7.50 to $12) and plenty of fresh seafood, most of it baked or fried ($8.95 to $12.95). There's surf and turf, of course; prime ribs are available on the weekends. Complete luncheons of the same genre are $5.95.

Lunch, 11:30 to 4; dinner from 5.

The Garden Cafe, 483 Main St., Chatham.

An outdoor oasis of greenery at the rear of a complex of shops called the Swinging Basket, this is a fine spot for lunch or snacks on a sunny day. Filled with the Cape's trademark blue hydrangeas and colorful flowers, the gardens are tended by the Rodman family, who bought the complex in 1983 and created a garden from the overgrowth. Patrons sit on kitchen chairs at umbrella-covered tables, sip a glass of beer or wine, and order a salad, soup, quiche, or sandwich — even a ploughman's lunch — or desserts like fresh peaches and ice cream.

Open daily 11 to 9, mid-June through September.

Queen of Tarts, 409 Main St., Chatham.

This tiny spot is immensely popular for breakfast or a light lunch. Except in summer when it's too busy and only coffee and pastries are served, Leah Tillinghast concocts such delights for breakfast as sourdough pancakes with fresh strawberries and a homemade English muffin sandwich with cheese and fried egg that could be called egg McChatham. Lunchtime brings croissants filled with chicken and vegetables or asparagus and cheese, plus sandwiches made with sourdough French or oatmeal whole wheat breads.

Open daily 7:30 to 3, Sunday to 11. Closed January to mid-February.

Diversions

From Chatham's choice location at the elbow of Cape Cod, all the attractions of the Cape are at your beck and call. People who appreciate Chatham tend to head north to Orleans or into Wellfleet and the Truros, if they leave Chatham at all.

Beaches. Chatham has more beach area and shoreline than any other Cape Cod town, but much of it is privately owned or not easily accessible. Those with boats like the seclusion of the offshore sandbar at the southern tip of the Cape Cod National Seashore, a barrier beach which shelters Chatham from the open Atlantic. Swimming is available by permit at such town beaches as Harding Beach on Nantucket Sound, or the sheltered "Children's Beach" at Oyster Pond. Those who want surf and open ocean head for Orleans and the Coast Guard and Nauset state beaches.

Monomoy National Wildlife Refuge. Accessible only by a short boat trip from Morris Island, this wilderness island stretching south into the Atlantic is a haven for birds — 309 species, at latest count. It's a major stopping point for migratory waterfowl along what ornithologists call the Atlantic Flyway.

Museums. The Old Atwood House (1752) on Stage Harbor Road, owned and maintained by the Chatham Historical Society, is one of the town's oldest houses. Among its offerings are seashells, Sandwich glass and the nationally known murals of Alice Stallknecht Wight. Changing exhibits illustrate Chatham life through photos, paintings and artifacts. The museum is open for limited afternoon hours in the summer for a nominal fee. Also open afternoons in the summer is the 20-year-old **Railroad Museum,** the former town depot now filled with more than 8,000 models, relics and photos, plus a 1910 caboose.

Shopping. Some of Cape Cod's finest shops are located along tree-lined Main Street; just stroll along and poke inside any number that appeal. We've always been partial to the **Tale of the Cod** at 450 Main, a wonderful collection of rooms filled with interesting gifts. Almost across the street is the Swinging Basket complex of boutiques; a highlight is Dick Rodman's **Afterhouse Gallery** with its imported English antique pine furniture. **Mark, Fore & Strike** has classic apparel. **Chatham Cookware** is one of the finest kitchen stores and food shops we've found; you might see a cooking demonstration or stop for refreshment on the outdoor side deck. Out Bridge Street near Stage Neck Road is the **Sail Loft,** which has fine clothing for the suaves.

Extra-Special ————————————————

Band Concerts. It's hard to imagine in sophisticated Chatham, but upwards of 6,000 people turn out for the Friday evening band concerts, a town tradition every July and August, in Kate Gould Park. The 40 instrumentalists, most of them townspeople who rehearse weekly during winter, are joined by the multitudes for rowsing singalongs. The natural amphitheater is good both for listening and for watching the children (and often their elders) dance to the music.

Boats are docked at waterfront area near Nantucket's Commercial Wharf.

Nantucket, Mass.
Island of History and Romance

Stepping onto Steamboat Wharf after a 2 1/2-hour ferry ride 20 miles out into the Atlantic is a bit like stepping onto another land in another time.

"This is the island that time forgot," announces one of Nantucket's visitor guides. "Steeped in tradition, romance, legend and history, she is a refuge from modernity."

Accompanied by brick sidewalks, towering shade trees and gas lamps, the cobblestone streets lead you past more fine old sea captains' homes still standing from Nantucket's days as the nation's leading whaling port than most people expect to see in a lifetime. The more than 400 structures from the late 1700s and early 1800s that make up the historic district represent the greatest concentration in America, prompting the town's description as "an architectural jewel."

So much for the island that time forgot. The island's romance draws thousands of well-heeled visitors to a sophisticated side of Nantucket that is uniquely chic and contemporary. More distant than other islands from the mainland and yet readily accessible to the affluent, Nantucket is all the more exclusive.

That's the way island businessman-benefactor Walter Beinecke Jr. planned it when he created the Nantucket Historical Trust in 1957 and later co-founded the Nantucket Conservation Trust. His efforts led to the preservation of 6,100 acres of open space — one-fifth of the island's land total. Through his historic and real-estate interests, the village has been transformed into what New England Monthly magazine termed "a perfect oasis — neat, tidy and relentlessly quaint — for upscale vacationers."

It's a bit precious and pricey for some tastes, this town in which whaling fortunes were amassed and which now is predicated on tourism for the elite. (Once you get away from Nantucket village and Siasconset, the folks on the south beaches and west side of the island let their hair down). The week our family roughed it, so to speak, in a cottage on the beach at Surfside was far different from the fall weekend a decade later when we returned, as so many couples do, for a getaway in Nantucket village.

Nantucket is perfect for an escape — away from the mainland and into a dream combining Yankee history and the Preppy Handbook. You don't have to wear Nantucket pink trousers or dine at Le Chantecleer, although many do. Simply explore the village's treasures, participate in its activities, or relax and watch a select world go by.

Inn Spots

Jared Coffin House, 29 Broad St., Nantucket 02554. (617) 228-2405.

One of New England's grand old inns, the famed Jared Coffin House is the yardstick against which other Nantucket hostelries are measured. It's rather fancy and handsomely furnished with museum-quality pieces, and it's also active and busy — like a train station 24 hours a day, some islanders say.

The public rooms, restaurant, tap room with entertainment and outdoor patio are busy, that is, for this is a center for Nantucket life and a must visit for tourists, if only for a drink or to sample one of the restaurant's brunches or buffets.

The restoration of the island's earliest three-story house was accomplished by Walter Beinecke Jr. and the Nantucket Historical Trust, which acquired it in 1961 for $10,000, renovated and furnished it, and finally sold it in 1975 for more than $750,000, which is an example of the gentrification of Nantucket.

Innkeeper Phil Read and his wife Peg, an island native, who had been leasing it as an inn for 10 years before they purchased it, are active behind the scenes — he on the business end and she on the reservations — but this is a large operation with a staff to match.

The 58 guest rooms are scattered in six buildings, two of which are connected to the main 1845 Jared Coffin House. Three are in houses 30 feet on either side of the main complex. All have private baths and most have television.

Some guests prefer the seven twin and double rooms upstairs in Jared's former home, each furnished with period antiques, art works and island-woven fabrics. Others covet one of the three large rooms with queensize canopy beds and sitting areas in the 1700s Swain House attached to the main building, or, across the street, one of the six queensize canopy rooms in the 1821 Henry Coffin House or the 12 queensize canopy rooms in the 1841 Greek Revival Harrison Gray House.

The public areas are a sight to behold, the living room and library furnished in priceless Chippendale and Sheraton antiques.

Jared's, the inn's large main dining room, features classic American cuisine and changing seasonal menus. Dinner entrees are $19.95 to $24.95 for items like sauteed Nantucket bay scallops with tomatoes, garlic and herbs on spaghetti squash. Less formal dinners in the beamed, pine-paneled Tap Room downstairs are $9.50 to $13.50. Lunch on the patio might be the "Pride of New England" ($5), a choice of broiled jumbo frankfurter or deep-fried codfish cake with baked beans, brown bread and coleslaw.

A table d'hote breakfast begins at a fruit and juice bar and includes eggs Benedict for $6.75 and roast beef hash with poached eggs, $6.25.

Doubles, $85 to $125. Reduced rates with complimentary breakfast, January-March.

76 Main Street, 76 Main St., Nantucket 02554. (617) 228-2533 or 228-9151.

A costly restoration in 1984 upgraded the old White Eagle Inn into an elegant bed-and-breakfast in an 1883 sea captain's home and the only one on central Main Street, a residential section of stately 19th century mansions.

Innkeepers Stuart and Shirley Peters arrived in Nantucket by way of Wellesley, Japan and England. They restored the original cherry, oak and walnut floors which had been covered by rugs and papered the walls hidden behind layers of paint.

Finding what Stuart said had been "a real 1950s guest house with paneled rooms and shared baths," they added private baths for the 12 guest rooms, each furnished with queensize beds, upholstered chairs and antiques. Our attractive room at the rear of the first floor was adjacent to the kitchen; the sounds of breakfast preparation were a bit too close to let us sleep late.

The large front corner room on the main floor with four-poster bed and Victorian furnishings is a showplace, renting for $120 a night. Besides the other guest rooms on the second and third floors (plus an extra bathroom with shower for use of departing guests returning from the beach after they have checked out) are six family units in a motel-style annex with color TV and refrigerator.

Off a grand entry hall are a formal Victorian parlor for reading and the kitchen with dining area, where a continental breakfast of fruits and home-made muffins and breads is served. Outside are a sheltered courtyard and patio.

Doubles, $95 to $120.

Brass Lantern Inn, 11 N. Water St., Nantucket 02554. (617) 228-4064. The convenient location in a residential area near the ferry landing make this a good bet for people arriving without a car, carrying luggage, and not wishing to take a taxi several blocks.

Also an attraction are the eight luxurious contemporary rooms with large windows, queensize beds and modern amenities in an addition constructed in 1983 by innkeeper Benoit W. Garneau's son, a builder. These large rooms have private baths; some have cathedral ceilings and one extra-large room with seating area has two white wicker chairs, a skirted table and sofa bed.

The 10 older guest rooms in the front of the 1846 Greek Revival house vary in size. Two on the ground floor have private baths, four on the second floor share two, while four on the third floor share one bath and have a common sitting room.

Continental breakfast is served guests in their rooms between 8:30 and 9. Guests also have access to a main-floor living room with books and television.

Doubles, $65 to $110.

Carlisle House, 26 N. Water St., Nantucket 02554. (617) 228-0720. The 15 guest rooms in this 1765 house range from a large corner front with fireplace, queensize canopy bed with eyelet cover and rose spread to a small single with pencil-post bed and shower. A third-floor room with

Front room at 76 Main Street has canopied four-poster bed.

strawtop canopy bed and wicker furniture has an inviting, summery air. Most have private baths, and each has an antique bed with iron or brass headboard or canopied four-poster.

Nowadays in Nantucket, "people want more than a rooming house — they want a place to gather," says innkeeper Peter Conway. So he has provided an attractive common room with fireplace, a sun porch with wicker furniture where breakfast is set up buffet style in summer, a Victorian lounge looking onto the garden, and a pleasant back yard.

In the winter, breakfast is served at a huge trestle table by the original kitchen fireplace with its beehive oven and cauldron. Breakfasts include fresh fruits, homemade fruit breads and Portuguese bread. On Sunday afternoons, Peter might offer guests some wine or a bit of brandy.

Doubles, $55 to $95.

Four Chimneys Inn, 38 Orange St., Nantucket 02554. (617) 228-1912.
Said to be the largest of 126 homes erected by sea captains on Nantucket, this was built in 1835 and beautifully restored and decorated by innkeeper Betty Gaeta, an interior designer who recreated the whaling era throughout.

A grandfather clock and curving staircase are focal points of the center entry hall. A double drawing room has twin fireplaces, comfortable sitting areas and a piano.

Upstairs are 10 guest rooms with private baths, most with fireplaces and canopy or four-poster beds. Those on the third floor have good views of the harbor. Each is furnished with prized antiques and quilts. Some have armoires, rugs and porcelain from the China trade.

Continental breakfast includes unusual muffins. Hors d'oeuvres and setups are provided at cocktail hour.

Doubles, $85 to $150.

Ship's Inn, 13 Fair St., Nantucket 02554. (617) 228-0040.

Built in 1812 and furnished to the period, the 12 guest rooms at the Ship's Inn include 10 doubles with private baths and two singles sharing. Much of the furniture dates back to the days when Captain Obed Starbuck lived there between his ocean voyages, and some of the rooms — named for the ships he sailed — have seen better times.

On the main floor is a formal parlor with fireplace and oriental rugs. Downstairs is a cozy restaurant, the Captain's Table, with small-paned windows and a white fireplace in the center, where continental breakfast is served to guests. On the other side of the fireplace is the Dory Bar, with a bar made from an old dory and tavern games like backgammon and darts.

Highly regarded dinners are served in the restaurant. Chinese noodles with shrimp is a spicy cold appetizer at $5.95. Entrees ($12.50 to $15.95) include Nantucket bay scallops and broiled swordfish, billed as the biggest serving on the island. Chocolate brandy cake and frozen pudding ice cream with rum are among favored desserts. Dinner is served nightly except Tuesday, mid-April to mid-November.

Doubles, $85.

India House, 37 India St., Nantucket 02554. (617) 228-9043.

This 1803 house is what many an inn aspires to be — a small, out-of-the-way inn with good accommodations, a fine restaurant that's lively and popular (see Dining Spots), and a peaceful garden out back.

The front parlor can best be described as quaint. Five of the seven upstairs guest rooms have private baths and four-poster beds, and some have working fireplaces.

Besides serving dinner, the India House offers to the public daily a breakfast that it advertises as Nantucket's best. It's certainly one of its most creative, with such items as whiskey pears, bananas in brandied cream, fresh fish with herbed scrambled eggs, lemon French toast, broccoli-feta eggs and sweet potato pancakes.

Doubles, $60 to $85.

Roberts House Inn, 11 India St., Nantucket 02554. (617) 228-9009.

Built in 1846, this historic house in the heart of town has 21 new guest rooms plus six more in the Periwinkle House. Rooms are large with king and queensize beds, many with canopies and some with fireplaces. All are handsomely furnished with 19th century antiques and many are air-conditioned. The most deluxe has a kingsize four-poster bed with sitting room.

The inn has a small porch and a common entry, but few places to sit. Continental breakfast is served only to guests staying in the Periwinkle House.

Doubles, $95 to $140.

Dining Spots

Le Languedoc, 24 Broad St., Nantucket. (617) 228-2552.

Although the Grennan family have 20 guest rooms in four buildings, the attractive white building with blue shutters across from the Jared Coffin House complex is noted most for its dining.

The downstairs has a small dining room with checkered cloths. Upstairs are three small dining rooms with peach walls and white trim, windows

Second-floor dining room at Le Languedoc.

covered with peach draperies and valances, prints and posters framed in chrome, and Windsor chairs at nicely spaced tables bearing hurricane lamps with thick candles and vases, each containing one lovely salmon rose.

The hand-written menu is supplemented nightly by seafood specials. Our dinner began with an appetizer of smoked Nantucket pheasant with cranberry relish, very good and very colorful with red cabbage and slices of apples and oranges on a bed of lettuce. Other appetizers run from $4.50 for Black Forest mushroom pate to $7.50 for sauteed shrimp and escargots with pasta, pernod and garlic cream.

Good warm French bread compensated a bit for the lack of salad (a seasonal salad is $4 extra).

Of the entrees ($15 to $19), one of us sampled noisettes of lamb with artichokes in a rosemary sauce; the other had sauteed sweetbreads and lobster in puff pastry, in a sauce that included shiitake mushrooms, cognac and shallots. Nicely presented on piping hot white oval plates, they were accompanied by snow peas, broccoli, pureed turnips, yellow peppers, sweet potato and peach slices. Other interesting choices were sauteed medallions of venison in a sauce of lingonberries, green peppercorns and cassis; grilled duck breast in honey, soy, ginger and white wine, and grilled tenderloin in a black truffle sauce.

For dessert, we passed up strawberry pie and pears poached in a reduction of port to share a dense chocolate hazelnut torte spiked with grand marnier. The handwritten wine list of some 30 offerings seemed a bit strange and pricey (most from the mid-$20s to $70).

Le Languedoc is owned by the Grennan brothers, Neal, who is chef, and Alan. Michael Shannon, who runs the Club Car, sometimes cooks here on nights his restaurant is closed.

The inn has 20 bedrooms in four buildings, three on Hussey Street and a new one on Center Street. Doubles are $65 to $95.

Lunch in season, noon to 2; dinner nightly, 6:30 to 10.

21 Federal, 21 Federal St., Nantucket. (617) 228-2121.

New in July 1985 and an immediate smash success, this restaurant is renowned for its new "American grill cuisine."

Chef Bob Kinkead, who grew up in Wellesley and cooked in Cambridge and on the Cape, is into inspired creations. His pumpkin ravioli with Smithfield ham and sage was acclaimed in the fall, his grilled filet of beef with foie gras and black truffles was hailed at Christmas, and his changing pasta dishes and the mussels in light cream sauce were talked about all year.

Appetizers might be a trio of beef (carpaccio, bresaola and seared beef), grilled quail with shoestring sweet potatoes, lobster and oyster stew with shrimp quenelles, or salad of smoked duck and goat cheese with bacon dressing. Among entrees, lamb is served in three cuts (noisettes, rack and saddle), each with a different sauce and each said to be spectacular. A Mexican touch is added to dishes like the grilled salmon with coriander sauce and avocado relish.

Desserts include a trio of three chocolates and a bread pudding so extraordinary that our informant asked Gourmet magazine to get the recipe. Said informant and friends ate at 21 Federal three times during a week's vacation and couldn't believe everything was so good.

One of Nantucket's larger restaurants, 21 Federal is on two floors of a typical shingled house with white trim, designated by a brass plaque and elegantly decorated in Williamsburg style. The upstairs serves by reservation only; downstairs is first come, first served, and would-be patrons start queueing up about 5:45.

The patio luncheon is said to be a treat, as are the salads, breads and desserts available in the charcuterie near the side entrance.

Lunch, 11:30 to 2:30; dinner 6 to 10.

The Second Story, 1 South Beach St., Nantucket. (617) 228-3471.

The second floor of a building across from the harbor is all done up in pink walls and linen, pink and green floral overcloths, green napkins and green floors speckled with pink paint. Mismatched chairs with cane seats are at tables topped by mums in bud vases and enormous hurricane lamps enclosing candles. An alcove area beside the window onto the harbor is awash with comfy pillows.

It's all very striking and all very costly, especially at lunch, although dinners are comparatively more reasonable. That's also when the place is illuminated entirely by candles, and the setting could not be more glamorous.

The fare served up by chef-proprietors Patricia Tyler and David Toole is a mix of Mexican-Spanish, French, Italian and Cajun.

Their hand-written dinner menu changes nightly. Appetizers ($5 to $7.50) might be chilled scallops and avocado with a piquant salsa, a chilled sole and salmon mousse with a tomato mayonnaise, smoked goose breast with chevre and apples, littlenecks a la Diavolo, or Cajun duck liver and sausage timbale with shrimp sauce. We sampled the hot country pate, a huge thick slab of goose, duck, chicken and sausage, piping hot and bathed in a creamy green peppercorn sauce. Good monkey bread was hot as could be. Our Parducci chardonnay ($15) was chilled in a large silver ice bucket, and salt was in a crystal dish.

Entrees are priced from $16 for sole Deauvillaise or sweetbreads sauteed with ham, Madeira, mushrooms and creme fraiche to $19 for grilled noisettes of lamb with chutney sauce. The scallops au gratin (with avocado, tomato, garlic and cream) was a portion so ample that we needed neither salad (an extra $3) nor appetizer. The Thai shrimp with black bean and coriander sauce was super spicy and left the mouth smoldering long into the night.

For dessert ($4.50), the amaretto souffle turned out neither hot nor cold, but more like a mousse with only a hint of amaretto. Better choices might have been coeur a la creme with raspberry sauce or pears in puff pastry with caramel sauce.

Lunch, noon to 2; dinner 7 to 9, closed Mondays and January-March. No lunch in summer. Reservations required.

Straight Wharf Restaurant, Straight Wharf, Nantucket. (617) 228-4499.

Marian Morash of television and cookbook fame is the force behind this seasonal restaurant on the waterfront, one revered by some as their favorite on the island. Mrs. Morash wrote the encyclopedic Victory Garden Cookbook in 1982 with inspiration from her husband Russell, a television producer and weekend gardener, plus Jim Crockett and Julia Child.

Seafood is featured in this popular spot that is the height of chic and priced to match. The complex includes a fish market, a gourmet shop called Provisions and a contemporary restaurant, consisting of a large room with an outdoor deck and a crowded bar. Appetizers, light entrees and desserts are served in the bar. On warm nights, the doors to the deck remain open through dinner.

Menu items and prices vary throughout the season (entrees generally $19 to $23), but you can be assured Mrs. Morash will serve only what's fresh and creative. Her fans rave about almost everything: the smoked bluefish pate, grilled shrimp samurai, smoked pheasant with raspberry sauce and chilled guacamole soup for starters; the blackened sea bass (blackened fish is what they're best known for), soft-shell crabs meuniere, escalopes of salmon with ginger lime sauce, the grilled veal paillards for entrees; the arugula, endive and red pepper salad, and desserts like blueberry sorbet or lemon souffle with raspberry sauce.

Dinner, 6:45 to 10; bar from 4. Reservations required. Closed Mondays and October through mid-June.

The Club Car, 1 Main St., Nantucket. (617) 228-1101.

The red train car at the side of this luxurious establishment brightened by petunias in flower boxes outside the windows is a sedate bar that's open from noon daily and enlivened by a piano nightly. Beyond, the elegant dining room has cane-backed chairs with rose colored velvet cushions at crisp, white-linened tables. Large art works and a shelf of copper pans add color.

Chef Michael Shannon offers one prix-fixe dinner each night for $17.50, including choice of soup or salad and dessert. The entree when we visited was marinated duck legs bourguignon garnished with summer vegetables.

Otherwise, the menu is international in style but labeled in French (les potages du jour, les viandes). Les hors d'oeuvres include smoked trout with horseradish cream, octopus in the style of Bangkok, calves brains with balsamic vinegar and capers, and Beluga caviar, $4.50 to $28. The nine entrees run from $18.50 for the Indian curry of the day to $25 for rare breast of Nantucket Muscovy duck in a peppercorn and grand marnier sauce. Among other choices are scampi Dijonnaise, Nantucket swordfish with red pepper lobster butter, Wisconsin veal of the day, and rack of spring lamb with fresh herbs and a honey mustard glaze. The wine list and desserts are worthy of the rest of the menu.

Dinner nightly, 6 to 10; weekends only in off-season. Closed mid-December to Memorial Day.

Boarding House, 12 Federal St., Nantucket. (617) 228-9622.

The Boarding House provided our most memorable meal when we first visited Nantucket in 1972. It had just opened in the downstairs of a former boarding house on India Street and was the culinary hit of the summer. Jim Perelman took over from the original owners in 1978, and the Boarding House has moved to larger quarters around the corner at Federal and India streets. A la carte dinners are served upstairs in summer, but the downstairs room with an Italian feel, curved arches and a striking if strange mural of asparagus stalks and small crabs on a sandy beach is popular any time.

"We're a bit more moderately priced than some because we rely on local traffic throughout the year," says Jim, who runs a comfortable and unpretentious place.

For lunch (entrees, $4.95 to $5.95), we enjoyed a cup of mushroom and broccoli bisque served with a big chowder cracker, and scallops on a shell with tomatoes, herbs and tasty sauce, accompanied — rather oddly, we thought — by mashed turnips. The fettuccine Alfredo with three cheeses was terribly rich and terribly good. A limited selection of beers and wines by the glass are available.

Dinner entrees ($11.95 to $16.95) include swordfish with pecan butter, roast duck with raspberry and orange sauce, shrimp moutarde, saltimbocca, roast leg of lamb, steak Diane and chicken breast stuffed with gorgonzola cheese and pesto. Among desserts are orange cheesecake, lemon poppyseed cake and creme caramel.

Downstairs, lunch noon to 2:30, dinner from 6; upstairs in summer, dinner from 6. Closed January and February.

The Thistle, 20 Broad St., Nantucket. (617) 228-9228.

Along something of a restaurant row, this house with four small dining rooms just below Le Languedoc has been operated since 1978 by Howard and Carol Crocker. Table appointments vary between blue and white fabric mats and cloths, and non-smoking rooms are among the attractions.

Chef Sharron H. Vannerson, who has been with the restaurant since it opened, offers a typewritten menu of international cuisine featuring fresh seafood. It changes periodically and the appetizers and desserts are limited and somewhat unusual.

Dinner might begin with marinated artichoke and feta cheese salad, cheese mushroom souffle roll, cioppino or curried mussels and asparagus salad. Among the eight entrees ($17 to $19) the night we visited were shrimp with tomato, clams and artichoke hearts tossed with pasta, seafood in phyllo with a vermouth cream sauce, grilled swordfish with bearnaise sauce or mustard herb butter, roast duckling with raspberry sauce flambeed in grand marnier, and veal scaloppine with wild mushrooms and red wine.

Desserts ($5) might be fresh lime meringue pie or frozen macaroon souffle or, the night we were there, German sweet chocolate pie, apple-cranberry crumb pie and baba alla creme.

Dinner from 6:30; closed Monday and November-March.

India House, 37 India St., Nantucket. (617) 228-9043.

Candlelight dinners in the two small dining rooms in this historic, country-stylish inn and restaurant, a pleasant stroll from Main Street, are something of an event.

A changing prix-fixe menu ($26.50) offers choice of appetizer and green salad plus a limited selection of entrees. The fall offerings when we visited were roast loin of lamb with hunter's sauce, grilled tournedos beurre rouge, roast pork loin with fresh basil and garlic, and boneless duckling with apple cranberry sauce. A summer night might bring lamb India house, pesto pommery shrimp, veal medallions Czarina or a Cajun specialty.

Excellent American and French wines are offered, and the homemade pies and desserts are reported to be scrumptious.

Breakfast, Monday-Saturday 8:30 to 10:30, Sunday 9 to noon; dinner, nightly with seatings at 7 and 9:15. Dinner reservations required. Closed January-March.

The Woodbox, 29 Fair St., Nantucket. (617) 228-0587.

Billed as Nantucket's oldest inn, built in 1709, the Woodbox is a charming small restaurant with a limited menu, serving breakfast and dinner beside an ancient hearth.

The hand-written menu may have its misspellings, but locals say you can't go wrong with the food. Appetizers might be gravlax, country pate or scallop mousse with beurre rouge. For entrees ($16.95 to $20), how about ragout de ris de veau, fillet of halibut, lamb au porto or medallions of beef with green peppercorns and mustard? Entrees include seasonal salad, fresh vegetables and hot popovers.

Breakfasts here also are special, featuring popovers, a choice of omelets, pancakes and eggs Benedict.

Breakfast, 8:30 to 10:30; dinner, 7 and 8:45 seatings; closed Mondays and mid-October to mid-June. Reservations required. Beer and wine only; no credit cards.

Obadiah's, 2 India St., Nantucket. (617) 228-4430.

Native seafood is the specialty at Obadiah's, a crowded place with a big fireplace, candlelight and linened tables very close together in the downstairs of an 1840s sea captain's home.

Among the offerings from an extensive menu are such appetizers as scallops seviche ($6) and entrees ($10 to $16) like yellowtail sole, old-fashioned scallop broil, codfish curry, seafood stew, linguini with seafood and, of course, lobster in several variations, the most requested being baked stuffed. There are two veal dishes and pepper steak or steak Diane for those who prefer meat.

A local vegetable, rice or potato and a basket of Portuguese and cranberry breads comes with; many choose Obadiah's "bad, bad dessert" of dark chocolate cake with mocha frosting, topped with walnuts, coconut and whipped cream or Brant's pie of cranberry and raisins, from the limited choice.

Cobblestoned Main Street is decorated for Christmas.

Many of the same items at prices from $5 to $14 are served at lunch. Lunch, noon to 3; dinner 6 to 10; closed November to mid-April.

The Tavern at Harbor Square, Straight Wharf, Nantucket. (617) 228-1266.

Thoroughly casual and popular with tourists is this place owned by the Walter Beinecke Jr. interests in a shopping complex, with window tables, booths separated by glass dividers and an upstairs outdoor deck with a view of the waterfront buildings.

The dinner entrees are limited ($9.50 for chicken cordon bleu or shrimp scampi to $11.50 for broiled scallops), but for lunch or light meals it's fine. Potato skins, fried fish and oversized sandwiches are the rule, and the nachos deluxe with chili and vegetables (which we admired at a neighboring table and then ordered for ourselves) were $4 and more than enough for two.

Open daily, 11:30 to 10, May-October. Breakfast from 8 to 10:30 in summer.

Diversions

Nantucket's attractions run the gamut from beaches to history and architecture to art and antiques. Except for the beaches, almost everything the visitor needs or wants to do is right in Nantucket village, and easily reached on foot or by bicycle. A number of pamphlets detail interesting walking tours.

Fourteen buildings and exhibits of special interest are maintained by the **Nantucket Historical Association,** which offers a combination pass to 11 for $6.50. Among them:

The Whaling Museum, the largest complex and one most visitors pass just after they leave the ferry, is considered the nation's best after the New Bedford Whaling Museum. Originally a candle factory, an original beam press still is poised to render whale spermaceti into candles and oil. Rooms are devoted to scrimshaw, whaling equipment and objects brought home by seamen from the South Seas. A whale jaw with teeth, the skeleton of a 43-foot whale and whalecraft shops — a sail loft, cooperage, shipsmith and such — are among the attractions.

The Peter Foulger Museum next door recreates the town's early days, particularly the folk life of its population, from Indians to Quakers. Exhibits range from Nantucket silver and lightship baskets to artifacts from the Great Fire of 1846 and relics of the China Trade.

Fair Street Museum and Quaker Meeting House. Nantucket's art museum records the lives of early citizens in portraits. An upstairs gallery houses more recent works and special exhibitions. The adjoining Meeting House was built in 1838.

Farther from the center of town are the **Oldest House** (1686), the **Old Mill** (1746) and the **Old Gaol** (1805). Numerous other structures are under Historical Association auspices, but if you simply walk any of the streets fanning out from the center you'll stumble on your own finds. Do not miss central Main Street, particularly the three Georgian mansions known as "The Three Bricks."

Art Galleries and Antiques Shops. Besides beaches and good food, it's said that visitors are attracted to Nantucket by all the galleries and antiques shops. They certainly have a wide choice. One brochure is devoted to antiquing on Nantucket, and one of summer's big events is the annual antiques show in early August. Such Nantucket scenes as cobblestoned streets, deserted moors and rose-covered cottages in 'Sconset appeal to artists, whose works hang in galleries all along the wharves. Erica Wilson's needlepoint shop is a local attraction.

Shopping. Nantucket is a shopper's paradise and, were it not for the cobblestoned streets and salt air, you could as easily picture yourself in Lexington or New Canaan. Specialty stores with names like **Very Terry** (for terrycloth) and **Nobby Clothes** compete with the more traditional like **Murray's Toggery** and **Mitchell's Book Corner,** all across the several square blocks of "downtown" Nantucket. One of the best gourmet food and takeout shops anywhere is **Que Sera, Sarah** with the makings for great picnics at reasonable prices.

Extra-Special

Nantucket Lightship Baskets. The lightships that protected boats from the treacherous shoal waters off the south and east end of the island in the mid-18th century spawned a cottage industry indigenous to Nantucket. The crews of the South Shoal Lightship turned to basket-weaving to while away their hours on duty. Their duty ended, the seamen continued to make baskets ashore — first primitive and heavy-duty types for carrying laundry or groceries, later more beautiful handbags appealing to visitors. The latter were inspired by the Sayle family, who continue the tradition at their shop on Washington Street Extension. Today, Nantucket's famed baskets come in all shapes and sizes (including 14-karat gold miniatures) and seem to be ubiquitous in the shops and on tanned arms. The handbags have ivory carvings on top and carry hefty price tags. The Four Winds Craft Guild on Straight Wharf claims to have the largest collection.

Edgartown, Mass.
Fall for the Vineyard

One of the best things about visiting an island is the ferry ride over from the mainland. The ringing of ships' bells, the whistle as you depart, the hustle and bustle of getting cars on and off — it all adds to the anticipation of what is to come.

Even though the trip to Martha's Vineyard from Wood's Hole takes less than an hour, that's time enough to listen to the buoys clanking, and to watch one shore fade in the distance and another appear.

It's time enough also for a transition — to leave the mainland cares behind, before arriving at Vineyard Haven or Oak Bluffs and stepping into a different milieu.

The Vineyard is nothing if not varied. Oak Bluffs is a Methodist campground and Victorian beach resort, its many-splendored gingerbread cottages a rainbow of hues. At the other end of the island are the Indian-owned restaurants and shops atop windswept Gay Head, its cliffs a mosaic of colors and the East's mini-version of the Big Sur. In the interior of West Tisbury and Chilmark, the landscape is such that you might not even think you were on an island.

Then there's Edgartown, as up-to-date as a resort town can be but still reflecting a heritage back to 1642. It's a prosperous seaport village, which boomed during the whaling days of the 19th century and became a yachting center in the 20th century.

Long a retreat for the rich and famous as well as the rich and not-so-famous, Edgartown is best appreciated in the off-season. The crowds are gone, but the charms remain as autumn lingers at least through Thanksgiving. The beaches are deserted except for a few strollers. The waters are left for the fishermen and a few hardy sailors and wind-surfers. Many cottages and condos are battened down for the winter.

Autumn is the season that islanders and knowing visitors look forward

Waterfront view of Edgartown, including the Seafood Shanty.

Main 1860 house at the Charlotte Inn.

to, particularly in Edgartown, which is increasingly a year-round haven for retirees and escapees from the mainland. Here, many inns and restaurants remain open all or most of the year, but prices are reduced. You can be near the ocean in a moderate clime, and immerse yourself in a delightful community.

"Fall for Martha's Vineyard," the magazine ads entice in trying to boost autumn trade. It's hard to imagine how anyone wouldn't.

Inn Spots

Charlotte Inn, South Summer Street, Edgartown 02539. (617) 627-4751.

You register at a front desk so ornate that it is pictured in the centerfold of the Architectural Digest inn book. At one side of the main floor are a two-room art gallery and a shop that are destinations in themselves. Behind is a small, deluxe restaurant in which you dine romantically in an indoor-outdoor garden reminiscent of New Orleans or Europe. You relax beforehand on the side porch running the depth of the Summer House, rejoicing in the fountains and flowers and a scent resembling eucalyptus; the ice for your drinks comes in a green leather bucket. And later you retire to one of 24 guest rooms that are so lavishly and tastefully furnished as to defy expectation.

The Charlotte Inn compound which Gery and Paula Conover have developed from a private home he acquired in 1971 is nothing short of a masterpiece. Such an aura of elegance could make the inn seem aloof. But it turns out that the boyish-looking man talking to the painters is Gery (pronounced Gary), who might be mistaken for his 22-year-old son, and the youngish blonde helping out as a waitress at breakfast identifies herself as Paula. This is, after all, a very personal place, a reflection of Gery's desire to have an art gallery (he runs a restoration business as well) and of

Paula's flair with flowers, decorating and stitchery (she did many of the pillows and comforters that enhance each guest room).

Rooms are in the main two-story 1860 house, a rear carriage house with three suites that Gery built (without blueprints!) in 1980, the 200-year-old Garden House (so called because of its lovely backyard) across the street and, since 1985, the Summer House next door. The much-photographed deluxe suite upstairs in the Carriage House has an English hunting feel to it: a four-poster queensize bed, a mahogany sleigh bed redecorated as a sofa, a working marble fireplace, a beamed cathedral ceiling, thick beige carpeting and hunter green walls, a TV and stereo hidden away in a chest and a treasury of bric-a-brac from a gentleman's riding boots to one of the earliest cameras perched on a tripod in the corner. The suite rents for $250, and Gery says it's booked almost every night.

After seeing that and a sampling of other opulent rooms, we wondered about ours (the last available and at the other end of the price scale). No. 18 in the new Summer House had a private entrance off the wicker-filled side porch (we happened to be its only users on a couple of mild October days and nights). Although small, it was luxuriously comfortable, with a four-poster bed in front of shelves of books, two wingback chairs and many antiques.

A complimentary continental breakfast is served in the conservatory dining room and terrace which houses the inn's restaurant. Handsomely furnished with white linen, white bentwood and cane chairs, brick walls, skylights, paintings, lush ferns and a blooming hibiscus tree, it is truly charming. Classical music and a trickling fountain are the backdrop for fresh orange juice, tea or coffee and breads (perhaps raisin or cranberry) and muffins (walnut-sour cream, cheese, cranberry and apple) served with raspberry preserves and marmalade. More substantial breakfasts are available at extra cost, a choice of raspberry waffles or a sour cream and asparagus omelet, preceded by broiled grapefruit at our visit.

Dinners traditionally have been considered the priciest and most elegant on the island. The esteemed Chez Pierre, which had leased space in the inn for seven years, closed late in 1985 and the Conovers hoped to find a comparable chef and reopen for dinner by summer of 1986.

After dinner, you can wander around the art gallery, watch television or play games in the small fireplaced common room of the Garden House, or simply relax in the wicker rockers on the porch of the Summer House, taking in the sights of the illuminated Charlotte Inn compound and the sounds of the fountains and the church bells on the hour. What a way to end a day!

Doubles, $85 to $195; off-season, $32 to $135.

The Victorian Inn, South Water Street (Box 947), Edgartown 02539. (617) 627-4784.

Located across from the famous Pagoda Tree in an area of ship's captain's homes is the Victorian, with masses of impatiens in front of its striking exterior. It's as Victorian as can be (well deserving of its listing in the National Register) and also as luxurious as can be, from its elegantly furnished rooms to the gourmet breakfast served in the English garden out back.

Working quietly with great flair and taste over 10 years, innkeepers Marilyn and Jack Kayner have refurbished 14 guest rooms, all with private

English garden behind Victorian Inn backs up to Charlotte Inn property.

bathrooms (only one with tub) and inviting sitting areas, on the second and third floors. Pink, rose and green are the prevailing colors, and some of the sheets and shower curtains have patterns of roses. One room has two green velvet chairs in a bay window and a cedar chest topped with cushions at the foot of the bed. Another has kingsize bed with ruffled canopy, damask sofa, rose wallpaper and rose easy chair. Two on the third floor have tiny balconies offering glimpses of the harbor. A deluxe room at the rear has a porch with deck chairs and loungers overlooking the English garden and the carriage house of the abutting Charlotte Inn.

Decanters of sherry and the morning newspaper are among amenities.

Marilyn Kayner is famous for her granola at breakfast. Hearty eaters love her brandied French toast, soufleed eggs, banana or apricot crepes, and an English version of scrambled eggs and bacon — chipped bacon on top, served with toast points. The full breakfast is taken in a dining room with delicate pink wallpaper, polished floors and hanging plants or, in summer, outside at white tables shaded by blue umbrellas on a delightful brick patio amid the greenery and flowers of the English garden.

Doubles, $75 to $150. Closed November-March.

Point Way Inn, Main Street at Pease's Point Way, Edgartown 02539. (617) 627-8633.

Remodeled from a 150-year-old whaling captain's house, this 15-room inn offers a variety of fine accommodations and personality galore. The personality is that of owners Ben and Linda Smith, who landed in Edgartown Harbor in 1979 after a 4,000-mile sailing cruise and spent that winter turning the house into an inn reflecting the family interests through and through.

You'll enjoy the pictures of their 38-foot ketch, the Point Way (on which

255

they offer cruises off Florida or the Caribbean islands in winter), as well as the memorabilia of the Edgartown Mallet Club, a croquet group which Ben formed and which plays on the inn's lawn, all the yachting and golfing trophies, the photos of the Yale Whiffenpoofs of which Ben was a member, and the paintings by his mother, who was of the Boston School of Impressionists.

Each of the guest rooms, grouped off various stairways in separate sections of the house, has a private bath and half have fireplaces. Canopy and four-poster beds, colorful quilts, wing chairs, wicker or tweedy sofas, a couple of tiny porches and a large deck — it's a delightful mishmash that's comfortable as can be. Each room also has nice touches like stamped envelopes, pin cushions and candies.

The public rooms have oriental rugs, a brick fireplace, games and a wet bar. Yellow flowered tablecloths brighten the breakfast room, in which fresh orange juice, coffee cakes, muffins and bread are served buffet style. Cereal and yogurt also are available.

Lemonade and cookies plus clams — if guests have been successful on clamming expeditions — are an afternoon highlight in the ivy-covered outdoor gazebo, which is part of the mallet club. Guests as well as members can play croquet if they wish.

In 1985, the Smiths began sharing innkeeping duties with young new resident managers Casey and Amy Morton, who add their own energetic touch to the inn's personality.

Doubles, $80 to $150 (for a two-room suite with deck, private entrance and fireplace); off-season, $40 to $80.

Dr. Shiverick House, Pent Lane at Pease's Point Way, Box 640, Edgartown 02539. (617) 627-8497.

"The good doctor may be dead and gone, but people still come to Dr. Shiverick's house for a cure," says the brochure for this inn which opened in 1984 in a mansion built in 1840 by the town's physician. Today the cure is staying in the lap of luxury in a museum-quality home.

The owners, Philadelphia physicians who are descended from the Shiverick line, hired a leading Vineyard designer to restore the house into an inn reflecting the structure's heritage.

The doctor's widow had expanded the original Greek Revival home after a trip south during which she was taken with the grandeur of ante-bellum mansions, which explains the long, high-ceilinged entrance hall with its original mahogany staircase, inside the oak double-door entry.

Each of the 11 guest rooms has full baths and four-poster or canopy beds, a variety of art objects, fresh or dried floral arrangements, and Laura Ashley-style wallpapers and fabrics. One corner room has a lovely oriental carpet, eyelet-trimmed curtains and rose-colored lamps. The four-room suite on the third floor has a fireplace, kitchen and its own rooftop porch. A second-floor back porch with deck chairs is available for all guests.

Innkeeper Tena McLoughlin's collection of baskets is everywhere, some piled in the hall most picturesquely, and her handmade grapevine wreaths decorate many of the rooms. Many baskets are in the colorful living room.

The sunny Mediterranean-style solarium which serves as the breakfast room is a pleasant melange of tile floor, pressed-oak chairs, ferns, flowers,

Gazebo and croquet are features of Point Way Inn.

hanging bunches of herbs, and more baskets. A nearby farm provides fresh fruits for continental breakfast, which also includes yogurts, breads, jams and jellies. On Sundays, Tena might make French toast and sometimes, she says, "I sneak eggs in."

Doubles, $110; off-season, $65.

The Daggett House, 59 North Water St., Edgartown 02539. (617) 627-4600.

For a waterfront location, this bed and breakfast inn with 24 rooms in two houses and a cottage is unsurpassed in Edgartown. The long, narrow rear lawn with flowers, benches and umbrellaed tables slopes down to the water and a private pier next to the Chappaquiddick Ferry landing.

Guest rooms, all with private baths, are in the main 1750 Daggett House with its historic tavern downstairs, the newer (early 1800s) Warren House across Water Street, and the Garden Cottage, which has three double rooms. Rooms are comfortable, generally spacious and furnished with antiques.

After its location, the next best thing is the historic downstairs tavern room, which dates from the 1600s and above which the house was later built. It still looks the way an early tavern should look, with its unusual beehive fireplace chimney, dark beams, old tools and bare wood tables. Continental breakfast is complimentary; full breakfasts are extra.

Hidden near the fireplace in the tavern room is a secret staircase which provides steep, low-ceilinged access to an upstairs guest room with kingsize bed, gold wallpaper and a view of the harbor.

Off the entrance to the inn is a living room with sofas, wing chairs and television set. Among the 14 rooms in the Warren House are several efficiencies and suites.

Doubles, $50 to $120; off-season, $35 to $100. Only main house open all year.

Mid-19th century house has been converted into Governor Bradford Inn.

The Governor Bradford Inn, 128 Main St., Edgartown 02539. (617) 627-9510.

Young innkeepers John and Mary Kennan have restored and expanded a mid-19th century house on upper Main Street into an appealing inn of comfort and style. All 15 rooms on three floors have private baths, kingsize or twin brass beds, and ceiling fans, and some have Queen Anne wing chairs. The third-floor suite ($205), which John calls "a home away from home within a home away from home," has a sofa and coffee table, velvet wing chair and television.

The public rooms are exceptionally attractive. The garden room has white wicker chairs with green corduroy seats and a refrigerator with ice and setups. Sherry is provided guests in the formal front parlor full of Victorian antiques. Afternoon tea with cookies and cakes is served in the television room, done up in colorful gold and navy and oriental rugs.

Croissants and muffins are served in the breakfast room, which has bentwood chairs at round tables dressed in white linen. For a surcharge, John will dish up some acclaimed omelets or pancakes. The blue and white color scheme is taken from the willoware collection on display in the Sheraton china cabinet.

Doubles, $85 to $115; off-season, $50 to $85.

Chadwick House, Winter Street at Pease's Point Way, Box 1035, Edgartown 02539. (617) 627-4435.

Pure white with black shutters, on a nicely landscaped corner lot, this Greek Revival-style house built in 1840 has been an inn since 1979. It has two elegantly appointed front parlors and a cheery dining room where breakfast is served, plus six guest rooms (three with private baths and three sharing) upstairs, all with high ceilings, wide-plank floors, period furnishings and area rugs.

In 1981, innkeepers Eugene and Jean DeLorenzo added a two-story garden wing, extending the main house in an L-shape. Although the exterior is architecturally in keeping with the original, the interior is modern, containing a suite and eight bedrooms with private baths and wall-to-wall carpeting.

Jean DeLorenzo's china collection is featured in the public rooms. She also makes the pillows and does all the baking for the continental breakfasts — coffee cakes, bran muffins, and banana and pumpkin breads, for instance — served on flowered china in the fireplaced dining room.

A pleasant, shaded veranda beside a flower garden faces the ample grounds. One room in the original house also has its own veranda.

Doubles, $75 to $100; off-season, $40 to $65.

Dining Spots

Warriners, Post Office Square, Edgartown. (617) 627-4488.

The place to be seen in Edgartown since it opened in December 1984 in what was a private residence behind the Old Whaling Church, Warriners was so successful that it doubled its size with an addition in July 1985. Changing menus, fine wines and an elegant, home-like setting amid fine china and antiques combine for luxurious dining.

The decor consists of "all the favorite things we've seen and pulled together," owner Sam Warriner says. He obtained the striking Dudson china (with everything matching, even vases and salt and pepper shakers) from the Reject Shop in London and the heavy print mats for the English reproduction mahogany tables from another trip to England. It's little wonder that the dark-paneled main dining room with Queen Anne chairs, bow windows and brick fireplace with oriental fan in front has the look of an Englishman's library. Small brass lamps with pleated shades and vases of astromeria grace each well-spaced table, and china and books glow in a back-lighted corner cabinet.

Dinner might begin, as ours did, with a pate of duck accompanied by a beach plum chutney ($4.50), a ravioli of brie, escargots and basil, or pan-fried frog's legs provencale. Scotched duck and leek soup was the special of the night, followed by a carved loaf of fresh bread and a house salad of endive, lettuce and cucumber with a mild vinaigrette.

Entrees run from $13.50 for breast of chicken provolone with sun-dried tomatoes or sole a l'Americaine to $19 for Atlantic lobster and shellfish court bouillon. We liked the peppered duck steak mousseline with zinfandel sauce and the roulade of lamb brunoise with prosciutto, nicely presented with an array of brussels sprouts, cherry tomatoes and small red potatoes, and — an appropriate touch — garnished with a bunch of small wild grapes. The dessert tray included a tasty kiwi cake, sorbet with melon, a grand passion genoise with liqueur, butter cream and kiwi, creme celeste, a dish of four kinds of chocolate truffles and Sam's favorite chocolate mousse with fresh raspberry sauce.

Accompanying all this was an excellent Clos du Bois pinot noir for $11, chosen from a magnificent wine list containing more than its share of bargains among pricier offerings up to $500. The house wines are $7.50 a bottle and available by the glass, as are several other select wines.

Dinner nightly, 6 to 9; closed Wednesday off-season. Reservations required.

Table in main dining room at Warriners.   Conservatory dining room at Charlotte Inn.

Martha's, 71 Main St., Edgartown. (617) 627-8316.

What could be more New Yorkish than Martha's, the arty, unbelievably colorful and crowded downstairs restaurant and the upstairs nightspot with a glassed-in waterfall behind the bar, tiny theater lights that flash on and off, and a small front porch where patrons vie in warm weather for the few tables overlooking the Main Street goings-on? It seemed an unlikely spot for the busload of elderly Midwestern tourists who jammed it the mid-October noon we had hoped to have lunch there.

Tables are smack dab together in the dining room, done with art deco flair in colors of peach, rose and green. They are topped with glass and vases of yellow lilies and votive candles in ornate holders. Banquettes in a wild peach and green print line the walls, and an unusually beautiful chandelier with globes shaped like lilies, made in Florence, hangs from the middle of the ceiling. Island artists' works are incorporated into the scheme; especially appealing are the tile work (even in the rest rooms) and cutout paintings by Margo Datz.

The lunch menu features many quiches and omelets; sandwiches, (hummus on pita is $3.95; lobster salad on French bread, $6.50), a pita pizza and huevos rancheros.

Dinners are more international and pricy, with entrees from $12.95 for vegetable stir-fry with Japanese tofu and a couple of chicken and pasta dishes to $22.95 for a bouillabaisse that mixes filet mignon tips with seafood in a rose-pernod sauce over a bed of angel hair pasta. With fish and seafood dishes, baked or sauteed ($13.95 to $18.95), you have a choice of six sauces.

At brunch you can order whole wheat pancakes with grand marnier butter or eggs Martha, with filet mignon tips on a croissant and hollandaise. Upstairs, in summer, a sushi platter is available for $14.50. There's a huge wine list, and the house wine, Principato, is $8 a carafe.

Breakfast-lunch and Sunday brunch, 10:30 to 3:30; dinner, 6:30 to 10:30.

260

Shiretown Inn, North Water Street, Edgartown. (617) 627-4283.

In season, the large indoor-outdoor dining room and covered terrace at the rear of the Shiretown Inn is one of the most popular spots in Edgartown. Pink linen and pink and green wallpaper provide a soft backdrop for the garden setting, and many diners like to have drinks in the garden or the Pub adjacent to the dining room.

Seafood is the specialty, particularly among appetizers (marinated whitefish and mussels supreme or smoked white marlin), and the inn boasts the best clam chowder on the island. Typical entrees ($11.95 to $19.95) are stuffed yellowtail flounder, sauteed shrimp romana, seafood brochette, rack of lamb Dijon, veal Martiniquaise and tournedos with avocado, crabmeat and bearnaise sauce.

Fancy ice creams are the dessert specialty, among them the Shiretown wonder: ice cream with hot fudge sauce, creme de menthe and shredded coconut.

Dinner nightly, 6 to 10, spring to mid-fall.

The Seafood Shanty, 31 Dock St., Edgartown. (617) 627-8622.

For dining, the best harbor view is from the popular open-air porch with water on three sides off this contemporary, three-level spot which is anything but a shanty. Unusual plastic chairs with deep blue wire frames, bare tables with blue and white mats and bare wood walls add up to an attractive nautical setting.

You pay for the location. Our lunch for two came to $26 for a cup of clam chowder and a spinach salad, plus a pasta salad loaded with seafood; the sunny Indian summer setting, we admit, was such that we lingered over a second beer.

The seafood dinner entrees are fairly standard, from $10.95 for broiled bluefish to $16.95 for a fried seafood platter; rolls and salad or coleslaw, baked potato or french fries accompany. After all this, who needs the desserts, which are standard anyway?

Lunch daily, 11:30 to 3; dinner, 5:30 to 10:30; May-October.

The Wharf, Dock Street, Edgartown. (617) 627-9966.

A sprawling spot with deck, dining room with windows toward the harbor and a pub, this is popular for casual and light meals. A seafood salad and fried oysters vie with the raw bar as attractions at lunch. Lobster and a fisherman's platter with fried calamari, scrod, clams and oysters are among dinner entrees ($11.95 to $15.50). Nachos and specialty drinks are featured in the Pub.

Lunch daily in season, 11:30 to 4:30; dinner, 5:30 to 10:30; pub open all year.

Zachariah's, at the Kelley House, Kelley Street, Edgartown. (617) 627-4394.

Although the country-style decor of this large, two-level dining room with spindle-back chairs and frilly curtains reflects its location between buildings in a hotel-motel complex, the menu is among the island's more innovative.

Dinner entrees ($12.50 to $19) include Cajun popcorn shrimp, chicken duxelle with sauce Albuferia, blackened sea bass with lemon herb butter, and panneed veal with czarina sauce. Toll house pie, Indian pudding and carrot cake are on the limited dessert menu.

Caribbean onion tarts are popular as lunch and dinner appetizers. Also on the lunch menu, which changes daily and charges hotel prices, are things like Cornish pasties, a croissant filled with chicken salad and a lobster roll for $9.25.

Lunch daily, noon to 2; dinner, 6 to 9; Sunday brunch, 11 to 2.

Navigator Restaurant and Boathouse Bar, 2 Lower Main St., Edgartown. (617) 627-4320.

Part of the Harborside Inn motel and time-sharing complex, this establishment has an unmistakably nautical feeling and good views of the harbor. Downstairs in the Boathouse bar filled with artifacts from old whaling ships, the beams are hung with lobster buoys, harpoons and ship's lights, the freestanding fireplace cuts the evening chill and there's a patio for outdoor lunches and boat-watching. Upstairs in the Navigator Room, you look out over the harbor or the inn's gardens.

Dinners run from $12.95 for chicken rosemary to $19.95 for loin lamb chops; the fish of the day is broiled or baked stuffed. Lunch in the Boathouse Bar ($5.25 to $7.95) might be shrimp in a basket, a croissant filled with seafood newburg or a seafood tettrazini.

Open 11 a.m. to midnight, early May to early October.

Andrea's, Upper Main Street, Edgartown. (617) 627-5850.

Islanders always include Andrea's, which serves classic northern Italian cuisine, in their list of favorite restaurants. The setting is a large white house, built in 1890, with a wide front porch, a side garden patio where lunch and brunch are served in summer, and a downstairs bar-lounge and wine cellar.

The airy dining rooms have bare wood floors and large windows framed by lacy white curtains. Deep green tablecloths contrast with the white walls. The fare is about what you'd expect: pastas in full or half portions, and seafood, chicken, veal and beef dishes from $11.95 to $22.95. Hot and cold appetizers include melon and prosciutto, clams casino and mozzarella in carozza.

Lunch or brunch, Wednesday-Sunday 11:30 to 2; dinner nightly except Monday, 6 to 11.

Savoir Fare, Post Office Square, Edgartown. (617) 627-9864.

For a light lunch on the deck, or to pick up a picnic or beach lunch, try this little spot near Warriners. Innovative sandwiches, salads (poached salmon with mangos and dill sauce is one), pates and desserts are on display in glass cases, and everything looks so fresh and good that it's hard to choose.

Ratatouille quiche, white bean cassoulet, stuffed grape leaves and King Pao chicken all beckon. A sandwich of brie, avocado and sprouts with creamy garden dressing is $3.95; a French bistro lunch is $5.95 for pate, French bread, cornichons and a selection of mustards. Coffee beans and the vinegars of Chicama Vineyards are sold, as are all kinds of breads, meats and cheeses.

For dessert, a slice of chocolate pecan pate is $2.50, or you could get a piece of cointreau fudge cake or a tropical chocolate coconut bar.

Open daily, 8 to 8 in summer; 10 to 7 off-season; closed January-March.

Extra-Special

Chicama Vineyards, West Tisbury. (617) 693-0309.

The wild grapes that gave Martha's Vineyard its name are now being cultivated by ex-Californians George and Catherine Matheisen and winemaker son Tim, who makes "the kinds of wines we like to drink," Catherine says. They specialize in dry viniferas, among them a robust zinfandel, a new white zinfandel and the first Martha's Vineyard-appelation merlot. Much of the winemaking operation is outside and rather primitive, as you might expect after negotiating Stoney Hill Road, a long mile of bumps and dirt that we'd rename Stoney Hole. Several hundred people make the trek on a busy summer day and relish the shop's choice of wine or herbed vinegars, dressings and jams, all neatly displayed in gift baskets and glass cases lit from behind so the herbs show through. In the fall, the Christmas shop also offers festive foods, wreaths and hot mulled wine. Open daily, 11 to 5, Sunday 1 to 5.

Vinegars on display at Chicama Vineyards.

Diversions

Edgartown is an eminently walkable town and everything (except some of the beaches) is within walking distance, which is fortunate for in summer the place tends to be wall-to-walk people, bicycles and cars. The shops, restaurants and inns are compressed into a maze of narrow streets leading from or paralleling the harbor. Interspersed with them and along side streets that live up to the description "quaint" are large white whaling captains' homes, neatly separated from the brick sidewalks by picket fences and colorful gardens. Here you see and sense the history of a seaport village preserved from the 19th century.

Walk around. Don't miss the churches: The Old Whaling Church, the tall-columned Greek Revival structure that doubles as the Performing Arts Center (Robert J. Lurtsema was on the docket when we were there); the little St. Andrew's Episcopal Church with wonderful stained-glass windows and a cheery interior; the imposing First Federated Church with old box pews and a steeple visible far at sea. Other highlights are the newspaper offices of the revered Vineyard Gazette in a 1764 house across from the Charlotte Inn, the towering Pagoda Tree brought from China as a seedling in a flower pot early in the 19th century and now spreading over South Water Street to shade both the Victorian and Harborside inns, the Old Sculpin Art Gallery showing works of various artists, and all the sea captain's homes of diverse architectural eras along Water and Summer streets in particular.

The Dukes County Historical Society, at School and Cooke streets, is a block-sized museum complex worth a visit. The 12 rooms of the 1765 Thomas Cooke House are filled with early island memorabilia. You're apt to see historians at work in the Gale Huntington Library of History, through which you pass to get to the Francis Foster Museum, which has a small maritime and island collection. Outside is a boat shed including a whaleboat, fire engine and old wagon, plus the original Fresnel lens from the old Gay Head Lighthouse, mounted in a replica of the lighthouse lantern and watch room, and still lighted at night.

Beaches. Katama Beach, the public part of South Beach along the open south shore three miles south of Edgartown, has excellent surf swimming, a tricky undertow, shifting dunes and a protected salt pond inhabited by crabs and scallops. A shuttle bus runs from Edgartown in summer. Non-surf swimming is available at the Joseph A. Sylvia State Beach, a narrow, two-mile-long strip between Edgartown and Oak Bluffs. Back toward Edgartown is Bend-of-the-Road Beach; its shallow waters are good for children. In town is Lighthouse Beach at Starbuck's Neck, on the harbor a short walk from North Water Street and seldom crowded.

Chappaquiddick Island. Reached by a 25-cent and five-minute ferry ride from Edgartown, it has a public beach facing the Edgartown Harbor at Chappy Point, plus the Cape Pogue Wildlife Refuge and Wasque Reservation beaches. These are remote and secluded, three miles from the ferry — best reached by car as bicyclists may find it difficult negotiating some of the sandy roads (but parking is limited). On the way you'll pass the forested Mytoi Trustees Preservation and the Chappaquiddick General Store and gasoline station, surrounded by abandoned cars and the only commercial enterprise of size on Chappaquiddick.

Shopping. Main Street and adjacent streets are crammed with interesting stores. **The Fligors'** (billed as the Vineyard's most delightful store for 27 years) is an intriguing maze of rooms and levels that make it almost a department store; gifts, dolls, resort clothing, toys, Christmas shop, a fantastic basement sale room — you name it, Carol and Richard Fligor probably have it. **A Gift of Love** is an elegant gift store. **Cork Corner** has some one-of-a-kind clothes, including quilted jackets and hand-done skirts with cats all over them. The **Unicorn Tales Bookshop** also offers funny cards and island memorabilia. The **Edgartown Woodshop** has colorful rag baskets, two-family birdhouses and feeders made of bark. The **Golden Door** has Far Eastern arts and treasures. The **Divine Yard** fashion outlet sells White Stag at half price. **Handworks** offers teeny things for doll houses among a large assortment of gifts and crafts. The **Bird House** boutique, the **Vermont Shop, Tashtego** and the **Country Store Collections** are others we liked.

If you get bushed from all this shopping and walking, rest awhile on the benches atop the Memorial Wharf pavilion, a salubrious vantage point for contemplating the harbor.

Newport waterfront, as viewed from dining deck at Clarke Cooke House.

Newport, R.I.
A Many-Splendored Place

For the visitor, there are perhaps five Newports.

One is the harborfront, the busy commercial and entertainment area along the wharves and Thames Street. This is the heart of Newport, the place to and from which the Tall Ships and America's cup winners sailed, the place to which the tourists gravitate.

Another Newport is a world apart. It's up on fabled Bellevue Avenue among the mansions from the Gilded Age. Here the Astors, Vanderbilts, Morgans and others of America's 400 built their summer "cottages," palatial showplaces designed by the nation's leading architects. Here near the Casino at the turn of the century was a society summer resort unrivaled for glitter and opulence.

A third Newport is its historic Point and Historic Hill sections, which date back to the 17th and 18th centuries when Newport was an early maritime center. Here are more Colonial houses than in any place in the country, and some of the oldest public and religious edifices as well.

A fourth Newport is the windswept, open land around Ocean Drive, where the surf crashes against the rocky shore amid latter-day mansions and contemporary showplaces. This is the New England version of California's Pebble Beach and Seventeen-Mile Drive.

And then there's the rest of Newport, a bustling, Navy-dominated city which sprawls north along Aquidneck Island, away from the ocean and the other Newports.

Join these diverse Newports as history and geography have and you get New England's international resort, a wondrous mix of water and wealth, of architecture and history, of romance and entertainment.

265

You can concentrate on one Newport and have more than enough to see and do, or try to savor a bit of them all. But likely as not, you won't get your fill (unless you tire of fighting the crowds of a summer's weekend). Newport will merely whet your appetite, its powerful allure beckoning you back.

Inn Spots

The Inn at Castle Hill, Ocean Drive, Newport 02840. (401) 849-3800.

Gnarled trees on a hillside, reminding us of the olive groves in Portugal, make the approach to the Inn at Castle Hill a bit mysterious as well as picturesque. And when you reach the brown shingled inn at the crest of the hill, the view of Narragansett Bay and the Atlantic is breathtaking.

Calling itself a "country inn by the sea," Castle Hill seems rather more sophisticated than that, with its fine restaurant and Victorian air. Well-aged oriental rugs and well-cared-for wood paneling and carving abound; the fireplace of inlaid wood in the sitting room, where a fire is usually lit, is a sight to behold.

Seven of the ten rooms in the inn have private baths; the smaller three rooms that were in the servants' wing share two baths. Most are huge, and smashingly decorated in her inimitable style by Ione Williams of the Inn at Sawmill Farm in Vermont, with splashy coordinated prints.

In one room, the peach covering of a loveseat and chair, beside a bay window that appears to be perched right over the ocean, is matched in the peach chair set in front of the dressing table in the large bathroom. Other bedrooms have chestnut or pine paneling, chaise lounges, Victorian furniture and plush carpets, and most have wonderful views. On the third floor is a suite with sitting room; another room is all green and white and wicker, and even the clawfoot bathtub is wallpapered. The Nun's Room in the former servants' quarters, transformed from a large closet, has enough room to accommodate a twin bed and a sink "for the person who can't afford our rates," says innkeeper Paul McEnroe.

He collects and displays the paintings of Helena Sturdevant, a Newport artist early in the century.

In the lovely little breakfast room, named after Alexander Agassiz, the naturalist who was first owner of the house, continental breakfast is served to inn guests all year, buffet style from April to October. The inn's bar is a stunner and its restaurant widely acclaimed (see Dining Spots).

In summer, six motel-like units are available in the Harbor House, just in front of the inn; 18 cottages (typical New England tacky beach cottages, says the innkeeper, but they're rented a year in advance) right on the water are available by the week.

Doubles with private bath, $85 to $160, depending on season; shared bath, $50 to $80; suite, $110 to $200. Harbor House, $65 or $90. Beach cottages, $500 or $550 weekly.

Admiral Benbow Inn, 93 Pelham St., Newport 02840. (401) 846-4256.

Located on Newport's Historic Hill on the first street in the country to be lit by gas lamps, this gray clapboard house built in 1855 by a retired sea captain has both an historic and a nautical air.

Innkeeper Maggie Wiggins said new owners Bruce and Jean Berriman were having canopy beds made for many of the guest rooms, already

266

Guest room at Inn at Castle Hill has windows onto Narragansett Bay.

outfitted in brass beds and one grand four-poster. The 15 guest rooms on three floors have antique bureaus, cozy armchairs and Victorian settees, tall windows with print curtains and private bathrooms with showers. Some of the upper rooms have harbor views, and Room 12 has a deck overlooking much of Newport.

In winter, the first-floor guest room in the curved front section is transformed into an inviting Victorian parlor where afternoon tea is served. Continental breakfast (homemade breads and muffins) is served downstairs in a walkout basement with deck chairs, a wood stove, and stone walls covered with nautical flags.

The inn has a distinctly maritime flavor (it's named for the inn in "Treasure Island"). Quite a collection of antique English barometers is on display (and for sale) in the front hall and downstairs common room.

Doubles, $75 to $95; $45 to $55 in winter.

Wayside, Bellevue Avenue, Newport 02840. (401) 847-0302.

There's no street number, no advertising nor brochure, and the sign on the gate is so discreet that many miss it. In the midst of the mansions along fabled Bellevue Avenue and looking very much at home is Wayside, the beige brick Georgian summer cottage built by Elisha Dyer of New York, almost across from the Elms and just down the street from the Astors and Vanderbilts.

After a time as a dormitory for Salve Regina College, it was converted into an inn in 1976 by Al and Dorothy Post. Here, you can partake of Newport's gilded past, staying in a gigantic room amid Victorian furnishings at prices that are out of the past as well.

Enter Wayside through heavy doors under the portico into the foyer, its 15-foot-high ceiling, oak parquet floor and paneled walls setting the stage for things to come. Coffee and pastries are served on a wicker table here at breakfast. To the right is the Library, a bedroom with a tall carved fireplace crowned with an ornamental Florentine mantel. The room is so vast that the front has a queensize bed and armoire, the center section has a comfortable seating area available for meetings and television-watching, and built-in bookshelves are on all sides.

A beautiful quarter-cut oak staircase leads to seven more guest rooms off a wide hall on the second floor, each with private bath and each seemingly bigger and more impressive than the last. Crystal knobs on the doors, inside and out, are among the extravagant touches. Twelve-foot-high ceilings dwarf the canopy beds in the rooms, which have colorful wallpaper, shiny wood floors and pleasant sitting areas, usually with wicker furniture (Dot, says her husband, is a wicker nut). The largest room, Number 5, has two double beds, a wicker table and a grouping of two upholstered chairs and a rocker. The bathroom for Number 6 is almost as large as the bedroom.

The third floor has three more guest rooms, each with in-room wash basins and vanities but sharing two baths. One bedroom, fashioned from a storage area, has a sitting room and, up a few stairs, a "crow's nest penthouse" containing a brass bed.

All rooms have small black and white TVs for those who "want to watch the news," Al says. Children are welcome at this inn, and cribs are available.

A swimming pool behind the inn beckons on summer days.

Doubles, $55 to $65; $40 to $50 in winter.

The Inntowne, 6 Mary St., Newport 02840. (401) 846-9200.

This new inn built in 1980 after a fire destroyed the original structure is aptly named — it couldn't be more in town, just off Thames Street, its side rooms facing on the busy main street and those on the third and fourth floors catching a glimpse of the harbor.

Run by Betty and Paul McEnroe of the Inn at Castle Hill, this also reflects the decor of Ione Williams of Vermont's Inn at Sawmill Farm. All 26 rooms are different, but oh-so-decorated in colorful and contemporary matching fabrics (right down to the shower curtains and wastebaskets), thick carpeting, canopy beds, upholstered wing chairs and wicker furniture.

A fourth-floor corner suite has a pencil post bed, a sofabed and two upholstered chairs. A twin room is flanked by a narrow patio, which has two wrought-iron chairs against a brick wall. Terrycloth robes are provided in the only room with a hall bath.

The inn's Restoration House a couple of doors away at 20 Mary St. has a basement apartment with kitchen, sitting room and bedroom. Upstairs are six more rooms and suites, several with kitchenettes and small balconies, individualy decorated in white on gray, blue on white, white on taupe — you get the picture.

A continental breakfast of croissants, muffins and fresh orange juice is served in a small dining room amid oriental rugs and antiques. Tea and cookies are served there every afternoon (you can buy your teacup if you like).

The small front sitting room, with sofas and chairs in colorful chintz, has shelves of books and magazines for reading. Off the inn's fourth floor is a large plant-filled sundeck, popular on sunny days.

Doubles, $90 to $115 (suites and apartments, $125 to $140); $70 to $80 in winter.

268

Mill Street Inn, 75 Mill St., Newport 02840. (401) 849-9500.
Inn purists might find this inn austere, but we rather like its European atmosphere. A 19th century brick mill restored in 1985 and now listed on the National Register of Historic Places, it has 23 deluxe guest suites.

The vast expanses of white walls are fine backdrops for contemporary paintings and posters, modern sofas and chairs, industrial gray carpeting, vases filled with fresh flowers, wet bar areas and television sets. In a few rooms, original brick walls and beams tone down some of the white. Beds are queensize, fans whir on the ceilings, and baths are gleamingly white-tiled with pedestal sinks and Neutrogena amenities.

Eight duplex townhouses on the second floor have living room down and bedroom above, opening onto decks raised just enough so you can sit on the chairs and still see the water and the Newport bridge.

Ficus trees lit with tiny white lights, a free-standing staircase made of white piping and a sleek sitting area mark the lobby. Pastries and coffee are served in a basement breakfast room with stone walls and built-in benches.

Three meeting rooms are available for conferences, this inn being somewhat geared to the business market. There's a free parking garage underneath.

Suites, $125 to $135; townhouses, $150; winter, $75 to $85 and $95.

The Yankee Peddler Inn, 113 Touro St., Newport 02840. (401) 846-1323.
A 19th Century Greek Revival mansion-turned boarding house-turned inn offers 15 guest rooms on three floors plus five more in a carriage house, all but two with private baths.

Owner Don Glassie's collection of paintings and posters is prominent in the halls and rooms. The queensize continental beds are turned down to show their sheets, each in a striking print that matches the four pillows on top. Comfy comforters top the sheets. Rooms vary from suites with two bedrooms to smaller rooms, one with the smallest corner bathroom imaginable. Each is comfortably furnished with wicker chairs or maybe a posh sofa or chaise lounge.

The third floor opens onto a deck where you can sit on old dark green wooden garden chairs and gaze toward the harbor.

A continental breakfast of English muffins, raisin toast and bagels is served in the basement common room, looking properly ancient with fieldstone wall, old pine floors and a corner sitting area in front of a small TV set.

Doubles, $55 to $85; suites $95; $35 to $55 in winter.

The Willows, 8 Willow St., Historic Point, Newport 02840. (401) 846-5486.
"Fun and fantasy, that's what a vacation is all about," says Pattie Murphy, owner of this five-bedroom inn in two small attached houses — one pre-Revolutionary and one an 1840 Greek Revival — in the Historic Point section. And she sees to it that her guests get it. In black tie, she serves continental breakfast in bed at 9 a.m. to her guests after playing appropriate music and broadcasting appropriate information about Newport over the intercom system. Guests gather in the pink Victorian parlor, where Pattie,

a Newport native, has hung portraits of her ancestors on the walls and serves as concierge every afternoon.

Upstairs there's a wet bar area with refrigerator, glasses of all sorts and a multitude of magazines.

Four guest rooms, all decorated with romance in mind, are on this floor, and on the third floor is the very private Captain's Loft, its Victorian bed of wood inlaid in a waterfall pattern. In the Victorian Wedding Room the brass bed is canopied in lace curtains; the furniture is handpainted teak, the spread and curtains are a pretty chintz and the carpet is deep rose. The other rooms are the French Quarter, the Canopy Room and the Colonial Wedding Room, which has a kingsize brass cannonball bed and much lace. All have private baths and romantic touches: satin toeshoes hang from one bed, a dove from another. Stuffed animals or dolls are on most beds. At night while you're out at dinner, Pattie turns down the covers, puts mints on the pillows, dims the lights and leaves champagne glasses and a silver ice bucket in the room. Definitely not the place to bring the children!

Doubles, $88 and $98; $68 and $88 in winter.

Finnegan's Inn at Shadow Lawn, 120 Miantonomi Ave., Middletown 02840. (401) 847-0902.

Quite a surprise on a busy street just off Route 114 on the Newport-Middletown line is this elaborate and ornate Victorian mansion with gingerbread trim, set well back from the road.

Spotlights illuminate an enormous twisted tree at the side; the circular stained-glass designs in the windows suggest opulence inside, and a columned veranda with wicker furniture upholstered and pillowed in pink and green invites dalliance.

Built in 1856 and listed on the National Register, this was opened as an inn in 1983 by Dan and Mary Finnegan and their daughter and son-in-law. The dark paneled library on the left is where morning papers are put out daily and games are played at night. The Tiffany lighting, 15-foot ceilings and inlaid floors recreate an earlier era.

Across the grand hall is the dining room, where continental breakfast is served on a lace-covered table under the French crystal chandelier. Gold brocade draperies set off the high, arched bow windows, one of them a lovely stained-glass affair.

Upstairs on the second and third floors are eight large guest rooms, individually decorated with Victorian details. But the emphasis is on modern furnishings: mostly kingsize beds, wall-to-wall carpeting, color television,

Finnegan's Inn at Shadow Lawn.

Dennis House in historic Point section.

small refrigerators, comfortable sitting areas and tiled bathrooms. At the end of the second-floor hallway is a small front parlor.

A rear cottage has three smaller guest rooms and an apartment. Doubles, $70 to $90.

Extra-Special

Dennis House, 59 Washington St., Newport 02840. (401) 846-1324.

In this town which has so much religious history, it's a treat to stay in the rectory in front of St. John's Episcopal Church. Its pastor, the Rev. Henry Turnbull, takes in guests in his imposing 1740 sea captain's house in the historic Point. Five air-conditioned rooms and one suite on the second and third floors, all with private baths, are comfortably outfitted with period furnishings and beds with down quilts and pillows. The guests' rear entrance leads up to a small common room filled with books and games; a continental breakfast is served there. Father Turnbull lives on the handsomely appointed main floor, which he's willing to show guests. Doubles, $65 to $85.

Dining Spots

The Black Pearl, Bannister's Wharf, Newport. (401) 846-5264.

Our favorite all-around place in Newport — and that of many others, judging from the crowds day and night — is the informal tavern, the fancy Commodore's Room and the umbrella-topped deck that comprise the Black Pearl.

Up to 1,500 meals a day are served in summer, the more remarkable considering it has what the manager calls "the world's smallest kitchen." Waitresses vie with patrons for space in the narrow hall that runs the length of the building; white-hatted chefs and busboys run across the wharf, even in winter, to fetch fresh produce and fish — even champagne — from the refrigerators in an outbuilding.

It's all quite colorful, congenial in spirit and creative in cuisine.

You can sit outside under the Cinzano umbrellas and watch half the world go by while sipping a zesty bloody mary or sampling Newport's best clam chowder (creamy, chock full of clams and well herbed, served with a huge soda cracker) for $1.75 a cup, $3 a bowl. You also can get a Pearlburger with mint salad in pita bread and good fries for $4.50 and a variety of other sandwiches, salads and desserts.

Inside is the hectic and noisy tavern, serving the outdoor fare as well as heartier offerings that can serve as lunch or dinner. In winter, we thoroughly enjoyed our lunches of eggs Copenhagen (smoked salmon instead of ham) and Florida snapper. Among desserts, we remember a delectable brandy cream cake, a dish of golden grand marnier ice cream and an apple-raisin bread pudding. Last time we were there, we watched as a woman at the next table tried to finish (but couldn't) a huge slice of blueberry pound cake with lemon icing, just out of the oven and "awesome," said the waitress. Espresso as strong as it should be or a cup of cappuccino Black Pearl ($3), with courvoisier and kahlua, set you up for the rest of a winter's day.

Candlelight dinners in the Commodore's Room are great, the lights of the waterfront twinkling through small paned windows. The beamed sloped ceilings, dark green walls and white linen topped with vases of freesia make up an attractive dining room.

Chefs Marjorie and J. Daniel Knerr use light sauces and stress vegetables and side dishes. Entrees run from $12 for chicken sauteed with lemon butter to $19.50 for pepper steak. Shrimp, scallops and lobster in a light sauce Americaine, soft-shell crabs meuniere, duckling sauteed with green olive sauce, veal sauteed with mushrooms and served in a champagne sauce and medallions of lamb in a mustard sauce are among the offerings. Appetizers ($4.50 to $5.75) include oysters, escargots and lobster mousse.

Tavern and outdoor cafe open daily from 11 a.m.; dinner in Commodore Room from 6 p.m.

La Petite Auberge, 19 Charles St., Newport. (401) 849-6669.

Chef Roger Putier opened Newport's first classic French restaurant with classic French service in 1975 in the historic Stephen Decatur house, and has been thriving ever since. Smack against the sidewalk, the severity of the dark green exterior is warmed by roses climbing fences and trellises beside a small outdoor courtyard.

The inside seems indeed petite, most people never getting beyond the two intimate and elegant main-floor dining rooms, one with five tables and the other with four. But up some of the steepest stairs we've ever climbed are three more dining rooms, available for overflow or private parties. Out back is a little-known tavern where regulars linger over brandy.

Chef Putier's hand-written French menu is so extensive and his specials so numerous that the choice is difficult. His sauces are heavenly — from the escargots with cepes ($6.25), a house specialty (the heavily garlicked sauce demanding to be soaked up by the hot and crusty French bread), to our entrees of veal with morels and cream sauce and two tender pink lamb chops, also with cepes and an intense brown sauce.

Soups and appetizers ($3.95 to $6.50) include a fine Marseilles-style fish soup and a mousse of chicken livers with truffles. Entrees are priced from $13.95 for three fish dishes to $23 for lobster Americaine, and include classic poultry and meat dishes. Vegetables on our visit were green beans and creamy sliced potatoes topped with cheese. Desserts are classic as well; we enjoyed strawberries Romanoff, but regretted that the cafe filtre listed on the menu was really espresso.

Dinner, Monday-Saturday 6 to 10; Sunday, 5 to 9.

The White Horse Tavern, corner of Marlborough and Farewell Streets, Newport. (401) 849-3600.

A handsome red clapboard structure houses the oldest operating tavern in the United States. Inside, the tavern is a cozy, fireplaced bar with a few bar stools and three tables, all dimly lit by candles in hurricane lamps. The rest of the 1673 structur, restored by the Newport Preservation Society, is an elegant, formal restaurant.

The setting is properly Colonial: a large hearth ablaze in the main downstairs dining room, wide plank floors and beamed ceilings, candles in hurricane lamps and wall sconces. Dark rose and white draperies complement the handsome burgundy and off-white china on the white-linened tables.

Service is formal and the prices steep, following the restaurant's acquisition a few years ago by five Texans with sailing interests. For a summer lunch, we enjoyed an interesting cold soup of yogurt, cucumber, dill and walnuts; a rather bland chicken salad in half an avocado ($6.50) and the fish of the day ($10.95), an excellent halibut in a sauce with grapefruit pieces and a hint of brandy.

Chef Stephanie J. Thayer's dinner menu is inventive and wide-ranging. Appetizers run from $4 for oysters remoulade to $8 for ratatouille of five wild mushrooms.

Entrees ($15 to $21) are served with vegetables (a plate of julienned carrots and squash, spinach, cauliflower and boiled new potato on our visit) and a simple salad of Boston lettuce — a radicchio salad with walnut dressing will set you back an extra $7. Try the filet of sole and lobster in American and Normandy sauces with truffles, the individual beef Wellington served with a perigourdine sauce, the noisettes of lamb sauteed with champagne and herbs, the veal with champagne cream sauce and wild mushrooms, or the sliced duck with chutney, cranberry and port wine. The changing desserts range from cheesecake to fresh fruit tarts.

The extensive wine list — which includes Italian, Australian, German and Spanish varieties as well as French and Californian, a number available by the glass — is supplemented by the captain's list of rare vintages. A list of dessert wines ends with vintage ports, three by the bottle and one by the glass.

Lunch daily, noon to 3; dinner, 6 to 9:30 or 10; Sunday brunch, noon to 3.

Window table at White Horse Tavern.

The Southern Cross, 514 Thames St., Newport. (401) 849-8888.

A sleek and slick avant-garde dining room was added upstairs in 1985 to the popular restaurant opened two years earlier by Australian Peter DeCaux in time for the America's Cup races. The expansion spreads out the crowds, opens up the main floor for less-congested dining and is altogether pleasing. The gray ceilings, walls and carpeting are accented by mirrors, nautical posters and a few large plants. Unusual track lights illuminate the fresh flowers in vases set on mirrors and the striking black and white china, a different pattern at each table.

New chef Gregory Souza's fare features "the art of new American cuisine with a touch of Down Under." Dinner entrees ($10 to $19) are an eclectic mix: lamb Florentine, seafood fettuccine, baby New Zealand lamb chops with rosemary, peasant bouillabaisse, grilled swordfish with citrus butter, and scallops sauteed with lime and ginger. Start with deep-fried brie or gravlax and end with a classic Pavlova or chilled passionfruit souffle.

The drink list includes fine Australian wines, ports and beers. A special edition of Sidney's Daily Mirror with the headline "Aussies Win Cup" is framed discreetly near the bar.

Dinner, nightly 6 to 10 or 11; Sunday brunch, noon to 3.

The Inn at Castle Hill, Ocean Drive, Newport. (401) 849-3800.

The most sumptuous bar in Newport is tucked away in the front corner of this fine inn, its tall windows taking in the grand views of bay and sunset as you sip a drink and snack on crackers with a zippy spread.

Beyond is a three-sided dining porch with rounded walls that juts out toward the water, all very inviting with white tables and chairs and flowered seats, plus a fancy small dining room where breakfast is served in winter, and a large formal dining room, all richly paneled but for one wall of deep blue and rose wallpaper.

Chef James Mitchell's continental menu with a touch of nouvelle is highly regarded. Dinners could begin with artichoke bottoms stuffed with goat cheese, escargots in pastry, a selection of cold smoked fish, lobster mousse or an assortment of chilled seafood served with remoulade sauce, priced from $5 to $12.50.

Entrees ($17 to $22.50) include veal kidneys flambeed with cognac. sliced duck with raspberry or green peppercorn sauces, veal cutlet with two shrimp and a garlic butter sauce, a trio of beef, veal and pork medallions served with separate sauces, and Dover sole or native lobster. We can vouch for a fine filet of sole stuffed with scallop mousse and an excellent tournedos au poivre from meals past.

Dinner nightly except Sunday, 6 to 9; lunch, Tuesday-Saturday noon to 2:30 in summer; Sunday jazz brunch on the lawn, noon to 4; closed for dinner January-March. Jackets required for dinner.

The Clarke Cooke House, Bannister's Wharf, Newport. (401) 849-2900.

A 1790-vintage Colonial house offers an informal menu downstairs in the bistro-like Candy Store Cafe and formal dining upstairs on several levels, including a breezy, canopied upper deck with great view of the waterfront. In these rarefied heights, the staff's demeanor is more haughty and the prices more expensive than need be, but as the clipping from "W" out front attests, the Clarke Cooke is one of those places with style, as defined by W.

Consider the appetizers ($5.25 to $10.25): pate of duck tenderloin with fresh foie gras and truffles, ravioli of lobster and morels, escalopes of fresh foie gras deglazed with red currant vinegar and apple butter, or canape of steak tartare. Entrees start at $15.75 for escalopes of salmon and top off at $22.50 for sauteed breast of pheasant with a mushroom sauce. Rack of lamb persillade and steak au poivre are in the $21 range.

Owned by Locke-Ober of Boston, Clarke Cooke features Locke-Ober's Indian pudding a la mode for dessert, along with chocolate grand marnier mousse, maple walnut creme brulee and something called Snowball in Hell

Dinner, nightly 6 to 10, weekends only in winter; cafe, 11:30 to 10 in season.

Le Bistro, Bowen's Wharf, Newport. (401) 849-7778.

With large windows on the airy second and third floors looking toward the water, Le Bistro is fancier than a run-of-the-mill bistro. The newly redecorated second-floor dining rooms have an air of elegance, and the winter 1986 menu was regional American. Chef-owners John and Mary Philcox continue their tradition of a fine wine list and a series of prix-fixe dinners from regions of France.

Dinner entrees run the gamut from smoked loin of pork with cabbage pastry ($10.95) to grilled tenderloin steak with mustard butter ($19.50). In between are duck salmis with braised endive, chicken saute with raspberry vinegar, pasta with shrimp and scallops, and veal saute with morels and cream. Desserts, baked daily on the premises, include an Ivory Coast chocolate rum cake, walnut cake and Creole bread pudding.

For lunch from a menu on which everything sounds (and later looks) good, we enjoyed a fine salade Nicoise ($5.50) and a classic bouillabaisse ($8.95).

Lunch daily, 11:30 to 2; dinner, 6 to 11; bar menu served from 11:30 to 11 on the third floor.

Dave & Eddie's, Brick Market Place, Newport. (401) 849-5241.

Billed as a seafood grill and raw bar, this large and modern restaurant is known locally for its fresh seafood, and a blackboard at the entrance details where the day's catch is from (oysters from Virginia, mussels from Maine when we last were there).

All kinds of seafood, pastas and some meat dishes are served up on a sidewalk cafe, in a large bar and on two dining levels, appropriately nautical with shiny wood floors, large photographs of boats on the walls, white linen, and cane and chrome chairs. You can dine very well for under $10 at dinner and under $5 for lunch, or you can splurge for bouillaibaisse or lobster thermidor in the $17 range.

The appealing wine list is remarkably low priced, most of the whites from $7 to $14.

Lunch daily, 11:30 to 4; dinner, 4 to 9:30 or 10:30; closed Tuesday in winter.

Main Brace, 109 Long Wharf, Newport. (401) 849-4397.

Opened in 1984 and an immediate hit, this large bar with informal restaurant moved down the street early in 1986 to even larger quarters vacated by the Harbor Front restaurant. Here, owner Mitchell Uzwack envisioned less of a tavern and more of a dining room than in his original facility where the long bar took up half the downstairs. A more formal restaurant was planned for the lofty second floor under a 200-year-old ceiling, while the oyster bar ("the best in all Rhode Island," Mitch claims) would continue to serve the adjacent outdoor deck.

You can order steamed mussels or seviche for $3.95, lobster or oyster stew (or combination thereof) for $5.95 or tavern lobster for $16.95. At dinner ($9.95 to $17.50), you also can have grouper with lobster sauce, grilled salmon with hollandaise, pasta with seafood tossed in virgin olive oil or San Francisco cioppino.

Lunch and oyster bar, daily from 11:30 to midnight; dinner from 6, Sundays from 4.

Diversions

The Mansions. Nowhere else can you see such a concentration of palatial mansions, and nine are open to the public under individual or the collective auspices of the Preservation Society of Newport County. If you can see only one, make it Cornelius Vanderbilt's opulent 72-room **The Breakers,**

although romantic **Rosecliff** of "The Great Gatsby" fame and the museum-like **Elms** would be other choices. If you've seen them all, as we have, you may like best the Victorian **Kingscote,** which looks lived-in and eminently livable. **Hammersmith Farm,** the childhood summer home of Jacqueline Kennedy Onassis and the Kennedy summer White House in the early 1960s, has more of a country feeling, a salubrious setting overlooking Narragansett Bay and lovely grounds and gardens. Schedules and prices vary, but all are open daily at least from May through October; some are open weekends in winter.

Historic Sites. Newport has more than 400 structures dating from the Colonial era. **Touro Synagogue** (1768), the oldest place of Jewish worship in the country, has fascinating though limited guided tours. **Trinity Church** (1726) at the head of Queen Anne Square has the only remaining central pulpit and the second oldest organ in the country. The **Quaker Meeting House** (1699) is the oldest public building in Newport. **St. Mary's Church** (1848), where Jacqueline Bouvier was married to John F. Kennedy, is the oldest Catholic parish in Rhode Island. The **Redwood Library** (1748) is the nation's oldest library building in continuous service. **The Old Colony House** (1739) is the nation's third oldest capitol building and still used for public ceremonies. The **Hunter House** (1748) is considered one of the 10 finest Colonial homes in America, while the **Wanton-Lyman-Hazard House** (1690) is the oldest house still on its original site. The **Samuel Whitehorne House** (1811) is a Federal showplace. The **Old Stone Mill** may have been built as early as 1100 by the Vikings. The military is represented in the Revolutionary fortification at **Fort Adams State Park** and the Artillery Company of Newport museum, as well as the Naval War College museum.

Water Sites. Ocean Drive winds along Newport's spectacular rocky shoreline, between Bailey's Beach where the 400 swam (and still do) and Brenton Point State Park, past clapboard estates and contemporary homes. The Cliff Walk is a must for a more intimate look at the crashing surf and the backs of the mansions. Narragansett Bay is visible along the nine-mile trip run by the Old Colony & Newport Railway to **Green Animals,** the delightful topiary garden in Portsmouth. King Park along Wellington Avenue has a sheltered beach with a view of the Newport waterfront; the ocean surf rolls in at Easton's Beach.

Sports sites. Yachting reigns across the Newport waterfront; the America's Cup Gallery, the Museum of Yachting at Fort Adams State Park and the wharves off Thames Street and America's Cup Avenue appeal to sailing interests. In the landmark Newport Casino is the **International Tennis Hall of Fame,** housing the world's largest collection of tennis memorabilia and the Davis Cup Theater, where old tennis films are shown; outside are 13 grass courts for tournaments and public use.

Shopping. Innumerable and oft-changing shops line Thames Street, the Brick Market Place, Bannister's and Bowen's Wharves, Christie's Landing, the Perry Mill Market and, uptown, fashionable Bellevue Avenue. If the past is an indication, there will be more when you're there. Some of our favorites are the **Spectrum,** representing American artisans and craftsmen; **Cabbages & Kings** for gifts and accessories that appeal to those who still live in Newport's "cottages," and **Stone Bridge Dishes** and **Indesigns,** for contemporary kitchenware and gifts.

Old Lighthouse Museum is landmark at Stonington.

Watch Hill and Stonington
Vestiges of the 19th Century

They face each other across Little Narragansett Bay from different states, these two venerable towns so different from one another.

Watch Hill spreads out across a point at the southwesternmost tip of Rhode Island, a moneyed seaside resort of the old school and something of a mini-version of Newport. "Still echoing with the elegance of past years" (according to the brochure of the Inn at Watch Hill), Watch Hill indeed has enjoyed better days, although the large brown shingled "cottages" remain respectable, the shops fashionable and the atmosphere clubby. It is here that Long Island Sound gives way to Block Island Sound and the Atlantic, opening up the surf beaches for which Rhode Island's South County is known.

Stonington, on the other hand, is a peninsula cut off by travel and time from the rest of southeastern Connecticut. Quietly billing itself as "a place apart," it's an historic fishing village and an arts colony. The old houses hug the streets and each other, and the Portuguese fishing fleet adds an earthy flavor to an increasingly upscale community. Better than anywhere else along the Connecticut shore, the Borough of Stonington lets you sense times gone by.

These two choice vestiges of the 19th century are linked — in terms of geography — by the small Rhode Island city of Westerly, through which you drive from one to the other, unless you go by boat.

In recent times, Watch Hill and Stonington have been upstaged by Newport and Mystic, and thus bypassed by many of the trappings of tourism, particularly in terms of overnight accommodations. Neither town wants — nor can handle — crowds. Each in its own way clings to its past.

Inn Spots

Shelter Harbor Inn, Route 1, Westerly, R.I. 02891. (401) 322-8883.

The best choice in the area for both lodging and dining is this expanding farmhouse dating to the early 1800s, set back from the highway and off by itself not far from the edge of Quonochontaug Pond.

The original three-story main house contains a fine restaurant (see Dining Spots), a sun porch with a bar, a small library with the original fireplace and 10 guest rooms, plus a new rooftop deck which has a hot tub and water view that you must see to believe. Suffice to say that it's a scene straight out of California. The barn next door has been renovated with 10 more guest rooms, plus a large central living room on the upper level opening onto a spacious redwood deck A small carriage house adds four more guest rooms.

All rooms have private baths, many have king or queensize beds, and about half have color TV. As innkeepers Jim and Debbye Dey continue to upgrade and expand with a contemporary flair, their nicest rooms now are those recently renovated or added upstairs in the main house. Three on the second floor have wonderful terraces with a view of Block Island Sound in the distance. A particularly nice room with brick fireplace, brass screen, rose carpet and terrace is a steal for $72 a night.

Out front are two paddle tennis courts. In summer, Jim Dey runs guests across Quonochontaug Pond in a motor boat for a day at what he calls the finest beach along the Rhode Island shore.

A full breakfast, sometimes apple or banana pancakes, is served guests.

Doubles in summer, $60 to $72.

Narragansett Inn, Bay Street, Watch Hill 02891. (401) 348-8912.

In the understated Watch Hill style, this large, unassuming white wood structure with waterfront terrace and dining room has 20 guest rooms which the owners call unpretentious and rustic.

Notes their welcome letter to guests: "We are an inn, not a modern motel. We lack many of the conveniences associated with the large chains — like no TV and no phone; in some cases no bath or toilet. However, we have the most fabulous view of the sunset on the East Coast."

Eight rooms on the second floor have private baths, while the rest share. Only a few in the front have views of that sunset across Little Narragansett Bay. Colorful quilts brighten what are otherwise plain, old-fashioned rooms, many without chairs.

The inn serves light lunches ($3.95 to $5.50) in the downstairs cocktail lounge and on the popular outdoor Sunset Deck overlooking the harbor. Dinner, considered the most elegant in Watch Hill, is served in the main dining room, where butcher-block tables, captain's chairs and picture windows lined with planters set a contemporary style. Appetizers ($3.95 to $5.50) are primarily seafood standards (clams casino, shrimp cocktail). Entrees run from $8.95 for broiled flounder or fettuccine with vegetables to $12.95 for prime rib or sirloin steak; three preparations of lobster are priced daily.

Doubles, $40 to $55; open late May to mid-October.

The Inn at Mystic, Route 1, Mystic, Conn. 06355. (203) 536-9604.

Located on the Stonington side of Mystic with a glorious view across 13 acres of landscaped hilltop grounds toward Long Island Sound, the white-pillared Colonial Revival mansion built in 1904 by the widow of one of the owners of the Fulton Fish Market is an island of serenity above busy Route 1.

Part of the Mystic Motor Inn and Flood Tide restaurant complex, the inn offers five luxurious, antiques-filled guest rooms in the mansion in which it is said that Lauren Bacall and Humphrey Bogart spent their honeymoon, plus three in the Gatehouse, nestled in the orchards and looking as if it were transplanted from England.

The beautifully furnished public rooms in the mansion are full of grand arrangements of flowers picked from the gardens, large oriental carpets and crystal chandeliers. They are available to guests, who are served breakfast there in winter. The modern bathrooms with each guest room contain

Entrance to Inn at Mystic.

whirlpool soaking tubs and spas. Some rooms have canopy beds and working fireplaces.

The gardens, laid out in the English style, are stunning. You can relax on the white wicker and hot pink furniture on the wide front porch overlooking the rock gardens and see Long Island Sound in the distance.

Three meals a day are served in the well-regarded **Flood Tide** restaurant, down the hill near the motor inn. The continental menu specializes in seafood and roast duckling (dinner entrees, $10 to $20).

Doubles, $105 to $135.

The Inn at Watch Hill, Bay Street, Watch Hill 02891. (401) 596-0665.

Something of a misnomer, this strip of motel-type units above the shops along Bay Street was totally renovated in 1982 from what was once a ramshackle rooming house with 32 rooms.

You enter from a hilltop parking lot at the rear, register at a tiny shingled house that serves as an office, and descend to one of 16 spacious rooms, each with contemporary furnishings and sliding doors opening onto small balconies above the street, with the municipal parking lot and harbor beyond.

Rooms have bare wood floors and white brick walls. They're plain but pleasant, all with full baths and color TV, and certainly located in the midst of Watch Hill activity. Some are new suites and some are original, a few have an extra sink and a refrigerator, and prices vary accordingly as well as by day of week and time of year.

Doubles, $65 to $110. Open May-October.

Dining Spots

The Harborview, Water Street at Cannon Square, Stonington. (203) 535-2720.

Candles in the hurricane lamps in the dining room are lit even at noon at this dark and romantic restaurant from which you can glimpse Stonington harbor through small-paned windows. The darkness of wood paneling and the blue-clothed tables is brightened by pink napkins and fresh flowers.

Classic French food is the specialty of owners Jerry and Ainslie Turner, who try to visit Brittany every year to catch up on the latest in haute cuisine. Among 15 dinner appetizers ($3.95 to $6.95), we especially recommend the crevettes remoulade, a dinner plate full of five huge shrimp on a bed of tender lettuce covered with a piquant sauce, and a sensational billi-bi soup, creamy, mussel-filled and redolent of herbs.

Entrees ($10.95 to $15.95) include a Marseillaise bouillabaisse, sauteed shrimps in a pernod cream sauce with artichoke hearts and green pepper, Jamaican shrimps sauteed with dark rum, kiwi fruit and lime, and veal prepared three ways. We liked the veal sweetbreads in a vol-au-vent pastry and the veal scallops in a calvados cream sauce, a portion large enough for two, served with julienned vegetables and tiny new potatoes, still in their jackets and swimming in butter.

Many dinner items are available at lunch (entrees $5.50 to $8.95). The popular rustic bar offers daily specials and reasonably priced entrees, and we like the lavish Sunday brunch buffet ($10.95), which has unusually interesting hot dishes and enough food to keep one full for a couple of days.

Lunch, 11:30 to 3; dinner 5 to 10; Sunday brunch, 11 to 3; open daily in summer; closed Tuesday in winter.

Shelter Harbor Inn, Route 1, Westerly. (401) 322-8883.

The highly regarded dining room at the Shelter Harbor Inn was expanded in 1985 by a large addition with dining on two levels. The original dining room with stone fireplace has bare floors, country curtains and bentwood chairs at white-linened tables topped with hurricane lamps and colorful mums in carafes. Beyond is the new upper level, which has rough wood beams and posts, brick walls, comfortable chairs with curved backs and white linens. The lower dining level has large windows looking onto the back lawn, and another small room with several more tables and a fireplace.

The food is worthy of the setting. At Sunday brunch, we loved the pasta imperial, with gobs of crabmeat, and a smoked salmon omelet.

At dinner, be sure to try the Rhode Island johnny cakes (75 cents) and, among appetizers ($2.95 to $3.75), the honey mustard scallops with peppered bacon or the smoked bluefish with horseradish. Entrees run from $8.95 for

New dining room has views onto lawn at Shelter Harbor Inn.

broiled scrod or hazelnut chicken with orange thyme cream to $14.95 for lobster. Highly rated are the seafood pot pie chock full of shrimp, scallops and lobster, plus the roast duckling with the inn's tart beach plum sauce and the veal with wild mushroom sauce. You can even get finnan haddie poached in milk with bacon.

Desserts in the $2 range include genoise, chocolate mousse cake and blueberry crisp as well as a white chocolate hazelnut cheesecake. The interesting wine list offers such bargains as Firestone merlot for $11 and Chateau Montelena zinfandel for $17.

Some of the same items are available at lunch. We'd begin with the country pate or clams casino and try as main courses the calves liver in Madeira sauce or chicken with raspberries ($4.95 to $6.95).

Lunch daily, 11:30 to 2:30; dinner, 5 to 10; Sunday, brunch 11 to 3, dinner 4 to 9.

The Terrace, Mystic River Marina, Masons Island, Mystic. (203) 572-0632.

Some of the Connecticut shore's most innovative food emanates from the second floor of a nondescript building where sea breezes blow through open windows. Opened in 1984, it's owned by Sue Davis, whose breakfasts at Kitchen Little, a tiny establishment up the Mystic River just past Mystic Seaport, are legendary.

A short and appealing menu is augmented by specials from a different cuisine each week of the summer months the Terrace is open. Dining is by candlelight at tables covered with white linen, napkins of every pastel shade imaginable and fresh field flowers, and service is unusually caring and competent.

From the regular menu you can choose among five appetizers, priced from $2.50 for seafood chowder to an astonishingly reasonable $4.75 for a chilled half lobster with tarragon mayonnaise; we enjoyed the shrimp and mushroom strudel and the deliciously spicy cold linguini with snowpeas, scallions and Szechuan dressing (almost a meal in itself). A super fresh salad was served with choice of dill blue cheese or herb vinaigrette dressings from small sauce boats.

The seven main entrees ranged from $9.95 for roasted half chicken with honey-thyme barbecue sauce to $13.75 for pan-fried tenderloin of beef with green peppercorns and cream. We liked the medallions of pork, a beautifully presented dish garnished with snowpeas and bathed with a delicate brandy and butter sauce, and — from the week's Chinese specials — fireworks chicken, a huge mound of spicy shredded chicken and vegetables, which wasn't as incendiary as we wished. Fresh fruit mousse and an exotic fruit salad that included kiwi, papaya and mango were exceptional desserts.

Special cuisines vary from Creole and West Indian to Greek, provincial French and Mideastern. Patrons bring their own wine and can sip their own pre-dinner drinks on a small deck while watching the passing boating activity.

Dinner only, Tuesday-Sunday 5:30 to 9:30, June-Labor Day Weekend.

Noah's, 113 Water St., Stonington. (203) 535-3925.

The price certainly is right at Noah's, the popular family-style operation that has expanded into a second dining room with service bar at the rear.

When did you last find soup for $1.05 or homemade clam chowder for $1.15, broiled flounder with salad and vegetable for $6.95 and desserts like German chocolate pie or Tartuffe di chocolate (this is a good place for chocolate freaks) for $1.50? Those are dinner prices; an omelet for breakfast is $1.60 and a fruit and cheese plate for lunch, $3.25.

The blackboard specials are as appealing as the regular menu: blackfish stew for $2.95 at lunch, regional and ethnic specialties nightly. Such luncheon salads as Greek country or farmer's chop suey in the $3 range are masterpieces. The most you can pay is $11.50 for a large filet mignon. Save room for the chocolate yogurt cake or what one customer volunteered was the best dessert he'd ever had: fresh strawberries with Italian cream made from cream cheese, eggs and kirsch.

Owners Dorothy and John Papp have decorated their storefront restaurant colorfully with pastel linen tablecloths and fresh flowers. They have a full liquor license, with most wines under $10.

Open for breakfast, lunch and dinner daily except Monday.

The Skipper's Dock, 66 Water St., Stonington. (203) 535-2000.

The owners of the Harborview took over the off-again, on-again restaurant on the fishing pier behind their fine French restaurant in 1985 and reopened with two interior dining rooms and a smashing outdoor deck, right over the water.

The name was borrowed from the original Skipper's Dock in Noank, established in 1929, which provided some of the historical-nautical motif, but the food bears the distinctive touch of the Harborview. The striking mural of Stonington Harbor at the entrance was done by Breezy Turner, daughter of the owners, and fellow members of her eighth-grade art class at Pine Point School; it's a beauty.

The young staff in dark blue shirts and khaki skirts or shorts scurry between the new kitchen and either of the informal, paneled dining rooms (one with a skiff suspended from the ceiling) or the always-crowded deck.

282

Start with fish house chowder, a pile of grilled mussels, chilled oyster cocktail or a bowl of Stonington steamers ($1.95 to $5.95). Besides black-board fish specials, you can continue with a kettle of Portuguese fishermen's stew, hot scallops on the half shell, grilled marinated shrimp or lobster ($10.95 to $15.95), the latter the price for the clambake with lobster, mussels, steamers and corn on the cob. Choices for non-seafood eaters are filet mignon with rum butter, loin lamb chops with minted pear and barbecued chicken Caribe. Ice cream puff with mocha ice cream and pina colada cheesecake are among the desserts. Wines are reasonably priced by the glass or liter.

Lunch, daily 11:30 to 4; dinner from 4; closed in off-season.

1 South Broad Cafe, Route 1, Stonington. (203) 535-0418.

Tricia Shipman and Judy Colucci, waitresses and bartenders for years in area restaurants, decided they would rather be working for themselves, and in 1983 opened their own place in a small shopping center.

It's tiny and cheerful, with forest green ceiling, Laura Ashley-look wall-paper and striped cafe curtains, bare wood tables adorned with zinnias in antique bottles as well as bottles of ketchup and Dijon mustard, and a big old Wurlitzer in the corner. Billed as "an eating and drinking cafe," it has a bar almost as big as the dining area.

Outside the front door is an old bathtub where herbs for the innovative cuisine are grown. Everything is done from scratch, even the tortilla chips for the nachos, which, claims one of the owners, are the best in the state. A blackboard lists the day's dishes, which change frequently and are inter-national in nature (even the eggrolls and wontons are homemade). Cheddar and vegetable chowder, grilled mussels, stuffed mushrooms, tostadas, nachos and super nachos, shrimp and tortellini salad, deli sandwiches and inter-national burgers were listed when we visited.

The most expensive entree was shrimp and asparagus on fettuccine, $9.95; sole Savoy, sliced steak with bearnaise sauce and scallops gruyere over angel's hair pasta were some of the others. The bouillabaisse ($8.95) and paella are renowned. Desserts could include a macademia nut torte and grand marnier mousse.

The nicely-priced wine list is mainly Californian; Cuvee blanc de blanc is $1.75 a glass.

Lunch daily except Sunday, 11:30 to 3; dinner nightly, 5 to 10 or 10:30.

Peter's, 142 Water St., Stonington. (203) 535-3910.

Almost across the street from the immensely popular Noah's restaurant is this smaller version opened in 1985 by Peter Nania. An L-shaped counter and five butcher-block tables are the spartan setting for what Peter bills as an innovative, informal restaurant. He started with breakfast and lunch, and then served dinner on weekends.

For breakfast, the Crazy Peter McMuffin is a toasted English muffin with Canadian bacon, fried egg and cheese ($2.25); French toast made with Portuguese sweet bread is $2.75.

Lunch prices are pleasant as well: sandwiches from $1.25 to $3.50 (for open-face chicken with brie and almonds); entrees from $2.75 for chili with corn bread to $3.95 for grilled breast of chicken with tarragon butter. Dinner items include stuffed flounder, lasagna, fried clams and lobster, with

Owners Jerry and Ruth Mears at Abbott's Lobster in the Rough.

prices generally under $6.95. A beer and wine license was pending.

Breakfast 7 to 11, lunch 11:15 to 2:30, dinner 6 to 9, Thursday-Sunday, seasonally; closed Monday.

Just Delicious, 2 Fort Hill, Watch Hill.

The best seafood and baked items in Watch Hill are served up in this no-nonsense establishment with a few inside tables and an expanded outdoor deck beside the beach. It's a glorified shack run in summer only by Frank Lattuca, who teaches at the University of Massachusetts hotel school. The pastries come from his wife's new Just Baked Pastry and Deli out on Bay Street; we can vouch for her chocolate almond pastry. Fried seafood plates are in the $5 to $7 range, good clam fritters are $3, and an oversize lobster roll is $6.50. You can BYOB for a twilight supper.

Open from 9 a.m. to 9 p.m., June to September.

Extra-Special

Abbott's Lobster in the Rough, 117 Pearl St., Noank, Conn. (203) 536-7719.

If it's lobster you're after, make the short trek west through Mystic to the quaint shore town of Noank, where the busiest place day and night is Abbott's. Here, seated at brightly colored picnic tables placed on mashed-up clamshells, you watch the passing parade of marine traffic in and out of Mystic Harbor as you feast on the freshest of seafood. You order at a counter inside and take a number; bring your own drinks and appetizers to tide you over while you wait. The lobster comes with a bag of potato chips, coleslaw, melted butter and the obligatory bib. Also available are steamers, mussels, clam chowder, shrimp, lobster or crab rolls and hot dogs for the kiddies. We think this is the neatest lobster pound south of Maine.

Open daily, noon to 9, May-September.

Diversions

Watch Hill and Stonington are small, choice and relatively private places off the beaten path. The crowds head east to Rhode Island's South County beaches, particularly the vast Misquamicut State Beach where the surf thunders in, or west to Mystic, where Mystic Seaport and the Mystic Marine Aquarium join to make up Connecticut's largest tourist attraction.

Stonington Borough. We cannot imagine anyone (except children, perhaps) not falling for the historic charms of this once-thriving seaport, founded in 1649 and not all that changed since the 19th century. The last commercial fishing fleet in Connecticut is manned by the resident Portuguese, who stage a colorful Blessing of the Fleet ceremony every mid-July. To savor fully the flavor, walk the two narrow streets through the borough. Along with their cross streets, they are lined with historic homes, many of them marked by the Stonington Historical Society and some occupied by the likes of John Updike, Eve Merriam, Peter Benchley and L. Patrick Gray. The house where artist James McNeil Whistler painted Whistler's Mother later was home for Stephen Vincent Benet. Edgar Allen Poe and Capt. Nathaniel Brown, who discovered Antarctica, also lived here. Much local memorabilia is on display in the fine **Old Lighthouse Museum,** full of whaling and fishing gear, articles from the Orient trade and an exquisite dollhouse, at the end of Water street (open daily except Monday, May-October; adults $1).

Watch Hill. This staid, storied resort community protects its privacy (parking is limited and prices are high), but things do get busy on summer weekends. Stop for a tart, thirst-quenching lemonade at the old-fashioned Olympia Tea Room (serving three meals a day since 1916). Youngsters line up at the entrance to the Watch Hill Beach for 25-cent rides on the Flying Horse Carousel, established in 1879 and thought to be the oldest merry-go-round in the country.

Napatree Point. If you find a place to park, hike out to Napatree Point conservation area, extending half a mile beyond the Watch Hill parking lot. The walk to the ruins of a Spanish-American War fort at the far end opposite Stonington can take an hour or a day, depending on beachcombing and bird-watching interests. Privately owned but open for nature lovers, it's a refuge for waterfowl and tidal creatures.

Shopping. Along Water Street in Stonington are several special shops. At the **Hungry Palette,** silkscreened and handprinted fabrics can be purchased by the yard or already made up into long skirts, wrap skirts, sundresses and colorful accessories like Bermuda bags. **Quimper Faience** deals exclusively in handpainted French earthenware. **Grand & Water** sells interesting antiques and gifts (check the handmade lampshades and the boxes handpainted by Clare Bray). **Icefire** has gifts and clothing. **Downstairs at the Harbor View** offers antiques, accessories and vintage jewelry. In Watch Hill, the **Ocean Shop** and **John Everets** specialize in clothing and resort wear; **Harvey's** offers linens and gifts, and **McMonogram** has personalized bags, aprons, sweaters and such. Apparel is featured at the **Mayan Shop,** actually three in one and including a gourmet-kitchen shop.

Between expeditions, you might stop in North Stonington at **Stonecrop Vineyard,** where Tom and Charlotte Young run Southeastern Connecticut's first farm winery and offer wine tastings and tours during the summer.

Essex and Old Lyme, Conn.
River Towns and Charms

Nearing the sea after lazing 400 miles from the Canadian border, the Connecticut River wends and weaves between forested hillsides and sandy shores. Finally it pauses, almost delta-like, in the sheltered coves and harbors of Essex and Old Lyme before emptying into Long Island Sound.

A sand bar blocked the kind of development that has urbanized other rivers where they meet the ocean. Indeed, the Connecticut is the nation's biggest without a major city at its mouth.

It is this tranquil setting in which historic Essex was settled in 1635, its harbor a haven for shipbuilding in the past and for yachting today. From Essex the first American warship, the Oliver Cromwell, was launched in the Revolution. From Essex, leading yachtsmen sail the Atlantic today.

Touted by the New Yorker magazine as "a mint-condition 18th century town," Essex relives its heritage in the River Museum on Steamboat Dock, in the boatworks and yacht clubs along its riverfront, in the lively Tap Room at the Griswold Inn, and in the lovely old homes along Main Street and River Road. That Essex is more sophisticated and serene than most river towns is its special appeal.

Across the river from Essex is Old Lyme, which has less of a river feel but exudes a charm of its own. In a pastoral setting that now is part of an historic district, artists gathered at the turn of the century in the mansion of Florence Griswold, daughter of a boat captain. The American Impressionist movement was the result, and the arts are celebrated and flourish here to this day.

Just inland from old Essex along the Falls River are Centerbrook and Ivoryton. They and Old Lyme provide a setting in which fine inns and restaurants thrive. Up river are Deep River, Chester, Hadlyme and East Haddam, unspoiled towns steeped in history.

You still have to drive the long way around to get from one side of the river to the other, unless you take the tiny ferry which has been plying between Chester and Hadlyme for 200 years. The Valley Railroad's excursion steam train and riverboat link the towns as in the past, offering visitors scenic ways to see both river and shore.

Inn Spots

Griswold Inn, Main Street, Essex 06426. (203) 767-0991.

The Griswold Inn has an historic appeal matched by few inns in America. There's the requisite tap room containing a steamboat-Gothic bar, potbellied stove and antique popcorn machine — New York magazine said it "may be the best-looking drinking room in America." Unpretentious meals and an unexcelled Hunt Breakfast are served in four dining rooms that are troves of Americana. And the floors in some of the 22 guest rooms list to port or starboard, as you might expect of an inn dating to 1776 when it was built as Connecticut's first three-story structure.

Commandeered by the British during the War of 1812, the inn was found to be long on charm but short on facilities. Today, most of the 22 guest rooms in the main inn, the annex and a house have private baths, but are

Griswold Inn in Essex, as viewed from Griswold Square shops.

unabashedly simple and old-fashioned. One upstairs front room facing the
street has beamed ceiling and sloping floor, twin beds, marble-topped table
and a small bath with shower. Three suites are a cut above; the Oliver
Cromwell has a living room with two sofas, coffee table and fireplace, four-
poster bed in the bedroom with a dressing table up a step, a kitchenette
and a small porch from which you can look over rooftops to the river.

A continental breakfast buffet of juice, coffee and Danish pastry is served
in the dark paneled Library, its walls hung with an important collection of
Antonio Jacobsen marine oils. There's much to see in the other dining
rooms as well: the Currier and Ives steamboat prints in the Covered Bridge
Room, actually fashioned from a New Hampshire covered bridge; the
riverboat memorabilia in the Steamboat Room; the musket-filled Gun Room
with 55 pieces dating to the 15th Century. Put together, they rank as one
of the outstanding maritime art collections in America.

The atmosphere may upstage the food, which is country New England,
fresh and abundant. "We have no pretenses," says the informative Innkeeper's Log. "Our menu is printed in English. We call fish fish and beef
beef." The menu is a mixed-bag of seafood, fish and game, priced at night
from $8.95 for broiled scrod to $16.95 for T-bone steak. Steak and kidney
pie, braised lamb shanks with lentils, roast duckling with brandied currant
sauce, fried catfish and barbecued ribs are among the offerings.

The inn's patented 1776 sausages are served in four versions at lunch
($5.50). You also can get shirred eggs or Welsh rarebit, salade Nicoise or
a bucket of steamers or mussels, $3.95 to $8.95. Seventeen wines, many
available in half bottles, are ordered by the bin number.

The "Gris," as it's known to locals and visitors from near and far, serves
hundreds of meals a day, and the Sunday Hunt breakfast is an institution
(an enormous buffet of dishes ranging from kippered herring and creamed
chipped beef to eggs and grits).

Before and after dinner, the Tap Room is a happy hubbub of banjo
players, a singalong pianist and sea chantey singers, depending on the night.
There's always something going on (innkeepers Bill and Vicky Winterer are

287

partial to holidays), and the Gris is nearly everyone's idea of what an old seaside tavern should be. You can snack from the raw bar, sample popcorn from the old red machine, hoist a few brews and readily imagine you've been transported back 200 years.

Lunch, daily noon to 2:30; dinner, 6 to 9 or 10; Sunday, Hunt Breakfast 10:30 to 2:30, dinner 5 to 9.

Doubles, $64; three suites, $75 to $90.

Old Lyme Inn, Lyme Street, Old Lyme 06371. (203) 434-2600.

With nine sumptuous guest rooms, an addition opened in the fall of 1985 has transformed what was basically an acclaimed restaurant with a few rooms into a full-service inn of distinction.

The new north wing has been added so tastefully that the casual passerby in Old Lyme's carefully guarded historic district wouldn't know it was new. On two floors, the rooms are individually decorated in a plush Victorian theme — canopy and four-poster beds with Marblehead mints perched atop their oversize pillows, comfortable sofas or chairs grouped around marble-topped tables, and large gleaming white bathrooms outfitted with Dickinson's Witch Hazel (made in Essex) and herbal shampoos. The new rooms are so attractive they make the five smaller rooms in the older part of the inn seem almost dowdy by comparison.

Innkeeper Diana Field Atwood has furnished guest rooms and public areas alike with Empire and Victorian pieces acquired at auctions, tag sales and antiques shows. Many of the inn's outstanding paintings represent the Old Lyme School of artists who were based at the Florence Griswold House across the street.

Guests have use of Sassafras's Library (named for the inn's aged cat), which has a marble-topped fireplace and television. The Victorian bar dispenses drinks, shellfish from a raw bar, light snacks, special coffees and dessert pastries.

Coffee cake is served for continental breakfast in the Rose Room. Lunch and dinner are available in three formal dining rooms (see Dining Spots).

Doubles, $75 (older rooms), $85 to $105 (new rooms).

Copper Beech Inn, Main Street, Ivoryton 06442. (203) 767-0330.

Long rated highly as a restaurant (see Dining Spots), the Copper Beech was aiming for the luxury market in lodging in 1986. Nine guest rooms were scheduled for a May opening in an old carriage house behind this imposing mansion shaded by the oldest copper beech tree in Connecticut.

Louise Ebeltoft and her husband Paul, both former IBM executives, purchased the inn in 1981 from Jo and Robert McKenzie, who had put it on the map as a restaurant. The Ebeltofts redid one of the five upstairs guest rooms, had a brief stint also operating the Gull restaurant in Essex, and now Louise is devoting her energies to the expanding inn, stamping it with her personal touch.

The nine new guest rooms were being decorated in country French style much like that of the master suite in the inn. Each has a jacuzzi bathtub and French doors onto an outdoor deck overlooking landscaped gardens. Second-floor rooms have cathedral ceilings.

Rooms in the main inn are attractive as well. Decorated in rich shades of blue, the suite has a striking floor-to-ceiling fabric canopy enveloping

New addition expands lodging capacity at Old Lyme Inn.

the kingsize bed, a loveseat in front of the fireplace, a chaise lounge across the room and a large table for two in the front dormer window.

Another room is bright and cheery with wicker furniture and brass bed. All the rooms have good-looking furnishings and antiques as befits a mansion once occupied by an ivory merchant.

There's a small sitting area upstairs in the spacious hall. In season, one of the most pleasant places to relax is the large greenhouse behind the inn, nicely outfitted with colorful garden furniture and an abundance of plants. It's popular for cocktails or after-dinner drinks.

Guests are served continental breakfast in the Copper Beech Room, where there are blue oriental carpets on the floor and tables spaced well apart, and views of the great tree through the windows.

The inn's limousine will pick up and deliver guests to and from the airport or the Essex Yacht Club.

Doubles, $90 to $125 in carriage house, $70 to $95 in inn.

Bee and Thistle Inn, 100 Lyme St., Old Lyme 06371. (203) 434-1667.
Stately trees, gardens all around and a flower-bedecked entrance welcome visitors to this cheery yellow and white frame inn, set on five acres bordering the Lieutenant River in the historic district of Old Lyme. Built in 1756 with subsequent additions and remodeling, the structure is a delightful ramble of parlors and porches, dining rooms and guest rooms.

It is this scene that attracted Bob and Penny Nelson in 1982. Wishing to leave the corporate life in northern New Jersey, they were looking to buy a traditional New England inn. A broker told them of one they weren't familiar with along the Connecticut shore. "It was only two hours from home so we decided to go look," Bob Nelson recalls. "We walked in the front door, saw the center entrance hall and graceful staircase and said, 'This is it.'"

Dining porch at Bee and Thistle Inn.   Living room at Riverwind.

With sofas to sink into and fireplaces ablaze, the parlors on either side of the entry are inviting. On sunny days, the enclosed porches beyond are great for lingering over breakfast or lunch. The Nelsons have refurbished most of the inn's public spaces and guest rooms, and have upgraded the restaurant as well (see below).

Nine of the eleven guest rooms upstairs have private baths and all have fresh flowers and what Bob calls "country old" furnishings. Four-poster, fishnet canopy and spool beds are covered with quilts or afghans; some rooms have wing chairs and ruffled curtains, and one even has a washstand full of flowers. Nooks are filled with games and old books are all around.

Full breakfasts are available in the sunny dining porches, a great place to start the day. Breakfast in bed may be ordered the night before.

Doubles, $60 to $85, EP.

Riverwind, 209 Main St. (Route 9A), Deep River 06417. (203) 526-2014.

Innkeeper Barbara Barlow, who grew up in Smithfield, Va., and whose dad is a hog farmer there, serves up slices of the red, salty Smithfield ham for breakfast every morning to her guests. She found the dilapidated 1850 house in 1983 and spent a year restoring it, doing most of the work herself. The result is a winner: a cozy inn crammed full of antiques and folk art, including a noteworthy collection of pigs in all guises, all over the house.

The hams hang from the ceiling in Barbara's kitchen, where her cupboards are made of wood from a gristmill in upstate New York and her counter is a 200-year-old piece of hemlock. In the adjacent blue and white dining room, guests eat breakfast by candlelight at a lovely old harvest table from Virginia. Coffeecake, real Southern biscuits in the shape of pigs, fresh fruit in summer and hot curried fruit in winter, and her homemade jams and preserves are the fare. It's all set up buffet-style on an antique ironing board.

A comfortable living room with fireplace is also loaded with antiques and neat touches; a decanter of sherry is always out for guests. Quilts, wooden animals, hooked and woven rugs, a set of blocks shaped like houses spelling "welcome," a wonderful lighting fixture of wooden animals holding candles, a piano topped with all kinds of sheet music — it's an exceptionally welcoming room. In summer, the long narrow porch in front is set with white wicker furniture and looks as if it's made for Scarlett O'Hara.

On the first floor is the small Barn Rose room, with a fishnet canopy on the four-poster bed. A clawfoot tub is in the bathroom, where a picture of Piglet hangs above the sink.

Up steep stairs, lined with old preserve jars full of dried flowers, are three more guest rooms, two with modern baths and one with its bathroom across the hall. The Smithfield Room, all red, white and blue, has bluebirds stenciled around the walls. A stenciled floor and Barbara's grandmother's carved oak hall tree and carved oak headboard give Zelda's Room a decidedly Gatsby flavor. The Havlow Room, named for her parents' farm, has an early pine bed and crazy quilt. A wreath made of corn husks, and corn husk dolls depicting the Oz characters and Tom Sawyer, Aunt Polly and Huckleberry Finn are on the walls. There's also a small game room upstairs, where coffee is available in the mornings.

Barbara used to run an antiques shop in the inn but has moved it to the other end of town. Riverwind Antiques is now managed by a friend from Virginia.

Doubles, $60 to $70.

Dining Spots

Fine Bouche, Main Street, Centerbrook. (203) 767-1277.

For consistency and creativity, Fine Bouche stands at the head of the list in an area known for fine restaurants. It's also a relatively good value, young chef-owner Steven Wilkinson having reluctantly raised his fixed-price menu to $32.50 after holding at $29 for three years ("some people were saying we didn't charge enough — that there must be something wrong," he acknowledged).

Trained in London and San Francisco before opening his small French restaurant and patisserie in 1979, Steve since has been ranked among the top three or four chefs in Connecticut. But he remains unassuming and personable, chatting with patrons on a first-name basis and running special wine-tasting and culinary events.

Beyond the patisserie, service bar and a small reception parlor (note the two lighted glass cases containing interesting memorabilia from the owner's career) are two small interior dining rooms seating a total of 45. One has pictures of grapes and vines on cream-colored walls, and the other is darker with pretty green and flowered wallpaper and old French prints. A cafe-style wrap-around porch is particularly inviting with arched lattice-work over the windows, peach-colored walls and rattan chairs, their seats covered by a dark green chintz dotted with exotic lilies.

The menu for a winter lunch offered Swiss cheese or smoked salmon omelets for $6.50 and seven entrees for $7.95: veal with cepes, lamb curry, beef stroganoff, creamed cod, chicken crepinette and game stew with winter vegetables. Warm and flaky croissants are served with sweet butter at lunch; they also form the base for a selection of interesting sandwiches.

Steve Wilkinson is at his most creative on the dinner menu, which changes daily.

The $32.50 menu la degustation might start with a choice of rabbit terrine, oysters mignonettes, Irish smoked salmon with sour cream and three types of caviar, or a puff pastry with chicken quenelles and fresh asparagus in a tarragon and butter sauce.

The soup or fish course might be lobster bisque with cognac, bay scallops and zucchini in a light curry sauce, oysters with sole mousse baked in the shell with a cream and riesling sauce, or salmon with white wine, cream and shiitake mushrooms.

After a green salad comes the piece de resistance: perhaps grilled veal chops with fresh rosemary and grilled polenta, pepper steak with cognac, sauteed breast of duck with green peppercorn, cognac and cream sauce, or boned saddle of lamb with a red wine, vinegar and crushed peppercorn sauce.

Desserts are superlative, particularly the almond-hazelnut dacquoise and the marjolaine, a heavenly combination of almond praline, hazelnut meringue, creme fraiche and bitter Belgian chocolate. Those with more resistance than we can order a fresh fruit sorbet.

The a la carte menu offers a few additional choices. Entrees are $14 for calves liver to $19 for rack of lamb.

We'll never forget a dinner of warm duck pate in puff pastry, grilled oysters with herb sauce, sweetbreads and a filet of veal with mushrooms, Madeira and tarragon, and a rich genoise for dessert.

The superb wine list is especially strong on French, fairly priced from $8.50 to $175.

Lunch Tuesday-Saturday, noon to 2; dinner 6 to 9, reservations required.

Bee and Thistle Inn, 100 Lyme St., Old Lyme. (203) 434-1667.

Head chef Danny Capiello and his wife Sharon, both Culinary Institute of America graduates, have solidified this inn's place on the culinary map with inventive dishes stylishly presented.

Dining on the enclosed side porches overlooking the lawns is a treat. Ladderback chairs are at tables with blue and rose cloths or mats, baskets hang from the ceiling and windows open to let in the breeze. Thriving African violets, other plants and knickknacks are all around.

Luncheon choices in the $5 to $7 range include smoked English bangers, cold salmon salad on watercress, hot chicken salad baked with boursin cheese, pheasant in puff pastry, veal and pepper marinara served over toasted French bread, stuffed ham roulades and chilled asparagus, artichokes and baby shrimp in a Dijon vinaigrette.

Candlelight dinners are served on the porches or in a small rear dining room, where a harpist plays on Saturday nights.

Dinner entrees ($13.50 to $22.50) range widely from poached salmon in an anchovy and caper sauce through veal sweetbreads (garnished with artichoke hearts and roasted peppers, tossed in parmesan cheese and finished with marsala) to breast of pheasant sauteed with hazelnuts and green grapes. The "pesto in a pot" is a magnificent melange of five kinds of seafood on a bed of linguini; seconds from the pot are proffered and gladly accepted. The rack of lamb is heavily garlicked, embellished with sauteed broccoli

Chef-owner Steven Wilkinson outside Fine Bouche.

and cherry tomatoes and served with one of the chef's potato dishes with which he likes to experiment.

He also likes to experiment with appetizers ($4 to $6). Mushrooms might be sauteed with basil and cherry tomatoes and set in pastry cups ("trumpets") or their caps stuffed with pheasant and duck liver pate and set on roasted peppers and peapods vinaigrette.

The inspired desserts include "the inn's selection" (a plate of chocolate profiteroles, oatmeal lace cookies, apricot leaves and macaroons, when we visited), a melt-in-the-mouth lemon mousse, chocolate mousse cake and ice cream peanut pie.

The changing Sunday brunch includes crepes "overstuffed with a variety of the chef's ideas."

The wine list changes as well, with some interesting Californias available at reasonable prices.

Lunch, daily 11:30 to 2; dinner 6 to 8 or 9; Sunday brunch, 11 to 2; closed Tuesday.

Old Lyme Inn, Lyme Street, Old Lyme. (203) 434-2600.
Twice given a high three-star rating by the New York Times and its desserts featured in successive 1985 issues of Bon Appetit magazine, the Old Lyme Inn has been a mecca for traveling gourmets since Diana Field Atwood took it over in 1976.

The food is inventive and the setting is formal in three large dining rooms, all regally done up in gold and blue. Tables in the long, high-ceilinged main dining room are angled in perfect formation, a vase with one perfect rose atop each. Beyond are two more dining rooms, one with an intimate windowed alcove containing a table for four.

Chef Daniel McManamy cooks in the nouvelle style. Dinner appetizers ($5 to $8) run the gamut from pate maison and Irish smoked salmon to venison sausage and hickory-smoked pheasant with a raspberry and walnut vinaigrette. Seasonal salads ($3) might be avocado, watercress and grapefruit with a summer berry and yogurt dressing or spinach, radicchio and mushrooms with warm goat cheese and a hazelnut vinaigrette.

Entrees ($14.50 to $21) include roast Nantucket duckling, veal sweetbreads with a white wine sauce and pine nuts, poached salmon with a saffron cream sauce and fish quenelles, and medallions of lamb in puff pastry.

Pastry chef Joseph Klim's luscious raspberry cheesecake Japonnaise was pictured on the cover of Bon Appetit. Other desserts could be kiwi and strawberry tarts, chocolate mocha cake and filled pastry rings.

The lunch menu includes good salads (country smoked duck with romaine or smoked pheasant with mixed greens and raspberry vinaigrette), a two-bird (chicken and duck) salad sandwich, veal stew, broiled salmon and lobster ravioli ($7 to $10). We liked the curried cream of yellow squash soup and the Niantic scallops.

The wine list is choice, the median price being in the $30 range.

Lunch Tuesday-Saturday, noon to 2; dinner 6 to 9, Sunday noon to 9; closed Monday.

Copper Beech Inn, Main Street, Ivoryton. (203) 767-0330.

The level of dining at the Copper Beech dropped following the departure of founding innkeepers Jo and Robert McKenzie. But the level was raised again in 1985 by chef Paul Gaffney (who had been voted Connecticut's chef of the year when he was at the Booth House in New Milford).

New innkeeper Louise Ebeltoft has redecorated the main Georgian Room with rose carpeting and subdued beige floral wallpaper. It is lavish indeed, with chandeliers, wall sconces and crisp white napkins folded to stand tall. The dark Comstock Room with beamed ceiling looks a bit like the old billiards parlor that it was; in between is the prettiest little garden dining porch, its three tables spaced well apart amid the plants.

The dinner menu is more extensive than most. Twelve appetizers, for instance, start at $5.95 for country pate and rise to $18 for smoked foie gras with Dijon vinaigrette. In between are poached mussels, crepes a la creme fraiche with caviar, beef with curry and fresh chutney, and wild mushrooms wrapped in puff pastry.

Some of the more inspired entrees ($17.95 to $24.50) are roast duckling with a blueberry and creme de cassis sauce, sauteed lamb with fried garlic in a butter-brandy sauce, and veal sweetbreads with a sauce of pureed apple, cream and calvados.

Desserts in the $4 to $5 range include profiteroles and sacher torte.

Lunch, Tuesday-Saturday noon to 2; dinner, 6 to 9 or 10, Sunday 1 to 9.

Pelicans, 30 Main St., Centerbrook. (203) 767-0155.

The folks who brought us La Boca in Middletown, one of Connecticut's best Mexican restaurants, opened this light-hearted establishment in an eccentric looking fieldstone and stucco house with a modern addition in August 1985. The Mexican touch on the menu is obvious; a Caribbean touch is sporadic in decor and cuisine.

The main-floor dining room is airy and casual: bow chairs at tables with green or gray laminated tops on black pedestals, gray paper mats, shell-pattern cutlery and a spray of fresh flowers in a glass vase. A few large plants and pictures, many of pelicans, and that's it — except for the young staff casually attired in aprons adorned with, of course, pelicans.

The upstairs is more dramatic. Tall deck chairs, their seats perhaps four feet off the ground, are at various counters in or near the bar. A comfy lounge has rattan furniture endowed with pink and green cushions. The spacious high-ceilinged dining room has comfortable brown velvet and chrome chairs. Outside is a large deck for dining in summer.

The interesting menu features seafood (some Caribbean), gourmet pizzas, salads and sandwiches.

The pizzas are something else. One of capicola, roasted garlic and artichoke hearts ($5.40 at lunch, $6.95 at dinner) was great — the featherweight crust topped with so much garlic that we should have gone into hiding for the afternoon. After it, we craved one of the day's sorbets — golden and refreshing passionfruit, enough for two (as it should have been for the $3.25 price tag). Less successful was the luncheon special of very fishy tasting yellowfin tuna, accompanied rather boringly by a sprig of broccoli and a boiled potato. An extra-good mustard vinaigrette dressed a hard-to-handle salad of uncut greens, julienned carrots and a cherry tomato; the good crunchy French bread was served with those uncouth foil-wrapped pads of butter.

Essentially the same menu is served all day, with more sandwiches and salads at lunch, more pastas, pizzas and entrees at night. Roti of the day (a Caribbean specialty of curried seafood, chicken or beef with potatoes, wrapped in a soft flour tortilla shell with a yogurt cucumber sauce), empanada, tostada de pesce and occasionally baked red snapper or conch are available for dinner ($6.95 to $13.50). You also can graze on seviche, a lamb sausage pizza and a three-chocolate bombe.

Lunch daily, 11:30 to 2:30; dinner, 5:30 to 10; Sunday brunch, 11:30 to 3.

Oliver's Taverne, Plains Road (Route 153), Essex. (203) 767-2633.

For a change of pace, this establishment named for Essex's first ship, the Oliver Crombell, is a casual spot in a breathtakingly-high space in the former Hitchcock furniture store. The decor is mostly wood with a massive stone fireplace; the large hanging panels of stained glass in the three-story window catch the light. Upstairs is a large oak and mahogany bar from Cicero, Ill., at which Al Capone once drank, and a suave lounge area.

Huge sandwiches served with french fries, burgers, salads and a few entrees like quiche or scallops baked in a cheese sauce are $3.50 to $5.50 at lunch. Snacky things like nachos, potato skins, fried calamari and such are also offered at night, when entrees go up to $12.50 for a sirloin steak. Bailey's Irish Cream mousse cake and chocolate chip cookie pie are popular desserts.

Lunch daily, 11:30 to 5; dinner, 5 to 10:30; Sunday brunch, 11 to 4.

Diversions

Essex Waterfront. The **River Museum** at Steamboat Dock, restored in 1975 from an 1878 steamboat warehouse, is a memorial to the Connecticut River Valley, from which the first American warship was launched. The main floor has changing exhibits. Upstairs, where windows on three sides afford sweeping views of the river, the permanent shipbuilding exhibit contains a fullsize replica of David Bushnell's first submarine, the strange-looking American Turtle, plus a new model of a Dutch explorer ship that sailed up the river in 1614, given by the William Winterer family of the Griswold Inn. Old-timer Albert F. Dock, one of the Connecticut River Foundation founders and benefactors, often is around to share an insight or two. The museum is open Tuesday-Sunday from 10 to 5, April-December. The foundation property also includes a small waterfront park with benches and the 1813 Hayden Chandlery, now the Thomas A. Stevens maritime research library. Just to the south off Novelty Lane are the historic Dauntless Club, the Essex Corinthian Yacht Club and the Essex Yacht Club.

Uptown Essex. Besides the waterfront area, Methodist Hill at the other end of Main Street has a cluster of historic structures. Facing tiny Champlin Square is the imposing white **Pratt House** (circa 1648), restored and operated by the Essex Historical Society to show Essex as it used to be (open June-September, Friday-Sunday afternoons). The period gardens in the rear contain herbs and flowers typical of the 18th century. The society also operates the adjacent **Hill's Academy** (1833), an early boarding school which now displays historical collections of old Essex. Next door in its former dormitory is the Catholic Church and, next to it, the Baptist Church, one of only two Egyptian Revival structures in the country.

Old Lyme. One of Connecticut's prettiest towns has a long main street lined with gracious 18th and 19th century homes, including one we think is particularly handsome called Lyme Regis, the English summer resort after which the town was named. Lyme Street, once the home of governors and chief justices, is a National Historic District.

The **Florence Griswold Museum** is the pillared 1817 landmark in which the daughter of a packet boat captain ran a finishing school for girls and later an artists' retreat, when most of the rooms were converted into bedrooms and studios were in the barns by the river. Now run as a museum by the Lyme Historical Society, it has unique painted panels in every room; especially prized is the dining room with panels on all sides given over to the work of the Old Lyme artists, who included Childe Hassam. Across the mantel the artists painted a caricature of themselves for posterity. The arts colony thrived for 20 years and its works are exhibited in the second-floor galleries. The museum is open daily except Monday from 10 to 5 and Sunday from 1 to 5, June-October; Wednesday-Sunday from 1 to 5, November-May.

The **Lyme Art Association** gallery, next door to the Florence Griswold Museum, was founded in 1921 and exhibits three major shows each season.

Deep River, just above Essex and reached most scenically via the River Road, is a sleepy river town best known for its ancient muster of fife and drum corps every July. Portrayed lately by the New York Times as being on the verge of chic between Essex and Chester, its downtown has a couple of good shops — Celebrations, for neat cards and paper goods, and Pasta Unlimited, where pasta of all shapes and flavors (we liked the tomato basil) is made in the front window, and goodies like a white bean and ham salad with garlic dressing are available for takeout. Up North Main Stret near the old Piano Works is a new complex of storefront shops including On the Verge of Chic, Calla Lillies, Seconds to Go and Keyboard Pond flower shop, plus Riverwind Antiques.

Up river is the delightful town of **Chester,** an up-and-coming area of restaurants and shops; the restored **Goodspeed Opera House** at East Haddam, where lively musicals are staged in a Victorian structure beside the river, and actor William Gillette's eccentric stone **Gillette Castle** on a hilltop above the river at Hadlyme. All are well worth a visit.

Shopping. Most first-timers in Essex are impressed by the quality of shopping, much of it nautically oriented. One concentration is at Essex Square: **E.J. Danos & Co.,** an intriguing place advertising sports art and antiques, has decoys, ducks and birds of all shapes and sizes, plus hunter's caps and St. Mary's Woolens sweaters emblazoned with birds. **Seaflowers** is a whimsical garden shop with a mechanical cat lying in a basket in one window and a real one snoozing in a chair in the other window; it has great hanging wall baskets and exotic dried flower arrangements. The **Clipper Ship Bookshop** specializes in nautical volumes and has a fine children's department. For fashions, visit **the Talbots, the Country Shop of Madison, Parrot Limited, Silkworm** and **Camps.** At Griswold Square, the **Sweaterville** factory outlet is housed in the 1720 Timothy Starkey House. Other shops are **Toys Ahoy, Far Away Things, Connecticut River Tapestries, Individual Expressions** and the **Connecticut Mariner.** The soaring and colorful **Boat House** at Dauntless Boat Yard is contemporary, nautical and full of interesting gifts; **All Decked Out** offers sportswear for the yachtsman.

The Yellow Daffodil on Main Street, Centerbrook, is contemporary as can be, its showrooms filled with sophisticated cards, paper goods, glassware, toys, furnishings and such.

The Queen's Museum, an extraordinary gift shop run very personally by Alice and Bates Johnson at Champlin Square, is a must stop every time we're in Essex. It's one of those rare places where you covet almost everything. A china plate is lettered, "A fool and his money are soon invited everywhere." There are enormous stuffed fabric tulips, intriguing California necklaces bearing fish or fruit, placemats with historic scenes, tote bags and purses, dolls and lamps, but, says Bates, "the crafts set us apart."

Extra-Special

The Valley Railroad. Its whistle tooting and smokestack spewing, the marvelous old steam train runs from the old depot in the Centerbrook section of Essex through woods and meadows to the Connecticut River landing at Deep River. There it connects with a riverboat for an hour's cruise past Gillette Castle to the Goodspeed Opera House and back. The two-hour trip into the past is fun for old and young alike. Trips run daily in summer, mainly weekends in spring and fall and at Christmas. The Saturday evening Dixieland or country music cruises, three hours of jam-packed nostalgia, are a fun-filled Connecticut summer tradition. Adults, $7.95, train and riverboat; $4.95, train only.

Lake Waramaug provides backdrop for Hopkins Vineyard wines.

Litchfield-Lake Waramaug
Connecticut's Colonial Country

Nestled into the hills of Northwest Connecticut, picturesque Lake Waramaug boasts an Alpine setting that appealed enough to a couple of Austrian innkeepers to call it home. Nearby is Litchfield, the quintessential Colonial Connecticut town preserved not as a restoration in the tradition of Williamsburg, with which it has been compared, but as a living museum community.

The lake and the town, though ten miles apart, are linked by a mystique of timeless isolation.

Hills rise sharply above the boomerang-shaped Lake Waramaug. Its sylvan shoreline is flanked by a state park, summer homes, and four country inns. With little commercialization, it's enveloped in a country feeling, away from it all.

Litchfield, a small village whose importance long has transcended its borders, is perched atop the crest of a high ridge. Its beautiful North and South streets are lined with gracious homes and history (George Washington slept here, Harriet Beecher Stowe was born here, Ethan Allen lived here, the nation's first law school and its first academy for girls were founded here). The village is so preserved and prized that only recently has it attracted inns and the kind of shops that affluence breeds.

Between the hills and lakes are fine natural and low-key attractions — Connecticut's largest nature sanctuary, a world-famous garden center, two farm wineries, state parks and forests. Connecticut's entire Northwest Corner has much to commend it, but there's no more choice a slice than Litchfield and Lake Waramaug.

Inn Spots

The Boulders Inn, Route 45, New Preston 06777. (203) 868-7918.

Its setting just across the road from the lake, its handsome and comfortable sitting room and its fine kitchen make this the inn in which we would most like to stay in the area. Built as a private home in 1895, it has been a small inn since about 1950. Former Indianans Carolyn and Jim Woollen took over in 1979 and it is they who have given the inn its reputation for interesting dining (see below).

The five guest rooms in the inn are comfortable, with thick new carpeting in a deep sand color. Two corner rooms have twin beds; two others that face the lake have queensize beds, loveseats and cushioned window seats, and one in back has a sleigh bed and separate sitting room. All have private baths, as do the eight contemporary guest rooms in duplex chalets scattered along the hillside behind the inn. Each of the chalets has a deck, most with good views of the water; four have comfy sofas and chairs grouped around free-standing fireplaces, and are especially popular with the New Yorkers who comprise the bulk of the Boulders clientele.

Back in the inn, a basement game room offers ping-pong and skittles, a small den has a color TV and the inviting living room, with picture windows overlooking the lake (binoculars are provided), is a perfect mix of antiques and groupings of sofas and wing chairs in reds and blues. In one corner are a stereo with many records, and shelves of books. A Russian samovar dispenses tea in winter months, and guests also enjoy cocktails here.

Pinnacle Mountain, out back, has trails for climbing and hiking. In winter, cross-country trails abound and the lake usually freezes enough for skating. In summer, of course, swimming, sailing and canoeing are favorite pastimes, and a tennis court is on the grounds. If you feel lazy, just sit in the beach house's wicker swing and watch the changing moods of the lake.

Full breakfasts for inn guests are served on floral quilted mats at tables by the windows in the new six-sided Lake Dining Room. A help-yourself cold buffet is set up with fruit juices, prunes, melon in season, cereals and coffee cake. Eggs any style, omelets, French toast and pecan, apple or blueberry pancakes with bacon, sausage or ham can be ordered and are accompanied by English muffins or homemade whole wheat toast.

Doubles, $130 MAP, $92 to $96 winter mid-week.

Hopkins Inn, Hopkins Road, New Preston 06777. (203) 868-7295.

This landmark yellow inn astride a hill above Lake Waramaug is known for its setting and cuisine (see below), and we often recommend it when asked where to take visitors for lunch in the country. Its reputation was built by Swiss-born innkeepers Margrit and Rudy Hilfiker, and continued since the late 1970s by Austrian Franz Schober and his wife Beth.

Built in 1847 as a summer guest house, the Federal structure with several additions was converted from a boarding house into an inn in 1945, and the guest rooms have been considerably enhanced lately by the Schobers. Although still warmed only by small heating units (so used only from April through mid-November), the nine guest rooms on the second and third floors have been sparingly but comfortably furnished with brass or wood bedsteads, thick carpeting, floral wallpapers, chests of drawers and the odd rocker. Seven of the nine rooms have private baths, and two on the third floor share.

Guests share a couple of small main-floor parlors with restaurant patrons, and may use the inn's private beach on the lake. There are few better vantage points for lake-watching than the expansive outdoor dining terrace, shaded by a giant horse chestnut tree and distinguished by striking copper and wrought-iron chandeliers and lanterns. Breakfast is available for house guests.

Doubles, $33 to $40, EP.

The Inn on Lake Waramaug, North Shore Road, New Preston 06777. (203) 868-0563 or (800) 525-3466.

From private home to village inn to boarding house for summer guests, this has grown since the 19th century into a year-round destination resort with an indoor pool, sauna, whirlpool, game room, meals in two dining rooms or at the beachhouse dock, a lake beach, the Honeycomb gift shop and 25 guest rooms, five in the main inn and 20 in newly redecorated guest houses below. Since 1951, it has been run with warmth and energy by the Richard Combs family, descendants of the boarding house owner; following the death of their father in 1985, sons Jay and Chris have assumed leading roles.

This is the place for people who like a lot of activity, and the Combses — promoters of their inn and the region from way back — keep things busy with lake excursions on the inn's 50-passenger Showboat in summer and horse-drawn sleigh rides in winter.

Yellow webbed lawn chairs are lined up in rows all around the grounds, the better for watching all the goings-on, among them the antics of several horses, including Chester, a 40-year-old pony who grazes on the lawn.

All guest rooms have cable television and air-conditioning; eight in the guest houses have fireplaces, and many have canopy beds, maple furniture and upholstered chairs. The top of the line are the eight master bedrooms with canopy beds, working fireplaces and water views.

Dining is in a large, pleasant room all done up in blue or in an adjacent lighter, more airy room in pink. An extensive menu of standard appetizers and entrees (priced from $11 for roast turkey to $16.75 for tournedos Rossini) is supplemented by daily specials and a vast array of desserts and fancy coffees.

Doubles, $130 to $188, MAP; midweek and seasonal discounts available.

The Birches Inn, West Shore Road, New Preston 06777. (203) 868-0229.

Its dining room and secluded waterfront location are the attractions at this rustic inn run in Alpine style since 1977 by Austrians Heinz and Christa Holl.

Of the nine guest rooms, all with private baths, the most choice are the three in the lakefront cottage across the shore road, each sharing part of an extended back porch directly over the water. They're used seasonally, and one which is good for families has a loft area with four beds. The Holls live on the second floor of the inn, which has one large guest room with two double beds, an assortment of chairs and a large front window onto the lake. The other five rooms are in a guest house behind the inn.

The Inn on Lake Waramaug

Guests have use of the private beach and boat dock; canoes and bicycles are available for rent. They also join restaurant patrons in the cozy bar, pleasantly situated with an excellent lake view.

Christina Holl is the dinner chef; her wiener schnitzel and apple strudel are praised. Other specialties on the continental menu include Hungarian goulash soup, chicken Kiev, sauerbraten and pork Styrian style, among more traditional entrees like chateaubriand and seafood newburg platter, priced from $9.95 to $15.95. Sacher torte and strawberries Romanoff are a couple of the good desserts.

Lodging rates include a full breakfast and four-course dinner (European plan is available midweek or weekly only).

Doubles, $98 to $130, MAP.

Toll Gate Hill, Route 202, Litchfield 06759. (203) 482-6116.

The rural 1745 landmark home near the Torrington town line, in which Captain William Bull once took in travelers on the Hartford-Albany stage route, was handsomely restored and reopened as a small inn and restaurant in 1983. Inviting it is, hidden from the road in a forest of trees, its red frame exterior dimly illuminated at night and appearing to the traveler much as it must have more than two centuries ago. We only wish that one's grand entrance for dining or lodging didn't have to be through a small, narrow bar in which everything seems to stop (and everyone stares) as visitors arrive.

Once that hurdle is overcome, overnight guests are in for a treat, staying in one of six nicely decorated guest rooms on the second and third floors. The most choice are the three larger ones on the second floor, each with working fireplace. All are air-conditioned and have modern bathrooms, comfortable sitting areas with chairs or loveseats, pleasant Laura Ashley-style decor and color-coordinated fabrics. Innkeeper Fritz Zivic was planning to add four suites in a carriage house at the rear of the inn in 1986.

A small parlor for house guests is located on the second-floor landing next to the ballroom. Light breakfasts of juice, fruit breads and muffins are served in the rooms or in summer on the outdoor patio.

Doubles, $75 to $85.

Litchfield Inn, Route 202, Litchfield 06759. (203) 567-4503.

Set back from the road west of the village on a vast expanse of lawn in need of more landscaping, the Litchfield Inn is a new (1982) white Colonial-style inn with modern accoutrements, 32 guest rooms, a couple of restaurants, a banquet facility and plans for 70 more rooms, a banquet hall and a swimming pool-health club facility.

Furnished with early American reproduction pieces, single rooms, doubles and suites have private baths, color TV and air-conditioning, and some have wet bars. The formal main-floor sitting room is elegantly furnished, if a bit austere. More cozy is the Tack Room with fireplace and comfortable armchairs.

Lunch is served in the Tapping Reeve lounge and bar, or in the narrow, skylit Greenery. Dinner is in the Joseph Harris Room, properly decked out in hand-hewn beams, wide planked floors and nicely spaced tables. The menu suggests wines with each entree, which run from $9.95 for Yankee pot roast and glazed vegetables to $16.95 for filet mignon wrapped in bacon. Veal dishes are among the specialties, as are seasonal favorites like stuffed pork chops with McIntosh apple gravy or Cornish game hen with sausage stuffing.

Lunch daily, 11:30 to 2:30; dinner, 5:30 to 9 or 10, Sunday noon to 8. Doubles, $70.

Dining Spots

The Boulders Inn, Route 45, New Preston. (203) 868-7918.

Boulders make up a good part of the decor at this inn, jutting out from the walls of the intimate inner dining room as well as in part of the smashing new six-sided addition, where, through large windows, almost every diner has a view of Lake Waramaug. A spacious deck-terrace is the setting for lunch and cocktails during warm months.

Large paper Japanese globe lights hang from the ceiling; other light is provided by hurricane lamps on the white-linened tables. Bits and pieces of old china are displayed on shelves, and taped classical music plays in the background.

Six appetizers ($1.75 to $5.50) include avocado with mussels and scallops, terrine of duck and artichoke hearts lemonette. Dinner entrees ($10.25 to $15.25) could be veal with lemon and capers, boned duck breast maconnaise, broiled lamb chops with tarragon butter or Kashmir lamb in a sauce of tomatoes, ground almonds, yogurt and curry spices. We remember from a dinner a few years ago how tasty the chicken paprikasch was. Desserts include a wonderful brandied orange nut cake, creme caramel and an old favorite of ours, meringue glace Pavlova.

Dining room at the Boulders.

An extensive luncheon menu includes five or six hot dishes, one of which is a crepe du jour, delicious salads (curried chicken with fresh mango is one) and interesting sandwiches like mozzarella pesto and charcuterie plate. Prices are in the $4.50 to $6.75 range. Sunday brunch ($8.95) starts with a choice of appetizers like pears in port, California salad or a fresh pineapple sherbet boat and goes on to such entrees as blueberry blintz, lamb kidneys Madeira or sour cream and caviar omelet.

Jim Woollen, who mixes a dynamite martini, is proud of his reasonably priced and wide-ranging (several from Connecticut) wine list. A Robert Mondavi pinot noir '79, for instance, is only $11.

We heartily applaud the ban on smoking in the new Lake Dining Room.

Dinner, Memorial Day-Labor Day, nightly 6 to 8:30 (except Monday when an informal outdoor buffet is served on the terrace to inn guests). September and October, Tuesday-Saturday. Rest of year, Wednesday-Saturday. Lunch, noon to 2, summer only. Sunday brunch.

Toll Gate Hill, Route 202, Litchfield. (203) 482-6116.

Innkeeper Fritz Zivic, who founded the late Black Dog Tavern steakhouse chain in the Hartford area in the 1960s, features a changing menu of what he calls "light, unencumbered food" in two small, charming old dining rooms on the inn's main floor or upstairs in the ballroom complete with fiddler's loft for piano or other live entertainment.

The hand-printed dinner menu of a dozen entrees ($11.95 to $17.50) is supplemented by half a dozen blackboard specials: stuffed monkfish with crabmeat, veal gruyere, sweetbreads with mushrooms and buffalo ribeye steak the last time we were there. The wine list is choice and reasonably priced, the soups are creative and our dinners of shrimp in beer batter and broiled scallops with a white butter sauce were fine. The shellfish pie and roast duck with apple brandy or green peppercorn sauce also appealed.

The high, ladderback chairs are a bit uncomfortable, but the original tavern room with its dark wood, wide plank floors and well-spaced tables covered with beige linen, heavy silver and tiny lamps is attractive. Others prefer the formal dining room with fireplace and arched corner cupboard, while still others go for the piano music on weekends in the upstairs ballroom under a vaulted ceiling and brass chandeliers.

Brunch items are offered on weekends in addition to the daily luncheon menu, with many of the dinner appetizers, sandwiches and entrees like broiled sole, mixed grill, puff pastry or breast of chicken in a cream cognac sauce ($6.25 to $7.50).

Lunch daily, noon to 3; dinner, 5:30 to 9:30 or 10:30.

Hopkins Inn, Hopkins Road, New Preston. (203) 868-7295.

On a warm summer day or evening, few dining spots are more inviting than the large outdoor terrace under the giant horse chestnut tree at the entrance to the Hopkins Inn. With the waters of Lake Waramaug shimmering below and a bottle of wine from the Hopkins Vineyard next door, you could imagine yourself in the Alps, so no wonder Austrian chef-owner Franz Schober feels right at home.

Dining inside this 1847 Federal structure is a delight as well. Two dining rooms stretch around the lakeview side of the inn; the overflow goes to a paneled Colonial-style taproom up a few stairs. One dining room is Victorian, while the other is more rustic with barnsiding and ships' figureheads on the walls.

The blackboard menu changes daily, but always includes the Austrian and Swiss dishes of the chef's heritage and the prices are surprisingly reasonable.

You might start with pate maison ($1.75), baby trout or escargots ($4). Dinner entrees are $10.25 to $14.50 for dishes like wiener schnitzel or sweetbreads that we remember fondly from years past. In spring, you can get shad roe; Beth Schrober says her husband's roast pheasant with red cabbage and spaetzle is especially popular in fall. How about trout meuniere or backhendl with lingonberries, both in the $11 range? Vegetables are special, especially unusual things like braised romaine lettuce.

Regulars cherish the grand marnier souflee glace and strawberries Romanoff, the priciest desserts at $2.50 and $2.75 respectively; pear Helene and chocolate mousse are a bargain $1.75. The wine list has 20 cabernet sauvignons from $12 to $80 as well as four Swiss and two Austrian whites and an incredible list of bordeaux and burgundies. Finish with a flourish: Irish or Jamaican coffee at $2.50.

The luncheon menu offers many of the same specialties at lower prices. Entrees run from $5.50 for lamb curry to $9 for sirloin steak. It's no wonder the place is always crowded.

Lunch, Tuesday-Saturday noon to 2; dinner, 6 to 9 or 10, Sunday 12:30 to 8:30; closed Mondays. Dinner only in April, November and December. Closed, January-March.

Le Bon Coin, Route 202, Woodville. (203) 868-7763.

The small white dormered house along the route from Litchfield to New Preston is home for classic French cuisine, lovingly tendered by chef-owner William Janega, who moved from Le Parisien in Stamford with his wife and young sons to take over this off-again, on-again country establishment in 1983.

The dark, cozy barroom has French Impressionist paintings on the walls and Hitchcock chairs at half a dozen small tables. On the other side of the foyer is a dining room, barely larger but brighter in country French style. Colorful La Fleur china tops the double sets of heavy white linen cloths on each table.

Dinners might begin with country pate, a pastry shell of sweetbreads, mussels baked in escargot butter or smoked trout; if you can't decide, try the hors d'oeuvres plate for $7.25. The 14 entrees run from $11.75 for calves liver with onions to $18.95 for Dover sole with mushrooms and artichokes. Frog's legs, pepper steak, veal citron, roast duck bigarade and sweetbreads du jour are among the offerings. Desserts include sorbets, pear belle Helene and crepes Suzette for two.

Chef Janega is proud of his wine list and of his new front entry, decorated with wine casks, spigots and crate labels plus some handsome stained-glass windows.

Lunch and dinner daily except Tuesday, Sunday dinner from 3 p.m.

La Tienda Cafe, Sports Village, Route 202, Litchfield. (203) 567-8778.

Opened in 1982, this Mexican cafe quickly became so popular that co-owner Paul Haas moved into larger quarters across the street in 1984, and in late 1985 an addition increased seating capacity to 95.

A green neon cactus beckons in the window of the two-room cafe, the front room used for lunch. Glass tops the cloths of wide, bright stripes, on each table is a cactus in a small pot (all different) and colorful prints and rugs adorn the walls. Chairs are comfortable cane and chrome, and

Landmark 19th century hilltop structure houses Hopkins Inn.

hanging lamps are topped with straw covers. If you don't like country music, La Tienda is not for you — Willie Nelson and friends are played rather loudly at all times.

Crispy homemade tortilla chips and a fairly hot salsa are served. We found a lunch of Mexican pizza was almost more than one could handle: a flour tortilla topped with ground beef, cheese, lettuce, tomato, chilies, guacamole and sour cream. One half had hot peppers, the other mild. An order of burritos, one stuffed with cheese and scallions and one with chicken, was also delicious and hearty.

Both dinner and lunch menus have "north of the border" dishes, but who would come here for a strip steak? Black bean soup, flautas, Arizona-style nachos (topped with ground beef) and quesadilla are some of the appetizers ($1.95 to $4.50) and there's even a Mexican eggroll. Dinners include rice and refried beans, and are $6.50 for folded tacos to $9.50 for chimichanga. Everything may be ordered mild, medium or hot. Lime pie is the most requested dessert, but flan and sopaipilla are popular as well. On Monday and Tuesday nights, a Mexican buffet offers all you can eat for $7.95.

Carafes of margaritas, pina coladas or daiquiris are $8.50; pitchers of sangria $5.50, and many beers are available, including Lone Star of Texas, $1.25 on tap.

Lunch, 11:30 to 2:30; dinner, 4:30 to 9 or 10.30, Sunday 3 to 10.

The Rooster and the Hawke, Route 202, Litchfield. (203) 567-4539.

A neon Dom Perignon sign hangs in the window of this new restaurant, the outside gray with red trim and a sign, painted by co-owner Michele Murelli, of an adorable cow, house and red barn. Michele's maiden name, Gallicchio, means little rooster, and her former partner in her catering business was named Hawks, hence the name. And, she explains further,

305

she was born in 1957, the Chinese year of the rooster. She, her brother and two other young men are partners in the small restaurant with a decidedly country feel, an adjoining bar with roosters painted on the linoleum floor, and a retail store featuring food to go, plus Sarum teas, Silver Palate products and baskets, pottery and quilts by local artists.

At noon on weekdays a table in the middle of the room is set up with a buffet lunch for $5.95. A hot dish (perhaps Brunswick stew with buttermilk biscuits or prime rib with mushroom gravy) is supplemented with many platters of salads and breads. One may also order, from $3.75 to $7, things like baked sole, grilled reuben or open steak sandwich, chef salad or cold poached chicken.

At dinner you could begin with five onion soup ($2.25) or "our own onion rings" ($2.75). Entrees, from $7.50 for a small chopped sirloin to $15.50 for veal chop with wild mushrooms, include poached salmon, beer batter shrimp and Northern fried chicken.

Besides pecan pie, cheesecake and rice pudding, there's an awesome Toblerone chocolate sundae. House wine is Rene Junot, $2.25 a glass.

Cafe curtains, country tablecloths in browns and greens, pictures of cows, wreaths made of vines, dinner plates collected from near and far, and a fieldstone fireplace over which is a moose head convey a rustic feeling. Bills are presented on plates decorated with roosters.

Lunch, 11:30 to 2:30; dinner, 5 to 10 or 11, Sunday noon to 9; closed Tuesday.

Diversions

Lakes and Parks. Lake Waramaug State Park at the west end of the lake is a wonderfully scenic site, its picnic tables scattered under the trees right beside the water. The lake's Indian name means "good fishing place;" it's also good for swimming and boating, and blessedly uncrowded. On the north and east sides of the lake are the forested Above All and Mount Bushnell state parks. Not far from Lake Waramaug on the road to Litchfield (Route 202) is **Mount Tom State Park.** It has a 60-acre spring-fed pond for swimming and again picnic tables are poised at shore's edge. A mile-long trail rises to a tower atop Mount Tom.

White Memorial Foundation and Conservation Center. Just west of Litchfield are 4,000 acres of nature sanctuary bordering Bantam Lake. Thirty-five miles of woodland and marsh trails are popular year-round with hikers, horseback riders and cross-country skiers. This is a splendid place for observing wildlife, birds and plants in a variety of habitats. The Conservation Center in a 19th century mansion has a natural history museum with good collections of Indian artifacts, butterflies, live and stuffed animals, and an excellent nature library and gift shop. Grounds open year-round, museum April-November.

Topsmead State Forest. Flower gardens, nature trails and a 40-acre wildflower preserve where 200 species are marked, a pond and a picnic area are attractions at this 500-acre hilltop beauty just east of Litchfield. The 1920s Tudor-style summer home of Edith M. Chase, daughter of the Chase Brass founder, is open free in the summer, Monday-Friday 10 to 4.

White Flower Farm, Route 63, Morris. This institution south of Litchfield is a don't-miss spot for anyone with a green thumb. In fact, people come from across the country to see the place made famous by the catalog, wittily written by the owner under the pen name of Amos Pettingill. Eight acres of exotic display gardens are at peak bloom in late spring; twenty acres of growing fields are at their height in late summer. Greenhouses with indoor plants, including spectacular giant tuberous begonias, are pretty all the time. Shop and grounds open daily, mid-April through October.

Litchfield Historic Sites. The Litchfield Historic District is clustered around the long, wide green and out North and South streets (Route 63). The information center on the green has maps for walking tours, which are the best way to experience Litchfield. Note the bank and the jail with a common wall at North and West streets. Along North Street are Sheldon's Tavern, where George Washington slept, plus the birthplace of Harriet

Litchfield Congregational Church.

Beecher Stowe and the Pierce Academy, the first academy for girls. South Street is a broad, half-mile-long avenue where two U.S. senators, six Congressmen, three governors and five chief justices have lived. Here too is the **Tapping Reeve House and Law School** (1773), the first law school in the country. The house with its handsome furnishings and the tiny school with handwritten ledgers of students long gone are open mid-May to mid-October, Thursday-Monday noon to 4. The **Litchfield Historical Society Museum** at South and East streets has four galleries of early American paintings, decorative arts, furniture, and local history exhibits; open mid-April to mid-November, Tuesday-Saturday 11 to 5.

Wineries. Two of New England's premier wineries occupy hilltop sites overlooking the beauty of Litchfield and Lake Waramaug. **Haight Vineyard & Winery,** Connecticut's first farm winery just east of Litchfield, has moved from its original barn across Chestnut Hill Road to a new, English Tudor-style building with a large tasting room and gift shop. Guided winery tours and a 15-minute vineyard walk are among the attractions. You can pick up a bottle of award-winning Covertside white ($4.95) or a chardonnay ($7.95), plus a pink T-shirt ("Never bite the foot that stomps your grapes"), wine accessories, salad dressings and spices. Open Monday-Saturday 10 to 5, Sunday from noon.

Hopkins Vineyard, Hopkins Road, New Preston. A hillside location with good view of Lake Waramaug marks this family operation run by Bill and Judy Hopkins, dairy farmers turned winemakers. The rustic red barn offers a quick, self-guided tour from an upstairs vantage point and the fine Hayloft Gallery showing works of local artists. The gift shop sells wine-related items like baskets, grapevine wreaths and stemware, even handmade linen towels. The winery's cat Wonder Puss may be snoozing near the wood stove, upon which a pot of mulled wine simmers on chilly days. On nice days, you can sip a superior seyval blanc ($5.99) or Lakewide white ($4.75) in a small picnic area overlooking the lake. Open daily 11 to 5, May-December; weekends rest of year.

Shopping. Good shops have sprung up lately in the center of Litchfield and its western environs. Enter the **Mason Gift Shop,** just off the common, to smell the Arkansas potpourri called Scent of Spring but also to check out some delightful gifts. **The Litchfield Exchange,** where practically everything is handmade, **Cobble Court Book Shop** and the **Kitchenworks** are all worth visiting in the courtyard around the corner. Also near the green is **Workshop Inc.,** a boutique with trendy women's apparel and Mexican and South American imports, including straw hats and handpainted silk earrings; downstairs is a gallery with handwoven rugs, interesting pieces from Africa and a flock of stuffed sheep.

Litchfield Commons, a cluster of new shops in an attractive grouping around a brick walk, is worth a stop as you traverse Route 202 west of town. **Mother Goose** is an outstanding toy shop, and other shops have names like the **Haberdashers, Eagles Nest** for antiques and country accessories, **Puddlejumpers** for childrens' clothing and **Jonathan Peters,** too elegant for words, with white painted floors upon which are displayed exquisite table and bed linens from France and Italy, hand-painted dinnerware and baskets, and the most gorgeous wicker chairs, handpainted in soft summery colors (we did not dare ask the price). At the **Uncommon Strudel,** a bakery with five blue-clothed tables, you can get an inexpensive breakfast or lunch. A blackboard menu lists such things as French bread pizza and salad ($3.95), beef and vegetable pot pie and salad ($5.50) and Russian piroski and salad ($4.95). Pick up some banana chocolate chip or carrot raisin muffins, or, as we did, some buttery linzer torte to take home. **Truffles,** a restaurant including a greenhouse and outdoor dining, was due to open by summer 1986 (entrees to be in the $12 to $18 range).

New Preston, a hamlet just down the hill from Lake Waramaug, has the intriguing **Brittania Bookshop;** the Union Jack flies out front and all kinds of old British and Irish books are within. A worthwhile side trip is to **The Silo,** four miles west off Route 202 at Upland Road. Here, Ruth and Skitch Henderson run a cookery shop par excellence, and sponsor culinary classes plus changing arts and crafts exhibitions in their gallery.

Extra-Special _____

The Pantry, Washington Depot. (203) 868-0258.

One of our favorite places for lunch and shopping is this upscale gourmet shop just south of Route 202 in tiny Washington Depot (while waiting for a table, you could browse through the excellent **Hickory Stick Bookshop** nearby). A counter displays and a blackboard lists the day's offerings, from an extensive repertoire, and you can get anything to take out as well. The fare is innovative, with especially good soups, salads and desserts. Tables are set amidst high-tech shelves on which are just about every exotic chutney, mustard, vinegar, extra virgin olive oil and the like that you could imagine, as well as kitchenware and tableware, baskets and pottery. Open daily except Monday for lunch and Sunday brunch.

Enormous sculpture frames back of Aldrich Museum of Contemporary Art.

Ridgefield, Conn.
Yankee Enclave of Urbanity

The 1783 white clapboard, black-shuttered structure is not unlike many of the gracious old homes lining Ridgefield's long, wide and historic Main Street. But its interior is filled with modern art and its exterior is surrounded on three sides by modest to far-out sculptures.

This is the Aldrich Museum of Contemporary Art. And its futuristic statements amidst a bastion of Yankee tradition are symbolic of the broader community in which it resides.

Few towns have better preserved their heritage (certainly none so close to metropolitan New York), and few have so much heritage to preserve. Ridgefield was settled in 1708, and many of its early homes still stand along tree-lined Main Street, which remains blessedly unravaged by time. It was along this street where the Battle of Ridgefield was fought in 1777, and the 1772 Keeler Tavern which served as Patriot headquarters was operated as an inn until 1907.

Today, this small Yankee town has expanded into a prosperous ex-urban refuge of 20,000 living in historic, traditional and contemporary homes tucked away in 35 square miles of forested ridges and fields. Three luxurious, air-conditioned inns cater to weekenders who seek a bucolic escape not far from the city, as well as to increasing numbers of business visitors at corporate headquarters nearby. Visitors and residents are sustained by some of the East's finer restaurants, as well as a proliferation of casual but creative cafes and bistros. A number of small stores, mostly owner-operated, cater to affluent tastes.

Ridgefield proper, hidden off the beaten path between busy Connecticut Route 7 and the New York state line, has nary a motel nor a fast-food restaurant.

After all, this is not New York and not suburbia. Ridgefield's present has been gracefully shaped by its past. It is an enclave of Yankee New England, noticeably more so than neighboring towns, and proud of it.

Inn Spots

West Lane Inn, 22 West Lane, Ridgefield 06877. (203) 438-7323.

Since 1978, this grand early 1800s home next to the Inn at Ridgefield restaurant has been lavishing its creature comforts on overnight guests.

An entry foyer has oak paneling, deep pile carpeting and upholstered chairs in front of the fireplace. The dining room, in which guests are served continental breakfast, is as richly appointed as many a formal restaurant. The spacious guest rooms have one king or two queensize beds, wing chairs and-or sofas, scales and heated towel racks in the bathrooms, and color TV; some have working fireplaces. All the decorating — quiet and restful in varying shades of blues, rusts and beiges — was done by innkeeper Maureen Mayer in the style of a private home.

Fourteen rooms are in the main inn — four on the first floor, six on the second and four on the third, where there is a small sitting room. Turn-of-the-century grill work, a carved wood screen, an abundance of magazines and views onto the gardens provide much to look at.

Out back in a converted garage named "The Cottage on the Hill," six rooms have private rear balconies looking onto emerald green lawns. These rooms have kitchenettes; one with a living room and full kitchen with bedroom upstairs is like an apartment. Umbrellas are beside the doors in case it rains.

New in 1985 were three suites converted from the low-lying house between inn and restaurant, all very private behind redwood fence and green plantings. It is the former home of the innkeeper, who has moved across the street.

Two suites with living room, dining room, kitchen and bedroom are so versatile they can be rented as single, double or family units. Another has all the above plus a floor-to-ceiling fireplace and, our guide informed, "a dressing room for madame and an office for her husband."

On the inn's wide front porch are white wicker tables and chairs with yellow seats. Guests can have continental breakfast there in summer, or a snack from the inn's pantry from noon to 10 p.m.; an ice machine is discreetly tucked into a corner of the inn's front entry. You also can walk next door to the Inn at Ridgefield for lunch or dinner, or a drink in its small bar.

Doubles, $95 ($135 with fireplace, Sept. 15 through May); suites, $145 to $165.

Stonehenge, Route 7, Box 667, Ridgefield 06877. (203) 438-6511.

A country setting along a rural road set back from Route 7 — complete with swan pond and waterfall — makes Stonehenge a retreat for lodging as well as dining (see below). For city types, it's the perfect place for a country getaway — not at a country inn, as co-owner David Davis notes, but at an urbane "inn in the country."

All 13 rooms have private baths, color TV and sumptuous furnishings. Three rooms are upstairs in the main building, which was remodeled in 1947 from a country farmhouse into an English-style inn by a World War II veteran who had been stationed on the Salisbury Plain near Stonehenge. Each is very different in color and style, the nicest being the Windsor Room with bookcase, antique dresser, wing chairs and fireplace.

Six rooms have been grandly refurbished in the Guest Cottage, an unobtrusive T-shaped complex behind the inn. One has kingsize bed with spindle headboard, two shiny antique bureaus and bedside night tables, a wing chair under a reading lamp and formal draperies with matching-fabric valances around the several windows.

Beyond is the newly built, two-story Guest House with two master bedrooms, two suites and garages underneath in the rear. Bearing the English names Surrey, Devon, Cornwall and Kent, they can sleep four in kingsize beds and sofabeds and are particularly lush. The bridal suite has a large living room and a kitchenette where honeymooners can make their own breakfast if they wish.

Most guests prefer to take the inn's continental breakfast, including its own fine pastries, in one of the restaurant's dining rooms. Also available in the main inn is an antiques-furnished parlor with Victorian settees, books and a selection of current magazines. A swimming pool is available in summer.

Doubles, $90 to $125; two suites, $170.

The Elms Inn, 500 Main St., Ridgefield 06877. (203) 438-2541.

Ridgefield's oldest operating inn (1799) has evolved from the beige Colonial house built in 1760 and comfortably ensconced across from a town park. Today, the original inn is primarily a restaurant and most of the guest rooms are next door in the 1850 annex, which was totally refurbished in 1983 by innkeeper Violet Scala and her brother-in-law, Robert Scala, who oversees the restaurant.

Four rooms upstairs in the original inn are redecorated but retain their historic look, even to the vaulted ceilings and sloping floors. Violet Scala treasures the old beds made by her mother-in-law's uncle; one has a canopy with white ruffle around the top, and another is a hand-carved cherry bed with matching dresser. One room still contains a sink (plus private bath, as do all the rooms). Another has a separate sitting room with red wing chairs, glass-top table and oriental rug over the wide-plank floor. Two have stenciled birds on the walls.

The refurbished annex has 16 rooms and suites on three floors, all spacious, carpeted and containing color TV and telephones. Antique furnishings, velvet rockers, old samplers, a few four-poster beds and striking wallpapers convey a feeling of tradition and luxury. Many of the bathrooms have dressing areas, and suites have comfortable sitting rooms and two TV sets.

Across from the office is an elegant sitting room. Guests are served a continental breakfast of fresh croissants in their rooms.

Doubles, $85 to $95; suites, $105.

Dining Spots

Stonehenge, Route 7, Ridgefield. (203) 438-6511.

Ever since the days of its famed Swiss chef-owner Albert Stockli, Stonehenge has been synonymous with fine dining. Since his death in 1972, co-owners David Davis and Douglas Seville have continued the tradition.

The restaurant, on the building's lower level overlooking a picturesque pond on which swans glide, is comprised of a formal main dining room, a dark and cozy tavern, and a new enclosed dining porch in more contemporary style (with canopied outdoor deck above). The main room is made particularly gracious by rich wood paneling, heavy draperies, corner cases full of rare china and silver pieces, and ornate wood chairs with leather seats. The pink linened tables have fresh flowers and tiny red lamp shades over flickering candles in hurricane-type lamps.

We've enjoyed both lunch and dinner here several times over the years, and each meal has been memorable. Lunch is less expensive (entrees from $8.50 for curried chicken Madras or omelet of shrimp and scallops to $16.75 for medallions of venison or tournedos with bordelaise sauce).

At lunch, we've sampled the famous Stonehenge barley soup, an intense, bisque-like mushroom soup, the renowned shrimp in beer batter with pungent fruit sauce, brook trout meuniere, a beautifully arranged seafood salad in an avocado shell and an excellent chef's salad.

Dinners are a prix-fixe $34, with the shrimp in beer batter appetizer and roast rack of lamb carrying a surcharge. Or you can order some items a la carte — appetizers $5.75 to $8.50, entrees $21.50 to $24, and a changing selection of desserts, $5.50. We can vouch for the mushroom crepes mornay with gruyere cheese and the smoked sausage (smoked on premises, served

Formal dining room at Stonehenge.

with an extraordinary mustard wine sauce in a pastry crust), the roast baby
pheasant with lingonberries and the whole roasted squab chicken Grand-
mere, garnished with mushrooms and carrots and swathed in a rich brown
sauce.

The dessert selection is temptingly arrayed on a table near the dining
room entrance. We've liked the glazed strawberry tart and the chocolate
cake (requests for the recipe arrive almost weekly from across the country).

The wine list is broad, deep and fairly priced, with interesting selections
in the mid-teens and a page of rare vintages from $100 to $600.

Lunch, noon to 2; dinner, 6 to 9, Sunday 2:30 to 7:30; Sunday brunch,
noon to 2:30. Closed Tuesday.

Le Coq Hardi, Big Shop Lane, Ridgefield. (203) 431-3060.

Since Le Coq Hardi opened in 1982, it has received such rave reviews
that owner Barbara Lubliner branched out in January 1986 with a second
establishment in Stamford.

Patterned after the restaurants she likes in the countryside outside Paris,
Le Coq Hardi occupies the lower level of what once was the blacksmith
shop of a 19th century carriage factory. The low-ceilinged interior retains
the original fieldstone walls and rough-hewn beams and posts; half a dozen
tables are in an airy greenhouse out front.

Decor is intimate and contemporary: tables generally close together, pink
cloths and napkins, cane and chrome chairs, spotlit art works, massed
flowers and a collection of roosters as accents.

Dinner appetizers ($6 to $7) include salmon mousse, sweetbreads forestiere, poached oysters in spinach sauce with pernod, and smoked fish with
a tart mustard sauce. The soup was creamy almond last time we visited.

313

An unsweetened citrus sorbet clears the palate between courses.

Among entrees ($17 to $21) are poached Norwegian salmon, grilled monkfish with pink peppercorns, loin of lamb, sliced breast of duck, veal chop with plum tomatoes, filet of beef with four peppercorns and fresh game in season. Desserts start at $5.50 for grand marnier souffle with chestnut sauce, Paris-Brest, pears poached in wine or a selection of fine cheeses. The well-chosen wine list has some good values.

Our spring lunch was a culinary adventure that included a fine breast of chicken with lingonberries and an interesting salad concoction of scallops and vegetables (tomatoes, radishes, celery, zucchini, shredded lettuce and pieces of lime). The chicken dish was followed by a plain salad of mixed greens and a zesty vinaigrette. Warm loaves of mini French bread were served with tongs from a basket. Refreshing desserts were a souffle framboise and an apricot mousse with amaretto.

Lunch prices start at $8 for three kinds of omelets; other entrees run from $9 for duck liver in red wine sauce to $13 for three versions of veal or quail with red currant sauce.

Lunch, Tuesday-Friday noon to 2; dinner, 6 to 9:30, Sunday 5:30 to 8:30; Sunday brunch, noon to 2. Closed Monday.

The Inn at Ridgefield, 20 West Lane, Ridgefield. (203) 438-8282.
A profusion of flowers brightens the canopied entrance to this formal restaurant which was established in 1947, the same year as Stonehenge, and is included with Stonehenge in most lists of Connecticut's great restaurants.

Gregarious owner Henry Prieger greets patrons and Peter Walters plays quiet dinner music nightly, as he has for 17 years, on the grand piano at the entrance to the main dining room.

Three dining rooms plus a small bar are attractively furnished in turn-of-the-century style with rich fabric wallpaper, chandeliers and comfortable upholstered chairs at large, well-spaced tables. The striking pewter service plates are emblazoned with a picture of the inn.

The left side of the oversize dinner menu is fixed price at $36 and tends to the nouvelle, while the right side is a la carte and more traditional.

Prix-fixe dinners might begin with a pate of pistachio and truffles or smoked ham with exotic fruits. After soup du jour (often a fine lobster bisque) comes the entree, perhaps sliced duck with peppercorns and sweet and sour sauce or filet mignon with pistachios and truffle sauce. The dessert cart might contain a cheesecake, chocolate mousse, pear tart, apple-kiwi tart and such.

On the a la carte side, appetizers ($6.25 to $10.75) include smoked eel with a creamy dill sauce, breast of quail with lobster in two sauces, and Peruvian shrimp cocktail. Entrees run from $15.75 for frog's legs provencale and chicken Florentine to $24 for the inn's cold seafood platter on ice. The changing veal dishes, Dover sole and rack of lamb for two have been rated highly. Seasonal vegetables and a basket of bread come with.

Although much tableside flambeeing goes on, even at lunch, the only flaming dessert is crepes Suzette for two ($16). The lunch menu ($7.75 and up) has a smattering of dinner items plus omelet du jour.

Lunch, noon to 2:30; dinner, 6 to 9:30 or 10:30, Sunday 2 to 8:30; Sunday buffet brunch, noon to 2:30. Closed Monday.

Extra-Special

Chef Lenard, Main Street, Ridgefield.

Only in Ridgefield would a sidewalk vendor wear a floppy blue chef's hat from Bloomingdale's and dispense gourmet hot dogs in an operation he calls "Les Delices Culinaires de la Voiture." Michael Soetbeer serves up le hot dog, le hot dog supreme, le hot dog choucroute Alsacienne and le hot dog facon Mexicaine, among others, at prices from $1.25 to $3. What he says are the world's first gourmet hot dog rolls in pumpernickel, whole wheat, rye, sourdough and egg are custom-designed for him at a local patisserie. He offers cold sodas Americaines and Perrier with lime as well. From April to December, his cart is usually near the corner of Main and Prospect streets from 11 to 4 Monday to Saturday and sometimes Sunday.

The Elms, 500 Main St., Ridgefield. (203) 438-2541.

In a variety of dining rooms, Robert Scala oversees the tradition of solid American and continental cuisine built by his late father, John, a former master chef at New York's St. Regis Hotel.

At lunch, the chef's special might be arugula salad, or on another day, Belgian endive with radicchio. Those are about the only touches of nouvelle on a menu that ranges from $5.75 for omelets to $12.50 for a steak sandwich, the price including soup, beverage and ice cream or pears in burgundy. The day's specials were veal curry ($9.50) and venison steak ($14.50) the last time we visited.

Complete dinners, from escargots Bacchus or eggs a la Russe through soups to desserts are available, the price varying with the choice of four entrees ($20 for chicken Veronique to $29 for tenderloin of beef forestiere). The a la carte menu lists 15 appetizers ($2.50 for relish tray to $8.50 for clams casino or oysters Rockefeller).

Dinner entrees are mostly $15.95 to $19.95, broiled chicken at $11.75 and chateaubriand or rack of lamb for two at $42 being the exceptions. A curried sliced capon, veal marsala and English lamb chop with kidney and bacon are some choices.

Pastries, parfaits, cherries jubilee and crepes Suzettes for two ($10) are among the desserts, mostly $3 to $4. Robert Scala has expanded the American side of his wine cellar of more than 8,000 bottles; some of the changing offerings are attractively displayed on a large table in the main foyer.

Entertaining four nights a week in the Music Room for seven years has been composer-pianist Noel Regeney of nearby Bethel, who wrote the Christmas carol "Do You Hear What I Hear?"

Lunch, Monday-Saturday noon to 2:30; dinner, 6:30 to 9:30 or 10:30, Sunday 6 to 9; Sunday brunch, noon to 2:30.

Scrimshaw's of Ridgefield, 5 Bailey Ave., Ridgefield. (203) 438-1774.

The former storeroom of a hardware store was transformed in late 1985 into a bright, intimate seafood restaurant by young chef David Hammond and partner Vito Uva. And, in the tradition of Ridgefield, it was crowded from the start.

The long, narrow dining room has bare wide-plank floors, three-inch-thick blond pine tables made from bowling lanes and dark captain's chairs. Color comes from small vases of fresh flowers, fanned rose-colored napkins, and walls papered in a rose-colored print. Lanterns on the walls provide illumination and there's a growing scrimshaw collection in two corner shelves.

Local people praise the food and friendly service. Dave Hammond's menu is incredibly extensive and supplemented by daily specials which he says people prefer anyway. You can get mussels of the day or marinated squid, conch and octopus for appetizers ($2.95 to $5.95) and bouillabaisse. fisherman's platter or seafood marinara for entrees ($7.95 to $16.95). Among popular items are sea scallops en brochette, garlic shrimp, baked sole stuffed with broccoli and cheddar, a rich golden souffle sole and paella for two ($21.95).

Similar items plus salads and sandwiches are offered at lunch. Homemade cheesecake and Italian pastries are among desserts, and wines start at $11 with most in the mid to high teens.

Lunch daily, 11:30 to 2:30; dinner, 5:30 to 9:30 or 10:30.

Cafe Natural, 3 Big Shop Lane, Ridgefield. (203) 431-3637.

Breakfast, lunch and dinner (three nights a week) are served from a menu which changes weekly at this intimate place with old posts and beams and watermelon slices stenciled on the walls. Outdoor dining is provided at two umbrellaed tables beside the door.

Young chef-owners Beth and Mark Ostad offer picnics in baskets and take-out items as well as meals. The "El Marco" omelet (baked ham and sausage blended with three cheeses and seasonings, $4.95) is a great way to start your day. For lunch, how about half a seafood salad sandwich with the mushroom beef barley soup ($3.95), a pizzalini or garden grill special or the "super special" — ham, turkey and roast beef with Swiss cheese, fresh mushrooms, avocado and grilled tomato in a pita pocket ($5.75).

Desserts are irresistible: black and white espresso cake, apple walnut and chocolate satin pies, and carrot layer cake, all $2.50.

At dinner, you might start with smoked trout ($3.75). Main courses run from $6.50 for Caesar salad through chicken, pasta and pesto casserole or veal marsala to $9.95 for filet of sole Creole. Patrons are invited to bring their own wines.

Breakfast and lunch, daily 8 to 4, Sunday 9 to 3; dinner, Wednesday-Friday 6 to 9.

Gaddi's Restaurant, 5 Grove St., Ridgefield. (203) 438-1377.

The name is the same as that of his favorite continental restaurant in his native Hong Kong, according to Sanford F.K. Lau, who opened this appealing-looking establishment in October 1985 in quarters formerly occupied by Entrez-Vous. But any Far East resemblance stops there.

The expanded interior includes an L-shaped dining room and enclosed side porch seating 75 and a cocktail lounge with tables for 30 more. The prevailing gray color scheme (carpeting and walls) is accented with rose-colored linen (under glass), white and rose china, rose-colored Laura Ashley-type cafe curtains on the windows, and a few hanging plants and pictures.

The menu is fairly standard — potato skins to escargots bourguignon for appetizers ($3.95 to $5.25), chopped sirloin to surf and turf for entrees ($8.95 to $15.95). Red snapper amandine, chicken cubes sauteed with garlic, artichoke hearts and diced ham, and four vegetarian entrees also are offered.

Desserts include chocolate mousse, profiteroles and pastries. The wine list is strikingly inexpensive — a Monterey chardonnay for $12, chateauneuf du pape for $14 and only two offerings above the mid-teens.

Lunch, 11:30 to 3; dinner, 5:30 to 10.

Food For All Reasons, Copps Hill Common, Ridgefield. (203) 431-3578.

This spacious gourmet shop and delicatessen which really lives up to its name was opened in September 1985 by young chef Brian Hudson, who used to work with Martha Stewart in Westport. The food is as innovative as his exciting plans: a European-style stand-up espresso and wine bar, an outdoor sidewalk cafe, an ice-cream fountain, and cooking provisions and convenience foods for people who like to cook at home. He mentions natural cereals, low-fat and low-salt cheeses, applewood smoked hams, British bangers, ingredients for Japanese sushi and Indian dishes — "we literally want to be food for all reasons," he says.

Large deli-style counters line the walls. You place your order at the counter, and then proceed to one of six ice-cream-parlor tables near the front window. We enjoyed a lunch of mellow albacore tuna salad and spicy Waldorf turkey salad, washed down with a Perrier for a modest $3.50 tab. "Brian's board" of specials also offered curried lamb, mallard duck and veal with basil cream sauce, plus regular entrees from three-salad platters ($2.95) to beef stroganoff ($7.50). Brunch is available on weekends.

Open Tuesday-Friday 11 to 7, weekends 9 to 4; closed Monday.

The General Store Cafe, Ridgefield General Store, Copps Hill Common, Ridgefield. (203) 438-1984.

Opened in 1984 and already expanded, this inventive cafe has 14 small glass-over-linen tables on the bright lower floor of the new Ridgefield General Store and serves lunch only.

The blackboard menu changes daily. Soups usually are a clam chowder and one other: a hearty vegetable one day, a mulligatawny the next, accompanied by homemade cornbread. Main-course selections ($4.95 to $5.95) might be salmon and dill quiche, chicken pie or broccoli-spinach-cheese pie, all served with salad, or chef salad, Chinese chicken salad or lamb stew, all with cornbread.

Desserts (all $2) include an acclaimed bread pudding, orange chiffon pie, chocolate cake with a layer of cream cheese and mocha macaroon torte.

Lunch, Monday-Saturday 11:30 to 3.

Touchstone's, 470 Main St., Ridgefield. (203) 438-4367.

One entrance leads to the bar and another to the dining rooms outside this restaurant which has been around for awhile in the lower rear level of the Yankee Ridge Center shopping complex. Ceilings are beamed, oriental carpets hang on the white stucco walls, shelves are filled with books, and the atmosphere is cozy and casual.

So is the menu, which starts at $8.95 for linguini with clam sauce and ranges through veal, beef and seafood to $14.95 for blackened Cajun rib, a roast prime rib spiced with Cajun sauce. Sirloin steak and roast duck, both $11.95, come with bread, vegetable and garden salad. Apple walnut pie and chocolate mousse cake are among the desserts.

"Touchstone's famous thumbits" (sirloin tips on a wedge of garlic bread, topped with mushrooms and wine sauce, $5.95) is a feature of the lunch menu. Chicken gumbo soup, Mexican omelet and broiled sole with caper dill butter were specials the last time we visited.

Lunch, Monday-Saturday 11:30 to 3; dinner, 5 to 9 or 10.

Diversions

Aldrich Museum of Contemporary Art, 258 Main St. Controversial when it opened in 1964 under the private aegis of Mr. and Mrs. Larry Aldrich, the museum went public in 1969, won increasing support from the community and has earned a reputation of note. Although now in his 80s, Larry Aldrich keeps in touch with his museum, which remains committed to the new and avant-garde; to new visitors whom he overhears saying "I could do that" as they view the abstract art, he's prone to challenge, "go ahead and try." Much of the interior of the 200-year-old house has been stripped to provide three open galleries on each of the second and third floors; the expanses of white walls are perfect for the large canvases of modern artists lit by track lights. Exhibits change frequently; the eye-catching sculptures across the side and rear lawns do not. The museum is open year-round, Wednesday-Sunday afternoons, Friday-Sunday in winter. Adults $1; Fridays free.

Keeler Tavern, 132 Main St. Just up the street from the Aldrich but years away in feeling is Ridgefield's only house museum, on one of Ridgefield's original 24 proprietor's lots and once the summer home of architect Cass Gilbert. Preserved and furnished by a group of residents who "took furniture right out of our own houses," according to one, it has been open to the public since 1965. Timothy Keeler's 18th century inn and post office, an elongated structure erected in 1772, is given over to period furnishings explained by costumed guides. The two-acre enclave of history includes a garden house, its low white exterior contrasting with the moss green of the tavern, facing a brick-walled, trellised British-style garden, plus a cottage and a barn. Open Wednesday and weekends 1 to 4; closed January. Adults $1.50.

Shopping. Ridgefield's Main Street shopping area is confined to a couple of short blocks; many of the newer shops are tucked behind in Yankee Ridge Center or Big Shop Lane. Among the best: **Ashley's,** the **Silk Purse** and **RSVP** for fine accessories and gifts, and the **76 Colonial Gallery** for antiques and furniture. In recent years, Ridgefield's shopping has expanded to the outskirts along Danbury Road (Route 35 east). It is here that **the Talbots** and other chain and local stores are located. Some of the more interesting are in Copps Hill Common, a new complex of small shops in several buildings. Typical of the atmosphere is **Muriel's,** a women's fashion store in which the coffee pot is kept heated up front all day. Don't miss the new **Ridgefield General Store,** borrowing an old name but fully up to date with upscale toys, cards, gifts and kitchenware.

Open cocktail lounge occupies corner of vast atrium of Westin Hotel-Stamford.

Stamford, Conn.
The Gold Coast A-Glitter

Fairfield County has long been dubbed the Gold Coast, at least as far as the rest of Connecticut is concerned, and nowhere is that gold more glittering these days than in Stamford.

Facing Long Island Sound and surrounded by some of America's choicest residential real estate in Greenwich, New Canaan and Darien, this once-decaying city has come alive. Now the headquarters for more Fortune 500 companies than any city except New York, Stamford dazzles the eye with new mid-rise skyscrapers that have cast the downtown area into a Sunbelt sheen of gleam and glass.

Where corporate headquarters go, hotels, restaurants and shops are sure to follow.

In the mid-1980s, Stamford added nearly 2,000 rooms in five luxury hotels and a Texas-scale inn. Swank and pricey restaurants sprang up all around town. More than 100 fashionable stores opened in Stamford Town Center, the largest enclosed shopping mall between New York and Boston. Culture and entertainment proliferated with the opening of the Palace Theater, a branch of the Whitney Museum and the emerging Stamford Center for the Arts.

So suddenly "in" is Stamford that most of these attractions did not exist three or four years ago. Now many of the amenities that people expect of New York are available in Stamford.

A new convention and tourism bureau is attempting to position Stamford both as a city for New Englanders to visit without going into New York and as a destination area for the business and leisure market from afar.

319

"Stamford hasn't had a strong tourist image," said promoter John Mitovich. "You pick up a magazine and see other cities say, 'Come to Chicago,' 'Come to Dallas.' We're going to say, 'Come to Stamford.'"

If you're into urbane activities without the hassle of much larger cities, Stamford beckons. And, if you go beyond its facade, there's more to Stamford than glitter.

Inn Spots

The Inn at Mill River, 26 Mill River St., Stamford 06902. (203) 325-1900.

New England's fanciest new inn and restaurant opened in May 1985, thanks to a $15 million-plus investment and the interior design of James Northcutt of Los Angeles, who previously was involved in the Mansion at Turtle Creek in Dallas, the Campton Place Hotel in San Francisco and the Bel-Air Hotel in Beverly Hills. Situated at the edge of downtown across the Mill River from Bloomingdale's, the 92-room, European-style small hotel reflects what the designer calls "a Californian's view of Connecticut." To that we'd add a Texan's flair for high living.

But for the surprising neon sign (probably so you can find your way at night) atop the five-story honey-colored brick structure, you might not know from the outside that this was anything but another of Stamford's ubiquitous condominiums and apartments.

The interior exudes an aura of wealth, however, from the travertine marble floors to the shiny brass fixtures in the bathrooms, from the original art works on the walls (and on the ceilings of the elevators) to the Chippendale chairs in the public areas, from the Wedgwood china to the Reed and Barton silver in the Swan Court restaurant and Promenade lounge (see Dining Spots).

Each of the 42 "standard" rooms, which start at $115 a night, has a sitting area with loveseat and arm chair around a table, a bedside Lexar system for controlling everything from room temperature to the television set hidden in the armoire, ample closets with three kinds of hangers (thoughtfully, all removable), separate marble vanity and large, mirrored baths notable for French toiletries, thick terrycloth towels and courtesy robes. There are two telephones (one in the bathroom) and two lines, so a businessman can put one caller on hold while striking another deal.

Beds have down comforters, all-cotton linens and four enormous decorator pillows which are removed by the maid and replaced with mints during turn-down service at night. "It's like being in your own home," owner Todd Hoffman told us as he relaxed on an oversize bed, his head and back propped against the pillows, and demonstrated how to flick on the TV set from afar. "This is like heaven."

The California peach color scheme is coordinated with more shades of rose, cream and gray than one would expect from a color chart, so that each room is different and repeat visitors won't feel as if they're staying in the same room.

Unless, of course, they seek out Suite 300, in which the living room has a working fireplace, facing loveseats, many side chairs and a formal dining table. The suite has three baths, one with a jacuzzi, and two bedrooms upstairs, and rents for $575 a night. It and another penthouse suite and

The Library is an attractive public room at the Inn at Mill River.

several king deluxe rooms have outdoor terraces with views onto the little waterfalls of the tranquil Mill River.

Regular king deluxe rooms are about half a room bigger than standard rooms, the extra space providing most comfortable sitting areas. Some of the baths have rose marble pedestal sinks, and some of the beds are four-posters carved with welcoming pineapples.

Masses of exotic fresh flowers grace the lobby, Promenade bar and other public areas. The fireplaced Library is superlatively furnished, with pieces ranging from Georgian and Louis XV to Neiman-Marcus contemporary.

Breakfast is available in the Promenade, continental for $6.50 and the Mill River for $9.50. If you don't blink at $6.50 for a continental breakfast, you won't mind the same tab for a mixed green salad or a dessert at dinner.

Doubles, $115 to $125; deluxe, $140 to $160; suites, $250 to $575; weekends, $100 to $475.

Le Pavillon, 60 Strawberry Hill Ave., Stamford 06902. (203) 357-8100.

The Indian owners who operate out of Hong Kong spent $8 million transforming this large and solid apartment building for the elderly into a luxury European style hotel in 1983 and, on the inside, money shows. The Buddha of Prosperity sits behind the table at which you register (no hotel desk here); a glass of champagne is offered as you check in.

All 176 mini-suites (so-called because they have sitting areas) and suites are named for champagnes, cognacs and wines. All have refrigerators, king or queensize beds, arrangements of exotic flowers and original Indian or oriental art. Chinese robes, chocolate mints on the pillows and bedside brandies are among the amenities.

The restaurant (see Dining Spots) recently has been renovated and expanded. One-thousand-year-old Indian prayer books and enormous Indian art works are on the walls, and oriental plates and porcelain figures are all around. The former breakfast area is now a bar called "a quiet lounge."

For health and recreation, guests have free use of the Twin Lakes Swim and Tennis Club and the Fitness Connection Center of Stamford. Complimentary transportation is available to and from the club as well as to businesses in downtown Stamford.

Doubles, $115 to $155; weekend packages start at $55.

Westin Hotel-Stamford, 2701 Summer St., Stamford. 06905. (203) 359-1300.

Opened in October 1984 and billed as Connecticut's largest luxury hotel, the former Hotel Stamford Plaza gave up its independent ownership in February 1986 when it was acquired by the Westin chain.

It looks like something you'd find in a Sunbelt city. Glass elevators rise to 500 guest rooms on five floors, all built around a 30,000-square-foot atrium. Interior room windows look right onto the atrium, which gives the atrium a rather odd appearance, as does its ceiling of structural steel gridwork, rather like that of a hockey arena.

Down below all is lavish. In the reception corner, a sitting area has leather couches, marble tables, carpets in hues of rose and violet or blue and beige, and vases of the exotic flowers that seem to be a Stamford trademark. At the opposite corner of the atrium is an open cocktail lounge outfitted with curved and upholstered chairs. Another corner has a gift and sundry shop, while the last corner has the Terrace restaurant. Rotating art exhibits and lush greenery warm up the lower atrium walls and the vast expanses of floor in between.

An enclosed corridor leads out front to a wing with a few shops and service businesses and the hotel's two privately operated luxury restaurants, **Le Coq Hardi** and **Mr. Lee** (see Dining Spots).

Standard guest rooms have kingsize beds, separate closets and dressing areas, baskets of amenities in the bathrooms, sitting areas with work desks that double as dining tables and remote-control TV. Suites have sitting rooms with oriental or bamboo furniture, 45-inch television screens and a variety of beds, including one antique four-poster.

Thirty-three rooms and suites on the fifth floor are granted concierge status in what is called the Stamford Club.

A tiny indoor pool and whirlpool is in a windowless room off the Stamford Plaza Health Club, which has the most elaborate fitness facilities among Stamford hotels.

Three meals a day are served in the **Terrace,** under a lattice roof or partially open to the atrium. The extensive lunch buffet for $8.25 with changing hot dishes (sweet and sour pork and egg foo yong the day we visited) looked especially good. Dinner entrees run from $8.50 for ground sirloin burger to $25.95 for twin lobster tails.

Mystery weekends have caught on with the leisure market.

Doubles, $140 to $175; Concierge, add $25; weekends, from $55.

Sheraton Stamford Hotel & Towers, One First Stamford Place, Stamford 06902. (203) 967-2222.

Set in a glittering high-rise office park across the Connecticut Turnpike from downtown, the 505-room Sheraton opened in stages in late 1985 and

1986 and bills itself as Fairfield County's largest conference facility and Connecticut's largest hotel. The focal point is a sloping, three-story glass atrium of various levels linked by escalators, marble floors, lush plantings and sitting areas all done up in purples and plums.

Most of the guest rooms are on the third through tenth floors, some looking onto the lobby and others out toward Long Island Sound. A typical room has two double beds with restful beige spreads, a TV set hidden in the armoire, a round table and two chairs. Kingsize rooms include a chair with an ottoman.

A 109-room luxury level on the top two floors, called the Towers, has upgraded facilities and amenities, including an extra phone and television in the bathroom.

One wall of the 20-by-40-foot indoor pool opens onto an outside lawn for summer sunning. Exercise and steam rooms are adjacent.

Raspberry's, an unusually pleasant hotel restaurant with a motif of — what else? — raspberries, opens off the lobby. Its sidewalk-cafe ambiance gets progressively more formal as you move inward. Dinner entrees ($10.95 to $16.95) are supplemented by such nightly specials as Irish beef stew and paella.

The Magnificent J's, a luxury restaurant named for the J boats of the America's Cup races and full of extensive nautical memorabilia, including wall and ceiling murals of races, opened in March 1986 with an emphasis on seafood and mesquite grilling. **Celia's,** a multi-level lounge, is a lively spot with band music and a marble dance floor.

Doubles, $115 to $135; Towers, $155; suites, $200 to $240.

Holiday Inn Crowne Plaza, 700 Main St., Stamford 06901. (203) 358-8400.

The Holiday Inn's new top-of-the-line establishment, which opened in 1984 a long block from the Stamford Town Center, is designed with the individual traveler in mind.

Most of the public facilities are in or around an enclosed, three-story atrium, which is notable for its open swimming pool (the swimmer is on display for all to see, for better or worse), a noisy waterfall and striking prints on one wall, done by an artist friend of one of the employees. The atrium is also notable, we think, for the grand piano playing melodiously away in the mid-afternoon — by itself, it turns out, for this is a player piano, Stamford style (a live trio replaces it during cocktail hour).

The piano is in the large lobby bar, where continental breakfast is served in the morning. Open to the atrium, **Winslow's Cafe** serves three meals a day, including a lunch buffet for $6.95. Underneath the lobby is **Razzmatazz,** a lounge on several levels with a separate entrance, seafood bar and live entertainment.

Cezanne's, the formal and highly rated restaurant for lunch and dinner, is small (15 tables) and most elegant, with deep mushroom-colored walls, velvet chairs and banquettes, well-spaced tables, freesias in silver vases, and china with a pretty poppy pattern. A harpist plays on Friday and Saturday nights. Dinner entrees run from $13.95 for breast of capon with spinach and raspberry vinegar to $22.95 for lobster Savannah.

The 10th-floor concierge level has 41 rooms, including two suites. The kingsize room here is decorated in a residential look with loveseat, sofa, round table and two chairs; nightly turn-down service brings an after-dinner cordial.

The rest of the 384 rooms are furnished in Danish teak, some with sofas and some with chairs. Complimentary newspapers are outside each door in the morning, and two vans are available to take guests to business meetings or to area restaurants.

Doubles, $118; concierge, $140; weekends, $75.

Stamford-Marriott Hotel, 2 Stamford Forum, Stamford 06901. (203) 357-9555.

Stamford's first major hotel (1977) and its most conveniently located (right downtown, across from the Stamford Town Center) was being expanded and upgraded early in 1986 to match its new competition. Two hundred rooms were added in wings on both ends of the 18-story structure, raising the total to 505. The original lobby was remodeled and brightened with lighter colors and marble floors, and a new lobby was added.

An exposed glass elevator rises up the exterior to a revolving rooftop restaurant with panoramic view of Long Island Sound (we were able to spot the towers of Manhattan during a sneak preview).

The new guest rooms are billed as Marquis grade or better, and the 305 original rooms with kingsize or two double beds decorated in earth tones were upgraded as well. A concierge level on the 14th floor has the usual amenities.

The indoor-outdoor pool is one of Stamford's nicest, with an outdoor deck beside. Universal equipment and saunas are nearby.

The new wing includes the **Forum,** an enormous lounge with multi-screened video and an elaborate sound system, said to be the liveliest night spot in Fairfield County. The main-floor restaurant was being renovated, and the major emphasis was placed on **Le Carrousel,** the rooftop restaurant set to revolve one full turn every 68 minutes. Planned by the same designer who did New York's Windows on the World, it was to be the setting for very expensive continental dining.

Doubless $125; Concierge, $138.

Dining Spots

The Inn at Mill River, 26 Mill River St., Stamford. (203) 325-1900.

You would naturally expect New England's fanciest new inn to have a restaurant to match. You won't be disappointed, but you may be taken aback by the prices.

Both the curved, outer dining room with windows onto the front lawn and the larger interior dining room beyond are beautiful indeed: latticed walls in shades of the inn's prevailing peach and cream, oriental prints and Canton blue and white vases, nicely spaced tables covered to the floor in beige and white linens, upholstered arm chairs, Wedgwood china and Reed and Barton silver.

Dining here is a feast for the eye as well as the palate. Each dish is artfully composed in the nouvelle style, the complexities and combinations sometimes boggling the mind and baffling the tastebuds.

Chef Raymond Peron's winter dinner menu includes such appetizers ($8.50 to $11.75) as quail pate with port wine aspic, a terrine of Dover sole and sea scallops with cold mustard sauce, and a fricassee of snails, mushrooms and garlic. The shellfish soup is $7.25, the warm salad with sliced scallops is $10.75 and the house salad of greens with herbed vinaigrette is $6.

Entrees run from $18.50 to $28.50, most at the high end. Dover sole comes with mushrooms and lobster in puff pastry and two sauces, the medallions of veal in a mushroom cream sauce, the filet mignon with a black pepper and raisin sauce, the breast of free-range chicken with raspberry vinegar. Changing vegetables accompany. The extensive wine list is geared to those on expense accounts, generally starting in the $20s.

Desserts are marvels, as they ought to be for the tariff ($5.25 to $6.75). Among them are a raspberry mousse, a chocolate terrine with creme Anglaise, tarte tatin, chocolate charlotte with fresh berries and one we particularly liked, a trio of fresh fruit sorbets accompanied by a coulis of raspberries.

The lunch menu is similar to the dinner and only slightly less pricey (appetizers, $6.50 to $9.25; entrees, $13.50 to $18.50). We remember a remarkable summer lunch starting with three-vegetable mousse (a scoop each of yellow squash, pureed red pepper and spinach in a garlicky gazpacho sauce), continuing with Atlantic sea bass surrounded by a fan of paper-thin slices of tomatoes and zucchini, and finishing with a silky, moist cheesecake topped with raspberries and a raspberry tart on the side. Perfection, but we sure were glad someone else was paying the tab!

Lunch, Monday-Saturday 11:30 to 2; dinner, 6 to 10, to 9 on Sunday; Sunday brunch, 11 to 2.

Aux Beaux Jardins, Le Pavillon, 60 Strawberry Hill Ave., Stamford. (203) 357-8100.

The enlarged and remodeled restaurant at Le Pavillon is more striking than ever, enriched with historic Indian prayer books on the walls and shelves filled with Eastern plates and porcelains. Pinpoint lights highlight the striking floral arrangements (birds of paradise last time we were there) on each well-appointed table in the two serenely lovely dining rooms.

Alas, prices are enriched as well, having nearly doubled in the two years since we stayed there. Dinner entrees ($18.50 to $24.75) include such treats as Norwegian salmon in phyllo dough with champagne sauce, poached grouper with lobster medallion, veal chop stuffed with a duxelle of mushrooms in a Madeira sauce, and chicken breast stuffed with wild rice, served with Chinese vegetables in an orange sauce. Shrimp with vodka sauce and tomato soup with gin are among the more exotic starters.

At one springtime lunch we enjoyed a dynamite gazpacho, an artichoke salad marinated in raspberry vinaigrette, Szechuan pork and grilled lamb chops with honey mustard sauce.

Lunch, noon to 2:30; dinner, 6 to 11; Sunday brunch, 11 to 3. Reservations required.

Le Parisien, 323 Hope St., Stamford. (203) 964-0404.

Country French is the cuisine and decor of this popular. out-of-the-way restaurant owned by Christian Milonas and his chef from Paris, Jean-Jacques Gabrillargues. An 80-year-old friend painted the murals of Paris scenes that brighten the stucco walls of the main dining room, made intimate by plates hung on the exposed beams, mounted copper skillets, copper pots full of flowers, glass lamps, candles and wall sconces.

The classic French menu is extensive but not intimidating, and supplemented by nightly specials like veal saute in raspberry vinegar with truffle sauce or salmon poached in champagne caviar sauce. Other entrees ($14 to $18) include roast quail with grapes, trout sauteed with lemon and capers, breast of duck in orange and pepper sauce, and sweetbreads with wild mushrooms.

Appetizers ($4 to $8) are classic and simple: escargots, littlenecks au naturel, cold mussels, pate maison and such. The pastry baker from Paris is known for delights on the dessert trolley, and you also can get souffles, mocha mousse and ice cream with chestnuts. Most of the 120 wines are from France and reasonably priced.

Lunch, Monday-Friday noon to 2; dinner, 6 to 10, Sunday 5 to 9.

Bourbon Street, 20 Summer St., Stamford. (203) 356-1467.

With all the French restaurants in Stamford, it might come as a relief to find a newcomer that doesn't take itself too seriously. We happened to visit Bourbon Street during Mardi Gras, were served by "The Fonz" (all the staff were costumed, some rather bizarrely) and had a good time at lunch, watching hundreds of bobbing purple, yellow and green balloons decorating the place. A banjo player was wandering around, and the jollity was contagious.

Bourbon Street is a mix of all those New Orleans restaurants with tile floors, dark wood, big raw bar, dining areas separated by brass rails, lots of mirrors and coat hooks, and a very busy bar. Tables are covered with glass, which we don't appreciate, but some of the glass covers are handsomely etched with piano notes.

Except for rock-hard rolls, we had a fine lunch of a house specialty, coconut and beer batter shrimp, served with good hot mustardy fruit sauce; a delicious file gumbo chock full of oysters, clams, mussels and scallops, and a smallish Creole-style stew from the trunnion kettles. At $5.95 for the stew with oysters, we thought the gumbo, which had more seafood, was a better bargain at $3.95.

Dinner entrees range from $11.95 for cappellini a la Antoine to $17.95 for rack of lamb. Blackened redfish, chicken with crayfish, two quails stuffed with wild rice and oysters bonne femme are some. You could begin with seafood boudin or Cajun popcorn (shrimp).

Many of the appetizers and salads are the same as at lunch, when entrees are $5.95 (for omelet of the day) to $9.95 for grilled strip steak. Among sandwiches are oyster and andouille po' boys, $6.95 and $7.95.

All kinds of goodies, like smoked trout or salmon, shrimp remoulade, seafood cocktail Louisiana and Baton Rouge brigade (a sampling of everything), come from the raw bar.

Desserts include creme caramel a l'orange, chocolate sabayon cake and chocolate pate with praline sauce. Wines are reasonable (pouilly fume for

Water views are available from almost every table at the Rusty Scupper.

$11.95), a glass of Cordon Negro champagne is $3, and the bloody marys are good and spicy.

Lunch, Monday-Saturday 11:30 to 4; dinner, 5 to 10 or 11.

Rusty Scupper, 104 Harbor Plaza Drive, Stamford. (203) 964-1235.

Most visitors are unaware of Stamford's waterfront at hard-to-find Shippan Point (pronounced Ship-PAN, if you ask for directions). A few restaurants are tucked amid office parks and condos in this harborfront area, which is as upscale as downtown.

The best all-around, we think, is this new edition of the Rusty Scupper chain. From almost every table in the angled, multi-level two-story structure one may gaze onto the boat-filled harbor. In summer, the tiered, outdoor deck is the place to be, and the upstairs lounge is the place for locals to be at all times. Decor is contemporary and unobtrusive, light and airy.

The typical Rusty Scupper menu offers all things for all people, with a simplicity in cuisine and pricing that is refreshing for Stamford. Dinner is preceded by pumpernickel and white breads (ours were a bit stale) and large spinach or mixed salads with choice of dressings and an offer of a pepper grinder. A special of poached salmon and the shrimp tempura were fine, and when we couldn't decide between the mixed vegetables or red skinned potatoes, our waiter offered both. These people are accommodating, and so are the prices ($10.95 for the shrimp, $12 for a Glen Ellen char-donnay).

Lunch, Monday-Friday 11:30 to 2; dinner, Monday to Saturday 5:30 to 10 or 11, Sunday from 4.

Le Coq Hardi, 2711 Summer St., Stamford. (203) 357-0098.

The namesake of the widely known Ridgefield restaurant opened in the Westin Hotel-Stamford in January 1986. Head chef Carl Wright moved to Stamford to ensure its success, bringing with him much of the menu and style of the smaller Ridgefield enterprise.

Devotees of the original Le Coq Hardi will recognize this place, with its specially designed stone wall at the back, its pink and deep rose color scheme, and the paintings and prints of roosters on the walls. Here, praise be, the tables are not quite so close together as in Ridgefield.

The menu is French nouvelle and its contents quite different at lunch and dinner. Dinner appetizers ($7 to $25) include snails and cepes served en brioche, a mixture of seafood in raviolis, and duck liver in aspic. Entrees run from $18 for poached salmon with lobster sauce or sliced duck with hazelnut sauce to $23 for spring chicken steeped in black truffles or rack of lamb with basil and "a hint of orange." Rolled filets of Dover sole stuffed with pike mousse, ragout of lobster with fresh herbs and vegetables, and roast quail stuffed with truffles are other creations.

Lunch entrees are inventive as well, priced from $11 to $16. The wine list is extensive, rising from a muscadet for $12 to a 1957 Chateau Margaux for $580.

Lunch, Monday-Friday noon to 3; dinner nightly from 6.

Mr. Lee, 2711 Summer St., Stamford. (203) 357-1108.

Condominium developer Johnson Lee lays claim to serving the finest Szechuan cuisine in Connecticut, although some oldtimers consider the best Chinese food in Stamford to be found across the street at the unpretentious-looking Hunan Wok.

Visitors likely will be impressed by the elegant, sumptuous decor of the second Mr. Lee, which opened in August 1985 in the Stamford Plaza Hotel, now the Westin Hotel-Stamford. Johnson Lee spares little expense in his design, although he leaves the day-to-day operations of his restaurants here and at the original in New Canaan to his sons.

In something of a coup, Zhi An Gui — considered one of China's "Big Ten" master chefs — came from that country early in 1986 to serve as master chef at Mr. Lee's for two years in a cooking and cultural exchange. As it happens, he was head chef at the Green Hotel in Kunming, Johnson Lee's hometown, but has served many Chinese leaders and given Chinese culinary demonstrations around the world. Not limited to one region, his cuisine is what is called Chinese National Food, light and natural. Daily specials reflecting it are offered at both the Stamford and New Canaan restaurants.

Dinner entrees ($10.95 to $30) include such Mr. Lee specialties as orange beef, orange chicken, crispy sea bass, Shanghai shrimp, crab a la king, sea scallops and beef, and Bejing duck. Jade lobster, Mongolian lamb and firecracker prawns also appeal. Many dinner dishes are available at lunch, at considerably lower prices.

With fine Chinese art on the walls, high-back velvet chairs and crisply linened tables set with fine china and heavy silver, the two main dining rooms are so serene and the staff so formal that patrons might be reluctant to follow the Chinese tradition of sharing dishes. That would be unfortunate.

Lunch and dinner daily.

Extra-Special

The Japanese Kitchen, 909 Washington Blvd. (203) 325-0404.

The somewhat dreary Stamford YMCA contains a serendipitous surprise, one of the best and cheapest Japanese restaurants in the Northeast. The small dining room, to the right of the main entrance, is nondescript. But the windows are covered with rice paper, and from a tiny kitchen behind the lunch counter emit aromas that have your mouth watering in anticipation. The large platter of sushi (about $12) is as good as anything we have had in New York, and extra pickled ginger (our downfall) is available. We love the tempura and the sukiyaki, and even the miso soup is better than usual. The deluxe sushi platter is by far the most expensive dish on the menu; most are in the $3 to $7 range. Lunch, 11:30 to 3; dinner, 5 to 8; closed Sunday; no credit cards, no liquor.

Le Mistral, 110 Harbor Plaza Drive, Stamford. (203) 359-1890.

Part of Harbor Place along with the Rusty Scupper, this lacks the marina view and its outdoor deck looks onto the parking lot. It also apparently suffers an image problem as the offspring of a Greenwich patisserie-restaurant called Versailles.

Owner Maurice Versailles changed the name from Versailles Too to Versailles to finally, in its latest incarnation in March 1986, Le Mistral. A cappuccino machine tops the pastry case in front; the rest of the place is casually chic with light peach and white table linens, fanned orange napkins and modern cane chairs.

When we visited just before the name change, the anglicized French menu was small but select, and getting more so. Prices were to rise, more seafood was to be added, and a liquor license was at hand. Based on what we heard and saw, Le Mistral had considerable promise.

Lunch, Monday-Friday 11:30 to 3; dinner Monday-Saturday 6 to 10; closed Sunday.

The Davenport, 84 West Park Place, Stamford. (203) 357-0281.

The main floor of the old Davenport Hotel was carefully restored into a Victorian bar with oak paneling and brass railings, and a sophisticated, skylit restaurant with fireplaces and art works on the walls. It looked rather like a new-old hotel dining room, which is exactly what it is, upon its opening in February 1986.

Shrimp and oysters Louisiana, veal medallions sauteed with morel sauce, and charcoal-grilled duck with cassis and peppercorn sauce were among the entrees ($10.95 to $17.95) on the initial dinner menu. So were meal-sized salads, pizzas and hamburgers. Cajun meat loaf and smoked duck salad appealed for lunch.

Lunch and dinner daily; brunch on Saturday and Sunday, noon to 3:30.

La Bretagne, 2010 W. Main St., Stamford. (203) 324-9539.

Newly ensconced in a former Chinese restaurant near the Old Greenwich line (and with something of an old continental feel) is one of Fairfield

County's more enduring French restaurants. The three dining rooms are formal, fairly brightly lighted and enhanced by paintings done by the owner's wife.

Again the menu is classic French. Dinner entrees are $16 to $20 and the kitchen is known for its seafood dishes, especially mussels served three ways as appetizers. Dover sole, bay scallops, poached salmon with choron sauce and sweetbreads are among recommended choices. Desserts are standard French.

Lunch, Monday-Saturday noon to 2:30; dinner, 6 to 9:30 or 10:30; closed Sunday.

Diversions

Stamford Town Center. This enclosed downtown mall changed the nature of Stamford and put it on the serious shoppers' map when it opened in 1984. A maze of levels, escalators and winding marble corridors in which you can easily lose your bearings (and we always seem to), it is nevertheless a wonderful mix of generally high-style shops: **Brooks Brothers, FAO Schwartz, Abercrombie & Fitch, Charles Jourdan, Courreges, Laura Ashley, Brookstone,** both **the Talbots and Country Store of Concord,**

Jaeger, Doubleday, and **Black, Starr & Frost.** Anchor stores are **Saks Fifth Avenue, Macy's** and **J.C. Penney.** If you can negotiate the spiraling ramp to the high-level parking garage, you'll find seven floors of metered parking for a quarter.

Other shopping. Stamford has **Bloomingdales, Lord & Taylor** and **Gimbels** stores, as well as several shopping plazas along Summer Street and High Ridge Road. It also has the famous **United House Wrecking Co.,** a huge outdoor place that's a tourist attraction in itself. Antiques-hunters go wild and interior decorators come up with rare finds among the five acres of relics, nostalgia and just plain junk.

Whitney Museum of American Art, Atlantic Street at Tresser Boulevard. The new Fairfield County branch of the New York museum, located on the first floor of the Champion International headquarters building, has changing exhibitions. Across the street is the emerging $12 million **Stamford Center for the Arts,** to stage symphony, theater and ballet productions.

The Bartlett Arboretum, 151 Brookdale Road. Garden enthusiasts find plenty to interest them at the state-owned arboretum run by the University of Connecticut. It's at its showiest in spring when its magnificent azaleas and rhododendrons are in bloom, but even in winter the rare trees and hardy greenery invite inspection. Five miles of trails traverse the 63 acres of woodlands and gardens. Open free, daily from 8:30 to sunset.

Index to Inns and Restaurants

Also by Wood Pond Press

Getaways for Gourmets in the Northeast. The first book by Nancy Webster and Richard Woodworth is for anyone who likes good food and wine. It guides you to the best dining, lodging, specialty food shops and culinary attractions in 18 areas from the Brandywine Valley to Montreal, Bucks County to Bar Harbor, the Finger Lakes to Cape Cod. Published in 1984. 306 pages to read and savor. $10.95.

Weekending in New England. The best-selling travel guide by Betsy Wittemann and Nancy Webster details everything you need to know about 18 of New England's most interesting vacation spots: nearly 1,000 things to do, sights to see and places to stay, eat and shop year-round. Published in 1980; fully updated and revised in 1984. 248 pages of facts and fun. $8.95.

The Best of Daytripping & Dining. The latest book by Betsy Wittemann and Nancy Webster, this is a companion to their original Southern New England and all-New England editions. It pairs 25 featured daytrips with 25 choice restaurants, among 200 other suggestions of sites to visit and places to eat, in Southern New England and nearby New York. Published in 1985. 186 pages of fresh ideas. $7.95.

These books may be ordered from your local bookstore or direct from the publisher, pre-paid, plus $1 for each book. Connecticut residents add sales tax.

Wood Pond Press
365 Ridgewood Road
West Hartford, Conn. 06107